Women and Politics in Canada

Women and Politics in Canada

Heather MacIvor

broadview press

Canadian Cataloguing in Publication Data

MacIvor, Heather, 1964–
Women and politics in Canada
Includes index.
ISBN 1-55111-036-9
1. Women in politics - Canada. I. Title
HQ1236.5.C2M33 1996 305.43'32'097 C95-933385-1

Broadview Press
Post Office Box 1243, Peterborough, Ontario, Canada K9J 7H5

in the United States of America:
3576 California Road, Orchard Park, NY 14127

in the United Kingdom:
B.R.A.D. Book Representation & Distribution Ltd.,
244A, London Road, Hadleigh, Essex. SS7 2DE

Broadview Press gratefully acknowledges the support of the Canada Council,
the Ontario Arts Council, and the Ministry of Canadian Heritage.

PRINTED IN CANADA

Contents

Foreword

It is surprising, given recent developments, that this book is the first introductory text about women in Canadian politics. Like many others who have have taught university-level courses on women and politics, I have tried, without success, to find a single, affordable textbook that brought together the main themes of my course: feminist theory, women in Canadian society, and women's place in the political system. There have been collections of articles and a host of monographs on various aspects of women and politics, but no single text that pulled it all together. My mother brought me up to believe that if you want to get something done, you have to do it yourself, and so I did. The text I wanted for my students is now in your hands.

This book was written with the first-year student in mind; it is not intended as a substitute for more specialized works in any of the subject areas. The sheer quantity and range of books, articles, theories, and empirical studies in the field of women and politics are impossible to convey in a single text. My hope is that this book will stimulate the reader to pursue further study in women's studies, in political science, or in both. The excellent work available in these fields will repay further reading.

I wish to thank a number of individuals for their assistance during the hectic period in which this book was written. I thank Don LePan and Michael Harrison at Broadview Press, for their faith and support; no first-time author could have asked for better treatment than I have received from them. My colleagues at the Department of Political Science, University of Windsor, have been most encouraging, as have colleagues in the Women's Studies Faculty Group. Professor Martha Lee has been my friend and my co-worker, and equally valuable in both capacities. Professor Heather Smith at the University of Northern British Columbia has been both critical and enthusiastic about feminism. My mother has been there during the high and the low points. I owe a tremendous debt to Stephen Murphy, my coach, guinea pig, psychiatrist, cheering section, moral support, and so much more. I want to dedicate this book to all women and men with the courage to question accepted wisdom, break out of stereotypes, and be whoever and whatever they want to be.

Introduction

Why Do We Need a Book about Women and Politics?

Canadian women have made a number of breakthroughs in the past century. Women can vote in elections. Two major national parties have had female leaders. Rita Johnston of British Columbia was premier briefly in 1991, and Catherine Callbeck of Prince Edward Island became the first female premier elected by the voters in 1993. In June 1993 Kim Campbell became the first woman prime minister of Canada. Women run businesses, lead established churches, and teach in universities. In addition to these new choices, most women still perform the traditional roles as well: spouse, parent, daughter, sister. The expansion of women's life choices has been rapid, reflecting broader social changes that have been unsettling for most people.

Despite these breakthroughs, many women are still at a significant disadvantage in Canadian society. They are underpaid relative to men, even when they hold the same qualifications. They are not assured of reproductive freedom. Abortion rights are fragile, and completely safe, reliable contraception is not yet a reality. Women are still regarded as threatening aliens when they enter male-dominated occupations.

Women are still sometimes treated as less intelligent beings, as sex objects, and as male property. When women try to adapt or to break out of women's traditional roles, or to combine them with other roles, they face hostility. When women work hard and achieve some measure of power, they are ridiculed as "bitches," derided as "pushy," their sexuality is questioned, and their qualifications are belittled.

The "second wave" of the women's movement began the development of modern feminist theory and provoked an extraordinary degree of women's activism on their own behalf. During that time, economic and social developments have drawn women out of their homes and into the paid workforce and created profound changes in Canadian families. Women's lives have been transformed in a dazzlingly short time. These changes are visible to people who have lived through them, but they may not be as apparent to people born since 1970. Yet it is impossible to understand Canadian society in the 1990s without understanding why these changes happened and what they mean for the future.

The disciplines of sociology, economics, and history have recognized the importance of these economic and social changes, reflecting them in their curricula. Political science has been slower in many respects. Recent history has shown that political elites and institutions often lag behind changes in society and the economy, resisting for years or even decades until they are finally forced to confront the alterations in their environments. Watching the Canadian political system respond to the women's movement and women's mass entry into the workforce, and to their implications for the rest of society, has been like watching an ocean liner pull a U-turn: it can be done, but it is a very slow process that has to overcome a lot of resistance along the way.

The same is true of political science. The resistance within the discipline is finally starting to break down, as evidenced by the presence of courses on women in most political science departments, and by the efforts of many instructors in mainstream courses to integrate material on women into their reading lists and lectures. But some hostility remains, and there is considerable resentment in some quarters about the amount of resources presently devoted to women and to feminist approaches in political science. (Some of the reasons for that resistance will be explored in chapter 1.)

Outline of the Book

This book is intended to be a political science text as well as a women's studies text. It differs from most other political science textbooks in at least one important respect: it relies on a feminist definition of "politics." Part 1 of the book explores the effects of feminism on political science. As we will see in Chapter 1, the traditional understanding of "politics" was quite narrow: a clearly defined sphere of activity that did not include the family, the economy, popular culture, or any other sphere in which women were visible. In short, politics was understood to be an exclusively masculine activity.

Chapter 2 explores women's responses to this and other traditional ideas, responses that are grouped together under the label of "feminism." Women's reactions to the traditional view of politics are varied. Some women accepted the idea of a sharp distinction between politics and private life. Others rejected the "public-private dichotomy" because it trapped women in a narrow range of domestic pursuits and kept them from developing their other abilities. Still others have argued that the dichotomy is a myth because women are equally oppressed in all areas of society, public or private. In the past thirty years, the period usually described as the second wave of feminism, feminists opposed to the dichotomy have adopted a slogan: "The personal is political." We will explore the implications of this phrase in Chapter 2.

Part 2 of this book will come as a surprise to readers who expect a book about women and politics to be entirely concerned with parties, legislatures, and policy-making. These chapters on women in the economy, the family, the justice system, and the mass media are nonetheless a necessary prelude to later chapters on women in formal political institutions. We cannot understand women's status in Parliament or political parties until we have examined their place in the economy and the family. Nor can we ignore the feminist redefinition of politics, which requires that we examine power relations in all areas of women's lives, not just vis-à-vis the state. Therefore, in Part 2 we will look at the ways in which women's status in Canadian society has changed, and failed to change. Chapter 3 deals with women in the economy, Chapter 4 with the family, Chapter 5 with women's experiences of the justice system and the Charter of Rights, and Chapter 6 with women in the mass media and popular culture.

Part 3 is concerned with Canadian political institutions and women's participation in them. We will examine women's patterns of political participation, the gendered division of labour in political parties, the barriers confronting women who seek nomination to the House of Commons, and the difficulties for women in executives and judiciaries. It is too easy to point to Audrey McLaughlin and Kim Campbell and say, "See? There's no problem for women in politics. If they can do it, any woman can do it." The truth is very different. Women with dependent children, partners, and the typical "woman's job" have little chance of a political career – although the case of Audrey McLaughlin suggests that this pattern may be changing.

Part 4 looks at the relationship of women to the policy-making process in Canada. Chapter 10 examines the effects of past and present public policy on the lives of Canadian women. Many of those effects have been negative, not because of a deliberate conspiracy but because male policy-makers have been unwilling or unable to take the facts of women's lives into account. In other cases, policy has been based on the traditional assumptions about women that we will discuss in Chapter 1 – the gendered division of labour and the public-private dichotomy – in such a way as to reinforce those assumptions.

Chapter 11 looks at some of the ways in which women have tried to shape public policy, to remove some of its harmful aspects, and to make policy sensitive to the different experiences of men and women in Canadian society. Chapter 12 offers five case studies of public policy in Canada, to illustrate the ways in which "women's issues" have been either kept off the policy agenda or tied up in knots of political controversy. The themes that run throughout the book – the silencing, belittling, stereotyping, and sexualizing of women – are clearly evident in the Canadian state's treatment of those issues that are of particular (but not exclusive) relevance to women.

Part 1: Feminism and Political Science

IN THIS SECTION WE WILL EXAMINE THE TREATMENT OF women in the study of politics. We will also look at the more general ideas about women in Western political and social thought, and at the ways in which women have responded to those ideas. Chapter 1 situates the study of women and politics within the broader discipline of political science, a discipline that reflects the sexism inherent in Western thought. Since men have put stylus to clay, or pen to paper, they have portrayed women in a narrow range of roles or types. Women have been seen as somewhat less than fully human, as walking temptations to sin, and in other unflattering lights. These descriptions do not constitute an accurate account of women, either historically or psychologically. Women have been reflected through the distorting prisms of male fear, anger, and bafflement.

One of the more damaging aspects of this distortion has been the absence of women from much of Western thought. Feminist responses to the Western tradition have been dedicated as much to making women visible as to correcting the misleading images of women that appear in the records of Western thought. Adrienne Rich has asked, "What does a woman need to know? Does she not, as a self-conscious, self-defining human being, need a knowledge of her own history, her much-politicized biology ... a knowledge of women's rebellions and organized movements against our oppression and how they have been routed or diminished?"[1] She argues that without a knowledge of their own past, "women live and have lived without context, vulnerable to the projections of male fantasy, male prescriptions for us, estranged from our own experience because our education has not reflected or echoed it."[2] She concludes that "not biology, but ignorance of ourselves, has been the key to our powerlessness."[3] The purpose of Part I is to begin to overcome that lack of knowledge.

Notes

1. Adrienne Rich, "Taking Women Students Seriously," in Adrienne Rich, *On Lies, Secrets and Silence: Selected Prose 1966–1978* (New York: Norton, 1979), 240.
2. Ibid.
3. Ibid.

Chapter 1: The Study of Politics and the Study of Women

Chapter Summary

This chapter is an introduction to the principal themes of Western thought as they apply to women. The discussion focuses particularly on social and political thought. The chapter begins with a brief description of political science, for those readers who are not majoring in the subject, and concludes with a discussion of the place of women in the discipline in the 1990s.

Chapter Outline

- What Is Political Science?
- Women in the History of Political Thought
- Feminist Critiques of Political Science
- Women as Practitioners of Political Science
- Conclusion

What Is Political Science?

The discipline of political science traces its origins back to Plato (c. 423–347 B.C.) and Aristotle (384–322 B.C.), who first asked systematic questions about power and government and wrote down their answers. By the late twentieth century, there were four primary streams in the study of politics in the West.

The first stream is political thought. Here the writings of the great political thinkers of the past, from the ancient Greeks and Romans to the nineteenth-century liberals and socialists, are analyzed and explained. The second stream is the "formal-legal" description of political institutions. Much of that description is based on national constitutions and other laws. Formal-legal study may focus on one country, or it can be used to compare countries and to deduce general principles of similarity or difference. The third stream is "political behaviour," which dominated political science following World War II. Opinion surveys and other "scientific" tools are used to discover and explain patterns of voting behaviour, and patterns of political values and beliefs. The fourth stream is "international relations," which studies the interactions among sovereign states: war, diplomacy, and international institutions such as the United Nations.

All four streams of political study define "politics" very narrowly, in terms of formal power structures. Political scientists focus on the study of government and public policy, with the study of political behaviour largely confined to voting and political parties. As the century progressed, political theory became increasingly abstract. It also became increasingly polarized between Marxists and non-Marxists, with little constructive dialogue among different schools. None of these trends and controversies in political science had any impact outside the rarefied circles of the academy; but they reduced its ability to offer real solutions to the increasingly intractable political problems in the real world of the late twentieth century.[1]

Women in the History of Political Thought

Despite their different subjects, techniques, and philosophical leanings, all of the major streams of political science have one thing in common: until very recently, they treated women as irrelevant. Women were "defined out" of political science, because they had no place in politics as it had traditionally been understood. Politics was about voting, from which women were excluded until this century. It was about the power of governments, in which women could not participate. It was about war and diplomacy, where women had no place. It was about the history of political thought, in which women were either invisible or treated with contempt. Because political science has been about power, and power has been perceived as a masculine attribute, women have traditionally been irrelevant to political science – both as subjects of study and as scholars.

The ancient Greeks and Romans, the "fathers" of Western political thought, held profoundly negative beliefs about women. Some of these beliefs arose from the problem of *paternity*. It was impossible to prove that a man was the father of his wife's child, so there was a strong male fear of women's sexuality. The solution to the problem was to strictly control women's bodies, so that women would not engage in illicit sexual activity. Women were physically restricted and taught that their sexuality was dangerous. They could not become independent in any way; their bodies and their material goods were owned by their fathers and then their husbands. If an unmarried or widowed woman had no father, her brother or son became her legal guardian. Not surprisingly, given their lifelong legal status as minors, women were believed to be childish, irresponsible, and irrational.

These beliefs were reinforced by the widely accepted view that men and women were naturally different. These differences were not neutral; men and women were not "separate but equal." Women were perceived as inferior in every respect: mentally, physically, spiritually, and morally. The idea that men and women were opposites fit well with the structure of ancient Greek thought, which saw the world as a set of *dichotomies,* or pairs of opposites: reason versus passion, civilization versus nature, mind versus body, order versus chaos. The purpose of political life was to ensure the triumph of the virtues – reason, civilization, mind, and order – over their opposites. These dichotomies came to reflect the more basic dichotomy of sex. In other words, they became *gendered.* Women were associated with, even defined by, the vices: passion, nature, body, chaos. Men were defined by the virtues: reason, civilization, mind, order. Therefore, it was extremely important that men keep their women in line.

Aristotle argued that women's inferiority made them unfit for citizenship, and for any kind of public activity such as law or business. Their proper sphere was the home, where their husbands could dominate them as their weaknesses required. The idea of sexual equality would have outraged Aristotle. He thought of male domination as the natural result of women's inherent irrationality and weakness. In one of his works on reproduction, he argued that "we should look upon the female state as being as it were a deformity, though one which occurs in the ordinary course of nature."[2] Aristotle's ideas, particularly the gendered dichotomies, reflected those of his culture and his time. They profoundly influenced the ideas of the ancient Romans and, after their rediscovery in the thirteenth century, the attitudes of the Christian church.

The creation myth of the ancient Greeks included the story of Pandora, the first woman, who first brought sorrow and trouble to man. Pandora was told not to touch a large box, but in her weakness she succumbed to curiosity and opened it. Out flew the Furies, and man's earthly paradise was ended. The Pandora myth finds strong echoes in the Old Testament book of Genesis, in which Eve's curiosity and temptation caused the Fall of Man. The message is clear: woman is untrustworthy; she is the fount of all sin and sorrow. In the Hebrew tradition woman was created to be man's servant, caring for his home and obeying his orders. Despite the more egalitarian message of Christ, his followers reverted to the old attitudes soon after his death: in the first century A.D. Saint Paul wrote in his Epistle to the Corinthians that "the head of every man is Christ; and the head of the woman is the man."[3]

Eve's sinfulness became the pretext for a host of repressive laws against women. Their sexuality was particularly feared. Many of the Church Fathers had an exaggerated terror of sexual sin, which they translated into a fear and loathing of women. They portrayed women as temptresses, best avoided if a man was to lead a holy life. Women were also seen by some theologians as inherently sinful, untrustworthy, and irrational. Saint Augustine (A.D. 354–430) argued that because of their unruly nature, women needed to be kept in line by their fathers or husbands, with physical force if necessary. These ideas ruled women's lives during the Middle Ages, when church and state were essentially the same. The only bright spot for women was the cult of the Virgin, which became popular in the late Middle Ages (c. 1200–1300). This cult believed that women were capable of the highest virtue, though only if they were beautiful and passive. While this was clearly an improvement over women's treatment elsewhere in Western thought, it did nothing to improve their daily lives.

The Renaissance (c. 1400–1600) could have ended these old notions about women, as it challenged old religious faiths and brought a new faith in the unlimited potential of the human being. Unfortunately, the rational human being heralded by the Renaissance was explicitly male. The Renaissance was sparked, in part, by the rediscovery of Aristotle's writings, which had been lost for centuries. Saint Thomas Aquinas (c. 1225–1274) wrote a synthesis of Christian and Aristotelian ideas, called the *Summa Theologica,* which influenced Christian thought for several hundred years. Aristotle's notions of natural and inherent female inferiority fit very nicely with Judeo-Christian assumptions of natural female sinfulness and servitude. This synthesis had both religious and secular implications. By the time of the Renaissance, state power was growing separate from church power; the classical ideas about women would influence politics and laws as well as scripture.

The foundations of the modern world were laid during the "Enlightenment," in the seventeenth and eighteenth centuries. Enlightenment ideas about the value of the individual, and about state power deriving from the agreement of the population rather than the divine right of kings, have become the unspoken assumptions that shape our lives. The Industrial Revolution, which began in England in the late eighteenth century, was made possible by the spirit of intellectual freedom and scientific inquiry that characterized the Enlightenment. Despite these intellectual and material upheavals, one aspect of Western thought remained relatively unaffected by the "age of reason": attitudes toward women. The "rational individual," the hero of the intellectual inquiry of the Enlightenment, was clearly male.

Three principal changes were wrought by the Enlightenment and the Industrial Revolution, each of which affected women's lives profoundly. The first was the triumph of capitalism over the old agrarian economies of Europe. Capitalism is an economic system in which one class, the bourgeoisie, owns the means of production (land, factories, and so forth) while the other, much larger class, the working class or proletariat, owns nothing but its own labour power. The working class must sell its labour power to the bourgeoisie for money in order to survive.

Capitalism rests on a number of ideas that emerged from the Renaissance and the Enlightenment. The most important of these is the value of the individual in the material world. It was no longer regarded as sinful to work for one's own advancement in this world, rather than putting one's energies into ensuring eternal bliss in the next world. Nor was it seen as sacrilegious to reject the social and economic status into which one had been born; individuals were now free to pursue their own advancement instead of resigning themselves to their lot in life.

The one exception to these new opportunities was the *gendered division of labour*. Women were expected to marry, produce children, work in the house, obtain and prepare food, and do all the chores necessary to look after a family. There has been a gendered division of labour throughout human history, since men hunted game and women collected plants and small animals closer to home. Later, women began to grow plants and men began to herd flocks. The gendered division of labour changes with the economy, but its existence remains constant. There is a narrow range of tasks that women may legitimately perform, all of them domestic: cooking, child care, sewing, and cleaning. The jobs outside the home are reserved for men. As we will see in Chapter 3, even when women have worked outside the home their jobs reflect the gendered division of labour inside the home: nursing, child care, food preparation, cleaning. We will return to the gendered division of labour several times in the course of this book.

The second change introduced by the Enlightenment and the Industrial Revolution was the idea of the modern state — that is, a secular state based on the consent of the governed. The state is not divinely created, nor does the individual have a sacred duty to obey it. The Enlightenment philosophers believed that the power of the state arose from the assent of its citizens, and that if it did not follow the wishes or needs of those citizens they had a right to overthrow it.

The divine right of kingship yielded to the liberal notion of a division between the state and civil society. Under divine absolutism the king had the right to intervene in all areas of public or private life. Liberals sought to replace this absolute ruler with a strictly limited state that was barred from interfering with the homes and businesses of its citizens, the "private sphere." We will refer to this division between the public and the private sphere as the "*public-private dichotomy.*" The notion of a "private sphere" is central to the operation of a free market system. Its guiding idea is that all individuals have certain rights and freedoms, which belong to them by virtue of their humanity — that is, their reason. If the state violates those rights, or passes laws the citizens do not like, it can justifiably be removed. The American Declaration of Independence is perhaps the clearest expression of this liberal attitude.

The idea that the public and private spheres of life are separate and distinct has been gendered as effectively as the earlier Greek dichotomies. Woman is private. She belongs in the home, with the family. Man is public: aggressive, rational, suited to the pursuits of politics, law, business, and warfare. The belief that women are naturally suited to the private sphere has been justified by appeals to religion as well as those of tradition. Today, after three centuries of liberal influence, it is still commonly assumed that women's place is in the home, and that a woman who steps into the public sphere is doing something unnatural and unwomanly. Although these attitudes have been eroding in recent decades, they remain very much in force.

The third key aspect of the Enlightenment and the Industrial Revolution was the idea that man differs from the other animals, not because of his soul, but because of his reason. Man is a thinking being, whose reason can penetrate the mysteries of the earth and give him dominion over nature. From this insight flowed the scientific enquiry and the belief in the power of technology over the environment that made possible not only the Industrial Revolution, but eventually the space age and the power to destroy the planet.

Despite these three important developments in Western life and thought, the Enlightenment and the Industrial Revolution perpetuated the ancient tradition of misogyny – albeit in new forms. The new emphasis on reason only served to exaggerate women's perceived inferiority to men. At least during earlier centuries, when the emphasis was on the soul, women could claim some measure of spiritual equality. But the old ideas about women's lack of reason prevented them from participating fully in the Enlightenment.

Women's exclusion from intellectual circles directly affected only a very few. But the Industrial Revolution changed all women's (and men's) lives profoundly and permanently. Families that had supported themselves on tenant farms were thrown out of their homes as landlords enclosed their estates for the production of wool. Former peasants flocked to the booming industrial and port cities, seeking work in the new factories. Clothing and implements were no longer produced by women at home, but factory produced on a mass scale; the resulting products were sold for cash either at home or overseas. Working-class men and women received a pittance for long hours of hard and dangerous work, lived in tenements, and saw their young children sent to workhouses. Their former self-sufficiency was destroyed by a new system that forced them to work to earn money, so that they could buy the food and other necessities that they had once produced themselves.

As the Industrial Revolution progressed, the home and the workplace appeared to become increasingly separate. The public-private dichotomy was firmly entrenched, along with the new gendered division of labour: men went out to work for money while their wives stayed home. These ideas did not reflect the reality of working-class life, in which women and even children had to go out to work to keep the family from starving. (The gendered division of labour still held, however; when the women returned from the factory, they were expected to cook and clean and look after the children.) Despite their unreality, the gendered division of labour and the public-private dichotomy exerted, and continue to exert, a powerful influence over the middle-class men (and some women) who dominate our economic, social, political, and cultural lives.

As we have seen, a gendered division of labour is a constant feature of human history. Since the eighteenth century, Western men have been expected to go out to work every day for a "family wage" while their wives stayed home with the children. Even today, when women constitute over 40 percent of the paid labour force, the gendered division of labour persists. Women are heavily concentrated in traditionally feminine jobs. Men, meanwhile, are free – subject to financial constraints – to pursue whatever career they want, as long as it is not perceived as a "woman's job." Men are expected to perform powerful jobs requiring superior physical strength or intellectual ability: engineers, doctors, lawyers, administrators, miners, lumberjacks, construction workers.

The gendered division of labour is partly based on biology; women are weakened by childbearing, and a nursing woman does face a few physical restrictions. But for the most part, the gendered division of labour has been based on taboo, custom, and prejudice. Aristotle's dichotomies, in which women were associated with body and passion and men with mind and reason, still have the power to legitimize the arbitrary division of men and women into different occupations. With modern medicine, machinery, and education, there is no reason why women cannot do most of the jobs men do, whether or not they have children. Yet despite its weak foundations, the gendered division of labour persists.

It still seems natural to us when we see female nurses and male doctors, and it is still a little surprising to see male secretaries and female professors.

We have seen how the Aristotelian dichotomies became gendered, so that the virtues – mind, reason, civilization, order – became associated with men and their opposites – body, passion, nature, chaos – with women. The liberal dichotomy between the public and private spheres was also a gendered dichotomy: men were associated with the public sphere, women with the private sphere. The belief that women had no place in public life was hardly new; it was present in the "democracy" of ancient Athens. But it acquired new force in the nineteenth century, because the Industrial Revolution had apparently split the economy from the family. The production of goods now took place outside the home; "work" was something that took place in an office or a factory, not in the house. In reality, of course, the family and the economy are intimately related. We will return to this issue in Part 2. What is important to note at this stage is the power of the gendered public-private dichotomy, and the new form taken by the gendered division of labour during the Industrial Revolution. These two social structures continue to shape attitudes toward women, as well as women's daily lives, in the 1990s.

Feminist Critiques of Political Science

In the past quarter century, Western political science has been attacked by a number of traditionally excluded groups. These groups have criticized political scientists for overlooking their concerns and for perpetuating hurtful stereotypes. They include women, gays and lesbians, African Americans, and people of developing nations. Feminist scholars have been particularly vocal, and their critiques have attracted some support from other political scientists. White academic feminists have attracted more attention than women of colour, or lesbians, or "Third World" women, largely because they are more privileged within the academy as a whole (though not yet as privileged as white heterosexual men).

Feminist critiques of political science have focused on sexist language, concepts, and techniques. Margrit Eichler offers a useful critique of political science research in her book *Nonsexist Research Methods*.[4] She describes seven problems that characterize most social-scientific research about women. The first is *androcentricity*, which means viewing the world from a male perspective. Androcentric research ignores women and assumes that only men exist in politics; or it can be misogynistic, as when it assumes that men are the archetype of political actors and women are an inferior variation. The second is *overgeneralization*. This is the practice of studying men and then applying the results to both men and women. The third is *gender insensitivity,* in which sex is ignored as a socially important variable. This is probably the most common of the problems identified by Eichler. The fourth problem is the issue of *double standards*. When a researcher describes identical behaviour by men and women and explains it differently for each sex on the basis of sex stereotypes, he or she is guilty of the double standard. (A classic example is the traditional literature on voting. A man who does not vote in an election may be described as rational, whereas a woman non-voter is likely to be condemned as apathetic.[5]) The fifth problem is *sex appropriateness,* in which attributes belonging to all humans are associated with only one sex. (For example, women are described as naturally nurturing while men are portrayed as aggressive.) The sixth problem is *familism,* which assumes that everyone in the family is affected in the same way by a particular social event. Familism does not take into account the different degrees of power and other resources belonging to each individual in the family. Finally, there is the problem of *sexual dichotomism,* an overemphasis on the differences between men and women to the exclusion of similarities between them. Sexual dichotomism also leads us to overlook the differences *among* men and women.

This list is not intended as an indictment of all non-feminist political scientists. (Indeed, I would argue that some feminist scholarship is characterized by sexual dichotomism, double standards, sex appropriateness, and even androcentrism.) Rather, it is intended to remind us of the insidious effect of sexism on supposedly value-free research. Feminist scholarship seeks to expose these defects in existing political science literature, and to eliminate them from our own work.

The importance of eliminating gender bias in political science research goes far beyond the university. To the extent that public policy is influenced by the findings of political scientists, it is essential that we provide an accurate account of the lives and experiences of both men and women. Otherwise we run the risk of penalizing those women whose lives have been misinterpreted because of sexist assumptions. Many public policies relating to families have been based on the old ideas of the gendered division of labour and the public-private dichotomy, leaving women without adequate pensions, child care, and income security. (We will return to this issue in Chapter 10.)

The rise of feminism in political science will strengthen the discipline, because it will require us to question our own biases and to examine issues that have been ignored. In the words of one feminist political scientist, the women's movement "brought gender into focus, and made people ask questions where previously there had only been assumptions."[6] This is a welcome self-examination of a discipline that had been growing somewhat stagnant in recent years.

Women as Practitioners of Political Science

Throughout this book, we will encounter a recurring pattern of women's presence in organizations: "the higher, the fewer." Within any hierarchical structure, as one looks from the bottom to the top the numbers of women diminish. Women are concentrated on the bottom rungs of the ladder, while men dominate the top rungs. The discipline of political science is a case in point. In the 1989–90 academic year, 44 percent of Canadian students registered for bachelor's degrees in political science were female. In the same year, only 32 percent of master's students in political science were female, and 29 percent of doctoral students.[7] Fewer than 20 percent of university instructors in political science were female.[8] It is clear that a disproportionate number of female students drop out of political science at the lower levels, instead of pursuing a career in the discipline. There are a number of possible reasons for this, including the nature of the discipline itself or an aversion to an academic career. Whatever the reasons, the diminishing proportion of women at the higher levels of political science should alert us to problems in the discipline.

The small number of women who teach and conduct research in the field of political science is a cause for concern. A female professor in a male-dominated discipline can be a role model for female students, inspiring them to strive for excellence. In addition, most of the research on feminism and women in politics is undertaken by female professors; fewer female professors means a smaller contribution to our knowledge of these subjects. But it must be acknowledged that political science is not always a very welcoming discipline for women. According to one classic critique of the discipline, "That politics is a man's world is a familiar adage; that political science as a discipline tends to keep it that way is less well accepted, but perhaps closer to the truth."[9]

Conclusion

In this chapter we have discussed the following key points.

1. Political science has traditionally defined politics as a male activity, and defined women out of politics.

2. The Greeks set up a series of dichotomies between the virtues and the vices; women were identified with the vices, men with the virtues. The Greek idea that women were irrational, untrustworthy, and inferior was reinforced by the founders of the Christian church.

3. The Enlightenment and the Industrial Revolution created capitalism, the idea of the modern secular state, and the emphasis on reason as the distinctively human attribute. Capitalism altered, but did not abolish, the gendered division of labour; the modern state brought with it the public-private dichotomy; and the emphasis on reason reinforced women's exclusion from the male public world.

4. The discipline of political science has been challenged in recent years by excluded groups, including women. The sexism inherent in much of the work in political science must be eradicated, both for the sake of academic accuracy and because faulty public policy may be based on flawed political research.

5. Female political scientists are few and far between, although this is beginning to change.

In the next chapter, we will see how women have responded to some of the traditional beliefs described in this chapter.

Notes

1. See Ricci, *The Tragedy of Political Science*.

2. From Aristotle, "On the Generation of Animals," excerpt in Mahowald, *Philosophy of Woman*.
3. Quoted in Agonito, *History of Ideas on Woman*.
4. Eichler, *Nonsexist Research Methods*.
5. Janet Siltanen and Michelle Stanworth, "The Politics of Private Woman and Public Man," in Siltanen and Stanworth, *Women and the Public Sphere*.
6. Virginia Sapiro, "Gender Politics, Gendered Politics: The State of the Field," in Crotty, *The Theory and Practice of Political Science*, 165.
7. Statistics Canada, *Universities: Enrolment and Degrees, 1990*.
8. Statistics Canada, *Teachers in Universities, 1989–90* (Ottawa: Minister of Industry, Science and Technology, 1992). There are no specific figures for female teachers in political science, but the figure for the whole field of social science was 19.5 percent. Given the fact that women are more numerous at all levels in psychology and sociology than they are in political science, it is reasonable to assume that the percentage of women in political science is below the average for women in social science as a whole.
9. Susan Bourque and Jean Grossholtz, "Politics an Unnatural Practice: Political Science Looks at Female Participation," in Siltanen and Stanworth, *Women and the Public Sphere*, 103.

References and Further Reading

Agonito, Rosemary, ed. *History of Ideas on Woman: A Source Book*. New York: Perigee, 1977.

Anderson, Bonnie S., and Judith P. Zinsser. *A History of Their Own: Women in Europe From Prehistory to the Present*. New York: Harper & Row, 1989.

Black, Naomi. "'The Child Is Father to the Man': The Impact of Feminism on Canadian Political Science." In Winnie Tomm, ed., *The Impact of Feminism on the Academic Disciplines*. Waterloo: Wilfrid Laurier University Press, 1989.

Bullough, Vern L. *The Subordinate Sex: A History of Attitudes toward Women*. Baltimore: Penguin, 1974.

Clark, Gillian. *Women in the Ancient World*. Oxford: Oxford University Press, 1989.

Coole, Diana. *Women in Political Theory: From Ancient Misogyny to Contemporary Feminism*. Sussex: Wheatsheaf, 1988.

Crotty, William, ed. *The Theory and Practice of Political Science*. Evanston, IL: Northwestern University Press, 1991.

Eichler, Margrit. *Nonsexist Research Methods: A Practical Guide*. Boston: Unwin Hyman, 1988.

_____. "Not Always an Easy Alliance: The Relationship between Women's Studies and the Women's Movement in Canada." In Constance Backhouse and David H. Flaherty, eds., *Challenging Times: The Women's Movement in Canada and the United States*. Montreal/Kingston: McGill–Queen's University Press, 1992.

Gardner, Jane F. *Women in Roman Law and Society*. Bloomington, IN: Indiana University Press, 1986.

Lovenduski, Joni. "Toward the Emasculation of Political Science: The Impact of Feminism." In Dale Spender, ed., *Men's Studies Modified: The Impact of Feminism on the Academic Disciplines*. Oxford: Pergamon Press, 1981.

Lucas, Angela M. *Women in the Middle Ages: Religion, Marriage and Letters*. New York: St. Martin's Press, 1983.

Mahowald, Mary Briody, ed., *Philosophy of Woman: An Anthology of Classic and Current Concepts*. 2nd ed. Indianapolis: Hackett, 1983.

Moller Okin, Susan. *Women in Western Political Thought*. Princeton: Princeton University Press, 1979.

_____. "Gender, the Public and the Private." In David Held, ed., *Political Theory Today*. Stanford: Stanford University Press, 1991.

Pateman, Carole. "Feminist Critiques of the Public/Private Dichotomy" and "Feminism and Democracy." In Carole Pateman, *The Disorder of Women*. Stanford: Stanford University Press, 1989.

Pateman, Carole, and Elizabeth Gross, eds. *Feminist Challenges: Social and Political Theory*. Boston: Northeastern University Press, 1986.

Randall, Vicky. *Women and Politics: An International Perspective*. 2nd ed. Chicago: University of Chicago Press, 1987.

Ricci, David M. *The Tragedy of Political Science: Politics, Scholarship, and Democracy*. New Haven: Yale University Press, 1984.

Siltanen, Janet, and Michelle Stanworth, eds. *Women and the Public Sphere*. London: Hutchinson, 1984.

Statistics Canada. *Universities: Enrolment and Degrees, 1990*. Ottawa: Minister of Industry, Science and Technology, 1992.

Vickers, Jill. "Sexual Politics and the Master Science: The Feminist Challenge to Political Science." In Geraldine Finn, ed., *Limited Edition: Voices of Women, Voices of Feminism*. Halifax: Fernwood, 1993.

Chapter 2: Sexual Politics and Feminist Responses

Chapter Summary

We begin this chapter with a discussion of the power imbalance between men and women in our society, often called *sexual politics* or *patriarchy,* and the structures of gender that perpetuate it. The rest of the chapter concerns women's responses to these inherited social conditions. The first response is feminist thought, the purpose of which is to reveal, explain, and eventually eliminate patriarchy. Feminist thought is divided into four approaches: the currents approach, the strategic practice approach, the integrative feminist approach, and the identity feminist approach. The second response is the women's movement, which is usually divided into the "first wave" (the fight for the vote) and the "second wave" (from the 1960s to the present). The chapter argues that this division is misleading, and provides a brief history of women's activism in the past century and a half. The division between feminist thought and the women's movement is not intended to suggest that the two are separate. Indeed, one of the hallmarks of the women's movement has been a unity of theory and practice. We will see in this chapter, and elsewhere in this book, how the ideas of feminism have influenced the ways in which women have tried to overcome the inherited structures of gender inequality.

Chapter Outline

- Sexual Politics and Feminist Responses
  Sex versus Gender
  Patriarchy
- Feminist Responses
  The Currents Approach
  - Liberal Feminism
  - Radical Feminism
  - Marxist and Socialist Feminism
  The Strategic Practice Approach
  Integrative Feminism
  Identity Feminism
- The Women's Movement
  The Suffrage Campaign and the "Persons" Cases
  The "Second Wave"
- The 1990s: Backlash or Revisionism?
- Conclusion

Sexual Politics

The term "sexual politics" has a number of possible meanings. The first meaning is that *sexual relations are power relations.* This is a revolutionary idea in a culture dominated by images of romantic love. In Harlequin Romances the young woman is swept off her feet by the handsome hero, rescued from loneliness or danger, and carried off to live happily ever after. The idea of sexual politics suggests that this rosy image is misleading; "romance" masks a harsher reality in which men dominate women physically, economically, and psychologically. The relations between men and women are based not on love and tenderness, but on power and submission. Men seek to control women's minds and bodies. They sometimes use physical force, but more often they use demeaning images of women in the mass media and pornography, lower pay, and the denial of reproductive freedom.

Second, the phrase "sexual politics" breaks down the dichotomy between the public and the private. It implies that the separation between the two is a fiction, one that perpetuates women's subordinate place in the family. Crimes such as wife battering and marital rape should be seen as legitimate subjects for legislation and public prosecution, not as personal matters to be ignored by the state and the police.

The idea that *all men* seek to dominate and control *all women* is highly problematic, as we will see in our discussion of radical feminism. But the phrase "sexual politics" retains some value, because it alerts us to the power imbalances that *do* exist between men and women. We will now turn to a brief discussion of two issues that are directly related to the concept of sexual politics: the question of sex versus gender, and the idea of *patriarchy*.

Sex versus Gender

One of the key issues in feminism is the distinction between sex and gender. *Sex* is generally understood as a biological phenomenon. Men and women differ from each other in their primary sexual and reproductive characteristics, and in their secondary sexual characteristics (e.g., women have larger breasts and less body hair than men). Sexual definition is therefore relatively straightforward, although there have always been a few individuals who defied easy categorization (hermaphrodites and, more recently, transsexuals). For the most part, a person is either male or female, and that's that.

Gender is more difficult to define precisely. In its essentials, gender is the set of *non-biological* factors that differentiate men from women in any given culture. These factors include appearance (hair length, clothing, make-up), body language, social behaviour, attitudes towards the self and the world, and expectations for success in various endeavours (e.g., parenthood versus paid work). Male and female gender patterns vary among cultures, although there is one common thread: women are expected to be quiet and passive, men to be strong and aggressive.

Collectively, these non-biological factors constitute *gender roles*. A role, in this sense, is a pattern of behaviour that an individual adopts in response to social expectations. Little girls are taught by the media, and by the approval of grownups, that they should behave differently from little boys. Women who exhibit patterns of behaviour expected of men are regarded with deep suspicion, and vice versa. It is not always easy to pinpoint a specific gender role, but it is easy to see when one has been violated. The gender equivalents of "male" and "female" are "masculine" and "feminine," which are harder to define precisely. It is certainly possible for a woman to behave in a "masculine" way and for a man to behave in a "feminine" way, but short of major surgery, one is born male or female and remains that way for life.

In practice, the issue of gender is extraordinarily complex. There are now multiple roles available to men and women in North America, and the number appears to be growing. For men, the approved traditional roles embody responsibility, hardness, and the triumph of strength and reason over "weakness" and emotion. One author lists four such roles: the Frontiersman, the Soldier, the Breadwinner, and the Expert.[1] Women have also been confined to a few roles, not all of them approved by the culture: the Wife and Mother, the Whore, the Spinster, the Working Girl (often combined with the Spinster), the Widow, the Maiden. The greater the degree of chastity and self-sacrifice inherent in the role, the more approval society has traditionally bestowed upon those women who embody it. Any hint of women's independence from male control has been condemned. As we saw in Chapter 1, the idea that men are (or should be) strong and women are (or should be) weak has characterized Western culture for centuries.

It is not entirely clear where our ideas of masculinity and femininity came from, although there are a number of historical, psychological, and anthropological theories.[2] Whatever the origins of these ideas, we are disposed to defend them vigorously. Any individual who fails to live up to the cultural expectations of gendered behaviour attached to his or her biological sex, deliberately or otherwise, faces concerted pressure to conform. This is one of the sources of resistance to the women's movement.

Each individual in a culture absorbs these gender roles and stereotypes in a process of *socialization*. We acquire the gender-based expectations of our societies in childhood, and we continue to develop them as we mature. Families, the media, peers, role models, and other agents of socialization collectively convey the behaviour and attitudes expected of males and females. Gender-role stereotyping appears to be at its peak in adolescence and early adulthood, as individuals search for partners and begin families. Once their children have been socialized into the prevailing gender roles, middle-aged parents may relax their efforts to live up to gendered assumptions; women may begin to worry less about their appearance, while men may put less emphasis on appearing to be strong and unemotional.

For most of us, these gender roles and stereotypes are so deeply ingrained that we are usually unconscious of them. Much of the "consciousness-raising" activity during the second wave of the women's movement was designed to make women aware of the cultural expectations that governed their lives and constricted their choices. Assumptions about the relative abilities and potential of boys and girls still influence primary and secondary education, as well as instruction in universities and colleges. Girls have always been discouraged, whether subtly or openly, from appearing to be "too smart" to attract boys. The eyelash fluttering and fiddle-dee-deeing of Scarlett O'Hara may seem comic today, but many women still feel pressured to hide their intelligence from men at one time or another.

Despite the women's movement, these gender roles and stereotypes still shape our lives in profound ways. A majority of nursing, secretarial, and home economics students are still women; a majority of math, computer science, chemistry, and engineering students are still men. The gender roles and stereotypes have been under assault for three decades, but they have been in place for millennia. It will take a long time to break down thousands of years of cultural conditioning, assuming that this can be done at all.

Patriarchy

The concept of *patriarchy* is central to much feminist analysis. The word "patriarchy" literally means "rule by the fathers." Patriarchy is the concentration of social, economic, cultural, and physical power in the hands of men, and the consequent oppression of women. Most definitions of patriarchy acknowledge that this power is not shared equally among men; a small male elite controls other men as well as women. It would be wrong, therefore, to assume that the man sleeping on the sidewalk outside the White House is as powerful as the man sleeping inside the White House. However, some analyses of patriarchy imply that a homeless man is higher on the social pecking order than a homeless woman, all other things being equal, by virtue of his greater physical power.

During the second wave, feminists have begun to draw attention to the existence and the consequences of patriarchy. According to the feminist analysis of patriarchy, men dominate the political system, the economic system, culture, the military, sports, academia, and all other important arenas of public life. In addition, they have had the right to do whatever they wanted to their families in their own homes, protected by the wilful blindness of the male-dominated justice system and the belief in the public-private dichotomy. Despite the inequalities among men, all men benefit to some extent from the patriarchal system, just as all women – even the wealthiest and most powerful – are damaged by it in various ways.

The issues we have just discussed – sexual politics, sex and gender, and patriarchy – are central to an understanding of the second wave of the feminist movement. Women have used these concepts to build powerful critiques of the sexual status quo, and of the way in which they have been treated in the Western tradition. We turn now to a discussion of four types of feminist response to women's subordination: the currents approach, the strategic practice approach, the integrative feminism approach, and the identity feminism approach. We will begin with a definition of feminism.

Feminist Responses

What is feminism? In practical terms, there are as many understandings of "feminism" as there are feminists – and anti-feminists. For many anti-feminists, feminism is a godless, anti-family, pro-abortion, man-hating ideology that threatens "our" way of life. Many people who might be sympathetic to feminism are turned off by anti-feminist rhetoric. We have all said, or heard someone else say, "I'm not a feminist, but ..." The person speaking may support some of the goals of the feminist movement, such as freedom of choice on abortion, publicly funded child care, or pay equity, but she (and the speaker is almost always a she) is afraid of being mistaken for a baby-killing, witchcraft-practising badly dressed shrew – in other words, the stereotype of a feminist that we have been fed by the media and by those who oppose changes to traditional gender roles. The eagerness to disclaim any attachment to feminism or the women's movement is widespread and, given the stereotype just described, understandable.

In reality, feminism is a set of diverse ideas with a few key points in common. First, feminists believe that women are not treated as well as men in our society. They point to violence against women, the wage gap, and the under-valuing of women's work in the home as proof for this claim. Second, feminists believe that women *should* be treated as well as men: their work should be valued fairly, whether at home or elsewhere, and their right to make choices concerning their own lives should be respected. In other words, a woman should have the same opportunities and autonomy as a man. She should be safe in her own home and on the streets; she should not have to see demeaning images of her gender in popular culture; and she should be judged on the basis of her abilities and not according to stereotypes of women.

Beyond these general principles, feminists differ on just about everything. Some feminists are pro-choice; others are strongly opposed to abortion. Some feminists believe that women should have access to publicly funded, high-quality child care so that they can pursue careers outside the home, while others believe that women should stay home to care for their children. Some feminists are lesbians; most are heterosexual. Some well-known feminists are highly educated professionals and artists, but any woman can find useful ideas in feminism. This chapter is an introduction to feminist thought, not a comprehensive discussion. Readers are urged to consult the list of works at the end of the chapter.

The Currents Approach

Most accounts of feminist theory divide it into three or four major "currents": liberal feminism, radical feminism, Marxist feminism, and socialist feminism (these last two are sometimes coupled, sometimes treated separately). This approach to the subject has the virtue of neatness and clarity, which explains its popularity among academics. But it has come under increasing criticism in recent years from feminists who object to that very neatness and clarity.[3]

In real life, critics argue, most feminists are not consistently liberal, or radical, or socialist, in their analyses of women's oppression. Instead, they borrow ideas from each current to construct their own personal philosophies. Therefore, the three or four currents of thought are not as distinct in practice as they are in academic descriptions. Furthermore, the currents approach is inadequate because it is too abstract, and does not take into account the lived experiences of most women (especially those who do not belong to the white, middle-class academic tradition). Nor does it permit an understanding of feminist politics and practice in the real world.

Despite these flaws, the currents approach is still the most popular method of teaching feminist theory. We will therefore begin with a brief description and analysis of each of the principal currents.

∾ Liberal Feminism

Sources The beginnings of liberal feminism are usually (though, as we will see, inaccurately) traced back to the eighteenth century and the rise of liberalism in Europe. Liberalism is a body of social, political, and economic ideas that arose in reaction against the feudal absolutism of the Middle Ages and the Renaissance. Its central ideas, which we will discuss in greater detail below, include a belief in the equal rights of all human beings and a faith in educated human reason. Many of these ideas have been adopted by liberal feminism. Nevertheless, it is a mistake to assume that women were incapable of devising these ideas by themselves. Similar notions had appeared in feminist writings as early as the fifteenth century, two hundred years before the birth of liberal thought.

The earliest surviving feminist works in Europe were written by French courtier Christine de Pizan (1365–c. 1430).[4] Pizan was an independent woman, a widow who earned a living by writing. She argued that women were equal to men in natural intelligence, and only appeared to be inferior because they were denied a proper education. She also believed that the subordination of women in marriage was unfair, and that it permitted many husbands to beat or starve their wives and children with impunity. These ideas were revived in the sixteenth and seventeenth centuries, inspired by Christian doctrines of equality of the soul as well as by the nascent ideas of liberalism. Englishwoman Mary Astell (1666–1731) argued that men and women were equal on the basis of their shared humanity, and pointed to England's Queen Anne as an example.[5] These ideas were condemned in their own day and were all but erased from the records of European history.[6] As a result, the credit for penning the first feminist theory is usually given to another Englishwoman, Mary Wollstonecraft (1759–1797), who published *A Vindication of the Rights of Woman* in 1792.

Wollstonecraft shared the beliefs of earlier feminists that women were innately as intelligent as men and that the deprivation of equal rights and opportunities weakened women's reason.[7] She was a member of a radical sect in London, which had embraced the ideas of liberalism in an extreme form. Whereas her predecessors had called for private schools for "ladies," Wollstonecraft advanced a more unusual proposal for a state-run education system in which boys and girls would be given equal opportunities. She attacked the idea (which had recently been made fashionable by Jean-Jacques Rousseau) that women were naturally inferior to men, and predicted that if women were taught useful skills and earned their own living they would be as rational as men. She also condemned the cruelties of marriage under a social system in which women had no legal rights. Much of what Wollstonecraft wrote in 1792 is still echoed in the feminist writings of the 1990s.

Wollstonecraft wrote her treatise in the years immediately following the French Revolution. Liberal ideas were spreading throughout Europe and were creating profound change in political and economic life. Nevertheless, Wollstonecraft's demand that liberal principles be extended to women met with ridicule, abuse, and vicious slanders against her character. These liberal principles have changed substantially during the past three hundred years, but their core remains largely consistent over time. We will focus on three key aspects of liberal thought that have profoundly affected not only its own development, but that of liberal feminism as well.

Key Concepts The first key aspect of liberalism is the *liberal conception of human nature*. For liberals, humans are distinguished from the animals not by their divine soul, but by their reason. Reason is a higher quality, separate from and superior to the body. Reason is also an individual quality; hence the liberal focus on the individual person. Other political ideologies focus on groups of people; for example, nationalism emphasizes the rights of a tribe or nation of people who share a language, culture, and history. For liberals, humanity is a collection of independent, essentially autonomous rational beings, pursuing their distinct self-interests as identified by their reason. This emphasis on the individual leads liberals to stress the rights and freedoms of each person instead of their obligations to a larger community. Those rights and freedoms are ultimately based on the person's capacity for reason; hence those persons with apparently limited reason (including children and the insane) have generally been granted fewer rights than rational adults.

The second key aspect of liberalism is *the public-private dichotomy*. As we saw in the previous chapter, liberals challenged the divine right of kings to control all aspects of human life. They argued that each person had a private sphere of life into which the king (and later the state) could not legitimately intrude. As we also saw, this dichotomy has been explicitly gendered since its emergence in the eighteenth century: men belonged in the public sphere, women in the private. As liberalism has changed in the past three centuries, the boundary between public and private has shifted substantially; liberals have moved from an insistence on a strictly limited state to an acceptance of necessary state intervention in society and the economy. But liberals remain firm in their belief that there must be limits on state activity; otherwise individual liberties would be swallowed up.

The third key aspect of liberalism is its symbiotic relationship with *capitalism*. For liberals, private property is the basis of individual freedom. The state should not own the means of production, or intervene in the economy, except where strictly necessary. It became clear in the nineteenth century that unregulated capitalism led to massive human suffering, as factory owners paid men, women, and children the lowest possible wages and charged them high prices for necessities. Families left their farms and moved to the slums of the new industrial cities, living in filth and poverty. It was apparent even to the staunchest liberal that the state had a responsibility to ensure fair wages, decent working and living conditions, and reasonable hours of work. Most Western countries now have mixed economies, in which the state regulates the private sector and owns some of the means of production.

These three features of liberalism have shaped (and, some argue, fatally weakened) liberal feminism. As the name suggests, liberal feminism shares many of the key ideas of liberalism. Liberal feminists want equal rights and opportunities for women. They work to reform existing political and economic structures in order to achieve those goals. Liberal feminist ideas lead naturally to efforts to influence the state, through lobbying, running for office, and other mainstream tactics. Women's campaigns for equal pay, employment equity, and greater female representation in politics are liberal feminist in inspiration and tactics. Most female politicians are primarily liberal feminists, to the extent that they are feminists at all, as are many other women involved in the institutionalized wing of the women's movement.

History The liberal current of feminism dominated feminist thought until the late 1960s. In the nineteenth century it was advanced by John Stuart Mill and his wife Harriet Taylor Mill.[8] They wrote *The Subjection of*

Women (though until recently only John was credited as its author), a blistering attack on the inherited privileges of men. John Mill agreed with his wife that marriage was a destructive arrangement for women, depriving them of their liberty, their property, and any rights that they might have exercised as single women. He did not entirely accept her belief that women should combine work inside and outside the home, being more committed to the public-private dichotomy. Mill was the greatest English liberal of the nineteenth century, but *The Subjection of Women* has never had the influence of his other, more mainstream writing.

During the first wave of the women's movement, the struggle for women's suffrage between 1880 and 1920, "equal rights" feminism[9] (as liberal feminism was then called) was one of the primary inspirations for the suffragettes. (There were others, as we will see below.) The equal rights feminists did not argue that women would transform politics, as some of their sisters did. Instead, they argued that women deserved the vote, as a matter of simple justice. Women were equal to men in the eyes of God, and many (widows and single women) owned enough property to qualify for the vote under the restrictive conditions of the nineteenth century. Why not allow them the right to vote?[10]

The liberal feminist analysis of women's oppression focuses on tangible issues like legal rights and pay scales. In her 1963 best-seller *The Feminine Mystique,* which many observers credit with beginning the second wave, Betty Friedan added new concerns to the list: the gender roles within which women (and men) were trapped, and the images of women in the media that reinforced those gender roles.[11] Liberal feminists began to talk about socialization, the ways in which little girls and little boys are trained to become feminine and masculine respectively. Liberal feminists criticized the media and the education system, as well as the economic and social conventions that turned women into housewives and men into wage-earners.

Friedan's book was largely aimed at middle-class suburban women who could afford to stay at home. This middle-class bias has been integral to liberal feminism since Wollstonecraft and the Mills. Friedan's solution to "the problem that has no name" – the boredom and frustration of intelligent women stuck in the suburbs – was for these women to get out of the house, back to school or into paid employment. At the time, liberal feminists did not consider all of the implications of this solution:

the lack of child care, the difficulties of combining employment and family, or the discrimination women faced in the workplace.

Twenty years later, after hundreds of thousands of women had entered the labour force (most for reasons of necessity, not liberation), these implications had become clear. In her 1981 book *The Second Stage,* Friedan acknowledged the incompleteness of her earlier analysis.[12] She called on women to re-evaluate their goals, and to pressure governments for the policies and services they needed in order to achieve full equality: child care, maternity leave, and equal pay (see Chapter 3).

Strengths The strengths of liberal feminism are its focus on tangible goals and its appeal to many women (and men) who are alienated by other streams of feminist thought. Instead of working in isolation to raise consciousness, institutionalized liberal feminists work within the system for changes in policy. Liberal feminism is consistent with the prevailing political culture of Canada, which gives it substantial legitimacy in the political system and society at large and enhances its chances of success as a lobbying movement.[13]

Weaknesses The weaknesses of liberal feminism arise from the three key aspects of liberalism discussed earlier. The liberal conception of human nature poses serious problems for feminists.[14]

First, it holds that all human beings are possessed of equal rights based on their capacity for reason. But as we saw in the previous chapter, women have universally been considered to be less rational than men. Therefore, women's rights have been of far less concern than men's rights.

Second, the split between the mind and the body denies the possibility that men and women experience the world differently. For a liberal, human nature is universal, not gendered. Such a conception of human nature denies the very basis of feminism. In addition, the dualism of mind and body blinds liberals to the importance of the material basis of life: food, shelter, sex, and reproduction. This means that liberal political theory cannot deal with the realities of women's (and men's) lives, or with the oppression that constrains women's opportunities.

Third, the idea that human beings are autonomous, purely rational individuals seeking their own self-interest without being influenced by the society around them does not conform to the experience of women. Most people, in fact, are deeply influenced by their culture and their society, no matter how rational they may be. In particular, the liberal focus on the individual obscures the *systemic* barriers to women's achievement in society, the economy, and political life.

Fourth, liberal feminism is criticized for its ambivalence toward the public-private dichotomy. Most radical and socialist feminists reject this dichotomy out of hand. Liberal feminists are torn between a desire to reject the gendered aspects of the dichotomy and a wish to preserve the sphere of individual liberty outside the purview of the state.[15] We have already discussed the effects of the dichotomy on women's lives (Chapter 1), as we will throughout this book. One final point: the dichotomy has been a barrier to women's efforts to use the state to redress inequalities in the home and the economy, and particularly in efforts to prevent and punish domestic violence.

Finally, liberal feminism is attacked for its acceptance of capitalism. The free labour market has never been a reality for women; women have always been disadvantaged by the "family wage" and the "pink-collar ghetto" (see Chapter 4). Liberal feminists have now come to realize that the state must intervene in the economy if the wage gap is to be overcome. Socialist feminists argue that legislated reform is not enough; the capitalist system inevitably oppresses and exploits women, and must be destroyed if women are to achieve full equality.

Conclusion Liberal feminism is no longer the only major current of feminist thought. In the past quarter century it has been substantially influenced by the insights of radical and socialist feminism, although it has remained reformist in its approach. Liberal feminists remain central figures in the women's movement. The strength of liberal feminism in Canada has been its ability to form coalitions with other groups; we will examine the inclusiveness of the Canadian women's movement in Chapter 11.

∾ Radical Feminism

Sources Most people, when they hear the phrase "radical feminism," conjure up a mental picture of a mob of fierce, androgynous women yelling furiously about the iniquity of men. In fact, the word "radical" in "radical feminism" does not mean "extreme" or "way out." It comes from the Latin word for "root." In radical feminist theory, the oppression of women by men is seen as the root of all other power inequalities in society. In addition, women's sexuality and ability to reproduce are at the root of both women's power and women's oppression. Radical feminism is the only current of feminist theory that owes nothing to male theorists; it is entirely the creation of women, in the late twentieth century.

Radical feminism emerged in the United States and Britain in the late 1960s and early 1970s, partly in reaction against liberal feminism and partly out of rage against sexism.[16] Most of the early radical feminists had been involved in the civil rights and anti-war movements, where they had encountered the same sexist discrimination and belittling they had suffered in traditional institutions. They quit the male-dominated movements and set out to create their own. The first radical feminist organizations were small "consciousness-raising" groups, modelled on the Maoist practice of "speaking bitterness."[17] The members were mostly young, alienated from "the system," and impatient for change.[18] They condemned the institutionalized liberal feminists as too old and too slow; they rejected the politic of "mainstreaming" and adopted a strategy of "disengagement" (see below). Today, despite the influence of its analyses on liberal feminism (especially in Canada), radical feminism tends to remain outside the established structures of power, in local groups working to help women on a small scale.

Key Concepts Because of this dispersion, and the lack of a single uniform radical feminist theory, it is dangerous to overgeneralize about what radical feminism says.[19] But there are some common threads in radical feminist analyses. First, all radical feminists agree that "distinctions of gender, based on sex, structure virtually every aspect of our lives and indeed are so all-pervasive that ordinarily they go quite unrecognized."[20] The goal of radical feminism is to make women aware that these distinctions of gender exist – hence the importance of consciousness raising – and that they injure women in all areas of their lives. Women are raped, beaten, exploited, and treated as second-class citizens entirely on account of their biology.

Second, these distinctions of gender are enforced and perpetuated not by nature, but by men. Hence, men are the oppressors of women. Radical feminists argue that "men derive concrete benefits from their oppression of women, and [therefore] feminists must struggle against rather than with men in order to achieve liberation."[21] In addition, "Radical feminists argue that, because men oppress women, feminists must struggle against men and so must acknowledge the need for separatism and a polarization of the sexes."[22]

Third, most radical feminists believe that despite their subordination to men, women have a unique sexual and reproductive power. Only women can conceive and give birth. However, the relationship between women's biology and women's oppression is a complex one in radical feminist thought. Some radical feminists argue that men's fear of this awesome female power led to the creation of patriarchal structures. Others believe that women's oppression began when men realized their own role in procreation and determined to keep their women away from other men who might impregnate them. In other words, women's ability to give birth is a unique power that leads to enforced powerlessness at the hands of men.

On the other hand, a few radical feminists have argued that women are weakened and made physically dependent on men by the demands of pregnancy and childbirth, and that this is the root of women's oppression within the biological family. Most radical feminists agree on one aspect of this debate: they object to the control of women's sexuality and reproduction by doctors and technicians – which some call the "male medical establishment," despite the growing number of women in medicine – and they call for a more natural approach to pregnancy and childbirth (including the recognition of midwives).

Fourth, radical feminists reject the public-private dichotomy. We have seen that the most famous slogan of the radical feminist movement, "The personal is political," has two meanings. The first is that there is no difference between women's oppression in the private sphere and women's oppression in the public sphere; therefore the liberal notion of a separation between the two is mistaken. In addition, the idea of the dichotomy has blinded us to the realities of domestic violence and sexual abuse, which radical feminists have succeeded in making visible. Second, "The personal is political" means that all relationships between people are based on inequalities of power.

As we saw earlier, the notion of "sexual politics" suggests that even intimate sexual relationships are constructed according to patriarchal norms of subordination and domination. Therefore, the old liberal notion that a man's home is his castle is not only wrong, but dangerous. Society and the state must intervene to prevent physical and sexual abuse of women and children within the family.

Fifth, radical feminists believe that all women share certain experiences, by virtue of their shared biology. This belief is reflected in the radical feminist concept of "sisterhood." The concept of sisterhood implies that all women, whatever their time and place, have suffered similar forms of oppression. As we will see below, this concept has attracted much criticism in recent years, mostly from socialist feminists.

Unlike liberal feminism, radical feminism does not consider the mind to be separate from the body. Women and men experience the world differently, and they think and reason differently as a result. Radical feminists also downplay the importance of rational thought, arguing that mental constructs like logic and the application of abstract rules are masculine in nature. Women are more intuitive and spiritual, in touch with nature and the earth. Finally, instead of focusing on the individual, radical feminism examines the patriarchal structure of society to identify systemic discrimination against women based on their sex.

History Although we have said that radical feminism emerged in the late 1960s, this is not entirely true. During the first wave, as we have seen, many women involved in the various reform movements were motivated by their belief in the responsibilities and virtues of motherhood. This "maternal feminism" grew out of a conviction that women were morally superior to men, and that their biological drive to bear and nurture children made them natural enemies of warfare, poverty, alcohol, and other evils that afflicted Canada early in this century (and since, of course).

One of the central figures in the suffrage movement, Nellie McClung, stated the case for maternal feminism succinctly: "The woman movement ... is a spiritual revival of the best instincts of womanhood − the instinct to serve and save the race. ... Women are naturally the guardians of the race, and every normal woman desires children. ... It is woman's place to lift high the standard of morality."[23]

Such sentiments (minus the words "race" and "normal") are expressed by many radical feminists today, particularly those active in the anti-nuclear and environmental movements.[24]

The emergence of modern radical feminist theory in the 1960s and 1970s can be traced to three books. The first, Simone de Beauvoir's *The Second Sex,* was published in French in 1949 and in an English translation in 1953.[25] *The Second Sex* broke new ground in feminism and in existential philosophy. De Beauvoir argued that sex was distinct from gender, and that women's oppression was a product of gender. In other words, the oppression of women is man-made, not natural. There is nothing in female biology to explain woman's secondary status in all human societies, especially in the twentieth century, when brute strength is no longer required for survival.

According to de Beauvoir, woman is made, not born. She is seen as "the Other" – alien, the object, inferior to man and to the male standard of humanity. Woman's apparently inferior character is shaped by her lack of opportunity and resources, not by any innate inferiority; in this respect de Beauvoir echoes Astell and Wollstonecraft. Woman's biology, particularly her reproductive capacity, does create certain inevitable differences between men and women: "her relations to her own body, to that of the male, to the child, will never be identical with those the male bears to his own body, to that of the female, and to the child."[26] But difference does not necessarily mean inferiority. De Beauvoir argued that men and women have to transform the structures of gender in order to create equality between the sexes in spite of their immutable differences.

The next two milestones in radical feminism appeared in 1970. Kate Millett's book *Sexual Politics* is a scholarly study of sexual themes in twentieth-century French, American, and English literature, and today it appears quite mainstream,[27] but in 1970 it was revolutionary. Millett revealed the power relations inherent in men's depictions of sexual acts. She agreed with de Beauvoir that patriarchy was created by men and that we are brought up to consider it natural. Little girls are trained to accept their gender roles, largely through the fiction of romantic love. But sex, as portrayed by respected male authors like Norman Mailer and D.H. Lawrence, is not romantic. It is an expression of man's power over woman, his physical, psychological, and economic strength prevailing over her (apparently natural) weakness. Millett's book provided the foundation for the modern analysis of patriarchy, exploded the myths of women's inferiority, and revealed the various forms of coercion hidden behind the rosy myths of romantic love.

The other radical feminist breakthrough of 1970 was Shulamith Firestone's book *The Dialectic of Sex: The Case for Feminist Revolution*. Firestone applied the Marxist method of historical materialism to the history of patriarchy, drawing an analogy between the economic class struggle – the oppression of the proletariat by the bourgeoisie – and the "sex class" struggle. She argued that women's biology was at the root of women's subordination.[28] Women in the state of nature had been weakened by pregnancy, childbirth, and the demands of nursing children. As a result, they became dependent for survival on men. Men took advantage of this dependence to create the universal structures of subordination that have persisted for millennia, long after the biological reason for them has elapsed. These structures include the myths of romantic love and the ideal marriage, and the "male" culture that keeps women passive and constantly struggling to meet impossible standards of sexual attractiveness. How to overcome this oppression and exploitation of women?

The most controversial solution proposed by Firestone was to eliminate women's role in reproduction altogether. Women could escape the oppression of the "sex class" system through a technological revolution. Women would seize the means of reproduction. Children would be conceived in glass dishes and gestated in glass wombs. The genital differences between men and women would cease to matter, and human beings would become essentially androgynous:

> Just as the end goal of socialist revolution was not only the elimination of the economic class *privilege* but of the economic class *distinction* itself, so the end goal of feminist revolution must be, unlike that of the first feminist movement, not just the elimination of male *privilege* but of the sex *distinction* itself.[29]

The biological parentage of children would be unknown, so that individual women would not be bound by the demands of child care. Instead, the children would be looked after by society as a whole. This utopian vision has attracted a great deal of criticism, often distracting attention from the powerful analysis that makes up the bulk of the book.

A more realistic solution proposed by Firestone is the creation of looser "family" structures, like Israeli *kibbutzim*, where groups of adults and their children would live together with the children the collective responsibility of all of the adults. Writing in 1970, with a growing social acceptance of unmarried adults living together, Firestone was optimistic that such a development would occur more or less naturally. In the 1990s, this prediction seems almost as utopian as the "glass wombs." There is now clear evidence that no matter how "loose" family structures become, women retain most of the day-to-day responsibility for children; and the looser the family structure, the less emotional and financial responsibility men take for their offspring.

Radical feminist theory has blossomed since 1970, but the principal themes and debates can still be traced back to these three pioneering works. In recent years the debate between the critics and the advocates of childbirth has intensified. In addition, radical feminism has spawned lesbian feminism, feminist separatism, and eco-feminism.

Lesbian feminism is essentially a celebration of women's love for women, and a critique of the "compulsory heterosexuality" inherent in Western concepts of sex and marriage. Feminist separatism is the belief that women can only escape their oppression by building an alternative lifestyle. Women live together, establish feminist collective businesses, and create relationships and families with other women. Finally, eco-feminism is an attempt to synthesize the radical feminist understanding of women's closeness to nature with the ecological analysis of the destruction of the planet. It argues that women must save the Earth from the masculinist "will to death," the male-created and male-dominated technologies that are depleting the planet's resources and poisoning its ecosystem.

Perhaps the most influential radical feminist analysis of the 1970s is Susan Brownmiller's history of rape.[30] Her analysis can be summed up in two famous sentences: "From prehistoric times to the present, I believe, rape has played a critical function. It is nothing more or less than a conscious process of intimidation by which *all men* keep *all women* in a state of fear."[31] This argument has influenced much later radical feminist analysis, as well as the work of socialist feminists like Catharine MacKinnon and Andrea Dworkin (see below).

Strengths The strengths of radical feminist theory include its willingness to name men as the beneficiaries of patriarchy; its insight that all aspects of women's lives are political; its synthesis of mind and body; and its ability to see beyond the separate experiences of individual women to perceive the systemic discrimination against all women. As we will see, these aspects of radical feminism are also its greatest weaknesses.

First, the naming of men as the enemy is a strength because it allows radical feminists to explain why the structures of patriarchy have persisted throughout human history. Like a police detective investigating a murder, they have asked, "Who benefits?" And the answer is that although they are usually unconscious of it, men have benefitted greatly from women's subordination. Women have been paid less than men yet forced to work harder than men; women have reproduced the species with little effort on the part of men; women have been trained to consider men their superiors; women have been the silent victims of men's violence and abuse. Without such a recognition, the persistence of patriarchy is inexplicable.

Second, the idea that "the personal is political" has also been a strength of radical feminism. By exposing the falsity of the public-private dichotomy, radical feminists have brought the issues of family violence and sexual abuse into the open, where we can deal with them. They have weakened – though not yet eliminated – the idea that a husband's right to privacy is greater than his wife's right to physical security. Radical feminism has also taught us that power inequalities between men and women are universal, despite the Harlequin Romance myths of romance and ideal marriage.

The synthesis of mind and body is a third crucial element of radical feminism. As we saw earlier, the mind-body dualism of liberal feminism implies that the physical realities of life are irrelevant to social and political theory. For radical feminists, the body is *the* crucial fact. Women and men live in different bodies, and their lives are very different as a result. Radical feminists have forced political theorists (and politicians) to come to grips with such physical facts as violence against women and the medicalization of childbirth. They have also reminded us that politics does not exist in some ethereal realm over and above the sordid realities of daily life. The body *is* political. How else can we explain the efforts of governments to control women's fertility and sexuality?

Finally, Catharine MacKinnon's analysis suggests that sex is not just about biology; our minds are actively involved in determining what is erotic.[32] As a result, we are culturally conditioned to find certain qualities sexy: cruelty and domination in men, passiveness and dependence in women. This erotic conditioning reinforces patriarchy, by inducing women to collude in its survival. MacKinnon's analysis goes somewhat beyond the single-minded focus on biology that often weakens radical feminist theory (see below).

Fourth, radical feminists reject the individualism of liberal theory in order to examine the structural and systemic problems confronting all women. This approach allows us to perceive the patterns in women's experience. And those patterns force us to acknowledge that if a woman is underpaid relative to a man in a similar job, it may not be entirely her fault. The reason may be a sexist employer who believes that women should be paid less because they're working for "pin money," or a school system that discouraged her from pursuing further qualifications, or a society that undervalues women in all aspects of their lives. Such an approach can help to build the self-esteem of women who are accustomed to blaming themselves for their lack of success.

Weaknesses There are four principal weaknesses of radical feminist theory: its basis in biological determinism; its assumption that all women are fundamentally the same and all men are the same, while men and women are fundamentally different; its lack of real historical analysis; and its neglect of the non-sexual aspects of women's lives. *Biological determinism* means the explanation of human social behaviour purely on the basis of sex, or race or ethnicity, or any other inborn characteristic. Human beings are considerably more complicated than a biological determinist analysis suggests, and in any case our knowledge of human biology is not sophisticated enough to explain all of the nuances of individual behaviour and thought. Radical feminism falls into the error of biological determinism because it implies that men are genetically predisposed to violence while women are naturally nurturing.

If this claim about male and female nature is accurate, three conclusions follow. First, there is no point in trying to change men's behaviour; patriarchy is programmed into their genes, and no amount of persuasion will overcome it. Second, there is no purpose in holding men responsible for their sexist actions, including violence against women, because they can't help it. Third, if men are inherently flawed, then women have no choice but to separate from men altogether. This may make some women more comfortable in the short term, but in the long run the species is doomed.

None of these conclusions holds much water. Nor is it credible to argue that *all* men are the enemy. Thousands of Canadian men are trying to come to grips with the women's movement and to overcome their own masculine conditioning. Others are sympathetic to the aims of feminism but are alienated from it because they are tired of being portrayed as villains. Some of those men might have been valuable allies had they not been put on the defensive by radical feminist rhetoric – or by the caricatures of radical feminism in the media. Finally, as Alison Jaggar has argued, biological determinism is simply not valid: "the human biological constitution is not a pre-social given, remaining constant throughout the changes in human social life. It is a result as well as a cause of our system of social organization."[33] Jaggar criticizes the radical feminist belief that "sex differences determine certain forms of social organization," arguing instead that "certain forms of social organization *produce* differences between the sexes."[34]

Recent anthropological studies have demonstrated that men's domination over women is not universal. Nor is it caused by biology. Instead, "male dominance evolves as resources diminish and as group survival depends increasingly on the aggressive acts of men."[35] Power accrues to "whichever sex is thought to embody or to be in touch with the forces upon which people depend for their perceived needs."[36] The ability to give birth empowers women in some cultures, while the ability to kill empowers men in other cultures. "Conceiving power in this way, one can say that in some societies women have more power, or men have more, or both sexes have an approximately equal amount."[37] The conditions that favour male abilities over female abilities, for example a scarcity of resources, are not the product of human biology. They are set by the environment and by relations with neighbouring peoples. The study of anthropology suggests that the biological determinism inherent in radical feminism is a misrepresentation of women's (and men's) lived experience.

Second, radical feminism falls into the trap of *sexual dichotomism* (see Chapter 1). Women are treated as one homogeneous group and men as a very different (also homogeneous) group. This approach overlooks the differences among women, including those of race, class, and sexual preference. At the same time, it overstates the things that separate men and women from each other, while understating the common humanity that unites us. Radical feminism also ignores the fact that some women are more powerful than some men. It would be difficult to argue, for example, that Margaret Thatcher and Kim Campbell were less powerful than the men who took out their garbage.

The problems with this argument go beyond a few exceptional individuals. As more and more Canadian women achieve success in law, medicine, politics, and academia, it becomes increasingly clear that white, middle-class heterosexual women are very privileged people. Their male counterparts are more privileged, but many other groups (including working-class African Canadian or native Canadian men) are, on average, much less fortunate. Radical feminism has not dealt sufficiently well with issues of race and class, and its analysis of power remains unsophisticated as a result.

Third, radical feminism is essentially ahistorical. This means that it does not explain patriarchy on the basis of genuine historical fact, which causes it to overlook the differences among women at different historical periods. Even Firestone, who based her analysis on Marxist historical materialism, claims that human biology is identical across history and throughout the world. But more recent studies have demonstrated that as seemingly immutable a biological experience as childbirth can vary substantially from one time and place to another.

Some radical feminists have argued that the various misogynist practices of different cultures are somehow equivalent, that workplace sexual harassment in Canada in 1993 is as much a crime as seventeenth-century Chinese footbinding or contemporary Somalian clitoral mutilation. This is a remarkably parochial and patronizing argument. Women have suffered relatively little in Canada in recent years, compared to the witch-burnings of the not too distant past and the terrible suffering of women elsewhere in the world today. This is not to deny that millions of Canadian women suffer indignities and exploitation on account of their sex, but we must put those problems in perspective. Little is gained, and much credibility is lost, if we forget how lucky most Canadian women are in comparison with the girls of rural India who are never sent to school with their brothers, or the child prostitutes of Bangkok.

Fourth, radical feminism is essentially silent about the non-sexual aspects of women's lives. It can tell us little about the economic exploitation of women, or about the reasons why the gendered division of labour took the particular forms that it did in different societies. If all women share similar experiences based on their sexuality, why are more than half the doctors in the former Soviet Union female while the female proportion of Canadian doctors is substantially smaller? Why did Canadian women move into the workforce in such unprecedented numbers in the 1970s and 1980s? Why are there so few women in the House of Commons? Radical feminism can suggest a few broad answers to these questions, and those answers are not without value. But they are not sufficiently specific to provide an acceptable explanation in social science.

Radical feminism has profoundly influenced feminist theory. As we acknowledge its weaknesses and excesses, we should also be grateful for its strengths. It can be exhilarating to encounter radical feminist theory for the first time, reading women's words of pride and anger and power. But radical feminism is limited by its single-minded focus on the biological aspects of women's lives. It is also weakened by its tendency to condemn men as criminals and exalt women as innocent victims. Common sense and daily experience tell us that some men are not misogynist pigs. And the idea that "woman" equals "victim" is not only defeatist, it ignores the strength and the power displayed by women of all cultures. We must remember that despite their oppressive aspects, institutions like the church and the family have been a source of strength and sustenance for women. The radical feminist critique offers some important insights, but its fatalism and its condemnation of "male culture" should not be taken too far. The creation of socialist feminism, which we will examine in the next section, is an attempt to profit from the strengths of radical feminism while avoiding its weaknesses.

∾ Marxist and Socialist Feminism

Marxist feminism, like liberal feminism, is the result of women's attempts to apply male-derived analyses to the problem of gender inequality. Marxism is the theory of history and economics created by Karl Marx (1818–1883) and his long-time collaborator Friedrich Engels (1820–1895). Marx and Engels produced a complex and richly detailed body of work, very little of which deals directly with women. Nonetheless, several of their ideas have been adapted by later feminists to explain the subordination of women. We will briefly discuss a few of the key Marxist concepts: capitalism, class struggle, false consciousness, alienation, and historical materialism.

Sources Marxism is a critique of capitalism and liberalism. Marx and Engels exposed the exploitation that underlay the capitalist system, using the analytic concept of *class*. Capitalism, for Marx, is the stage of world history in which one class owns the means of production and the other class owns nothing but its labour power. The members of the proletariat have no means of survival except to sell their labour power to the bourgeoisie. The bourgeoisie use this labour power, in combination with the other factors of production (land and capital), to produce commodities.

For example: An industrialist employs ten workers in his factory. Each worker produces 100 widgets per day. It costs $5 to produce each widget: $1 in overhead, $1 in capital costs, $1 for materials, and $2 for labour. Therefore each worker earns $200 per day, or $2 for each of 100 widgets. The industrialist then sells each widget for $10, making $10,000 from the sale of a day's worth of widgets, for which the workers were paid a total of $2,000. But instead of passing along the profit (which Marx called *surplus value*) to the workers, the industrialist keeps it. Therefore the people who do the actual work earn $200 per day, while the factory owner earns $5,000 a day. If the worker complains about this state of affairs, he or she can be fired and replaced by another worker from the *reserve army of labour* (the unemployed).

At the root of capitalist exploitation, for Marx, is the institution of private property. If the bourgeoisie did not have the right to own the means of production for their own private benefit, then everyone would collectively own (and profit from) the means of production, and the worker would not have to sell his or her labour to earn a living. Collective ownership of the means of production is *communism*. Communism can only come about when the working class becomes a class-for-itself, that is, a politically aware and united class, which overthrows the bourgeoisie and seizes the means of production. The proletariat does not become a class-for-itself, according to Marx and Engels, because they are the victims of *false consciousness*. They have swallowed the myths and lies of liberal thought, the dominant ideology that keeps them from uniting in common cause and that tells them capitalism is the only possible way to organize economic production.

Another key Marxist concept is *alienation*. In an early manuscript, Marx argued that when a worker sells his labour-power to the bourgeoisie, he alienates himself from the product of his labour, which belongs to the employer. For Marx, the human being is not distinguished from animals by his reason; he is distinguished by his capacity for labour. Therefore when man is alienated from the product of his labour, he is alienated from his very essence. He is also alienated from his fellow humans, with whom he competes for a wage, and from his species-being (his identification with his fellow humanity). Under communism man would no longer be alienated from his essence, from his labour, or from his fellows; he would own the product of his labour, because it would not be necessary for him to sell his labour power in order to live.

A final Marxist concept is the idea of dialectical historical development, also known as *historical materialism* or *economic determinism*. For Marx, history is constantly evolving. The motor of history, the force that keeps it moving forward, is the improvement of the means of production. Technology brings advances in production, which in turn affect the relations of production (the relations between owner and worker). For example, the advent of the steam engine and the cotton gin ended the feudal agricultural production of the Middle Ages and brought about the Industrial Revolution. The workers left the land and moved to the new industrial towns to work in the factories owned by the bourgeoisie who had invested in the new technology. The workers no longer owned and worked their own land, freely selling or consuming their own produce; they were now selling their labour power to the bourgeoisie in exchange for a small money wage. Their wives and children were also put to work in the factories, or in the mines that produced the coal to run the engines.

On top of the means and relations of production, which Marx called the *base,* is the social *superstructure.* This includes the political system, the dominant ideology, and the prevailing social norms and beliefs. Liberalism is the dominant ideology of capitalism; it either hides or justifies the exploitation inherent in private ownership of the means of production. Representative parliamentary government is the political structure belonging to capitalism; it hides the fact that the state acts primarily in the interest of the bourgeoisie, and legitimates the political and economic system through the device of periodic elections.

This materialist model of history has a number of implications for the Marxist concept of human nature. Marxists reject the liberal model of human nature based on *reason* in favour of a social model of human nature based on work (*praxis*). The nature of women, like that of men, is historically determined. Therefore, there is no universal human nature. To understand why people think and behave as they do, we must look at each society at each particular historical stage. Within each society, there is one primary division: class. Gender was not a primary feature of Marx's thought, which poses problems for Marxist feminists.

Nevertheless, Marx (and especially Engels) did offer some account of women's oppression. For them, the explanation of women's oppression lies in the sexual division of labour. Unfortunately for later Marxist feminists, neither Marx nor Engels provided a satisfactory historical explanation for the sexual division of labour. In other words, they never really answered the question of why women have traditionally been relegated to the home and hearth while men worked for money. In a capitalist system, the role of women is to remain in the home consuming commodities, reproducing the labour force and serving, when needed, as a cheap reserve army of labour. But there is little analysis of pre-capitalist societies to try to explain how this division of labour came about. As Alison Jaggar has argued, "The traditional Marxist categories were not designed to capture the essential features of the sexual division of labour, and it is doubtful whether they are capable of doing the job."

Despite these problems, a distinct strand of Marxist feminism has emerged. Its core is the assumption that all forms of oppression, including the oppression of women, would be eliminated by the destruction of capitalism and of private property in a communist revolution. In the shorter term, Marxists have argued that the key to ending women's oppression was to end the gendered division of labour. If only women were in the labour force, instead of at home, their oppression would be diminished if not entirely ended.

Unfortunately for Marxists, a majority of women are now in the paid workforce yet oppression continues both inside and outside the workplace. This is not to dismiss the Marxist analysis of women's work entirely; as Rosemarie Tong notes, it has helped us to understand "how the institution of the family is related to capitalism; how women's domestic work is trivialized as not *real* work; and, finally, how women are generally given the most boring and low-paying jobs." In particular, it is important for us to realize that "women's work is the necessary condition for all other labour, from which, in turn, surplus value is extracted. By providing current (and future) workers not only with food and clothes, but also with emotional and domestic comfort, women keep the cogs of the capitalist machine running."

Strengths One of the central debates in Marxist feminism is the question of whether women constitute a class. Traditionally, women have been perceived as *divided* along class lines; bourgeois women and proletarian women belong to different classes. Yet the core project of Marxist feminism has been to unite women in common recognition of their shared oppression, with the ultimate goal of women's full participation in the coming revolution. It is not clear how this project is to be realized. Marxist feminists have had little to say about the family, focusing instead on work outside the home, although they have made a strong argument that women's housework has been trivialized by men. This focus has led to a Marxist feminist campaign for wages for housework.

There is no consensus about whether this would free women from oppression or turn women's work into just another commodity. To the extent that Marxist feminists have analyzed gender relations inside the home, they have focused on the concept of alienation. Women are alienated, as men are, from the forces of production; but women are even more alienated, because many of them are trapped inside separate houses with no connection through labour to the species-being. Marxist feminists have also given us some insights into the slowness of Western corporations and governments to provide adequate maternity leave and child care for women working outside the home: capital does not benefit from them, therefore it will not provide them.

Weaknesses There are a number of problems within Marxist feminism. One of these is the inability of the concept of class to provide an adequate analysis of women's oppression. Women do constitute a class in a sense, because they are distinguished from men by the gendered division of labour. But in all other senses, women do not constitute a class. Most women now work outside the home, and many women are not part of classic nuclear families. Given these differences among women, it is difficult to find the consistency of experience that would designate them as a class. Another problem with Marxism is the gender-blindness (and implicit maleness) of its central concepts. Women inside and outside the home are all but invisible in non-feminist Marxist thought; as Sartre put it, for Marxists "the individual is born at the moment of applying for his first job."

According to Jaggar, the gender-blindness of Marxism actually reinforces the patriarchal status quo: "By obscuring women's oppression, Marxist theory provides a rationale for its perpetuation." Although the Marxist concept of human nature does not suffer from the liberal flaw of metaphysical dualism (because it recognizes the material aspects of human life), it does suffer from an implicit assumption that all persons are male. Marxist feminists have laboured heroically to overcome this assumption, but women are still seen as the exception in Marxism. Therefore, Marxism cannot explain such non-economic phenomena as misogyny and violence against women. Jaggar argues that Marxism, by defining humanity solely in terms of productive labour, in effect defines women out of humanity: "In fact, however, women's concern with the sexual, emotional and procreative aspects of human life speaks to needs that are equally deep and to human capacities that are equally capable of development."

Another flaw in Marxism is that it does not identify patriarchy as something caused by men and in the interests of men. Because it is the result of class differences, women's oppression is caused by the political, social, and economic structures inherent in capitalism, and not by men. This leads to the conclusion, mentioned earlier, that the way to end women's oppression is to overthrow the capitalist system.

But there is no reason why a communist revolution should eliminate *women's* oppression, as liberating as it might be for male workers. This is because Marxism has no real explanation for pre-capitalist discrimination against women, and no historical explanation for the gendered division of labour. Why, then, should we accept the argument that women's oppression will end with capitalism, since it did not begin with it? Could there not be a distinctively communistic form of women's oppression, as there have been distinctively agrarian and industrial forms of women's oppression? Marxism fails to sustain a credible feminist analysis because it does not deal effectively with women *as women.*

By the late 1970s, many feminists had acknowledged the limitations of both Marxist and radical feminist theory. They were not satisfied with the radical analysis that identified patriarchy as the single root of women's oppression, nor with the Marxist analysis that blamed it on capitalism. Socialist feminism emerged from the effort to synthesize these two approaches: to overcome the gender-blindness of Marxist analysis while simultaneously applying historical materialism to the analysis of patriarchy. Socialist feminism has also attempted to broaden feminist analysis beyond the issue of gender, to include issues of race, class, relations between the West and developing countries, sexual preference, and disabilities. All structures of inequality, whether capitalism, racism, patriarchy, or imperialism, are both distinct and intertwined. Therefore, the destruction of one source of inequality but not the others will not solve all of the problems identified by socialist feminists. At the very least, both capitalism and patriarchy must be eradicated if women are to overcome oppression.

Socialist feminism differs from radical feminism in at least four significant ways. First, while radical feminists assume that human biology is a universal given, socialist feminists argue that biology is, to some extent, socially constructed. The foundation of this argument is the Marxist notion of historical materialism. As the technology of production evolves, so does the *praxis* of each society. In turn, "the specific form of *praxis* dominant within a given society creates the distinctive physical and psychological human types characteristic of that society." These "distinctive types" include all aspects of human nature, even sexuality and reproduction. Socialist feminists point out that sex and childbirth can be experienced very differently according to their time and place. There is a psychological element to our experience of the body, which is determined by the dominant ideology and the *Zeitgeist* of one's geographical and historical place.

An illustration of this difference between radical and socialist feminism can be found in the work of Catharine MacKinnon. MacKinnon's analysis of sexual violence and pornography follows Brownmiller's argument about rape (see above), and adds a further dimension. For MacKinnon, as we have seen, sexuality is a social construct as well as a biological given. We as a society have eroticized domination and power. This argument may explain the prevalence of rape, sexual abuse, and pornography. It also suggests a possible reason why so many women collaborate with patriarchy instead of resisting it.

A second difference between radical and socialist feminism is the socialist recognition that the concept of "sisterhood" has at best limited application. As we have seen, socialist feminists are trying to integrate issues other than gender into their analysis of women's oppression. This attempt is long overdue. The white, middle-class bias of feminist theory has been criticized by women who felt excluded from the abstract discussions of the academics. Unfortunately, the effort to integrate other forms of oppression into the analysis of patriarchy leads inevitably to an even higher level of theoretical abstraction, because of the conceptual problems involved. Exactly what is the relationship between capitalism and patriarchy? Are they separate or linked? Are they distinct phenomena with separate causes or two heads of the same Hydra? Where does race fit in? Or sexual orientation? Or country of origin? Or imperialism? Socialist feminists have set themselves an extremely difficult task, and there will never be theoretical consensus within the current. But the attempt is still worth making, because it helps us to understand the ways in which "sisterhood" is modified or superseded by racial solidarity, class struggle, or nationalism.

The third difference between radical and socialist feminism lies in their analyses of reproduction. For radical feminists, women's role in reproduction is a physical fact, a link to the natural world. For socialist feminists, reproduction is also an economic fact. Sexuality and reproduction are not part of the social superstructure; rather, they are part of the economic base of society. *Reproduction* is a form of economic *production*. The ability to bear children is crucial to the survival of the economy, because it guarantees a future supply of workers and consumers. As a result, powerful interests in society – both the bourgeoisie, through their control of the state, and men, through their structures of patriarchy – have constantly tried to control women's bodies, as they would any critical productive resource. Under patriarchal capitalism, women are alienated from their bodies and their children, just as men are alienated from their labour and from the products of their labour. Women lack the power to control their own reproduction, both because of a lack of effective contraception and because they must often make choices about childbearing under conditions of economic hardship. Socialist feminists argue that the liberal rhetoric of "choice" concerning abortion rings hollow to a woman who wants to carry her pregnancy to term but cannot afford the medical care, the time off work, or the cost of raising a child.

Fourth, radical feminism offers few convincing explanations of women's acquiescence to patriarchy. Why do so many women not only conform to the power structures that oppress them, but reject the feminist analyses that could liberate them? There are two radical feminist answers. The first is Brownmiller's argument that men use rape to keep women in a state of physical fear. The second is that men use pornography and other hate literature against women to undermine their self-esteem and keep them in their place. Neither of these answers is entirely persuasive. The socialist feminist response takes the radical feminist analysis further, incorporating both the economic aspects of women's lives and the Marxist concept of false consciousness.

Socialist feminists point out that women are brought up to accept their assigned gender role. It is reinforced in the school, in the workplace, in the home, and in the images of themselves that women see everywhere around them. The low self-esteem that keeps women quiet and passive works to the advantage of both patriarchy and capitalism: patriarchy, because it forestalls possible challenges; capitalism, because it leads women to spend billions of dollars a year on clothing, diets, cosmetics, plastic surgery, and other accoutrements of the "beauty myth." A starving woman in high heels is a far easier victim than a healthy woman who can run, or fight back.

Perhaps the most important difference between socialist feminism and Marxist feminism is the more successful account of gender in socialist feminist analysis. Marxist concepts were not designed to encompass human categories other than class. Marxist feminism is handicapped by this gender-blindness; it can only attribute women's oppression to a non-gendered capitalist "system," without fully explaining how this system benefits from sexual inequality.

Socialist feminism asks many of the same questions as radical and Marxist feminism, and its answers are often more complete and more intriguing. It illustrates the links between women's oppression in the home and the office. It can tell us more about both the sexual and the non-sexual aspects of women's lives than either of its founding currents alone. Nonetheless, the contradictions at the heart of socialist feminism weaken its analytical effectiveness. Socialist feminism is still less than twenty years old, and its analytical power will increase as some of these thorny issues are resolved. It is becoming increasingly influential in Canada and Britain, where socialism is more legitimate as a body of thought than in the United States. This current of feminism will probably have the greatest effect on feminist theory into the twenty-first century, although liberal feminism will likely continue to dominate feminist practice.

The Strategic Practice Approach

Most of the major scholarship about the currents approach has come from the United States and the United Kingdom. Canadian feminists have made greater contributions to the other approaches to feminist thought. In their 1988 book *Feminist Organizing for Change: The Contemporary Women's Movement in Canada,* three Canadian feminists divide Canadian feminism into two categories, based not on abstract principles but on practical approaches to organization. These practical approaches are called *strategic practices*. One of the three authors, Linda Briskin, has elaborated on that analysis in a subsequent article.

The two types (or "poles") of strategic practice identified by Briskin and her colleagues are *disengagement* and *mainstreaming*. Disengagement is based on "a critique of the system and a standpoint outside of it" and offers "a vision of social transformation." It is the politic of grassroots feminism, the small local groups most often associated with radical and socialist theory. Disengagement includes a conception of feminist process, arising from a rejection of masculine principles of hierarchy and organization. It permits feminists to stand back from the existing power structures in society, which allows them to construct a profound critique of the status quo. At the same time, however, it risks alienating the large numbers of women who are needed to make effective change.

Mainstreaming is the politic of institutionalized feminism, including national and provincial feminist organizations and the women's auxiliaries of the political parties. Its principal strategy is to work within the system for practical changes in women's daily lives. It is most often associated with liberal feminism, although it is a mistake to simply equate the two. Mainstream feminists try to build broad coalitions and to attract the widest possible support for their agenda. As a result, they cannot risk alienating their potential constituency by making radical critiques of a system that many people accept.

According to Briskin, "Both mainstreaming and disengagement are necessary to the feminist vision. The goal for feminist practice is the maintenance of an effective tension between the two; the dilemma is the tendency for feminist practice to be pulled towards one or other pole." Either extreme poses a risk for the feminist movement: disengagement risks "marginalization and invisibility," while mainstreaming may lead to "co-optation and institutionalization." Therefore, feminist organizations must steer a course between the Scylla of inefficient feminist process and the Charybdis of temptation into upholding the status quo.

Briskin and her colleagues argue that despite the risks of each, an effective feminist politic requires the integration of the two poles of strategic practice. They also suggest that the socialist current of feminism is best suited to such an integration. Liberal feminists may be co-opted into the system, while radical feminists often choose a purely disengaged – and therefore marginalized – strategy. However, the strategic practice approach goes beyond the currents to provide a more accurate account of feminist organizing for change: "tactical political choices made on a daily basis reflect not only the set of abstract principles which inform feminist currents but also particular historical and conjunctural factors."

As circumstances change, feminist organizations will be pulled in different directions: sometimes towards mainstreaming, sometimes towards disengagement. For example, Vickers argues that the American feminist movement has been less successful than the Canadian movement because it has been more radical, more disengaged, and hence less effective in persuading governments to adopt its agenda. Without an account of feminism that takes these practical factors into account, we cannot explain the forms that feminist movements take at different times and in different places.

The strength of the "strategic practice" approach is that it reveals the constraints under which feminists operate in the real world. It also demonstrates that socialist feminists or liberal feminists may nominally agree on the ends of political change, but differ on the means or strategies by which to achieve those ends. This is an important insight for anyone who wishes to understand how feminism works in the real world, particularly if one wishes to know why some feminist movements are more effective than others.

Joyce Gelb uses a similar approach in her comparative study of women's movements and public policy in the United States, Britain, and Sweden. She argues that the American women's movement is characterized by *interest group feminism,* a politics of "networking and inclusiveness." The British movement, on the contrary, typifies "ideological feminism." Ideological feminism "is characterized by insistence on ideological purity and a reluctance to work with groups espousing different viewpoints." It is "decentralized and locally based, largely lacking a national political presence and impact. Fragmentation as well as enthusiastic commitment to sectarian (feminist) views typify this model."

Gelb's typology of feminist movements illustrates the differences between the two strategic practices identified by Briskin et al. Gelb argues that the American movement has been more effective in changing policy, while the British movement has been excluded from political influence by its own refusal to compromise. She attributes the differences between American and British feminism to a number of factors, of which the political structures are the most important. Because the American political system is more open to external influences, and to claims of equal rights, American feminists have had an incentive to work within the system and have met with considerable success in so doing. But the British system is closed and elitist, and the language of equal rights and opportunities is alien to its parliamentary tradition. Feminists have been frustrated by their contacts with the system and have withdrawn into their own alternative organizations. Gelb reinforces the argument of Briskin and her colleagues: in order to understand the strategic choices made by women's groups in their struggles for change, we have to examine both their internal structures and the environments in which they operate.

Integrative Feminism

Another Canadian feminist, Angela Miles, has constructed a third approach to feminist thought. Miles argues that the primary division within feminism is neither ideological nor strategic. Instead, "the most significant political division within the women's movement is between a feminism that is a full politics and speaks to the whole of society and a feminism that is essentially a pressure politics which speaks only to the relative position of women." Integrative feminism cuts across the "currents" described earlier: "There are radical, socialist, anarchist and lesbian feminists on both sides."

Miles agrees with socialist feminists that capitalism is inherently patriarchal, but she does not rely entirely on class analysis or the theories of feminism. She focuses on the ways in which feminists approach their project of changing society. She argues that it is not enough to make a place for women in the existing, male-structured system: "Equal access to rights and privileges in existing society ... is a partial programme." The only path to "women's and human liberation" is to create a new society, "an alternative to the dominant separative, individualist, competitive, materialist rationality of industrial patriarchal society."

The latter approach, *integrative feminism,* "is grounded in the special life experience, interests and concerns of women, and as such, expresses the marginalized and subordinated values associated with women and with the work of human reproduction – integrative values, such as nurturing, co-operation, connection, love, and mutual service." In other words, both men and women would be freer and more fulfilled if society were reoriented away from masculinist values to female values of love, nurture and fairness. Integrative feminism also means bringing together the various strands of women's activism to create a unified and non-hierarchical approach to social change. In this sense, it entails a rejection of both the currents approach and the traditional structures within which most conventional political activity takes place.

This integrative approach resembles the radical current of feminist theory in its emphasis on the "female" virtues arising from reproduction. However, Miles specifically denies that integrative feminism is "a biological claim of a vision innate in our female essence." Her approach also resembles the strategic practice of disengagement, because it stresses the importance of feminist process and structure. But integrative feminism differs from the other approaches in this chapter because it goes beyond narrower issues of ideology or strategy. It is a broader worldview, a blueprint for an entirely new society in which women are recognized as different from men, yet equally human. The equation of "man" and "human" would be replaced with a humanist vision in which women's experience is the basis for a full-scale transformation of social and personal life. Integrative feminism is a unity of theory and practice, which can encompass all feminist theories and all feminist practices (except the narrow equal-rights aspect of liberal feminism).

For Miles, feminism is the most revolutionary force in human history. It offers the potential for a thorough reconstruction of our lives. To the extent that integrative feminism resembles the strategic approach of disengagement, it might prove to be less effective in practice than in theory. However, Miles's experience with feminist organizing in rural Nova Scotia offers some clues to an effective integrative feminist practice. Miles reports that as women gather in their communities to discuss their lives and shared experiences, they become more conscious of their distinctiveness and their strength as women. This consciousness lays the groundwork for cooperative action on their own behalf, and on behalf of other oppressed groups in society. Thus integrative feminism in practice goes beyond the effort to end sexism; women's sense of social integration leads them to campaign against poverty, racism, and other forms of inequality that affect men and children as well as women.

It is doubtful whether the ends of integrative feminism, a complete reorientation of society, can be accomplished using the means of political disengagement. Even piecemeal change requires a full and sustained engagement with the existing political structures, an engagement that Miles's approach categorically rejects. Her model for change is essentially the consciousness-raising group (see below), which can help individuals to understand what needs to be changed but which cannot provide the organizational basis to fight for that change. Finally, integrative feminism is not really compatible with identity feminism, which we will discuss in the next section, because integrative feminism rests on the belief that "the shared oppression and interests of women provide a real basis for dialogue and cooperation." But Miles's ideas have had considerable influence on Canadian feminists, and they provide a good example of the more utopian strains of feminist thought. They also illustrate the unity of theory and practice that characterizes second-wave feminism.

Identity Feminism

As we have seen, the currents approach to feminism has been criticized for being overly intellectual and exclusive of women who are not white, middle-class academics. In recent years a new approach to feminism has emerged from the women who have been excluded from the academic currents. "Identity feminism" is based on lived experience, not abstract concepts. Black women, lesbians, native women, and other marginalized groups have constructed their own analyses of oppression. These analyses are both a challenge to the radical feminist concept of a universal sisterhood, and an enrichment of our understanding of women's lives. They represent the recognition that if the personal is political, then race, sexual orientation, physical condition, and origin are just as relevant to women's oppression as gender.

The division of women into categories – "black," "disabled," and so forth – is done for the sake of clarity, and is not meant to imply that a woman can belong to only one identity group. That would be absurd. Black lesbians, disabled immigrant women, and others with more than one of these identities may choose to give one more importance than another, or they may try to create a new, integrated identity based on their own unique experience. Many of these women are skeptical of "theory," because they have experienced it as an elitist tool of exclusion. They associate abstract thought with white, well-educated, privileged women. Because identity feminism is focused on the lived experiences of women, it cannot be summarized as easily as theory. Readers are strongly encouraged to read the words of these women for themselves.

Black feminism is the oldest stream of identity feminism. The best-known example of early black feminism (also called African-American feminism) is the famous speech by former slave Sojourner Truth to a woman's rights convention in 1851:

> That man over there says women need to be helped into carriages, and lifted over ditches, and to have the best place everywhere. Nobody ever helps me into carriages, or over mud-puddles, or gives me any best place! And ain't I a woman? Look at me! Look at my arm! I have ploughed, and planted, and gathered into barns, and no man could head me! And ain't I a woman? I could work as much and eat as much as a man – when I could get it – and bear the lash as well! And ain't I a woman? I have borne thirteen children, and seen them most all sold off to slavery, and when I cried out with my mother's grief, none but Jesus heard me! And ain't I a woman?

The black feminist tradition is based on the work of novelists like Alice Walker and Zora Neale Hurston and on theorists like bell hooks. It is defined by Patricia Hill Collins as "theories or specialized thought produced by African-American women intellectuals designed to express a Black woman's standpoint." It is a humanist tradition, an integrated critique of sexism, racism, imperialism, and class inequality. It goes beyond theory: "Black feminism [is] a process of self-conscious struggle that empowers women and men to actualize a humanist vision of community." This humanist vision encompasses a society without structural inequalities, without discrimination based on ascribed characteristics like colour or sex. As such, it resembles both socialist feminism and Miles's concept of integrated feminism.

One central document of black feminist thought is the 1977 "Statement" of the Combahee River Collective:

> We are actively committed to struggling against racial, sexual, heterosexual, and class oppression and see as our particular task the development of integrated analysis and practice based upon the fact that the major systems of oppression are interlocking. The synthesis of these oppressions creates the conditions of our lives. As black women we see black feminism as the logical political movement to combat the manifold and simultaneous oppression that all women of color face.

The collective traced the origins of black feminism to the civil rights movement, the second wave of the women's movement, and "the political realization that comes from the seemingly personal experiences of individual black women's lives." Its statement described the resistance of white feminists and of black men to black feminism, and argued that only black women could liberate themselves. It concluded with an acknowledgement that "we have a very definite revolutionary task to perform."

Other women of colour have constructed their own critiques of society based on their experiences of sexism, racism, and poverty. Asian and Hispanic women in the United States have written of their resistance to integration, their pride in their own cultures, and their hurt at the ignorance of those cultures in the society around them. All too often, white feminists display racism in their assumption that men of colour treat their wives and daughters badly, and that women of colour need the help of white women to overcome sexist oppression. Many women of colour reject both the patronizing attitude inherent in this assumption and the white feminist idea that all men are the enemy. bell hooks has argued that non-white women "have more in common with men of their race and/or class group than bourgeois white women." Many consider the struggle against racism, in the company of non-white men, to be prior to the struggle against sexism. Others see the two struggles as indivisible and simultaneous.

Immigrant women have in recent years begun to challenge our understanding of their identity. They have argued that "immigrant women" are not the same category as "women of colour," and that to assume that the two groups are the same reflects the racist assumption that only white people are born in Canada. Immigrant women range from refugees to wealthy entrepreneurs. They may be fluent in one or both of Canada's official languages, or unfamiliar with either. Many are sponsored by husbands or other family members and are thus ineligible for language or job training. Despite their lack of access to new skills, most immigrant women work outside the home, as domestics or industrial cleaners, in food preparation, or in the garment industry. Many work at home, sewing piecework for a few dollars. They are at the lowest levels of the workforce. Most immigrant woman who do not go out to work are isolated in their homes and, in the urban centres, within their ethnic communities. They are oppressed by class and race as well as sex. They are more vulnerable to domestic violence and other forms of mistreatment.

At the same time, many immigrant women find strength and pride in their links with other women from their home countries and elsewhere. Immigrant women have begun to organize on their own behalf and to demand representation within larger organizations. The National Organization of Immigrant and Visible Minority Women (NOIVMW) was founded in 1986 and represents over 500 groups across the country. Nevertheless, many of the women involved with these groups feel that their lives and concerns are invisible to the state and that they are far down the list of priorities. They are denied the information and resources they need to lobby effectively for change. Most immigrant women remain outside the small circle of activists; they are working, looking after their families, and coping with life in a society that seems very cold and foreign to many of them.

Canada's native women have also suffered from misconceptions caused by racism. Like other non-white women, native women cannot be lumped together into a single homogeneous group. They are a diverse set of women from different tribes, nations, reserves, clans, and language groups. Some live in relative affluence, whether in cities or on oil-wealthy reserves; others live in horrifying poverty on poor reserves or in urban slums. Some, like the Mohawks, live in matrilineal societies where the female elders make important decisions about the interests of the entire community. Others live in patriarchal societies where men dominate. There are severe social and health problems on some reserves, where substance abuse contributes to staggering rates of domestic violence and suicide.

In recent years, Canada's native women have begun to organize and to fight back. There were three native women at the constitutional table during the 1992 Charlottetown negotiations: Nellie Cornoyea, the government leader in the Northwest Territories; and Rosemarie Kuptana and Mary Simon from the Inuit Tapirisat. The Mohawk action at Oka in 1990 brought the power of Mohawk women to the national consciousness: the chief spokesperson for the tribe was not a man, but Ellen Gabriel from the Longhouse.

In 1985 native women succeeded in removing a notoriously sexist section from the Indian Act. The section had stipulated that Indian women lost their status when they married non-Indian men but that Indian men conferred their status on non-Indian wives. This meant that an Indian woman who married a non-Indian no longer had the right to live on her reserve, to receive financial support, or to be buried in the land of her people. Despite the injustice of this law, many native groups – dominated by men – wanted to keep the Indian Act as it was. They were concerned about the possibility that all the women and children who had lost their status under the law would want to return to the reserves, and some of them believed that the women should not challenge the power of the men to decide if they could stay on the reserve or not. In 1981 the United Nations Human Rights Committee ruled against the Indian Act, but that section was not removed until after the equality section of the Charter came into force in 1985. Unfortunately, the money that the federal government had promised to the band councils, to help house and support the returning women and children, did not materialize. Many problems persist for Canada's native women. But the coalitions that they built in the struggle against their loss of status will continue to support them in future battles for justice.

Lesbian feminism can be defined as "the shift from lesbianism as a sexual identity to lesbianism as a *political* definition." Like visible minority women, many lesbians have worked for years in cooperation with men; lesbians and gay men have fought against homophobia (fear of homosexuality) and heterosexism (prejudice against homosexuality). But lesbians are also oppressed as women, and their experience is often very different from that of gay men. Sharon Dale Stone claims that "in many respects, lesbians are much more threatening to the social order than gay men." She argues that "patriarchal society is ... built on the assumption that women exist to serve men. Lesbians, simply by existing, flagrantly challenge this assumption." Therefore, "lesbianism represents a profound threat to the patriarchal order – a threat that is qualitatively different from the threat that gay men are seen as representing."

This sense of "threat" to the established order is embraced enthusiastically by many lesbian feminists. Charlotte Bunch has written that "the Lesbian is in revolt. In revolt because she defines herself in terms of women and rejects the male definitions of how she should feel, act, look, and live ... Lesbianism threatens male supremacy at its core." For Bunch, politically conscious lesbianism is "central to destroying our sexist, racist, capitalist, imperialist system."

For lesbian feminists, heterosexuality is not "natural." It is an institution, maintained, like capitalism and racism, "by a variety of forces, including both physical violence and false consciousness." Lesbianism is a continuum of women's experience, ranging from sexual contact with women to a milder sense of "women-identification," which constitutes the principal form of resistance to patriarchy. This radical feminist approach is criticized by socialist feminists, who argue that women are oppressed by a number of economic factors, not just by "compulsory heterosexuality." But the idea that women who are emotionally and/or physically drawn to other women are not "sick" is a liberating one. It helps us to understand our own emotional ties with other women, and to see those ties as a source of strength instead of a symptom of "perversion."

Disabled women experience the world in different ways from other women. Their disabilities may be visible or invisible. It is estimated that between 12 and 18 percent of Canadian women have some sort of disability, and that nearly 400,000 of those are severely disabled. The Disabled Women's Network (DAWN) identifies the following problems for disabled women: they are significantly more likely to be victims of violence and sexual abuse; they do not have access to enough support services, particularly when they become mothers; their unemployment rate is nearly 75 percent; and they earn an average of 64 cents for every dollar earned by a non-disabled woman (which works out to less than 40 percent of the wages earned by the average man). These women are doubly disadvantaged: they face the same barriers to education and employment as disabled men, and they must also confront occupational segregation and the lower wages available to women. For disabled feminists, the condition of "disablement" is not just a physical fact, but a social construct. It is exacerbated by prejudices and stereotypes about disabled people: that they are helpless, less intelligent, and incapable of knowing and articulating their own needs.

Most of the organizations for disabled people are dominated by men, and women have been isolated and overlooked. Many disabled women are reluctant to become involved in feminist organizations; they are dependent on older caregivers and frightened of angering them. Others feel that their needs and concerns have been ignored by mainstream feminist organizations. For example, until recently the annual general meetings of the National Action Committee on the Status of Women (NAC) were held in non-accessible locations, with standing floor microphones and no simultaneous interpretation for the hearing impaired. This created considerable ill feeling between NAC (whose budget is stretched to the limit already) and the disabled women's groups who had scraped together the money to send delegates to the meetings.

DAWN was established in 1985 and has achieved some success in making disabled women visible, but its funding was eliminated in 1993. Nevertheless, its creation is a source of pride to many disabled women. JoAnne Doucette, one of DAWN's founders, claims that "disabled women are among the most marginalized people in society. Society devalues women and is designed for able-bodied people only. Given this, it is a tribute to the tenacity of disabled women that we have been able to sustain the momentum necessary for building DAWN."

It remains to be seen whether DAWN will survive. Whether or not it continues to speak for disabled women, the coalition that built the organization is a promising sign for the future. Disabled women have demanded and achieved recognition within the women's movement, and their issues are receiving more attention than they ever have. The passage of the 1986 Employment Equity Act, which is designed to assist women and disabled workers among others, demonstrates some awareness on the part of governments of the problems of disabled women.

Some feminists have criticized the growing emphasis on identity and personal experience within feminism. Linda Briskin argues that identity feminism "has translated into both a competitive hierarchy of oppression and an opposition to any kind of theory." This approach can blind women to the oppression that they share and to the systemic patterns that link the experience of all women. "Sisterhood" may not be "universal," but it is the only basis for a women's movement that is united enough to be effective. At the same time, Briskin charges that the "anti-intellectualism" fostered by identity feminism "promotes individualism, on the one hand, and on the other, promotes the identification of women, not with reason, but with nature – both of which are ideologies of patriarchal capitalism." While Briskin agrees that a feminist ideal of undifferentiated "sisterhood" is unrealistic, she is concerned that too much emphasis on personal experience will damage the women's movement in the long run. Other feminists, such as the British writer Lynne Segal, share these concerns.

This section has barely scratched the surface of identity feminism. Its purpose is to introduce readers to the variety of voices included in this fourth approach to feminism, and to begin to create an awareness of the lives of women who do not conform to the white, middle-class standard of mainstream academic feminism. We will now turn from a discussion of feminist thought to a brief history of the two most recent waves of the women's movement in North America.

The Women's Movement

Like the feminist theories discussed earlier, the women's movement itself is a reaction against sexual politics. The development of theory has fuelled the growth of the movement, with theory and practice united (to some extent) in a common goal: to name the problems facing women and find an effective means of eliminating them. We begin with the first wave, and the campaign to extend the franchise – the right to vote – to women in Canada.

The Suffrage Campaign and the Persons Cases

Until the 1920s, women in most Western countries did not have suffrage, or the right to vote in elections. (See Chapter 8, Appendix 1.) By the end of the nineteenth century, women in Britain, the United States, and English Canada had begun to campaign for suffrage. The "suffragettes" were mostly white, urban, and middle-class women. Their fathers, husbands, brothers, and sons had voted for decades, and they saw no reason why women should be excluded. Some women did vote in the early nineteenth century. The right to vote was technically based on property, not on sex, and those who owned enough property to qualify assumed that they were eligible to vote. But by the middle of the century all of the Canadian colonies had passed laws specifically forbidding women to participate in elections. The ban against women's franchise at the provincial and federal levels continued into this century, although women in many provinces could vote for school trustees and municipal politicians by 1900.

The Victorian era witnessed the rise of women's charitable organizations and campaigns to improve the moral tone of society. Middle-class urban and farm women in English Canada worked to combat the evils of alcohol and urban poverty. Gradually, as the nineteenth century drew to a close, they reached the conclusion that their campaigns would be taken more seriously by the men in power if women had the right to vote. Many suffragettes also believed that women were morally superior to men and would, if granted suffrage, elevate political life above squalor and corruption. Some of them were motivated by the desire for equal rights with men, acting on their own behalf to promote their own interests. Others saw women's suffrage as purely instrumental, a means to the end of improving English Canadian society.

Whatever the reasons of the individual women involved, by the beginning of the First World War the movement for women's suffrage had become impossible for politicians to ignore. The Dominion Women's Enfranchisement Association was founded in 1889. The National Council of Women (founded in 1893), which initially resisted suffrage for women, had endorsed the idea by 1910. Farmers' organizations supported the cause, as did organized labour, many Protestant clergymen, and many of the leading newspapers of the day. The tenacity with which successive federal governments clung to their anti-suffrage position illustrates the depth of resistance to women's equal participation in public life.

That resistance is the more surprising, from the standpoint of the 1990s, because the demands of the suffragettes were quite moderate. They did not want to break down the public-private dichotomy. They were not arguing for sex equality in all spheres of life. Most of them agreed with their opponents that women belonged in the home, differing only in their belief that voting *was* compatible with women's sacred place in the home and family. The first wave was much less radical in its analysis and demands than the second wave of the 1960s and beyond.

The opponents of women's suffrage argued that women were too weak to withstand the strains of politics; that they had no right to a voice in public affairs because they had no share in the nation's armed forces; that the Bible forbade women to engage in political pursuits; that the vote would destroy the harmony of the family; and above all, that "women did not want the vote and would not use it if they had it." The advocates of women's suffrage were able to effectively disprove each of these points, by biblical study, statistics on men's low voting turnout, the reassuring experience of nations where women already had the vote (such as New Zealand), and simple common sense. They also made their own case, based on the injustice of requiring women to pay taxes and then denying them the vote, and on the belief that women would bring a much-needed concern for health, peace, and morality to the councils of state. Male supporters of the cause proposed private members' bills permitting women to vote in Parliament and in the provincial legislatures, but they were always ridiculed and defeated by the opponents of votes for women.

The suffragettes were never a majority of Canadian women; the movement was small in numbers, and most women were not involved in the campaign. But the force of their case, combined with some political expediency during the First World War, eventually brought victory. In 1911 the federal Conservatives defeated the Liberal government of Sir Wilfrid Laurier and formed a majority government. Three years later Britain declared war on Germany, and Canada followed suit as a loyal ally. As the war went on, the supply of Canadian volunteer soldiers became inadequate for the needs of the war. The federal government decided that it had to introduce conscription, which meant the compulsory draft of eligible young men into the armed forces. Meanwhile, women had begun to play an active part in the manufacture of war supplies and in filling jobs vacated by men in uniform.

By 1917 the federal government knew that it had to hold an election, and it knew the election would be won or lost on the issue of conscription. The country was deeply divided: English Canada favoured conscription and Quebec strongly opposed it. The Conservative government joined with anglophone Liberals who had split with their francophone colleagues, to form a Union government. Every last vote would be needed to keep the Union in power after the 1917 election. The government wanted to permit servicemen overseas to vote, but it was extremely difficult to arrange an absentee ballot in wartime. The solution was to grant the vote to the wives and other close female relatives of active servicemen, together with nurses and other women who had performed military service. The vote was ostensibly a reward to those women who had sacrificed for their country, but the reality was more sordid than that: the government thought the women would vote on behalf of their absent heroes, and that they would be more likely to support conscription because of their personal stake in the conduct of the war.

Over half a million women were eligible to vote in 1917, and it was widely believed that their votes contributed to the re-election of the Union government. Their reward came in 1918 with the passage of the Women's Franchise Act: all women over the age of twenty-one became eligible to vote in all future federal elections. The Dominion Elections Act, 1920 granted women the further right to run for public office. The first woman MP was elected in 1921; fewer than a hundred followed her in the next seventy years. (See the appendix to this chapter for the dates of women's suffrage in the various provinces and Canada as a whole.)

One more battle was won in the 1920s, over the judicial interpretation of the word "persons." Specifically, did the word "persons" in law refer to women as well as to men? Or were men the only legal "persons," on the basis of legal precedent? This apparently simple issue consumed a great deal of political and judicial energy in Canada and Britain in the first third of this century.

The first "persons" case in Canada was brought in 1905 in New Brunswick. Mabel Penery French had all the qualifications necessary to practice law in that province, but she was barred from doing so because of her sex. The Supreme Court of New Brunswick ruled that women and men had separate spheres ordained by nature, and that the practice of law was clearly outside that sphere of activity suited to women. Fortunately for Mabel, the provincial legislature disagreed, and passed a law in 1906 that permitted the entry of women into the legal profession. She was admitted to the bar soon afterwards. Two similar cases followed, one by French herself in British Columbia in 1911 and the other by Annie Macdonald Langstaff in Quebec in 1915.

The "mother of all persons cases" was launched in 1927, when five Alberta women asked the federal government to appoint a woman to the Senate. Section 24 of the British North America Act (now known as the Constitution Act, 1867) stipulated that only "qualified persons" could be admitted to the Senate. This phrase was interpreted by the federal government to mean that only men could be senators, because women were not "persons" in the legal sense of the term when the Act came into force in 1867. The Supreme Court of Canada agreed, apparently because it felt that changes to the law should be made by Parliament, not by judges.

The Supreme Court's decision was appealed to the Judicial Committee of the Privy Council in London. Until 1949, this committee of the law lords in the British House of Lords was the final court of appeal for Canada. In October 1929 the Judicial Committee ruled that Canadian women were indeed "persons" under section 24 of the constitution, and for all other legal purposes. One year later the federal government appointed the first female senator, Liberal Cairine Wilson.

The Second Wave

It is commonly assumed that once the vote was won, and women were legally acknowledged as "persons," women's political activity ceased until the 1960s. More recent historical research, influenced by a broader definition of "political activity," has proven this assumption to be false. Between 1930 and 1960 women were involved in the women's auxiliaries of political parties, in unions, in social movements, and in a host of other activities that we now consider to be political. The number of women elected to Parliament and to provincial legislatures was tiny, but this is a misleading measure of women's involvement in politics. Organizations like the YWCA, the Canadian Federation of University Women, and the Fédération Nationale Saint-Jean-Baptiste continued to lobby on issues of particular concern to women and to build personal networks of committed women across the country. These networks would be invaluable in the early years of the second wave.

The difference between the two waves on the one hand, and the apparent trough between them on the other, is less a difference of kind than of degree. Women were still politically active after 1929, but their activities were eclipsed in the media and the public eye by a series of earth-shaking events: the Depression and the Prairie drought of the 1930s, World War II and the Cold War that followed, post-war reconstruction, and the baby boom of the 1950s and early 1960s. By the mid-1960s the complacency of the 1950s had been shattered by the assassination of John F. Kennedy, the violent resistance to the civil rights movement, the deep social divisions over the Vietnam War, and the emergence of a massive generation of adolescents.

Although these were largely American phenomena, they affected Canadians profoundly. Canadians also experienced the baby boom and racial tensions, and were shocked by the apparent social disintegration of their powerful neighbour to the south. The conditions were in place for an explosion of women's political activity on their own behalf.

In 1960 the Voice of Women was founded to express women's concern about the threat of nuclear war. In 1965 the Quebec women's movement celebrated the twenty-fifth anniversary of women's suffrage in that province. The following year a number of women's groups came together to form the Fédération des femmes du Québec. Also in 1966, thirty-two women's organizations in English Canada formed the Committee for the Equality of Women (CEW), whose purpose was to lobby for the establishment of a royal commission on the status of women. The two umbrella groups united in September 1966. Women in the French- and English-language media began to support the idea of a commission. Laura Sabia, the leader of the CEW, threatened Prime Minister Lester Pearson that one million women would march on Parliament Hill if he did not accede to her demands. It is commonly believed that this threat was the final straw for Pearson, though many scholars give the real credit to Liberal cabinet minister Judy LaMarsh. Whether the threat worked or not (Sabia later admitted that it was impossible to carry out), Pearson finally set up the Royal Commission on the Status of Women (RCSW) in 1967. It was scheduled to report to Parliament in 1970.

For several months the commission travelled across Canada, listening to women in shopping malls and church basements as well as hotel ballrooms and legislatures. Women who read or heard about these meetings in the media were astonished to hear their own personal experiences in the words of others. The RCSW was a gigantic national consciousness-raising exercise. It helped to build a bridge between the older, more traditional feminists of the YWCA and the VOW, and the younger, more radical feminists emerging from the campuses and the new social movements. The commission's report became the blueprint for the new women's movement that emerged during its gestation. The very existence of the RCSW had legitimized the demands that women were beginning to place on the state; the report focused those demands and gave them a basis in statistics and women's experience.

A quarter of a century later, the RCSW report has not been fully implemented. The clearest example of failure is the recommendation for a national child-care program. But many of the less expensive and controversial measures recommended by the RCSW have been put into practice, including measures to redress the wage gap and abolition of the women's auxiliaries in the Liberal and Progressive Conservative parties. Monitoring the government's action on the RCSW report was the principal motivation for the founding of the National Action Committee on the Status of Women in 1971, and the federal government itself established the Canadian Advisory Council on the Status of Women (CACSW) as an internal watchdog. All in all, the appointment and the work of the RCSW were seminal events in the "second wave" of the Canadian women's movement.

Since 1970, and particularly since 1980, the numbers of women in positions of political, economic, cultural, and legal influence have jumped significantly. The first female justice of the Supreme Court (Bertha Wilson) was appointed in 1982; the first female leader of a national political party (Audrey McLaughlin of the NDP) was elected in 1990; the first female leader of a governing provincial party (Rita Johnston, British Columbia) was elected in 1991; the first female premier elected by the people (Catherine Callbeck, PEI) took office in early 1993. Perhaps the most powerful symbol of change occurred in June 1993, when Kim Campbell took over as leader of the national Progressive Conservative party and prime minister. We are still a long way from gender equality, as the next section of this book will make clear. Nevertheless, it is appropriate to stop and look back at how far we have come, before we plunge into the problems of the present and the prospects for the future.

The 1990s: Backlash or Revisionism?

In the late 1980s and early 1990s there was much talk about a backlash against feminism (see Chapter 4). The second wave of the women's movement provoked a reaction from some groups and individuals who were not comfortable with changes to the status quo. This reaction was most evident in the political arena, though it was not confined to politics. When a social movement seeks to change something as fundamental as gender roles, it is normal for it to encounter resistance. Many men and women were at best ambivalent, and at worst actively hostile, towards feminism – or the caricature of feminism presented by the mass media.

At the same time, a number of women who claimed feminist credentials were calling for a revision of feminist thought. Their books sold well and generated considerable public and media debate. Some feminists regarded these women with deep suspicion, deriding them as agents of the backlash, or as self-promoters whose words and ideas played into the hands of the movement's enemies. But there is no question that the ideas of the feminist "revisionists" struck a chord, not only among anti-feminists or those ambivalent towards the movement, but also among some committed feminists who had become disillusioned with the excesses of radical feminist analysis.

The revisionists argue that radical feminism – particularly the idea that men are naturally aggressive and violent and women are naturally passive and nurturing – is not only mistaken but harmful. It teaches women to fear men, to fear even consensual sex as a form of violence, and to think of themselves as victims. According to Camille Paglia, feminism has taught young women that they are not responsible for their own mistakes. It has blinded them to the truth about masculine sexuality: that young men cannot (and should not be expected to) control themselves. If a woman is raped, she has only herself to blame for her naivety.

> Every women must take personal responsibility for her sexuality ... She must be prudent and cautious about where she goes and with whom. When she makes a mistake, she must accept the consequences and ... resolve never to make that mistake again. Running to Mommy and Daddy on the campus grievance committee is unworthy of strong women.

When this approach was criticized by other feminists, Paglia responded that "blaming the victim makes perfect sense if the victim has behaved stupidly."

Paglia's outspoken and often deliberately outrageous views have angered many people, particularly feminists. She claims that she is not anti-feminist; rather, "I am a feminist who wants to radically reform current feminism, to bring it back to common sense about life." Paglia's notion of "common sense" often appears cold, unsympathetic, and even masochistic. But though she may be the most extreme and controversial critic of radical feminism and its gender dichotomies, she is far from the only one.

Another critic of feminist dogma about violence against women is Katie Roiphe, whose experience as an Ivy League student in the United States provoked her to write a polemic against campus "date rape" policies. Like Paglia, Roiphe appears to accept male sexual assault and harassment as a fact of women's lives. Responding to a feminist author's attack on male professors who harass their students, thereby turning women into victims, Roiphe writes:

> She does not see that it is her entire conceptual framework – her kind of rhetoric, her kind of interpretation – that transforms perfectly stable women into hysterical, sobbing victims. If there is any transforming to be done, it is to transform everyday experience back into everyday experience.

Roiphe seems to be arguing that women should just learn to live with male sexual aggression as an everyday occurrence, and handle it as best they can: women are victimized not by men, but by feminists.

A third revisionist takes a more academic approach. Christina Hoff Sommers distinguishes between two types of feminist thinking: gender feminism (which corresponds to radical feminism) and equity (liberal) feminism. She argues that gender feminism has become dangerously influential in academia. The influence of gender feminism is dangerous not because it transforms women into victims, but because it leads to shoddy research and misleading "facts" in the service of an ideology. "These feminist ideologues are helping no one," says Sommers; "on the contrary, their divisive and resentful philosophy adds to the woes of our society and hurts legitimate feminism. Not only are women who suffer real abuse not helped by untruths, they are in fact harmed by inaccuracies and exaggerations." Sommers's argument is echoed by John Fekete, whose critiques of Canadian feminist research are sobering evidence of what can go wrong when ideology takes precedence over academic standards.

The most optimistic message comes from Naomi Wolf, whose first book *The Beauty Myth* is sometimes cited as an example of the illogical extremes of radical feminism. In her second book, *Fire with Fire,* Wolf takes a revisionist look at feminism in the 1990s. Like Paglia and Roiphe, she argues that radical feminism has erred in turning women into victims. Like Sommers, she divides feminism into two streams: victim feminism and power feminism. She argues that "over the last twenty years, the old belief in a tolerant assertiveness, a claim to human participation and human rights – power feminism – was embattled by the rise of a set of beliefs that cast women as beleaguered, fragile, intuitive angels: victim feminism." Victim feminism "has slowed women's progress, impeded their self-knowledge, and been responsible for most of the inconsistent, negative, even chauvinistic spots of regressive thinking that are alienating many women and men." It is a mistake, says Wolf, to "retreat into appealing for status on the basis of feminine specialness instead of human worth."

Wolf condemns Roiphe and Paglia for using "the occasional excesses of the rape crisis movement" to deny that sexual violence exists and that it genuinely endangers women. Instead of denying that some women are victimized by some men, Wolf wants to persuade women not to build their entire self-images around that victimization. Women should be strong individuals, taking responsibility for their own choices and using their power to change the world. They should not be passive children, rejecting culture, power, and logic as "masculinist" and avoiding heterosexual sex as a form of patriarchal violence. Aggression and nurturing are human qualities, not gendered qualities, according to Wolf. Therefore, both men and women should be permitted to develop all of their human qualities to the limits of their individual potential, instead of feeling restrained by the gendered dichotomies shared by radical feminism and traditional patriarchy.

The emergence of these feminist revisionists has provoked some debate within mainstream feminism. Some argue that the revisionists, despite their self-professed feminism, are unwitting dupes (or even active agents) of the backlash. Others welcome the return to "common sense" and a more critical attitude towards the excesses of "gender feminism." If the revisionists can succeed in attracting more women to the women's movement, and in reassuring men that not all feminists consider them rapists by definition, they will have done a tremendous service for all of us.

Every political movement has to reassess itself periodically, to make sure that its ideology is not overwhelming its standards of truth and its grip on social reality. By the 1990s, mainstream feminism was ripe for such a reassessment. Feminism must distinguish clearly between its friends and its enemies, or it will attract even more critics and lose its most valuable allies.

Conclusion

This chapter has discussed the following key points.

1. Relations between men and women are political, because they are power relations. Men have more power than women in all aspects of our society: economic, political, physical, cultural. This state of affairs is called patriarchy.

2. Men and women are expected to play gender roles in our society, which constrict their range of choices and prevent the complete fulfillment of their human potential.

3. Women have responded to patriarchy and gender roles with feminist analysis, and with the women's movement. Feminism can be divided into the currents approach, the strategic practice approach, the integrative approach, and the identity approach. The women's movement blossomed in the early years of this century, when women petitioned the political system for the vote. Following the achievement of the vote, and the resolution of the persons cases, women largely withdrew from conventional politics until the 1960s. The second wave has created much of the feminist thought described in the chapter, and some of the most important achievements of the women's movement to date.

The feminist theories discussed in this chapter, and the women's organizations inspired by them, have done a great deal to change the lives of Canadian women in the past hundred and fifty years. But they are not the only, or even the primary, reason for the great upheavals in women's lives over the past several generations. Young women in the 1990s lead very different lives, and face very different choices, from those of their mothers, grandmothers, and especially great-grandmothers. How have those changes happened? How can we explain them? Which changes are the most important for the future of gender equality? The next section of this book deals with those questions.

Appendix: Dates of Women's Suffrage and Eligibility to Run For Public Office

Jurisdiction	Date of Suffrage	Public Office
Manitoba	January 1916	January 1916
Saskatchewan	March 1916	March 1916
Alberta	April 1916	April 1916
British Columbia	April 1917	April 1917
Ontario	April 1917	April 1919
Nova Scotia	April 1918	April 1918
Canada	May 1918*	July 1920
New Brunswick	April 1919	March 1934
Prince Edward Island	May 1922	May 1922
Newfoundland	April 1925	April 1925
Quebec	April 1940	April 1940

* Female relatives of Canadian servicemen on active duty were allowed to vote in the "khaki election" of September 1917, because the government believed they would support its policy of conscription. All women over the age of twenty-one were enfranchised the following year, and voted federally for the first time in the 1921 election.

Note: The dates in this table do not refer to all Canadian women. Chinese and East Asian women did not receive full Canadian Citizenship citizenship (including the right to vote) until 1947, while aboriginal women living on reserves could not vote in federal elections until 1960.

Source: Catherine L. Cleverdon, *The Women Suffrage Movement in Canada* (Toronto: University of Toronto Press, 1974), p. 2.

Notes

1 Gerzon, *A Choice of Heroes.*

2 See Basow, *Gender Stereotypes and Roles,* chap. 5; Sanday, *Female Power and Male Dominance;* Gilligan, *In A Different Voice.*

3 See Bryson, *Feminist Political Theory,* 261–67 passim; Briskin, "Feminist Practice: A New Approach To Evaluating Feminist Strategy," in Wine and Ristock, *Women and Social Change,* 25–29 passim.

4 Anderson and Zinsser, *A History of Their Own,* 341–43.

5 Ibid., 344; Bryson, chap. 1.

6 See Spender, *Women of Ideas,* 50–68 passim.

7 Anderson and Zinsser, 346–49; Bryson, chap. 1; Jaggar, *Feminist Politics and Human Nature,* chap. 3; Tong, *Feminist Thought,* chap. 1.

8 See Mill and Mill, *Essays on Sex Equality;* Rose, *Parallel Lives,* chap. 3.

9 See Adamson et al., *Feminist Organizing for Change,* chap. 2; Cott, *The Grounding of Modern Feminism.*

10 See Cleverdon, *The Woman Suffrage Movement in Canada,* Introduction.

11 Friedan, *The Feminine Mystique.*

12 Friedan, *The Second Stage.*

13 Jill Vickers, "The Intellectual Origins of the Women's Movement in Canada," in Backhouse and Flaherty, *Challenging Times.*

14 See Jaggar, *Feminist Politics and Human Nature,* chap. 3.

15 See Moller Okin, *Justice, Gender, and the Family;* and Pateman, "Feminist Critiques of the Public/Private Dichotomy," in Pateman, *The Disorder of Women.*

16 Adamson et al., chap. 2.

17 Bryson, 183.

18 Jill Vickers, "Bending the Iron Law of Oligarchy: Debates on the Feminization of Organization and Political Process in the English Canadian Women's Movement, 1970–1988," in Wine and Ristock, 79.

19 For excellent accounts of radical feminism, see Bryson; Jaggar; Jaggar and Rothenberg, *Feminist Frameworks;* and Tong.

20 Jaggar, 85.

21 Ibid., 88.

22 Ibid.

23 Quoted in Adamson et al., 31.

24 Bryson, 208–11 passim.

25 De Beauvoir, *The Second Sex.*

26 Ibid., 740.

27 Millett, *Sexual Politics.*

28 Firestone, *The Dialectic of Sex.*

29 Ibid., 11.

30 Brownmiller, *Against Our Will.*

31 Ibid., 5.

32 MacKinnon, *Feminism Unmodified,* Introduction.

33 Jaggar, 109.

34 Ibid., 109; emphasis added.

35 Reeves Sanday, *Female Power and Male Dominance,* 210.

36 Ibid., 11.

37 Ibid.

References and Further Reading

Sex and Gender

Archer, John, and Barbara Lloyd. *Sex and Gender.* Rev. ed. Cambridge: Cambridge University Press, 1985.

Ashton-Jones, Evelyn, and Gary A. Olson, eds. *The Gender Reader.* Boston: Allyn & Bacon, 1991.

Basow, Susan A. *Gender Stereotypes and Roles.* 3rd ed. Pacific Grove, CA: Brooks/Cole, 1992.

Gerzon, Mark. *A Choice of Heroes: The Changing Faces of American Manhood.* Rev. ed. Boston: Houghton Mifflin, 1992.

Gilligan, Carol. *In A Different Voice: Psychological Theory and Women's Development.* Cambridge, MA: Harvard University Press, 1982.

Illich, Ivan. *Gender.* Berkeley: Heyday Books, 1982.

Kaufman, Michael, ed. *Beyond Patriarchy: Essays by Men on Pleasure, Power, and Change.* Toronto: Oxford University Press, 1987.

Lindsey, Linda L. *Gender Roles: A Sociological Perspective.* Englewood Cliffs, NJ: Prentice-Hall, 1990.

Mackie, Marlene. *Constructing Women and Men: Gender Socialization.* Toronto: Holt, Rinehart & Winston, 1987.

Rhode, Deborah L., ed. *Theoretical Perspectives on Sexual Difference.* New Haven: Yale University Press, 1990.

Salamon, E.D., and B.W. Robinson, eds. *Gender Roles: Doing What Comes Naturally?* Scarborough: Nelson, 1991.

Spender, Dale. *Man Made Language.* 2nd ed. London: Pandora, 1980.

Feminist Responses

The Currents Approach

∾ *General*

Adamson, Nancy, Linda Briskin, and Margaret McPhail. *Feminist Organizing for Change: The Contemporary Women's Movement in Canada.* Toronto: Oxford University Press, 1988.

Bryson, Valerie. *Feminist Political Theory: An Introduction.* London: Macmillan, 1992.

Charvet, John. *Feminism.* London: Dent, 1982.

Cott, Nancy F. *The Grounding of Modern Feminism.* New Haven: Yale University Press, 1987.

Grimshaw, Jean. *Philosophy and Feminist Thinking.* Minneapolis: University of Minnesota Press, 1986.

Jaggar, Alison M. *Feminist Politics and Human Nature.* Totowa, NJ: Rowman & Littlefield, 1988.

Jaggar, Alison M., and Paula S. Rothenberg, eds. *Feminist Frameworks: Alternative Theoretical Accounts of the Relations between Women and Men.* 2nd ed. New York: McGraw-Hill, 1984.

Kourany, Janet A., et al., eds. *Feminist Philosophies.* Englewood Cliffs, NJ: Prentice-Hall, 1992.

Spender, Dale, ed. *Women of Ideas and What Men Have Done to Them.* London: Pandora, 1988.

Tong, Rosemarie. *Feminist Thought: A Comprehensive Introduction.* Boulder: Westview, 1989.

∾ *Liberal Feminism*

Anderson, Bonnie S., and Judith P. Zinsser. *A History of Their Own: Women in Europe from Prehistory to the Present.* Vol. 2. New York: Harper & Row, 1988.

Eisenstein, Zillah. *The Radical Future of Liberal Feminism.* Boston: Northeastern University Press, 1986.

Friedan, Betty. *The Feminine Mystique.* Harmondsworth: Penguin, 1964.
———. *The Second Stage.* London: Abacus, 1981.

Mill, John Stuart, and Harriet Taylor Mill. *Essays on Sex Equality,* ed. Alice Rossi. Chicago: University of Chicago Press, 1970.

Moller Okin, Susan, *Justice, Gender, and the Family.* New York: Basic Books, 1989.

Pateman, Carole. *The Disorder of Women*. Stanford: Stanford University Press, 1989.

———. *The Sexual Contract*. Stanford: Stanford University Press, 1988.

Rose, Phyllis. *Parallel Lives: Five Victorian Marriages*. New York: Vintage, 1983.

Wollstonecraft, Mary. *A Vindication of the Rights of Woman*. Buffalo: Prometheus, 1989.

∾ *Radical Feminism*

Brownmiller, Susan. *Against Our Will: Men, Women and Rape*. New York: Bantam, 1975.

De Beauvoir, Simone. *The Second Sex*. London: Picador, 1988.

Firestone, Shulamith. *The Dialectic of Sex: The Case for Feminist Revolution*. New York: Bantam, 1970.

French, Marilyn. *Beyond Power: On Women, Men, and Morals*. New York: Ballantine, 1985.

Greer, Germaine. *The Female Eunuch*. London: Granada, 1981.

———. *Sex and Destiny: The Politics of Human Fertility*. London: Picador, 1984.

MacKinnon, Catharine A. *Feminism Unmodified: Discourses on Life and Law*. Cambridge, MA: Harvard University Press, 1987.

———. *Toward a Feminist Theory of the State*. Cambridge, MA: Harvard University Press, 1989.

Millett, Kate. *Sexual Politics*. New York: Ballantine, 1988.

O'Brien, Mary. *Reproducing the World: Essays in Feminist Theory*. Boulder: Westview, 1989.

Reeves Sanday, Peggy. *Female Power and Male Dominance: On the Origins of Sexual Inequality*. Cambridge: Cambridge University Press, 1981.

Segal, Lynne. *Is the Future Female? Troubled Thoughts on Contemporary Feminism*. London: Virago, 1987.

∾ *Marxist and Socialist Feminism*

Birke, Lynda. *Women, Feminism and Biology: The Feminist Challenge*. Brighton: Wheatsheaf, 1986.

Burstyn, Varda, and Dorothy E. Smith. *Women, Class, Family and the State*. Toronto: Garamond, 1985.

Mitchell, Juliet, and Ann Oakley, eds. *What is Feminism? A Re-examination*. New York: Pantheon, 1986.

Rowbotham, Sheila. *Woman's Consciousness, Man's World*. Harmondsworth: Penguin, 1973.

Wolf, Naomi. *The Beauty Myth*. Toronto: Vintage, 1990.

∾ *Other Approaches to Feminism*

Carty, Linda, and Dionne Brand. "'Visible Minority' Women – A Creation of the Canadian State." *Resources for Feminist Research* 17:3 (September 1988).

Collins, Patricia Hill. *Black Feminist: Knowledge, Consciousness, and the Politics of Empowerment*. New York: Routledge, 1991.

Cruikshank, Margaret. *The Gay and Lesbian Liberation Movement*. London: Routledge, Chapman & Hall, 1992.

Finn, Geraldine, ed. *Limited Edition: Voices of Women, Voices of Feminism*. Halifax: Fernwood, 1993.

bell hooks. *Ain't I a Woman: Black Women and Feminism*. Boston: South End, 1981.

———. *Feminist Theory: From Margin to Center*. Boston: South End, 1984.

Miles, Angela. *Feminist Radicalism in the 1980's*. Montreal: CultureTexts, 1985.

Miles, Angela, and Geraldine Finn, eds. *Feminism: From Pressure to Politics*. 2nd ed. Montreal: Black Rose, 1989.

Moraga, Cherrie, and Gloria Anzaldua. *This Bridge Called My Back: Writing by Radical Women of Colour*. New York: Kitchen Table, 1983.

Phelan, Shane. *Identity Politics: Lesbian Feminism and the Limits of Community*. Philadelphia: Temple University Press, 1989.

Rich, Adrienne. *On Lies, Secrets, and Silence: Selected Prose 1966–1978*. New York: Norton, 1979.

Segal, Lynne. *Is the Future Female? Troubled Thoughts on Contemporary Feminism*. London: Virago, 1987.

Spelman, Elizabeth V. *Inessential Woman: Problems of Exclusion in Feminist Thought*. Boston: Beacon Press, 1988.

Statistics Canada. *Selected Socio-economic Consequences of Disability for Women in Canada*. Ottawa: Minister of Supply & Services, 1990).

Stone, Sharon Dale, ed. *Lesbians in Canada*. Toronto: Between the Lines, 1990.

Vickers, Jill, Pauline Rankin, and Christine Appelle. *Politics as if Women Mattered: A Political Analysis of the National Action Committee on the Status of Women*. Toronto: University of Toronto Press, 1993.

The Women's Movement

Backhouse, Constance, and David H. Flaherty, eds. *Challenging Times: The Woman's Movement in Canada and the United States*. Montreal/Kingston: McGill–Queen's University Press, 1992.

Bouchier, David. *The Feminist Challenge: The Movement for Women's Liberation in Britain and the USA*. London: Macmillan, 1983.

Burt, Sandra, Lorraine Code, and Lindsay Dorney, eds. *Changing Patterns: Women in Canada.* 2nd ed. Toronto: McClelland & Stewart, 1993.

Cleverdon, Catherine L. *The Woman Suffrage Movement in Canada.* Toronto: University of Toronto Press, 1974.

Kealey, Linda, and Joan Sangster, eds. *Beyond the Vote: Canadian Women and Politics.* Toronto: University of Toronto Press, 1989.

Morris, Cerise. "'Determination and Thoroughness': The Movement for a Royal Commission on the Status of Women in Canada." *Atlantis* 5:2 (Spring 1980).

Prentice, Alison, et al. *Canadian Women: A History.* Toronto: HBJ Canada, 1988.

Wine, Jeri Dawn, and Janice L. Ristock, eds. *Women and Social Change: Feminist Activism in Canada.* Toronto: Lorimer, 1991.

The 1990s: Backlash or Revisionism?

Faludi, Susan. *Backlash: The Undeclared War Against American Women.* New York: Crown, 1991.

Fekete, John. *Moral Panic: Biopolitics Rising.* Montreal: Robert Davies, 1994.

Friedan, Betty. *The Second Stage.* London: Abacus, 1982.

Hewlett, Sylvia Ann. *A Lesser Life: The Myth of Women's Liberation.* London: Sphere, 1988.

Paglia, Camille. *Sex, Art, and American Culture.* New York: Vintage, 1992.

Roiphe, Katie. *The Morning After: Sex, Fear, and Feminism on Campus.* Boston: Little, Brown, 1993.

Sommers, Christina Hoff. *Who Stole Feminism? How Women Have Betrayed Women.* New York: Simon & Schuster, 1994.

Wolf, Naomi. *Fire with Fire: The New Female Power and How It Will Change the 21st Century.* Toronto: Random House, 1993.

Part 2: Women in Canadian Society

IN THIS SECTION WE WILL EXAMINE THE DAILY LIVES OF women in Canada: in their families, in the economy, in the justice system, and in the mass media and popular culture. The political activities of women cannot be understood until we see the patterns that recur in women's lives: the wage gap, the pink-collar ghetto wage gap, the feminization of poverty, the double shift double shift, the stereotypes of women that populate the airwaves.

These four aspects of women's lives are treated separately in these chapters, but they are closely linked in practice. The family has always been the bedrock of the economy, and as the structure of the economy has changed the structure of the family has adapted. Today the economy is taking new forms, and families are changing quickly in response. Yet the effects of these changes are being borne not by the state or by employers, but by the women who bear the largest burden of family responsibilities.

The family is also affected by the legal system, directly in the case of family law and indirectly by the criminal law. And all women, in all aspects of their lives, are influenced by the stereotypes of women that they watch on television and in movies, read about in their books and newspapers, and see in advertising of all types. Those stereotypes can diminish women's self-esteem, lower their expectations, and subtly discourage them from challenging the limits imposed on them by society.

Part 2 helps us to understand Part 3, on women's participation in politics. The pattern of women's political activity is determined by the rest of women's lives, particularly women's role in the economy and the family. This link between the personal and the political is an essential part of feminist theory, and a direct challenge to more traditional political science – which, as we have seen, has accepted the public–private dichotomy at face value. I believe that neither women's nor men's political activities can be understood in isolation from the rest of their lives, or from the social and cultural factors that limit their choices.

Chapter 3: Women in the Canadian Economy

Chapter Summary

Chapter 3 examines women's participation in the Canadian economy, and the ways in which that participation has grown and changed since World War II. More women are spending more years in the workplace than ever before. This has some advantages for women: more money, greater independence, the opportunity to provide for themselves and their children in the case of a marriage breakdown. But there are some disadvantages for women as well. First, women are paid less on average than men. Second, women are concentrated in a narrow range of jobs, many of which are dead end and low paying. Third, most women have to balance work responsibilities and their family responsibilities, without much assistance at home from either their male partners or public policy (e.g., child care).

Chapter Outline

- The Ideology of the Housewife
- The History of 'Women's Work' in Canada
  Women's Paid Work in Canada before 1900
  Canadian Women's Work in the Twentieth Century
- The Double Shift
  Conflict between Job and Family Responsibilities
  State Support for Canadian Mothers Working outside the Home
- Occupational Segregation and the Wage Gap
  The Pink-Collar Ghetto
  Explanations for the Wage Gap
- Occupational Health and Safety Issues for Women
  Immigrant Women and Ethnic Minority Women
  The Exploitation of Domestic Workers and Homeworkers
- Racism in the Canadian Workplace
- Conclusion

The Ideology of the Housewife

Historically, most Canadian women have either worked outside the home for money wages or worked on the farm to help support their families. This fact is often overlooked. Many Canadians believe that until recently the great majority of women were full-time housewives. The myths surrounding women's paid employment reveal that many people have difficulty accepting it. There is still profound resistance, in some quarters, to the idea of women – especially mothers – working outside the home. We have to explain that resistance before we can understand why the Canadian state has been so reluctant to recognize women's labour force participation[1] and to make policies that would help women to combine their family and work responsibilities.

Canadians born between 1945 and 1964, the "baby boomers," grew up believing that a particular gendered division of labour was "natural." Women were expected to be full-time homemakers who sent their husbands off to work and the children off to school, and then spent the day preparing the house for their return. There were women who worked outside the home, of course, but they were assumed to be unmarried, or widowed, or otherwise unfortunate enough to be forced to provide for themselves. Most people did not ask whether these women might have preferred to be independent, just as we did not ask whether the housewives were fulfilled by tending to the physical and emotional needs of their families.

Today, with the benefit of hindsight, we can see that this rosy image of the housewife was largely fictional – not a description of reality, but an *ideology*. An ideology is more than simply a mistake about the way the world really is. An ideology is a system of thought with a practical purpose: to shape the world as the followers of the ideology would like it to be. Like so many other ideas about women through the ages (see Chapter 1), the ideology of the housewife obscures the truth about women's lives behind a thick veil of misconceptions and prejudices. It does not reflect reality. Instead, it reflects the persistence of the public-private dichotomy and the gendered division of labour in the twentieth century. It prevents us from seeing reality accurately and responding to it effectively, or from seeing alternative ways of structuring the family and the economy.

The History of 'Women's Work' in Canada

The evidence for the inaccuracy of the housewife ideology is persuasive. In the first place, a substantial proportion of Canadian women have always worked outside the home for money wages.[2] Some families could afford to have the wife and mother at home, but most families were not so fortunate. Either the husband was unemployed, or he could not earn enough to meet his family's needs. The wife and mother had no choice but to work outside the home, usually in a boring, repetitive job that offered low pay, little security, and virtually no hope of promotion. The lifestyle of the housewife was largely confined to the middle classes. A working-class woman who was told that women belonged at home, caring for their families, must have suffered bitterly from anger and guilt.

In the second place, the prevailing belief from the 1950s to the 1970s that all women were (or should be) housewives directly contradicts twentieth-century economic trends. Throughout this century the proportion of women working outside the home has increased continually, a steady rise punctuated by sudden upsurges of demand (in wartime, for example). Related to this trend are a number of others, which we will discuss more fully in the next chapter: the trend towards later marriage; the decline in the number of children per family; and the rising divorce rate. There are also two economic factors: the erosion of the "family wage," to the point where a middle-class lifestyle has become virtually impossible on a single salary; and the rising monetary value of a woman's labour, which has made her time and energy more valuable to her family in the workplace than at home.

I do not wish to argue that all women *should* work outside the home. Many women choose to stay at home to care for their families, especially when their children are small, and that is the best choice for them. More women would make that choice if they could afford to. Other women find that they need the sense of self-esteem and other benefits from their employment, in addition to the money, in order to function well within their families. Whatever choices some women make, we have to remember the millions of women who have no choice: women who are forced to take low-paying, dead-end jobs, with little hope of promotion or higher wages, for whom the ideology of the housewife is a bitter irony.

Women's Paid Work in Canada before 1900

The first European economy in Canada was based on temporary settlement; men arrived in ships to collect beaver pelts and fish, which they quickly processed in their shore camps and took back to Europe. Permanent European settlements were not established until the French *habitants* began to arrive. The first married woman landed in 1617. The women of New France were not all peasants; many were middle-class women who had entered Catholic teaching orders, and came to New France to convert and "educate" the native populations. The other women who travelled to New France in the eighteenth century arrived seeking husbands and a new life in a pioneer settlement. Their lives were difficult in material terms; they had to work hard on the farms, often helping their husbands to clear the land and prepare it for planting. In addition to these shared tasks, women quickly found that they had brought the gendered division of labour with them from France. Women were still expected to care for the home and children, to prepare the food, to make and mend the clothing, and to obey their husbands and priests.

The harsh conditions of pioneer life eroded the gendered division of labour to some extent. This happened because the women had to pitch in with the heavy outside chores that would have been men's work in France, and because the fluidity of social conditions allowed women to take a larger role in public affairs. The Church, which was controlled by men, dominated the French colonies. But the nuns and lay women who came to New France quickly established institutions that played a vital role in society, and that gave their administrators great influence and visibility: schools, hospitals, charitable organizations. Indeed, until the 1960s most of Quebec's social services were still run by the Church. Nuns were a powerful symbol of women's competence and independence, probably the only such symbol available to young women in New France. But the convents were not open to *all* young women; a girl who decided to become a nun had to bring a dowry with her, and poor families often could not afford it. One of the few options for a girl who did not marry was to go to Quebec City or Montreal and become a prostitute.

When British settlers arrived in New France, which became British North America in 1763, their lives were quite similar to those of the French in most material respects. Women worked the fields, tended the homes and children, acquired and prepared food, and provided clothing. Married women could expect to give birth to seven or eight children, of which four or five might survive to adulthood. This may sound like a high level of infant and child mortality, but it was lower than those in France or Britain at the time, mostly because food was more plentiful in the New World.

The early nineteenth century saw some changes in women's lives, although the gendered division of labour remained intact. Cities and towns grew, and an urban middle class – lawyers, doctors, landowners, merchants – was evolving. Middle-class women in the towns had domestic servants, most of whom were female. Some of these women also worked in their husbands' shops. Working-class wives who had to earn money took in laundry or boarders, did sewing or weaving in their homes, or went out to work as domestics or tavern servers. Single women were largely confined to domestic service or prostitution.

Life in the rural areas continued much as before, although rising population and prosperity did make women's (and men's) lives less harsh and insecure than they had been previously. The gendered division of labour persisted, with regional variations. On the Atlantic and Pacific coasts, men went out in the fishing boats while women stayed on shore and processed the catch – first at home or on the beach, later in canning factories. The emerging grain economy of the prairies produced a more isolated type of rural life than that which grew up around the small subsistence farms of central Canada; women were forced to be both more self-reliant and, because of the need for cooperation in the face of a harsh environment, more dependent on their far-flung neighbours. Prairie life continued to be difficult and insecure long after the rural economies of Ontario and Quebec became settled and prosperous.

By the late nineteenth century, the central Canadian economy was changing. Industry was growing, drawing unskilled men and women from the farms into the rapidly expanding towns and cities. The garment and textile sector boomed, as did commercial baking and food preparation. As the cities grew, the demand for domestic workers also grew. The service sector was expanding as well, and with it the need for office workers, teachers, nurses, sales clerks, and other skilled people. Some of these new jobs were traditionally "female," such as seamstresses, maids, laundresses, food processors, teachers, and nurses. Others had been "male" jobs, but the demand grew more rapidly than the supply of male workers; this is true of most clerical and sales jobs. By the end of the nineteenth century today's "pink-collar ghetto" was already in place. The majority of women in the labour force worked in a handful of virtually all-female occupations, while men could aspire to a far wider range of employment.

Canadian Women's Work in the Twentieth Century

By 1900 the Canadian economy was becoming increasingly industrialized, largely because of government policies designed to make Canada self-sufficient in manufactured goods. The resulting changes in Canadian society were rapid and profound. Between 1901 and 1921 the urban population grew from one-third to almost one-half of the Canadian total. The urban working class grew quickly, as well as the urban middle class. Both men and women went to work in factories and offices. But attitudes towards women's work did not change with the changing conditions of women's lives. Most Canadians still believed that a woman's place was in the home, and that any paid work she might undertake was both temporary and secondary to her place in the family. Women's paid work was regarded as a necessary evil in times of economic expansion, when a reserve army of cheap labour was needed. In times of economic recession women's work was seen as a threat to men's jobs, which took priority because men were still seen as the primary breadwinners.

Despite these attitudes, more and more women continued to take paid employment. In the early years of this century most of these women were unmarried. Women who did not have husbands to support them had little choice but to work. Most such women who did marry quit their jobs, partly because their economic needs were less pressing, partly because of social taboos against married women working and, in some cases, because of laws that forbade employers to hire married women. These laws and taboos were based partly on the belief that women's reproductive systems could be damaged by working, and that married women should therefore be protected from the risk. Another factor was the belief that a married woman did not need to earn money, because her husband supported his dependents; therefore, she would be taking a job away from a male wage-earner who really needed it. This argument overlooked the fact that, even then, the kinds of jobs open to men and women were very different. Women's jobs were low paying, sometimes simply because they were perceived as "women's work"; they were tedious, repetitive, with bad working conditions, little regulation of hours or pay, and almost no chance of promotion. Many men's jobs were similar except for the pay, but other men had the chance to become managers, administrators, school principals, doctors, and foremen. These options were not available to women.

In theory, a male worker was paid a "family wage" that he used to support his wife and children. In practice, many working-class families had difficulty surviving on one income. Wages were low in the early part of this century. Ironically, one of the factors that kept family wages low was the existence of a reserve army of cheap labour that could be used to replace unruly workers or to meet demand in busy times, and could then be laid off without difficulty. That reserve army was made up largely of married working-class women. In other words, the wife had to work because her husband's wages were low; but his wages were low, in part, because his wife could do his job at a fraction of the cost. During the Depression this paradox became particularly cruel: employers could no longer afford men's higher wages, so many of them laid off men and hired women to replace them. Working women faced intense criticism for taking jobs away from male breadwinners, when the truth was that *they* were the breadwinners. The problem of low family wages was intensified when men drank or gambled away their earnings, leaving their wives and children destitute.

Most working-class women in the urban centres had a very limited choice of jobs. They could work as domestics, they could work in factories or laundry operations, they could work in food service, or they could do specialized dressmaking. Most factory women worked in garments, textiles, food, and tobacco production. Many of them were immigrants, who could not get other jobs because of language barriers and lack of training. The hours were long, with unsafe and unpleasant working conditions: unsanitary, badly lit, crowded, unventilated. The garment sweatshops, where women did piecework sewing for subcontractors, were especially notorious. The work was tedious, the pay low, and the job security tenuous at best. There were several strikes in the garment sector in the 1930s and 1940s; but the unions were dominated by men whose principal interest was to help their own members, not the women who worked the longest hours at the worst jobs.

Middle-class women found their work opportunities growing rapidly in the first two decades of this century, as office and service jobs expanded. It became customary for middle-class women to work until marriage, and some people argued that this work – particularly nursing or teaching – made them better mothers afterwards. It was not until the mid-1950s that middle-class women began to go back to work after their children had gone to school or left home. In the 1960s and 1970s the number of years women spent at home shrank steadily. By the 1980s the majority of women stayed in the labour force throughout their childbearing years (see Appendix 1). In the 1980s the labour force participation rate of married women overtook that of all women on average, while the participation rates of married women were, for the first time, almost as high as those of single women. (See Appendix 2.)

No matter what their class or occupation, women have always been paid substantially less than men with comparable training and responsibilities. In Toronto in 1870 female teachers earned an average of $220 to $400 annually, while male teachers earned between $600 and $700.[3] That pattern remained intact in the twentieth century. In the garment industries of Toronto and Montreal women earned just over half of men's earnings. The family wage system justified women's lower wages by treating women's earnings as a supplement to their husbands' incomes. The truth was often very different, as we have seen: many husbands could not or would not work, while others earned too little to support their families. In addition, many women – particularly in the cities – did not marry. The supply of men was inadequate to meet demand, partly as a result of the two world wars. Single women had no choice but to support themselves. Women who had children but no husband at home were in an especially difficult situation under the family wage system, because "families" were not defined to include sole-support mothers.

Women's lower pay was also explained by the low-level jobs that were open to them. Both teaching and the garment trade were dominated by women, but their chances for promotion were virtually non-existent and they risked losing their jobs if they married. Women were hired for these jobs because school boards and employers were anxious to keep their costs down, and women were much cheaper than men. Few people appear to have questioned this system. There were some women who ran businesses, such as small inns in their homes, or boarding houses; others helped their husbands to run stores.

The watershed in the history of Canadian women's paid labour was World War II. Women's role as a reserve army of labour in the Canadian economy was clearly apparent in the campaigns to recruit women into "men's" jobs while the men were fighting the war, and the subsequent campaigns to draw women back into their homes when the men returned. As in World War I, thousands of women – concentrated in Quebec and Ontario – went to work in munitions factories to meet wartime demand. Others took clerical jobs vacated by men. Many of these women were married, which contradicted the prevailing opinion that women should not "neglect" their husbands by taking paid work; after the government had drawn the available unmarried women into the offices, factories, and armed forces auxiliaries, it was forced to recruit married women. The results were dramatic. In 1939 there were over 600,000 women in the Canadian labour force, of whom 10 percent were married; by 1944 there were over a million women in the labour force, one-third of them married.[4]

Hundreds of thousands of women, married and single, held paid jobs for the first time. They earned their own money. Many held jobs that had traditionally been reserved for men. The boom in women's employment was justified by the government as a wartime emergency measure, but most of the women themselves did not see their jobs as a patriotic duty; they were drawn to paid work by the money – though they made only half to two-thirds of men's earnings, even in identical jobs. Social attitudes to women's paid employment did not change overnight; it was regarded as a necessary evil, not as an overdue recognition of women's abilities. But many of the women themselves experienced a change of attitudes. They realized that they could do a full day's work, even in a non-traditional field such as the armed forces or heavy industry, and that the myths about female inferiority on which they had been raised were simply not true.

Many of the women in wartime employment had children, which would normally have excluded them from paid work. But the federal government could not afford to keep mothers out of the work force, because of the severe labour shortages. The result was the federal-provincial Wartime Day Nurseries Agreement of 1942, under which Ontario and Quebec set up child-care centres for the children of female munitions workers.[5] Only a few thousand children were actually enrolled in these nurseries, but the recognition by governments that women needed help to manage family and work responsibilities marked a symbolic milestone in Canadian public policy.

After the war, the federal government had to persuade thousands of Canadian women to leave their jobs and return home. The groundwork was laid in 1943, with the appointment of the Advisory Committee on Reconstruction. The goal of the committee was to ensure that the men returning from military service would have the same types of jobs they had left in 1939 and 1940. It recommended a policy of "veteran's preference," under which ex-servicemen would have priority in hiring, and a series of policies to deal with the hundreds of thousands of women who would lose their jobs at war's end. These latter policies included: firing women from industry, clerical work, and government service; a government propaganda campaign to promote the status of housework as a full-time occupation; the termination of all incentives for women to work, including cancellation of the day nurseries program; a law barring married women from the federal civil service (which lasted until 1955); and training programs for women discharged from the armed forces. These programs stressed domestic service and other stereotypically female occupations, even for women who had learned trades or professions while on active duty. There was a solid foundation of attitudes for the government to build on: a 1944 Gallup poll showed that 75 percent of men, and 68 percent of women, believed that men should have preference in employment when they returned from serving their country.[6]

The government's efforts to reinforce traditional attitudes among women, to persuade them to give up their jobs and become "happy homemakers," were intensive. They included advertising campaigns on radio, in newspapers and magazines, and via the National Film Board. At the same time, scientific experts were telling women that their natural fulfilment lay in marriage and motherhood, and that they risked terrible physical and psychological problems if they persisted in their "unnatural" pursuit of paid employment – particularly if they remained single. What was often overlooked, as it had been after the First World War, was the number of women for whom this "natural" wedded state would never be possible because of male wartime casualties. For this and other reasons, many women refused to accept their new image as full-time homemakers; throughout the 1940s and 1950s over a quarter of Canadian women continued to work for pay.[7]

Commercial advertisers quickly followed the government's lead, presenting images of women as wives, mothers, "domestic engineers" and, above all, consumers. Wartime production capacity was shifted from munitions to consumer goods, and women were bombarded with inducements to purchase these goods for their families. In the years immediately after the war, young couples married, moved to the suburbs, and had unusually large numbers of children. The middle-class lifestyle quickly came to require two cars, a washing machine, a dryer, electric stoves and refrigerators, dishwashers, expensive furnishings and carpets, and other trappings of material success. The problem, for many such couples, was that this lifestyle could not be maintained on a single salary. The result, despite the constant bombardment of "happy homemaker" propaganda, was a slow but steady increase in the number of married women in the workforce. One 1955 study of working women, conducted by the Canadian Department of Labour, found that half were married and that most of those worked full-time.[8] Almost all worked because of economic necessity; they could not afford the consumer goods that they wanted on the husband's salary alone. Single women, widows, and women who were divorced or separated from their husbands, as always, had little choice; they had to work to support themselves. But the old attitudes died hard: a 1956 Gallup Poll found that 60 percent of Canadians believed that men should be given preference in hiring over married women (women were somewhat less certain than men, but not significantly).[9]

The trends that began to emerge in the 1950s, as women who had had children in the late 1940s returned to the paid employment of their single days, continued throughout the 1960s. The numbers of women in the labour force rose steadily, especially the numbers of married women.

By 1975 two-fifths of married women in Canada were either employed or actively looking for work; this figure had increased to over 60 percent by 1991.[10] Whereas middle-class women had previously worked before marriage and then quit for good, now they were returning to work after their children were in school. By the mid-1980s this pattern had changed again: the majority of working women with children did not leave the labour force while their children were small, but remained in the labour force throughout their adult lives. The 1991 census found that 68 percent of women with children at home were active in the labour force – and a whopping 78 percent of women aged 35–44 – compared to 60 percent of Canadian women overall. As we might expect, participation rates were lowest for women with more than one child and highest for women with school-aged children.[11] Between 1981 and 1993 the proportion of mothers employed outside the home rose from 49 percent to 63 percent.[12]

The primary reason for the increase in women's participation rate was economic: women's earnings became increasingly necessary to their families' economic well-being during the 1970s and 1980s. By 1981 women contributed over a quarter of average family incomes in Canada.[13] In addition, changes in the family meant that growing numbers of women were unmarried, separated, or divorced, often with children to support (see Chapter 4).

As of June 1995 women constituted 45 percent of the Canadian labour force.[14] The unemployment rate for men was 9.9 percent, while the unemployment rate for women was 9.2 percent. Until the 1980s women had greater difficulty than men in finding employment. But women's unemployment rates have been roughly similar to men's, or lower, throughout the last decade. This is largely due to the rise in part-time jobs, which attract more women than men (see below). One particularly worrisome statistic is the discrepancy in unemployment rates between male and female single parents. In June 1995 the rate for single fathers was 16.8 percent, 3.1 points lower than the rate for single mothers.[15] This means that single mothers are having a considerably harder time finding work than their male counterparts – an important reason for the poverty of many single mothers and their children.

Married women, like married men, were less likely than single people to be active in the labour force in June 1995. Sixty-two percent of married women were working or seeking work, compared to 59 percent of all women and 76 percent of married men. Women in the 25–44 age group were by far the most likely to enter the labour force, no matter what their marital status. Overall, 74 percent of men and 59 percent of women were active in the labour force (a difference of 15 percentage points).

The history of women's work in Canada demonstrates conclusively that the myth of the housewife is a middle-class fantasy. It does not match the reality of working-class or immigrant life at any time in our history, nor does it reflect the middle-class reality of the past quarter-century. Now that we know the real story, we can begin to explore the problems faced by the majority of Canadian women – married or single, with or without children – who work for a living.

The Double Shift

The "double shift" is the situation of women who work a full day at the office, store, or factory and then return home to face a messy house, a pile of laundry, and a hungry husband or family. Whether they work outside the home or not, women still carry most of the burden of household work, including child care. Women who go out to work have greatly increased their workload; their husbands, for the most part, have gained increased income and made few sacrifices.

In 1982, on average, a Canadian woman with a paid job and children spent 28 hours a week on household chores; the average weekly number of hours of housework contributed by her husband was 4.[16] In 1986 employed women in Canada with live-in male partners spent an average of 4.9 hours a day in paid work and another 4.9 hours in unpaid work: 2.4 hours of housework, 1.6 hours of child care, and 0.8 hours shopping and performing services for their families. Their male partners, on the other hand, spent an average of 7.7 hours in paid work and 2.4 hours in unpaid work: 0.8 hours on domestic work, 0.9 hours in child care, and 0.6 in shopping and services. Men also reported more free time: 3.9 hours per day for men, versus 3.6 hours for women.[17] By 1992 married women still spent an average of 1.4 more hours per day on domestic tasks than their husbands did.[18] Parenthetically, housewives with young children spend an average of 8.5 hours per day in domestic work.[19]

Conflict between Job and Family Responsibilities

Women are trying to find ways to combine work and family responsibilities. One such solution is to work *part time,* scheduling working hours while the children are in school. Part-time workers do the jobs of full-time workers, but they work fewer hours over the course of a week or month than a full-time worker normally would.[20] Women have always been more likely than men to work part time. In 1975 women made up 36 percent of all Canadian workers and 70 percent of part-time workers; by 1993, 45 percent of Canadian employees were women and 70 percent of part-timers were still female. Mothers are most likely to work part time: 28 percent of working mothers with children under 16 years of age worked part time in 1993, compared to less than 20 percent of women without children at home.[21]

At first glance, part-time work looks like the perfect compromise between the need to earn money and the need to look after children. In fact, of the part-time workers who cite family responsibilities as the reason for not working full time, 96 percent are women.[22] It should be pointed out that fewer than 10 percent of women working part time cited family responsibilities as the main reason – most of them aged 25 and 44 years – and that almost half of female part-time workers would prefer full-time work if they could find it. Still, the fact that women take a disproportionately large share of part-time work suggests that many find it an attractive option.

But part-time work has some serious disadvantages for women (and men). One is the low level of job security. Part-time jobs, particularly in the service industries, have a high rate of turnover. This is largely explained by the casual and temporary nature of many part-time jobs. A second disadvantage is the substantially lower hourly earnings of part-time workers compared to those of full-time workers. In 1986 the average hourly wage for part-time work was $8.19, compared to $10.83 for full-time work.[23] A third problem is that many work-related benefits, such as unemployment insurance, sick days, pensions, and maternity leave, are unavailable to part-time workers. Some employers "pro-rate" these benefits, giving part-time workers a fraction of benefits proportionate to their share of a full-time position, but most do not; there is no legislative requirement that they provide benefits, except for some pension coverage. In fact, it is often argued that employers are creating more and more part-time jobs precisely because these pay less and offer fewer benefits; the growth of part-time work is occurring in all Western countries, not just in Canada.

Another attempted solution to the conflict between family and work responsibilities has been the search for affordable, good-quality *child care.* In 1992 there were 2.7 million Canadian children whose families required some form of child care at some time during the week.[24] About one in ten of these children had access to affordable, licensed child care.[25] Licensed care centres and family homes must meet provincial standards of cleanliness. They must provide acceptable child/staff ratios, nourishing meals and snacks, and a variety of stimulating activities. The remaining children are left in child-care centres of variable quality; with relatives, friends, or paid baby-sitters; or in other ad hoc arrangements. Most women who put their children with unsupervised caregivers do so not because they are indifferent to their family's welfare, but because they simply have no choice. The number of supervised child-care spaces is increasing; in 1992 there were around 350,000 supervised spaces in Canada, more than triple the total in 1980.[26] But the rate of growth has slowed in recent years, and the number of spaces is still inadequate.

A third method of balancing work and family responsibilities is for the two parents (where there are two parents) to *work at different times,* so that one of them will always be home. According to a 1992 federal child-care study, 62 percent of couples with children use this approach.[27] It has significant drawbacks, including the inevitable strains on a marriage in which the two partners rarely spend time together. However, it can help to solve the problem of child care.

A final solution for some women is *home work.* In the nineteenth century, as we have seen, some Canadian women "took in sewing" to help make ends meet. In the 1990s thousands of Canadian women continue to sew piecework at home for the garment industry.[28] In addition, advances in computer and communications technology have made it possible for white-collar workers to do their jobs on home computers, linked to the office by fax and modem. In principle, home work promises to help women combine their domestic responsibilities with paying work. In practice, the situation is a very difficult one for both mothers and children. Women who sew at home find that they have little time and energy for their children, given the long hours and intense pressures during peak seasons in the garment industry.[29] Women who try to do data processing or other clerical work at home report similar problems. For some women, home work may be a partial solution; but it is no substitute for good-quality, affordable child care and other state services for working parents. We will now look at the availability of such services in Canada.

State Support for Canadian Mothers Working outside the Home

In June 1995, 118,000 female workers in Canada lost at least a week of work because of personal responsibilities.[30] The hours lost totalled 23 percent of all of the time lost by women workers in that month. By contrast, only 16,000 men lost a week or more of work time because of family responsibilities, accounting for lass than 3 percent of the total hours lost. These figures prove what most working women already know: when a child becomes sick or a babysitter cancels unexpectedly, the burden of domestic responsibilities falls on the woman, not on her male partner.

When a woman has to take time off work because of family responsibilities, she faces more than just a temporary inconvenience. Her commitment to her job may be questioned, and she could lose opportunities for training or promotion. In the long run her earnings are lower, her prospects for advancement narrower, than those of a male employee who knows he does not have to rush home to a sick child because his wife will take care of the problem. Women work an average of 33 hours a week, compared to 42 hours for men, largely because of domestic responsibilities. While many women do not want to work more hours, others feel that their careers are being hampered because they receive little help, from their partners or from the state, in balancing their paid work with their unpaid work at home.

What is the Canadian state doing to help parents balance their work and family responsibilities? To put it bluntly, the state is not doing nearly enough. Some western European states, such as Sweden and France, provide universal free (or heavily subsidized) child care in high-quality centres. Other states also offer generous maternity and parental leave provisions, which recognize that the first few months of a child's life are an especially important time for the parents to be at home. The purpose of these policies is to ensure a reliable supply of female workers in the short term, while maintaining a steady birth rate to replenish the workforce in the future. The general term for such policies is "pro-natalist"; they favour a higher birth rate, by ensuring that workers do not have to choose between their jobs and their families.

The only Canadian jurisdiction that has taken pro-natalist policies seriously is Quebec, whose governments have been deeply concerned in recent years about its low birthrate. Quebec has the most advanced child-care policies in Canada, particularly in the field of workplace child care. Other Canadian governments have taken a more short-sighted view, implicitly treating children as the individual burden or luxury of their parents, and not as a social responsibility for the future of the country. This attitude has been most clearly reflected in the failure of successive federal governments to introduce a national child-care program and to strengthen maternity leave programs. The result is that millions of Canadian women (and men) experience great stress and exhaustion from trying to juggle work and child care. They cannot choose to do without one or the other: they need to earn an income, and they want to raise a family. The failure of the Canadian state in this area is one of the most serious problems facing women, men, and children in this country.

Occupational Segregation and the Wage Gap

The Pink-Collar Ghetto

Occupational segregation, also called the *"pink-collar ghetto,"* affects most women workers. Women who work outside the home are heavily concentrated in a small number of occupations, most of them low paying, low status, dead end, and stereotyped as "female" jobs. This occupational segregation is directly related to the wage gap, which we will discuss below. In general, men have a much wider choice of occupations than women do. In 1991 women accounted for 87 percent of nurses and physiotherapists, 81 percent of clerical workers, 65 percent of teachers, 57 percent of service workers, 56 percent of social science and religion workers, and 46 percent of sales people.[31] In 1993, 86 percent of working women were in service-producing jobs, compared to 63 percent of men.[32] On average, goods-producing jobs, which are dominated by men (76 percent in 1991[33]), pay higher salaries and offer greater benefits. In particular, clerical, sales, and social service jobs tend to pay considerably less than jobs in primary industries, manufacturing, and construction. Therefore, "women's jobs" are low paying relative to "men's jobs."

How do we explain the fact that 71 percent of female workers are concentrated in traditional occupations?[34] First, we have to ask why women are attracted to those particular fields, particularly clerical, nursing, and sales. One reason may be that many women are more comfortable in jobs that women have traditionally held, where they will be surrounded by other women. Another may be that girls are encouraged to take courses that prepare them for these jobs but not for others: business, typing, accounting, and home economics instead of the "male" subjects of science and mathematics. A third reason might be that these jobs offer predictable hours, and often allow for shift work, which makes it a little easier for women with children to balance their work and family responsibilities.

Second, we have to explain why so few women are breaking out of those jobs into traditionally male fields. We know, from the experience of those women who have done men's jobs, that the reason is not a lack of ability. Instead, women who have been pioneers in male fields – such as engineering, construction, heavy industry, and primary resource industries – complain about intensive campaigns of harassment from their male colleagues and superiors. These campaigns include "sexual harassment, social ostracism by coworkers, lack of encouragement from supervisors, and punitive assignment to the worst part of the work."[35] Many women are worn down by this treatment and quit.[36] Many men, especially those who are not accustomed to working with women, refuse to allow a woman to give them orders. Others are reluctant to hire women because they don't want to spoil the working atmosphere, which sometimes resembles a boy's locker room. In a perfect world men would accept women as colleagues and superiors without difficulty or question; in reality, women in non-traditional positions face hostility on the job.

Explanations for the Wage Gap

As we saw in the first part of this chapter, women who have worked for money have always been paid significantly less than men. This wage gap has narrowed in recent years, but it remains unacceptably large. Appendix 4 charts the trends in women's earnings as a percentage of men's earnings over the past quarter-century. In 1967 a woman who worked full time, all year round, earned an average of 58 cents for every dollar earned by a full-time, full-year male worker. By 1993, over a quarter-century later, that figure had risen to 72 percent.[37] Despite the remarkable changes of that quarter-century – the influx of women into the labour force, the explosion in higher education and skills training among women, the apparent advances for women in the professions – women still made an average of 72 cents for every dollar earned by their male colleagues. The gap is smallest among the youngest workers, single workers, and those with some post-secondary education. But education still benefits women less than men: in 1993 a man with less than a Grade 9 education earned more, on average, than a woman with a post-secondary diploma (though not a university degree).[38]

The reasons for the wage gap are the subject of considerable debate. Some economists argue that the wage gap is not evidence of a failure in the labour market; rather, it proves that the market works fairly. They contend that women have less work experience than men; that women spend long periods out of the workforce caring for young children, thereby forfeiting training and promotion opportunities; that women have less education than men; and that women freely choose to take low-paying jobs so that they can spend more time with their families. This argument overlooks the facts that many women do not have children, and that many of those who do have children do not leave the workforce as a result. Given those facts, how much of the wage gap do these "explanations" really account for?

One study found that 45% of the wage gap was explained by "objective" factors: 6% was accounted for by women's longer periods out of the labour force; 8% by women's higher incidence of part-time work; 15% by women's lower levels of job experience; 2% by lower levels of formal education; 3% by absences for personal reasons; and 11% by men's preferential selection for on-the-job training. The remaining 55% of the wage gap can only be explained by discrimination against women on the part of employers.[39] It should be clear to alert readers that the "objective" factors are also related to discrimination: if women spend less time in the workforce, have lower levels of education and experience, and are given fewer chances for on-the-job training, these barriers to higher pay can only be understood as evidence of sexism in the labour market.

A recent Canadian study[40] offers additional evidence that the wage gap is caused by sexual discrimination. It followed the employment patterns of 1982 university and college graduates for five years, and examined the annual earnings of those who were employed full-time. The men and women in this study were virtually identical in age, educational preparation, and labour-force experience. There was no reason, on the surface, for a wage gap between the male and female graduates. But the study found that the men in the study earned more than the women in nearly every category of occupation and field of study, although the wage gap was smaller than in the labour force overall. Even more alarming, the wage gap actually increased from 1984 to 1987. Part of the gap was explained by occupational segregation. But the remainder – 67 percent of the gap between male and female university graduates and 80 percent of the gap between male and female community college graduates – could not be explained by any objective factors. The study concluded that this residual wage gap "offers circumstantial evidence of differential treatment in the labour market."[41]

One of the principal reasons for the narrowing of the wage gap, particularly for younger workers, is the substantial increase in women's educational opportunities. In 1993, 11 percent of women were university graduates, compared to 14 percent of men; in 1981 only 7 percent of women had university degrees.[42] Women are now a majority in Canadian universities: in 1991–92, 54 percent of university undergraduates were female (compared to 40 percent in 1972–73).[43] Women are still under-represented in mathematics, applied sciences and engineering, and physical sciences, but the proportions are rising. At the same time, women now make up 21 percent of university faculty, compared with 15 percent in 1977.[44] Women also make up a majority of community college students, though they tend to be concentrated in secretarial, nursing, social work, and educational programs.[45]

The wage gap has received a great deal of legislative attention, in the form of employment equity, equal pay, and "comparable worth" policies. It is still too early to say whether these policies have succeeded, or will succeed in the future.

Occupational Health and Safety Issues for Women

There is no room in this chapter to discuss all of the occupational health and safety concerns relating to women, including reproductive hazards and risks to fertility from certain types of industrial and office jobs. But we should note that studies of workplace conditions have tended to exclude women, because of the stubborn myth that most women do not work outside the home. (The home is actually one of the most hazardous workplaces, but there has been very little study of its hazards because of the equally stubborn myth that housework is not really work.) Therefore, we know very little about the effects of poor ventilation, long hours, repetitive stress injury, and other workplace hazards on women's bodies.

There are a few facts about women's jobs that we know with certainty. Women tend to work in narrow, confined spaces without moving, except for their hands and arms. They often have to respond quickly to the needs of others, which builds up stress.[46] Think of the jobs where women predominate: typists, supermarket cashiers, clerks in clothing stores, nurses, sewing-machine operators, teachers, telephone operators. These jobs do not appear to be particularly strenuous, but they can take a heavy toll on women's circulation, cardiovascular conditioning, back muscles, arms, hands, and eyes. In 1991, 61 percent of Canadian women believed that they had been exposed to a health hazard in the workplace in the previous year.[47]

We also know that many women are forced to work at high speed, and that their supervisors enforce rigid standards of accuracy.[48] Such jobs include food processing, garment assembly, and typing on microcomputers that are programmed to count the number of keystrokes per second. These jobs are highly stressful, often contributing to high blood pressure and heart disease, and can lead to serious accidents. Other jobs require long periods of standing, repetitive movements of the arms and hands, or hours at a stretch in smoky, poorly ventilated environments (e.g., service work in bars and restaurants).

The replacement of typewriters and keypunch machines by microcomputers has made some aspects of women's jobs easier, but low-level radiation from video-display terminals (VDTs) has been linked with reproductive hazards in some studies (though not all). Because of the variety of tasks a computer can perform, many clerical workers now spend entire days in front of the VDT; this contributes to a lack of motion, to eyestrain, and to repetitive stress injuries of the hands and wrists. Nurses suffer a high incidence of back pain and viral infections. In 1991, 36 percent of employed women reported health problems related to working on computers; 25 percent reported excessive stress from job demands; 24 percent complained of exposure to airborne dust or fibres, and 20 percent reported low air quality. Ten percent had been exposed to fumes or chemicals. These figures are cause for concern, though they are somewhat lower than the reported incidence of health hazards among male workers.[49]

Immigrant Women and Ethnic Minority Women

Most women who work outside the home experience occupational segregation and the wage gap. But there are also important differences among women's experiences, including the particular difficulties confronting immigrant women and women of colour. We will look at some of those difficulties in this section.

The Exploitation of Domestic Workers and Home Workers

Throughout the twentieth century, immigrant women arriving in Canada have been strongly encouraged to enter domestic service. In many cases, young women overseas were actively recruited by Canadian agents for the purpose of working in middle-class homes. At present, immigrant women and native-born Canadians of ethnic minorities constitute the majority of domestic workers. A second area of work that has been dominated by recent immigrants and ethnic minority women is the garment trade, especially piecework done at home.

Domestic work and home work share a number of characteristics, all of them damaging to the women who perform them.[50] The hours are virtually unlimited. The work is hard, repetitive, sometimes dangerous, often stressful, poorly paid, and almost entirely unregulated by federal or provincial labour codes. The women are isolated from other workers, which makes it difficult to discover their true working conditions and nearly impossible to organize them to demand better pay. There are few or no job-related benefits such as unemployment insurance or pensions. In the case of domestics, if they protest against poor working conditions they can be sent home and their families deprived of their earnings.

These jobs do not require language skills, which is the primary reason why so many immigrant women take them. There is very little skill or language training available to immigrant women, and little child care for those who do find training. Most government training programs for immigrants are targeted to male heads of families, on the assumption that only they will look for work. But the low wages that characterize the jobs open to recent immigrants usually force both spouses to work. In addition, the 60 percent of female immigrants who are sponsored by relatives are automatically ineligible for skills and language training; this is not explained to most women who apply for Canadian visas in their countries of origin.[51]

To make matters even worse, recent immigrants lack Canadian work experience; their formal training and experience overseas are often treated as irrelevant by Canadian employers.[52] The result is that the most menial service jobs (cleaning, cooking) and manufacturing jobs (sewing piecework) are heavily populated with recent immigrants: they end up doing the work that no Canadian will do if he or she has a choice. There appears to be an assumption among Canadian immigration officials that foreign-born women, especially those from Asia and Latin America, are unskilled and suitable only for domestic and garment work. This is both racist and inaccurate.

The Canadian government continues to recruit women overseas to do domestic work in Canada, a policy that began in the late nineteenth century. Since 1955, Canada has set up programs with other governments, such as Jamaica's, to bring women to Canada to work as domestics for at least one year in return for landed immigrant status. In 1973 the rules were tightened: domestic workers enter Canada on one-year work permits, which are usually renewed only once or twice; they cannot apply for landed immigrant status, and they have no rights under the law – not even the right to change employers. After a few years, during which they have almost no protection under federal laws or provincial labour codes (except in Quebec, Manitoba, and Ontario), they are sent home and replaced by other women.[53] They work long hours, many are exploited or even abused by their employers, and they are exempt from minimum wage laws in most provinces. Most accept the conditions of work because they need to send money back to their families in the Caribbean or the Philippines.

It would be absurd to suggest that all foreign-born women are cleaners or sewing-machine operators. But it would be equally wrong to ignore the clear evidence of their concentration in those types of jobs. One study of the Winnipeg garment industry in the 1970s explains how that concentration arose. The rules for employment training "refused subsidized language or training courses to any immigrant who could get a job without them. Because immigrant women could always get a low-paid cleaning or garment industry job in Winnipeg, they were pushed by [employment] counsellors and immigration officials to do just that."[54] Once the women were in the garment industry, they lacked the language skills, the resources, and the opportunity to get out and find better jobs.

Immigrant women, particularly women of colour from Third World countries, face legal, linguistic, racial, and gender barriers to employment. Nevertheless, most of them must earn money to help their families survive, especially in the expensive large cities where most recent immigrants live. Many such women work in family businesses, such as grocery stores and restaurants; others work in the domestic and garment jobs described earlier. The isolation of these women, particularly those with little knowledge of French or English, makes them essentially invisible to the rest of the Canadian population. But their problems are no less real and urgent because they are ignored.

Racism in the Canadian Workplace

Racism is a problem that Canadians have preferred to ignore. But the problem is real, and it will not go away by itself. The workplace is one of the most important arenas of racism, both because of its centrality in daily life and because the labour force participation rate for immigrant and visible minority women is higher than for other Canadian women. Members of visible minority groups in Canada face racial discrimination; women of colour face two sets of obstacles. Non-white men have a harder time finding work than white men; non-white women report higher unemployment than non-white men. I do not wish to suggest that racism is a greater obstacle to equality than sexism, or vice versa. The two forms of discrimination are intertwined in the experience of black, Asian, Latin American, and aboriginal women.

Conclusion

In this chapter we have examined the following key points.

1. More women work outside the home, for pay, than ever before in Canada. This is particularly true of middle-class women. Most of these women have little choice: they need the money because their husbands' "family wages" are insufficient, or because they have no other source of income.

2. This increase in women's labour force participation has not led to a reduction in their domestic responsibilities. Most women have to work a "double shift," one unpaid shift at home and another shift for money.

3. Women earn less money than men.

4. Women are concentrated in a narrow range of occupations, while men are not.

5.   Women are more likely to work part time than men, which leads to lower earnings and fewer benefits.

6.   Despite the increase in women's paid work, many people refuse to accept that work as a necessary fact of life. Women have repeatedly proven themselves to be as competent as men, but they still have to struggle against old prejudices about women's inferiority. Women with children also confront the idea that a mother who goes out to work is selfish and neglectful.

The future of women's work is not entirely positive. Women will continue to move into non-traditional jobs, and employment equity laws may help to break down the wage gap and occupational segregation. The recent recession has caused a possibly permanent decline in "men's jobs" – heavy industry and resource extraction – while leaving "women's jobs" – clerical, service, sales, and part time – either relatively unaffected or even more numerous. But there are warning signs that the future may simply bring new problems and obstacles. The rapid spread of microtechnology – computers and wordprocessors – in the office and other workplaces threatens the jobs of many women, particularly in the clerical and sales fields. Men's jobs are relatively unaffected by the computer revolution. Because most of the people in the higher-end computer jobs are men, microtechnology threatens to create a new gendered division of labour. As time goes on we will learn more about the effects of computers on women's work, including their occupational health and safety.

As Canada approaches the end of the twentieth century, we are making some significant breakthroughs for women in the Canadian economy. But we must not allow a few high-profile female corporate lawyers and doctors to distract us from the problems of most working women in Canada. Nor can we assume that the problems facing working women will simply go away without the direct involvement of the state – involvement that governments, fearful of spending and blinded by the ideology of the housewife, are reluctant to provide.

Appendix 1: Percentage of Canadian Women Employed, By Age of Youngest Child, 1981–93

Year	<3 Yrs	3–5 Yrs	Total < 6 Yrs	6–15 Yrs	Total < 16 Yrs
1981	39.1	46.8	42.0	56.6	49.5
1982	39.2	46.3	41.9	55.4	48.8
1983	41.7	47.8	44.1	55.2	49.7
1984	44.1	49.2	46.1	57.5	52.0
1985	46.6	52.1	48.7	59.0	54.0
1986	49.2	54.5	51.3	61.9	56.7
1987	50.4	56.3	52.8	64.0	58.5
1988	51.7	58.3	54.3	66.7	60.6
1989	54.4	60.9	56.9	69.6	63.3
1990	53.3	59.5	55.7	70.2	63.1
1991	54.3	60.1	56.5	69.0	62.9
1992	53.6	59.4	55.8	68.0	61.9
1993	54.4	59.4	56.3	68.8	62.5

Source: Statistics Canada, Housing, Family and Social Statistics Division, *Women in the Labour Force, 1994 Edition,* p. 52.

Appendix 2: Percentage of Canadian Women Employed, by Marital Status, 1981–93

Year	Single	Married	Separated/ Divorced	Widowed	Total
1981	58.1	46.8	58.9	17.5	47.4
1982	55.1	46.2	56.5	16.1	46.1
1983	55.3	46.8	55.5	15.7	46.5
1984	56.4	48.4	56.2	14.9	47.6
1985	58.1	49.6	56.5	15.0	48.8
1986	58.6	51.4	55.8	13.9	49.9
1987	60.4	52.6	57.6	14.2	51.2
1988	62.0	54.4	59.1	13.1	52.6
1989	62.4	55.5	60.2	13.3	53.3
1990	61.9	56.4	58.9	13.1	53.7
1991	59.0	55.9	56.4	12.2	52.6
1992	57.0	55.4	55.0	11.6	51.6
1993	55.1	55.8	53.1	11.8	51.4

Source: Statistics Canada, Housing, Family and Social Statistics Division, *Women in the Labour Force, 1994 Edition,* 51

Appendix 3: Labour Force Participation Rates of Single and Married Women, by Age of Dependent Children, 1981, 1989 and 1994

	1981	1989	1994
Husbands working	57.6	71 2	73.4
0–5 years	47.6	64.6	68.0
6–15 years	61.5	76.8	77.2
No dependents	61.7	71.9	74.1
No husband present	53.7	57.1	56.6
0–5 years	51.3	50.6	49.1
6–15 years	67.8	74.0	72.7
No dependents	45.4	49.3	50.3
All families	51.7	60.2	60.8
0–5 years	47.7	62.3	64.3
6–15 years	61.8	75.2	75.7
No dependents	48.4	53.3'53.9	

Source: Statistics Canada; Labour Canada Women's Bureau.

Appendix 4: The Wage Gap for Full-time Workers and All Workers, 1975–88

Year	Wage Ratio for All Workers	Wage Ratio for Full-time Workers Only
1967	46.1	58.4
1975	48.0	60.1
1979	51.2	63.3
1982	54.6	64.0
1988	57.4	65.3
1993	64.0	72.0

Source: Statistics Canada.

Notes

1   The labour force is the sum total of all persons who are either employed or actively looking for work.
2   See Prentice et al., *Canadian Women,* chaps. 3, 5, 9.
3   Ibid., 130.
4   Wilson, *Women, Families, and Work,* 81–82.
5   Prentice et al., 198–99.
6   Ibid., 303.
7   Ibid., 311.
8   Ibid., 313.
9   Labour Canada, Women's Bureau, *Canadian Attitudes Toward Women,* 75.
10 Labour Canada, Women's Bureau, *Women in the Labour Force 1990–91* (Ottawa: Minister of Supply and Services, 1991); Statistics Canada, Housing, Family and Social Statistics Division, Women in the Workplace.
11 Statistics Canada, Labour Force Activity of Women By Presence of Children, table 1.
12 Statistics Canada, *Women in the Labour Force: 1994 Edition,* 45.
13 Edward T. Pryor, *Canadian Husband-Wife Families: Labour Force Participation and Income Trends 1971–1981,* Statistics Canada Labour Force Activity Research Series Number 42 (Ottawa: Minister of Supply and Services, 1984).
14 Statistics Canada, *The Labour Force: June 1995* (Ottawa: Minister of Industry, 1995), B-2.
15 Ibid., B-22, B-23.
16 Kome, *Somebody Has To Do It,* 19.
17 *Women in the Workplace,* table 6.1.
18 *Women in the Labour Force: 1994 Edition,* 48; Statistics Canada, Family and Community Support Systems Division, *Dimensions of Job-Family Tension,* 11.
19 *Women in the Labour Force: 1994 Edition,* 49.
20 This definition of "part-time" is taken from Labour Canada, *Report of the Commission of Inquiry into Part-Time Work.*
21 *Women in the Labour Force: 1994 Edition,* 45.
22 Logan, "Voluntary Part Time Workers."
23 Canada, Library of Parliament Research Branch, *Part-Time Work.*
24 Statistics Canada and Health and Welfare Canada, *Canadian National Child Care Study: Parental Work Patterns and Child Care Needs.*
25 Statistics Canada and Health and Welfare Canada, *Canadian National Child Care Study: Where Are the Children?*
26 *Women in the Labour Force: 1994 Edition,* 49.

27   *Parental Work Patterns and Child Care Needs*, 14.

28   Johnson with Johnson, *The Seam Allowance*.

29   Ibid., 86–92.

30   Statistics Canada, *The Labour Force: June 1995*, B-39.

31   Ibid., table 1.12.

32   *Women in the Labour Force: 1994 Edition*, 14.

33   Ibid., table 1.11.

34   Ibid., 14.

35   Bergmann, *The Economic Emergence of Women*, 90.

36   Between 1976 and 1985 the number of women working in processing, machining, and fabricating jobs fell by 3.6 percent, compared to 1.6 percent for men. The number of women in material handling and crafts jobs fell by 12 percent, while the number of men fell by 5.4 percent. See Statistics Canada, *Occupational Trends among Women in Canada: 1976–1985*.

37   Statistics Canada, *Earnings of Men and Women in 1993* (Ottawa: Minister of Industry, Science & Technology, 1995), 13.

38   Ibid., 45.

39   Bergmann, 79. It should be pointed out that the Canadian wage gap statistics are based entirely on full-time workers, so the higher incidence of part-time work among women does nothing to explain the situation here.

40   Warnell, *The Persistent Gap*.

41   Ibid., ii.

42   *Women in the Labour Force: 1994 Edition*, 36.

43   Ibid.

44   Ibid., 27.

45   Ibid., 38.

46   Labour Canada, Women's Bureau, *Occupational Safety and Health Concerns of Canadian Women*, 10.

47   *Women in the Labour Force: 1994 Edition*, 60.

48   See Menzies, *Women and the Chip;* Gannagé, "A World of Difference."

49   *Women in the Labour Force: 1994 Edition*, 60.

50   See Silvera, *Silenced;* Johnson, *The Seam Allowance*.

51   Estable, *Immigrant Women in Canada*, 11.

52   Canada, *Report of the Commission on Equality in Employment* (Ottawa: Minister of Supply & Services, 1984), 49.

53   Estable, 30.

54   Annalee Lepp, David Millar, and Barbara Roberts, "Women in the Winnipeg Garment Industry, 1950s–1970s," in Kinnear, *First Days, Fighting Days*, 161.

References and Further Reading

Anderson, Doris. *The Unfinished Revolution: The Status of Women in Twelve Countries*. Toronto: Doubleday Canada, 1991.

Armstrong, Pat. *Labour Pains: Women's Work in Crisis*. Toronto: Women's Press, 1984.

Armstrong, Pat, and Hugh Armstrong. *The Double Ghetto: Canadian Women and their Segregated Work*. Rev. ed. Toronto: McClelland & Stewart, 1984.

Bergmann, Barbara R. *The Economic Emergence of Women*. New York: Basic Books, 1986.

Canada. *Canadian National Child Care Study: Parental Work Patterns and Child Care Needs*. Ottawa: Statistics Canada/Health & Welfare Canada, 1992.

———. *Canadian National Child Care Study: Where Are the Children? An Overview of Child Care Arrangements in Canada*. Ottawa: Statistics Canada/Health & Welfare Canada, 1992.

———. *Report of the Commission on Equality in Employment*. Ottawa: Minister of Supply & Services, 1984.

———. Library of Parliament Research Branch. *Part-Time Work*. Ottawa: Minister of Supply & Services, 1990.

Duffy. Ann, and Norene Pupo. *Part-Time Paradox: Connecting Gender, Work and Family*. Toronto: McClelland & Stewart, 1993.

Estable, Alma. *Immigrant Women in Canada: Current Issues*. Ottawa: CACSW, 1986.

Gannagé, Charlene. "A World of Difference: The Case of Women Workers in a Canadian Garment Factory." In Heather Jon Maroney and Meg Luxton, eds., *Feminism and Political Economy: Women's Work, Women's Struggles*. Toronto: Methuen, 1987.

Hochschild, Arlie. *The Second Shift: Working Parents and the Revolution at Home*. New York: Viking, 1989.

Johnson, Laura C., with Robert F. Johnson. *The Seam Allowance: Industrial Home Sewing in Canada*. Toronto: Women's Press, 1982.

Kinnear, Mary, ed. *First Days, Fighting Days: Women in Manitoba History*. Regina: University of Regina, 1987.

Kome, Penney. *Somebody Has to Do It: Whose Work is Housework?* Toronto: McClelland & Stewart, 1982.

Labour Canada. *Part-Time Work in Canada: Report of the Commission of Inquiry into Part-Time Work*. Ottawa: Minister of Supply & Services, 1983.

Labour Canada, Women's Bureau. *Occupational Safety and Health Concerns of Canadian Women: A Background Paper*. Ottawa: Minister of Supply & Services, 1991.

———. *Canadian Attitudes toward Women: Thirty Years of Change* Ottawa: Minister of Supply & Services, 1984.

Logan, Ron. "Voluntary Part Time Workers." In Statistics Canada, *Perspectives on Labour and Income*. Ottawa: Minister of Supply & Services, 1994.

Menzies, Heather. *Women and the Chip: Case Studies of the Effects of Informatics on Employment in Canada*. Montreal: IRPP, 1981.

Peitchinis, Stephen G. *Women at Work: Discrimination and Response*. Toronto: McClelland & Stewart, 1989.

Prentice, Alison, et al. *Canadian Women: A History*. Toronto: HBJ Canada, 1988.

Randall, Vicky. *Women and Politics: An International Perspective*. 2nd ed. Chicago: University of Chicago Press, 1988.

Silvera, Makeda. *Silenced*. 2nd ed. Toronto: Sister Vision, 1989.

Statistics Canada. *Labour Force Activity of Women by Presence of Children*. Ottawa: Minister of Industry, Science & Technology, 1993.

———. *Occupational Trends among Women in Canada: 1976–1985*. Ottawa: Minister of Supply & Services, 1986.

———, Family and Community Support Systems Division. *Dimensions of Job-Family Tension*. Ottawa: Minister of Industry, Science & Technology, 1994.

———, Household Surveys Division. *The Labour Force: June 1995*. Ottawa: Minister of Industry, Science & Technology, 1995.

———, Housing, Family and Social Statistics Division. *Women in the Labour Force: 1994 Edition*. Ottawa: Minister of Industry, Science &Technology, 1994.

———, Housing, Family and Social Statistics Division. *Women in Canada: A Statistical Report*. 2nd ed. Ottawa: Minister of Supply & Services, 1990.

———, Housing, Family and Social Statistics Division. *Women in the Workplace*. 2nd ed. Ottawa: Minister of Industry, Science & Technology, 1993.

Warnell, Ted. *The Persistent Gap: Explaining the Earnings Differential between Recent Male and Female Post-Secondary Graduates*. Statistics Canada Analytical Studies Branch, Research Paper Series Number 26. Ottawa: Minister of Supply & Services, 1989.

Wilson, S.J. *Women, Families and Work*. 3rd ed. Toronto: McGraw-Hill Ryerson, 1991.

Chapter 4: Women in the Canadian Family

Chapter Summary

Chapter 4 examines some of the changes in Canadian families in the twentieth century, and the reasons why the political system has not responded effectively to those changes. The chapter argues that there is only one "politically correct" model of the family at a given time, and that any type of family structure that deviates from that model may be denied equal recognition and assistance by the state. Currently, the approved model is a married mother and father with at least one child. In contrast, the past half-century has witnessed a steep rise in divorce rates, a decline in birth rates, fewer marriages, and an increase in the number of single-parent families. Chapter 4 examines the reasons for these changes, and their implications for women in Canada. We will not provide a definition of "the family" in this chapter, partly because the meaning of "family" is itself a political issue. Each reader must decide what a "family" is, and how it fits into her or his life.

Chapter Outline

Political Conceptions of the Family

Families are at the heart of women's lives. Most women receive great joy and satisfaction from their partners, their children, and often their parents and siblings. Feminism has often been caricatured, by its opponents, as the greatest threat to "the family." If the anti-feminist movement is "pro-family," as it claims, then by definition feminists are "anti-family." But this is a misleading image of feminism. Some feminists have criticized traditional family structures, describing them as oppressive to women and inherently exploitative. These critiques were necessary, however, because the prevailing idealization of "the family" in popular culture and political discourse was hiding thousands of individual tragedies: husbands who beat their wives, parents who sexually exploited their children, and women who were trapped in unhappy marriages with no legal means of escape.

Attacking such a potent social institution as "the family" required strong language and analysis. The result has been a persistent popular belief that all feminists are vehemently opposed to marriage, children, and the traditional division of labour within the home. Today, most feminists acknowledge the value of families and their central role in women's lives. But the institution of "the family" is falling apart in all directions, and feminists are being blamed for social changes that are *not* the result of the women's movement. In all likelihood, the breakdown of the traditional family has caused more women to embrace feminism, rather than the reverse.

For centuries, political and religious leaders have spoken of "the family" as though there were only one possible or approved family structure at any given time. In this century this approved structure has been the "traditional family unit": a mother and father, married for life, with one or more children. The husband is the sole wage earner and the head of the household, with all of the power that accrues to those roles. Any other configuration of people – an unmarried mother and father, a single mother and her children, two lesbians raising a child, or a heterosexual couple who choose not to have children – does not constitute a "family" in this socially approved sense, however strong their ties of mutual affection and responsibility.

Despite the prevalence of this family model in public discourse and policy, it no longer resembles the majority of real Canadian families. Married couples with children accounted for 52 percent of all families in the 1991 census,[1] but the majority of the women in those families worked outside the home.[2] In spite of this discrepancy between myth and reality, the ideology of the traditional family unit has been powerful enough to overcome lived experience and common sense. This ideology arose during the nineteenth century, as the urban middle class began to assume political power. The middle-class family model was thus enshrined in legislation and in cultural values, and has shaped our lives and our ideas ever since.

The economic changes in women's lives, which we discussed in the previous chapter, have been both the cause and the effect of profound changes in the family since the Second World War. Today more than ever, Canadian families come in a variety of shapes and sizes. Unfortunately for many of the women and children in "non-traditional" families, some powerful public figures continue to resist these changes, with negative results. In this chapter we will describe the current state of the family in Canada and explain the changes of the past few decades.

Changes in Canadian Family Structure

As we have already seen, less than a quarter of all Canadian families conform to the traditional model that is held up as the ideal, as the foundation for our society. We have been told, by public figures including former American vice-president Dan Quayle and members of the Mulroney government, that this erosion of the approved family structure is the underlying cause of a social breakdown. Is such a breakdown happening? If so, is it the fault of feminists? Or are the changes less threatening, and explained by a host of other causes?

Fewer Children

The number of children born to Canadian women has dropped throughout this century, except for the baby boom of the late forties, fifties, and early sixties. In 1959 the Canadian birth rate was nearly four children for every woman; in 1990 it was 1.7 children per woman.[3] Most of this drop in the fertility rate occurred in the younger age groups: women between 15 and 24 are having just over half as many babies as their counterparts did in 1970. The reason is that today's women are postponing childbirth considerably longer than women did in the 1960s and 1970s: the median age of mothers at the time of their first birth was 22.8 years in 1971, and 25.8 years in 1987. The fertility rate among women over 25 has increased significantly in the past twenty years.[4]

Later and Fewer Marriages

For both men and women, the average age at first marriage has risen since 1970. In that year, the average age of first-time bridegrooms was 25 years; in 1993 it was 28 years. Women in 1970 married for the first time at an average age of 22.7 years, and by 1993 that figure had risen to 26 years.[5] At the same time, fewer Canadians are marrying at all. In 1990 the Canadian marriage rate per 1,000 women was only two-thirds of the 1970 peak: 70 out of 1,000 single, widowed, or divorced women married in 1970, whereas 45 did so in 1987. This trend is mirrored in the rising number of common law couples. In the ten years between 1981 and 1991, the number of common law unions increased by 104 percent.[6] It is clear that many Canadians are turning away from legal marriage as an institution, or postponing it to live common law. Not all Canadians have given up on marriage, however; many divorced people remarry at least once. The number of divorced people as a proportion of all persons getting married tripled between 1970 and 1987 (from 6.9 percent to 20 percent).[7]

Rising Divorce Rates

One reason why so many divorced people are getting married is simply that there are so many divorced people. In 1970, 30,000 divorces were granted; that worked out to 621 divorces for every 100,000 married women. In 1987 there were 87,000 divorces, and the divorce rate had more than doubled to 1,372.2 per 100,000.[8] By the 1990s, 50 percent of marriages ended in divorce.[9] Canada has one of the highest divorce rates in the Western world, lower than that of the United States but higher than all European countries except Sweden and Denmark.[10]

The percentage of divorces that involved children declined over this period, from over half to roughly one-third; but because of the rising divorce rate, the actual number of children directly affected rose to over 50,000 per year.[11] In 75 percent of divorces involving children, the mother received custody; the father was the custodial parent in 14 percent, with the remainder going to other types of arrangements.[12] Although women are usually awarded custody, few are given adequate financial resources to look after their children (see below).

Single-Mother Families

One result of the rise in divorce rates and the decline in marriage rates is the growing number of so-called single-parent families. In this instance, the gender-neutral language is misleading; fewer than 20 percent of single-parent families are headed by men.[13] It is more accurate to refer to single-mother families, because this terminology alerts us to the special problems faced by these families[14] – in particular, lower wages for the parent-earner, if she can find a job at all. Unemployment among single mothers is higher now than it was in 1981;[15] it is twice as high among single mothers than it is among married mothers.[16]

The 1991 census identified 954,700 single-parent families in Canada, an increase of 34 percent over 1981.[17] Of these, 82 percent (786,400) were headed by women.[18] In 1961, 9 percent of all Canadian families were single-mother families; by 1991 the proportion had grown to 16.4 percent.[19] Single mothers are the least likely of all parents to be employed: only 52.2 percent of single mothers were employed in 1991, compared to 64.6 percent of married mothers and 71.3 percent of single fathers.[20] The average income of single-mother families in 1990 was $22,000, compared to $36,800 for single-father families and $57,200 for two-parent families.[21] Sixty percent of single-mother families, a total of 257,000, lived below the poverty line in 1990, compared to 27 percent of single-father families and 10 percent of two-parent families.[22] Many single-mother families rely on some form of paid child care; the lack of subsidized care available in Canada constitutes a formidable barrier to the employment and retraining of women in this situation.

Explaining the Changes in Canadian Family Structure

Women's Greater Earning Potential outside the Home

The major reason for these changes is the growing demand for paid female labour in the economy. When women had to choose between expanding their families and working to support the children they already had, many chose not to have more children. Public policies that might have helped women to balance their work and family responsibilities, such as maternity leave and child care, have been absent or inadequate (see Chapter 12). As a result, couples have decided to have fewer children than they might otherwise have had. Or they have postponed children until one or both partners were sufficiently established in their careers to afford the costs (in time and money) of parenthood.

In addition, when women had the chance to earn their own money, even if it was less than a man might have earned, marriage ceased to be an economic necessity and became an option that many women (and men) have refused to take. Many women (and men) spent years in post-secondary and professional education, preparing for careers, and postponed marriage as a result. Later marriage, combined with a greater commitment to paid work, results in fewer children. Finally, women's growing economic independence has made it easier for many of them to leave bad marriages.

It must be remembered, however, that because women earn less than men, and because many single mothers cannot find affordable child care while they work or go to school, divorce is the principal cause of the "feminization of poverty" – particularly for women with children. Therefore, while a divorce may put an end to emotional turmoil, for many women it leads to severe financial distress. This is particularly true of middle-aged women who have stayed at home with their children. These women have few job skills, and they must rely on spousal support from their ex-husbands. But because most support awards are inadequate, and because more than two-thirds of support awards are in arrears at any given time, such women may be left destitute by a marriage breakdown (see below).[23]

Improved Contraception

Another reason why Canadian women are having fewer children, and having them later in life, is the greater availability of birth control since the 1960s. Until 1969, distributing birth control devices was technically illegal in Canada.[24] The advent of the birth-control pill, along with improvements in barrier methods (condoms, diaphragms, and sponges), has made it easier for both men and women to prevent unwanted pregnancies. This is not to suggest that any of these methods is perfect; all can fail, even when used properly, and the pill has side effects that should make us cautious about its use over a long period of time. In addition, the cost of some contraceptives is prohibitive for many people.[25] But the contraceptives available in the 1990s are more reliable than those available during earlier periods of human history, and have contributed substantially to the decline in fertility rates among Canadian women.

Changes in Divorce Laws and Social Attitudes

Until the 1960s divorce was difficult to obtain in Canada. The first Canadian divorce law was a British statute, the Matrimonial Causes Act, which was adopted by the Province of Canada in 1857. Like most family-related legislation of the time, it reinforced women's economic and legal dependence on men. A husband could divorce his wife on the grounds of her adultery, without requiring further proof of wrongdoing on her part. But a wife could only be granted a divorce if her husband's adultery had been compounded by "desertion without reason, extreme cruelty, incest or bigamy," or by a conviction for rape or sodomy.[26] Until 1919 only Nova Scotia and New Brunswick had divorce courts; people living in other provinces had to seek divorce by a special act of Parliament.[27] The western provinces set up divorce courts in the 1920s, Ontario followed in 1930, and Prince Edward Island in 1945; but as late as 1968 people living in Quebec and Newfoundland had to go to the Senate to obtain a divorce.

For most of Canadian history, our divorce laws were among the most restrictive in the Western world.[28] There were two principal reasons for this. The first was that governments refused to liberalize the laws, to allow for more grounds or to facilitate the process of legally ending a marriage. A few bills did pass through Parliament, all of them minor. One example was the 1925 bill that provided that simple adultery was adequate grounds for divorce sought by either husband or wife. But all of these were private members' bills, sponsored by individual MPs instead of by governments. No government wanted to associate itself with the issue of divorce. As a result, the 1857 laws remained largely intact until 1968. In that year, when polls showed that a majority of Canadians were in favour of more liberal divorce laws,[29] the federal government finally passed a law establishing divorce courts in all provinces and broadening the grounds for a legal decree.

The second reason for the restrictive laws was the social climate of the nineteenth and early twentieth centuries, which was strongly opposed to family breakdown. The prevailing attitude in Canadian society, until the middle of this century, was that the traditional family was the bedrock of society and of the nation. Anything that threatened the stability and sanctity of the family, such as birth control, abortion, divorce, or premarital sex, was a threat to Canada as a whole. For example, the 1925 reform was greeted with fear and suspicion by the popular press of the time, which "constantly reminded women that it was their duty, honour, and privilege to preserve family stability for the benefit not only of the family but also of the nation."[30] As a result, divorce carried a powerful social stigma, and divorced persons were often ostracized by friends and relatives.

Not surprisingly, in light of these legal barriers and social attitudes, the number of divorces granted in Canada in the nineteenth century was very small: an average of three divorces per year between 1871 and 1875, rising to an average of eleven by the turn of the century.[31] Divorce was a difficult and expensive process, beyond the reach of the poor and the working class. This began to change in the aftermath of World War I, when social upheaval and the strains imposed by wartime provoked a boom in the number of divorces (see Appendix 2). Another boom followed World War II, as hasty wartime marriages were ended and older couples faced the results of prolonged separation. Divorce rates have continued to rise in the past half-century, as social attitudes have changed and as women have become less dependent on marriage for their economic survival. They peaked again following the 1968 liberalization of the divorce laws, as couples who had been separated for years finally got the opportunity to end their marriages in court. A higher number of divorces leads to greater social acceptance of family breakdown; that greater acceptance, in turn, leads more couples to accept the inevitability of divorce. The laws are eventually reformed to catch up with changing attitudes and social realities.

Since the most recent reform in 1986, Canadian divorce law has been among the most liberal in the Western world.[32] The 1968 law had stipulated two grounds for divorce: the fault of one party, including adultery, cruelty, or desertion, which could lead to a decree for the other party after one year; and an irretrievable breakdown of the marriage, in which a divorce could be granted after the parties had lived separately for three to five years. The 1986 law keeps some of the old principles, including the fault-based grounds of adultery and physical or mental cruelty. But it has also shortened the waiting period for uncontested divorces quite substantially. Whereas the 1968 act had required proof of separation for three to five years before filing for divorce, the 1986 Act requires proof of separation for only one year before the decree. In other words, the couple can start proceedings in an uncontested divorce after being separated for less than a year. The 1986 law, in the opinion of one legal scholar, has "altered the legal definition of marriage itself by making it a relationship terminable at will."[33]

The purpose of the 1986 law was to eliminate fault-based, adversarial divorces; the intent of the legislators was to reduce the emotional trauma of the divorcing spouses and their children. But the reformed law has had negative consequences for divorced women and their children. It has required judges, when determining the amount and duration of support awards, to "promote the economic self-sufficiency of each spouse within a reasonable period of time."[34] For many women who have stayed at home with their children for the duration of the marriage, particularly those with custody, economic self-sufficiency is an unrealistic goal. Nevertheless, courts are putting strict limits on the amount and the duration of spousal support awards, thus plunging thousands of women and children into poverty. Even in the 1990s government figures showed that a woman's income decreases by an average of 76 percent following divorce while the man's income grows by 42 percent.[35]

For the minority of Canadian women who receive adequate spousal support awards, the divorce law reforms of the 1980s did bring some good news. The Family Orders and Agreements Enforcement Assistance Act, which came into force in 1988, gives the federal and provincial governments the power to trace spouses who fail to pay their spousal and child support, or who abduct their own children in violation of court custody orders. The act also gives the federal government the power to withhold certain payments from the debtor spouse and pay them to the creditor spouse. Those payments include federal income tax refunds, unemployment insurance payments, and benefits under the Canada Pension Plan.[36] Such laws are urgently required: in Ontario in 1991, 75 percent of court-ordered support payments were in arrears.[37]

We have seen that Canadian families have changed dramatically in this century. Canadian women are marrying later, having fewer children, and carrying more of the financial and emotional responsibility for their children than ever before. Are these changes the result of feminism, as the "pro-family" movement claims? Clearly, Canadian women are not becoming the selfish, hedonistic, man-hating dupes of feminism caricatured by R.E.A.L. Women and other right-wing groups. If women are having fewer children in the 1990s than they did in the 1950s, this is partly because they have greater economic opportunities outside the home, partly because of the high cost of raising children, and partly because they have more control over their own fertility. If more women are divorcing in the 1990s than in the 1950s, the reasons are partly economic, and partly the result of changes in the legislation governing divorce and changing social attitudes towards marriage breakdown. If women are waiting longer to marry, or living common law, it is because they have more options now than their mothers or grandmothers did. To blame (or credit) feminism for all of these changes in women's lives is simply wrong.

Resisting the Changes

The changes described above – particularly the breakdown of the traditional family model and the growing independence of women – have provoked fierce resistance in certain sectors of Canadian society. A minority of men have tried to use the divorce courts and custody arrangements as a way to get back at their ex-wives. Some politicians have tried to turn back the clock to an idealized family that no longer characterizes Canadian society. They have been abetted and encouraged by a political and cultural backlash against the supposed excesses of feminism, personified in Canada by R.E.A.L. Women.

The Backlash

The backlash against feminism, according to author Susan Faludi, manifests itself in the mass media and in the political system.[38] The *media backlash* rests on two main ideas. The first is that "women's lib" has prevailed in all aspects of society: that women are now equal to men in the workplace, the political system, and the home, and there is nothing further for feminism to accomplish. The second idea is that these supposed triumphs of feminism have created terrible problems, both for individual women who were "deceived" by feminists and for society as a whole. Such alleged problems include an epidemic of infertility among career women, the near-impossibility of finding a husband after age 35, and a mass outbreak of depression and anxiety among women who try to combine their traditional roles with paid employment.

In her book about the backlash, Faludi demonstrates the untruth of both of these claims. In the first place, women are *not* yet equal to men; the wage gap is still in place, most women still work in the pink-collar ghetto, women are still drastically under-represented in politics. In the second place, the attention-grabbing stories about biological clocks, man shortages, and "superwoman burnout" are based on studies whose methodology is flawed and whose results are contradicted by other, more reliable findings. There is no epidemic of infertility among career women in their thirties; in fact, infertility is a growing problem for women in their twenties because of the effects of chlamydia and other sexually transmitted diseases. The headlines that screamed that single women in their thirties were doomed to eternal spinsterhood were based on a study that failed to observe proper demographic methods and whose conclusions were patently contradicted by reality. Yet because it was called the "Harvard-Yale" study, and because it made the covers of magazines such as *Time* and *Newsweek,* millions of women believed its findings. The idea that a forty-year-old single woman was more likely to be killed in a terrorist attack than to find a husband has found widespread currency in our culture, while the numerous studies that proved this to be untrue were largely ignored.

The mass media popularizes these ideas in "trend journalism," which seizes on anecdotal evidence or those flawed, sensational studies to proclaim a "trend" affecting women, regardless of the credibility of the data. The ideas also appear on television and in movies, such as *Fatal Attraction* and *The Hand that Rocks the Cradle*. These supposed entertainments send disturbing messages to women: don't work outside the home or your child will be left in the care of a psychopath; don't put off marriage while you pursue a career or you'll end up as a crazy single woman obsessively stalking a married man.

Even more damaging are the *political* aspects of the backlash: the appointment of Clarence Thomas to the Supreme Court of the United States, the cuts to public programs that fund child care and abortion, the movement to rescind employment equity laws, and the victory of the right wing of the Republican Party in the 1994 congressional elections. The principal architects of the political backlash are right-wing religious and political leaders, many of whom are women. Their core constituency is young men from blue-collar backgrounds, whose fathers supported their families with manufacturing jobs that are now disappearing. These young men know that their standards of living will probably be lower than those of their fathers, but they may not understand the real reasons why: the decline in North American productivity and the shift of labour-intensive work to low-wage countries such as Singapore and Malaysia. So they blame the nearest scapegoats: blacks, Hispanics, immigrants, or feminists who demand that women have equal access to jobs.

Faludi wrote about the United States, not Canada. But while it can be argued that the backlash has been more intense south of the border, there have been similar developments in Canada. In addition, the media backlash has been as visible here as in the United States, because of the dominance of American cultural products in the Canadian market (see Chapter 6). The political backlash includes the "family caucus" in the Mulroney government and the emergence of R.E.A.L. Women. There has been less of a constituency for a backlash in Canada, because the political culture does not appear to be as divided over social welfare and gender issues as in the United States. Employment equity and other policies aimed at gender equality have certainly attracted criticism, but there appears to be a stronger consensus in favour of fairness in Canada. Nevertheless, the changes in the Canadian family have provoked a powerful reaction in some quarters. The rest of this chapter will discuss that reaction.

Domestic Violence

I do not mean to imply that domestic violence[39] is a product of the backlash; there have been battered wives for as long as there have been marriages. Nor am I suggesting that every man who beats his wife is reacting to some abstract fear of gender equality. Men who beat their wives do so for purely personal reasons. But I have decided to discuss domestic violence in this chapter because it is the most extreme form of the power inequalities within the family that women have been fighting to eradicate, and that those groups resisting the changes have been (implicitly or explicitly) fighting to reinforce.

According to Health and Welfare Canada, one in every ten women in Canada – roughly one million – is abused by her male partner at least once a year.[40] This figure includes physical abuse, sexual abuse, and severe emotional abuse. Physical abuse includes hitting, choking, burning, cutting, stabbing, and shooting. Sexual abuse includes rape (vaginal, oral, and anal), forcing a person to perform unwanted sexual acts, or using sex to torture the other person psychologically (e.g., by flaunting infidelities or by constantly undermining a person's sexual confidence). Emotional abuse includes manipulation, psychological control, terrorizing, threatening, isolating the person from friends and family, insulting, undermining the person's self-esteem, and shaming.

The severity of emotional abuse varies considerably, so that it is not always easy to distinguish between something a healthy person might say in a moment of anger and an incident of abuse. What distinguishes an abusive incident is that it is part of a pattern of behaviour, a pattern that is remarkably consistent among abusers. The overwhelming majority of abusers, 93 percent, are men.[41] Violent and abusive women do exist; but the statistics from police, social workers, and health professionals demonstrate that only a small minority of violent offenders are female. At the same time, 92 percent of victims are female.[42]

Abusive men scar their partners for life, whether physically, psychologically, or both. A minority of these men actually kill their victims. In 1992, 38 percent of murdered women were killed by their husbands. Only 6 percent of murdered men were killed by their wives, often in self-defence.[43] The violence and emotional abuse tend to begin shortly after marriage, or even during courtship, and to escalate in a cyclical pattern throughout the relationship. For example, a man who calls his girl-friend a "slut" in a jealous rage may progress to hitting her, choking her, raping her, and finally killing her. There will be periods when he is calm and loving, alternating with periods of rising tension that finally culminate in an attack. The woman will not be able to predict when the attack will begin, and will be afraid of doing something wrong and setting him off. She will also tend to hide the truth from others as best she can, convinced that she is somehow to blame and that nobody would believe her if she did tell.

The loss of self-esteem and the debilitating terror suffered by battered women combine to produce a mental state called Battered Woman Syndrome. This syndrome is increasingly relied on by judges and defence attorneys during the trials of women who murder their abusive partners, to prove that they acted out of self-defense and knew of no other way to protect themselves or their children. Most battered women do not kill their husbands or partners; when they do, it is often to protect other family members, and the murder itself is usually unpremeditated.[44]

The phenomenon of domestic violence graphically illustrates the power inequalities within the traditional family unit. For most people, most of the time, those inequalities are hidden, or they may be reduced by the economic contribution of the wife. But for a million Canadian women every year the family unit is a place of danger, not safety. Research has shown that domestic violence is most common in families in which the wife does not work outside the home, and where the husband adheres most strongly to traditional attitudes about women.[45] There is no difference in the incidence of violence among people of different educational levels, although abuse is twice as likely in households whose total income is less than $15,000 per year.[46] Many incidents of abuse are triggered by the woman's attempt to assert a little independence, to demand some rights within the marriage. The man feels threatened, and he reacts with verbal or physical violence. The most common time for an abusive man to murder his wife is at the moment when she decides to leave him.

Men who beat their wives sometimes engage in other forms of abuse as well, particularly the sexual abuse of their children. This demonstrates the power relation that underlies and facilitates abuse: the exploitation of the less powerful members of the family by the most powerful. The man who brings home the money, owns the house, and controls the minds of his wife and children – through isolation, manipulation, and threats – is virtually omnipotent in his own family. He may feel scared and inadequate outside the home, as many abusers do, but within the home he exerts absolute control. This is a grotesque parody of the traditional patriarchal family, but we should recognize it as the logic of that family structure taken to its extreme conclusion. Healthy families are safe and loving places for men, women, and children; I do not intend to suggest that most traditional families are violent and abusive. But we must recognize that the traditional family unit does not guarantee the safety of its members, and that the power inequality that permits domestic violence is inherent in that approved family model.

Custody

A third arena for resistance has been the struggle over child custody following divorce. Until the nineteenth century, the children were the property of the husband and father; in the event of marital breakdown, he could dispose of them as he wished. By this century the attitude of the legal system had changed. In most cases of separation or divorce where a judge was involved, the children were awarded to the mother. This practice flows logically from the assumption that women were naturally nurturing and maternal, while men were unsuited to child care.

While the presumption of maternal custody signalled an improvement in women's legal status, it often leads to a decline in their economic status. As we have seen, single-mother families are the poorest sector of our society and account for the fastest growing segment of the poor. Nevertheless, among the 85 percent of couples who work out their own custody agreements without the involvement of a court order, the vast majority assign the children to the mother.

For the remaining 15 percent of divorcing mothers, the family court is becoming an increasingly threatening place. The 1986 divorce law made a number of changes to the law of custody. First, it enshrined the "best interests of the child" rule for judges in ruling on custody. In other words, the judge determines which parent is best equipped to provide for the child's physical and emotional well-being, and then awards custody to that parent. This rule is often interpreted in strictly material terms, which gives the wealthier parent – usually the father – an advantage.[47]

The second change in the 1986 law is a strong advocacy of joint custody. The law encourages judges and divorcing spouses to work out an arrangement that gives the child as much future contact with both parents as possible. Under a joint custody arrangement, one parent (usually the mother) has physical custody, but both parents share the legal right to make decisions about the child's welfare (e.g., schooling, health care). A number of judges have expressed reservations about the act's encouragement of joint custody, arguing that the court should not impose a continuing legal partnership on two people who cannot work one out for themselves. The Ontario Court of Appeal has agreed that it is wrong to impose joint custody on parents who do not wish to maintain contact with each other.[48] But a "fathers' rights" movement has recently emerged, campaigning to make joint custody mandatory. Fathers' rights activists claim that men are being denied access to their children by sole custody awards to mothers. The solution, they argue, is to require mothers to allow men to participate in the decisions about the raising of their children. The feminist response to this campaign has been swift and uncompromising. According to author Susan Crean, "Despite the established facts that men are the main perpetrators of violence and sexual abuse in families and rarely participate in housework or childcare, men's rights advocates would have us believe that the only thing preventing them from turning into kind and skilled parents after they leave the marriage is their ex-wives."[49]

The third principle of custody law introduced in the 1986 act is the so-called friendly parent rule. Section 16(10) requires judges to take into account the cooperativeness of both divorcing spouses in making custody decisions. The parent who appears to be the most willing to allow generous access to the other parent may have an edge in a battle over custody.[50] Like the principle of joint custody, the friendly parent rule looks better in theory than it does in practice. Women who are convinced that their ex-husbands abuse the children, whether sexually, physically, or emotionally, will naturally be unwilling to give them further access to their victims.[51]

The result of these new principles has been a decrease in the proportion of sole custody awards to women, from 86 percent in the 1970s to 78 percent in the 1980s.[52] The fathers' rights backlash against the presumption of sole maternal custody has not made the financial or emotional situation any easier for divorced mothers and their children. Instead, it has created a new potential for dispute and wrangling in the courtroom. In March 1995 Judge Rosalie Abella of the Ontario Court of Appeal ruled that "the custodial parent's best interests are inextricably tied to those of the child."[53] The decision allows custodial parents greater freedom to move away from their ex-spouses and to make other decisions affecting their children, unless the visiting parent can prove that those decisions would harm the children. The presumption that the best interests of the child are served by requiring contact with both parents is no longer the standard, at least in Ontario. This may give custodial mothers greater discretion in their own lives, but it could also lead to an increase in the number of fathers demanding joint custody or sole custody, to block their ex-wives from moving away with the children.[54]

The Political Use of 'Family Values'

The 1980s and early 1990s were a time of reaction in Western politics – a reaction against social and political changes that many conservatives believed had "gone too far." Those changes included the expansion of the welfare state, the breakdown of the traditional family unit, and the entry of women into the "public" arenas of the economy and politics. The Republican Party under Reagan and Bush was much more overtly concerned with family values than the Progressive Conservatives under Brian Mulroney appeared to be, at least on the surface. The fiscal policies of the Mulroney government did not lend themselves to a great deal of progressive policy-making; one key example is the cancellation of a long-awaited national child-care program in the 1992 federal budget. But the government's rhetoric (and sometimes its policy) on a number of social issues – family violence, employment equity, divorce, spousal support, violence against women – was consistent with the progressive approach of earlier Canadian governments.

This began to change after the 1988 election victory, when a group of Tory backbenchers and senators got together to form the Caucus Committee on Family Issues, familiarly known as the "family caucus."[55] In June 1992 the family caucus included thirty-five MPs and two senators, and could count on the support of six Cabinet ministers. The family caucus was a "private back-room fraternity" within the government, whose purpose was to protect "the traditional family unit" from "feminists, homosexuals, activist judges, special interest groups and the Charter of Rights."[56] According to a 1992 newspaper report, the family caucus has been remarkably effective in promoting its ideology of traditional family values. In recent months, it has scored victory after victory: eliminating tax breaks for common-law couples, killing a national day-care program, introducing a targeted system of child benefits, and ... trying to amend federal laws to include an official definition of the family, specifying that the couple must be male and female.[57]

The family caucus became increasingly influential within the government as the Progressive Conservatives tried to counter the growing popularity of the Reform Party in 1991 and 1992. The group met at least once a week, and lobbied the Cabinet to adopt its policies. The purpose of most of these policies was to make it easier for women to stay at home with their children, and to protect the traditional family unit (which they defined as a married mom and dad with children) from the forces of "individualism" (i.e., feminism and the Charter of Rights).

In addition to the family caucus, there were other pressures on the Mulroney government that led it to adopt particular policies. The pressures came from conservative provincial governments, particularly the Social Credit government in British Columbia; from the business community, demanding deficit reduction; and from the American government, which wanted a "level playing field" following the 1989 free trade agreement. Those policies had the effect of discouraging mothers from working outside the home, by eroding their existing social services and benefits and failing to introduce other necessary services and benefits.[58] The amount of money available for child support and child care was either frozen or reduced. Unemployment insurance changes introduced in 1990 and 1992 made it difficult for women in many female-dominated industries to qualify for benefits (including maternity benefits). Cuts to health care and social services increased women's family burdens, as elderly parents and the chronically ill were sent home to be looked after by mothers, daughters, and daughters-in-law.

The consistent thread running through these policies was the assumption that women could and would choose to stay at home with their families if their domestic responsibilities were increased, or if they faced additional barriers to working outside the home. The reality of women's lives was very different: most women who work outside the home, whether or not they have children, cannot survive economically without their paycheques. The happy stay-at-home mothers who were featured in magazine stories and advertisements in the early 1990s were affluent enough to be able to quit work; most women are not so fortunate. They felt the political and cultural pressures to stay at home with their children, and they felt deeply guilty about their absences during working hours, but they simply had no choice. The family values backlash of the early 1990s has not changed the lives of women or children for the better; it has simply added even more stress to women who must juggle heavy responsibilities both at work and at home.

The election of a Liberal government in 1993 did not improve the outlook for Canada's social services. The 1995 federal budget slashed transfers to the provinces for health, post-secondary education, and welfare. The Reform Party's leader, Preston Manning, presented his own "budget," declaring that the state should no longer provide services for children, the elderly, or the convalescent. He argued that "the family" should care for the vulnerable in society. In practice, of course, this means that *women* would look after the young, the old, and the sick. The family is not always the haven of peace and comfort that Manning implies, as we have seen. But the Reform Party's calls for a reduction in social services found an echo in the Progressive Conservative governments of Alberta, and Ontario, and may have contributed to the federal government's willingness to cut provincial transfers in order to reduce the deficit.

R.E.A.L. Women

In 1984 a small group of women held a press conference, announcing the formation of a new national women's group. This group, called R.E.A.L. Women (Realistic, Equal, Active for Life), was intended to be an anti-feminist counterweight to the National Action Committee on the Status of Women (NAC). The following year the group held its first national conference, claiming (without providing supporting evidence) to have 20,000 members.[59] In 1986 R.E.A.L. Women followed the example of NAC and held a day of lobbying on Parliament Hill. They held meetings with the Progressive Conservative and Liberal caucuses. They distributed their literature, met with sympathetic MPs, and held a press conference to boast of their political influence. In that same year they also tried to obtain funding under the Women's Program of the Secretary of State's Department, which was intended to fund activities and organizations dedicated to ending discrimination against women. Their application was turned down, but not before R.E.A.L. Women had managed to spark a great deal of debate over the merits of feminism and anti-feminism in public policy.[60] (See Chapter 11 for a discussion of the Women's Program.)

The group has presented briefs to royal commissions and parliamentary committees, often making professional and highly technical arguments that belie their claims to be "just housewives." In 1992 the group's founder and vice-president, Gwen Landolt, claimed that it had 45,000 members.[61] This is only slightly higher than the figures quoted in a R.E.A.L. Women brief to a parliamentary committee in 1986.[62]

R.E.A.L. Women has been perceived as a threat by Canadian feminists, because there may be a large potential constituency for an anti-feminist organization in Canada. For the "new right," the only way to save the traditional family unit is to shift the provision of social welfare services away from the state and back to the family, while simultaneously putting women back into the home to do this unpaid work. Returning women to the home would have the additional benefit of restoring male authority. The patriarchal power structure of the family has been disrupted by the entry of women into the workforce, which explains the opposition of the "new right" to "affirmative action, equal pay legislation, state sanction of abortion, birth control and gay rights protection."[63]

Any public policy that encourages or even permits women to become independent of men encounters fierce opposition from those opposed to any change in the traditional family unit. For example, in 1992 R.E.A.L. Women opposed legislation that required men to obtain the consent of women before initiating sexual activity, on the grounds that it would convict innocent men whose partners had changed their minds "long after the fact."[64] They argued that women who took control of their own sexuality, by making it clear to their male partners what they would agree to and what they would not, were behaving like prostitutes: "Only between prostitutes and their clients is there sometimes a cold-blooded discussion of the state of mind of the participants and exactly what they are consenting to, as envisioned in the legislation."[65] Finally, R.E.A.L. Women argued that if a woman was sexually assaulted, it was her own fault: "Women must learn to take responsibility for anything they can control – alcohol consumption, not being alone with a man where protection is not available, not wearing seductive clothing in appropriate situations, etc."[66] In other words, if a woman does not behave like a nun, a man is perfectly at liberty to sexually assault her without reprisals; by implication, the woman can control her own behaviour but the man should not be expected to control his.

Unfortunately for researchers, R.E.A.L. Women are less open with their finances and their membership records than NAC. It is therefore impossible to confirm or deny their claims about their membership and their funding sources, or to predict their future growth. More work remains to be done to determine the political potential of organized anti-feminism in Canada.

Conclusion

In this chapter we have discussed the following key points.

1.   Canadians are marrying later and having fewer children.

2.   Divorce rates are increasing.

3.   The number of single-parent (i.e., single-mother) families is growing.

4.   The reasons for these changes include the greater value and necessity of women's paid work, improved contraception, and greater availability of divorce.

5.   Despite the magnitude of the changes to Canadian families, governments have been reluctant to respond with policies to help them because of their preference for the traditional family unit (and because of fiscal constraints).

6.   Resistance to the changes has come from the media, the political system, and the family courts. Some men are reacting to the changes with violence, although the phenomenon of domestic violence has a number of additional causes.

In Chapter 1 we discussed the public-private dichotomy, which implies that the state and the family are completely separate. In this chapter, we have argued that the state and the family are *not* separate – that the family has been a highly charged political issue since Victorian times, and that the state has tried to protect the approved family model. The approved family model of the past fifty years, in which dad works for money and mom stays at home with the children, has broken down in recent decades as a result of economic, social, and legal changes. Resistance to that breakdown has come primarily from political and religious conservatives, many of whom blame feminism instead of the real causes, and who deny or ignore the ways in which the traditional family unit has perpetuated power inequalities. Even in non-violent families, the approved model has kept many women from fulfilling their potential as human beings.

As we said at the beginning of this chapter, it would be wrong to portray the family in a negative way. Families are central to Canadian society, and to most women's lives. Healthy, stable families are infinitely preferable to diseased, unstable families. No one can look upon the high incidence of family breakdown in our society without sadness for the people involved, especially the children. However necessary divorce may be to adults who wish to escape an unhappy marriage, it can have devastating effects on children. But the great value of healthy families should not blind our political leaders to the fact that many families are not healthy, nor to their responsibility to protect women and children who are trapped in violent and abusive homes.

It is also time for politicians to recognize that there are many types of healthy family, not just the politically approved model: that parents in a loving and nurturing family need not be legally married, need not be of the same sex, need not even share a home; that many women who work outside the home are happier than they would be at home, which means a healthier family as a whole; and that the power inequalities inherent in the traditional model are unnecessary and potentially lethal. It is also time for politicians to recognize that the traditional model no longer describes the majority of Canadian families, and to create policies that help the real families of Canada instead of trying to protect a single idealized type of family unit.

Appendix 1: Divorce in Canada, 1871–1900

	Annual Averages	Rate per 100,000
1871–1875	3	0.08
1876–1880	6	0.1
1881–1885	10	0.2
1886–1890	11	0.2
1891–1895	12	0.2
1896–1900	11	0.2

Source: Ursel, *Private Lives, Public Policy,* 366.

Appendix 2: Divorce in Canada, 1900–1990

Year	Judicial	Parliamentary	Total
1900	6	5	11
1905	26	9	35
1910	31	20	51
1915	35	18	53
1920	370	98	468
1925	418	132	550
1930	630	245	875
1935	1398	33	1431
1940	2307	62	2369

Source: Snell, *In the Shadow of the Law,* 10–11.

Appendix 3: Divorce in Canada, 1951–1990

Year	Divorce Rate	Number of Divorces
1951	n/a	5,270
1961	n/a	6,563
1967	n/a	11,165
1968	n/a	11,343
1969	n/a	26,093
1970	621.0	29,775
1971	607.2	29,685
1972	649.0	32,389
1973	719.7	36,704
1974	860.1	45,019
1975	942.4	50,611
1976	985.6	54,207
1977	988.9	55,370
1978	1004.0	57,155
1979	1028.7	59,474
1980	1053.7	62,019
1981	1129.2	67,671
1982	1164.4	70,436
1983	1125.2	68,567
1984	1061.9	65,172
1985	1003.5	61,980
1986	1255.2	78,160
1987	1372.2	86,985
1989	n/a	80,716
1990	n/a	78,152

Source: Ambert, *Divorce in Canada,* 21; Statistics Canada, Housing, Family and Social Statistics Division, *Women: A Statistical Profile;* Statistics Canada, *Marriage and Conjugal Life in Canada.*

Notes

1   Statistics Canada, *Report on the Demographic Situation in Canada 1992*, 27.

2   Statistics Canada, *Labour Force Activity of Women by Presence of Children*, table 1.

3   Ibid., 11.

4   *Report on the Demographic Situation 1992*, 50.

5   Ibid., 18; Statistics Canada, *Report of the Demographic Situation in Canada 1994*, 24.

6   *Report on the Demographic Situation 1992*, 27.

7   Ibid., 21.

8   It must be noted, however, that the 1987 figures are abnormally high because a reformed divorce law had taken effect the previous year. Not only were divorces easier to obtain after 1986, as this chapter explains, but it appears that many couples had been aware of the approaching changes and had postponed their divorces until after the new law came into effect. The number of divorces dropped to 80,716 in 1989 and to 78,152 in 1990. See Statistics Canada, *Marriage and Conjugal Life in Canada*, chap. 4.

9   *Report on the Demographic Situation 1994*, 30.

10   *Marriage and Conjugal Life*, 55.

11   *Women in Canada*, 19.

12   Ibid., 20.

13   Statistics Canada, Housing, Family and Social Statistics Division, *Lone-Parent Families in Canada*, 5.

14   Eichler and Lapointe, *On the Treatment of the Sexes in Research*, 15.

15   Statistics Canada, *Women in the Labour Force: 1994 Edition*, 46.

16   Ibid., 47.

17   Statistics Canada, *Lone-Parent Families*, table 1.1.

18   Ibid.

19   Ibid., table 1.2.

20   Ibid., table 2.1.

21   Ibid., chart 3.1.

22   Ibid., chart 3.2.

23   See Bissett-Johnson and Day, *The New Divorce Law*, 64; Payne, *Payne's Commentaries*, 184.

24   McLaren and McLaren, *The Bedroom and the State*, 9.

25   See Colodny, "The Politics of Birth Control in a Reproductive Rights Context," in Overall, *The Future of Human Reproduction*.

26   Prentice et al., *Canadian Women*, 147.

27   Snell, *In the Shadow of the Law*.

28 Phillips, *Putting Asunder,* 465.

29 Ambert, *Divorce in Canada,* 57.

30 Prentice et al., 255.

31 Ursel, *Private Lives, Public Policy,* n. 2.

32 Phillips, 565; Glendon, *Abortion and Divorce in Western Law,* 81.

33 Glendon, 81.

34 Divorce Act, 1985, s. 15(7)d, quoted in Douglas, *Spousal Support under the Divorce Act,* 4.

35 Paula Bourne, "Women, Law and the Justice System," in Ruth Roach Pierson et al., eds., *Canadian Women's Issues: Twenty-Five Years of Women's Activism in English Canada,* vol. 1 (Toronto: Lorimer, 1993), 340.

36 Bissett-Johnson and Day, chap. 9; Payne, 185; Wilton and Miyauchi, *Enforcement of Family Law Orders and Agreements,* pt. 1.

37 Bourne, 341.

38 Faludi, *Backlash.*

39 In this book the term "domestic violence" will refer to wife battering, not to the abuse of children or elderly parents.

40 Canada, Department of Health and Welfare, *Information from the National Clearinghouse on Family Violence: Wife Abuse.*

41 Statistics Canada, Canadian Centre for Justice Statistics, *Family Violence in Canada, i–ii.*

42 Ibid., *ii.*

43 Ibid., *i.*

44 See Walker, *Terrifying Love,* for case studies of battered women who killed their abusers.

45 See the review of the literature in Finkelhor, *Common Features of Family Abuse.*

46 *Family Violence in Canada, ii.*

47 Crean, *In the Name of the Fathers,* 29.

48 Bissett-Johnson and Day, 50–51.

49 Crean, 112.

50 Bissett-Johnson and Day, 58.

51 Crean, 77.

52 Ibid., 37–38.

53 Fine, "Court widens rights of custodial parents," *Globe and Mail,* April 5, 1995.

54 Ibid.

55 York, "Tory politicians form family compact," A1.

56 Ibid.

57 Ibid. The caucus's proposed definition of "a couple" was later included in proposed amendments to the Human Rights Act.

58 Alanna Mitchell, "June Cleaver–style moms back in fashion," *Globe and Mail*, A1.

59 Dubinsky, *Lament for a "Patriarchy Lost"?*, 30.

60 Pal, *Interests of State*, 147.

61 York, "Sexual assault legislation attacked."

62 Canada, House of Commons Standing Committee on Secretary of State, *Minutes of Proceedings and Evidence*, April 4, 1987, 21A:31.

63 Ibid., 34.

64 Ibid.

65 Ibid.

66 Ibid.

References and Further Reading

Ambert, Anne-Marie. *Divorce in Canada*. Don Mills: Academic Press, 1980.

Bissett-Johnson, Alastair, and David C. Day. *The New Divorce Law: A Commentary on the Divorce Act, 1985*. Toronto: Carswell, 1986.

Canada, Department of Health and Welfare. *Information from the National Clearinghouse on Family Violence: Wife Abuse*. Ottawa: Minister of Supply and Services, 1990.

Canada, Department of Justice. *Divorce Law: Questions and Answers*. Ottawa: Minister of Supply & Services, 1986.

Canada, House of Commons Standing Committee on Secretary of State. *Minutes of Proceedings and Evidence*. April 4, 1987.

Colodny, Nikki. "The Politics of Birth Control in a Reproductive Rights Context." In Christine Overall, ed., *The Future of Human Reproduction*. Toronto: Women's Press, 1989.

Crean, Susan. *In the Name of the Fathers: The Story behind Child Custody*. Toronto: Amanita, 1988.

Douglas, Kristen. *Spousal Support under the Divorce Act: A New Direction*. Ottawa: Library of Parliament Research Branch, 1991.

Dubinsky, Karen. *Lament for a "Patriarchy Lost"? – Anti-Feminism, Anti-Abortion and R.E.A.L. Women in Canada*. Ottawa: CRIAW, 1985.

Eichler, Margrit, and Jeanne Lapointe. *On the Treatment of the Sexes in Research*. Ottawa: Social Sciences and Humanities Research Council of Canada, 1985.

Erwin, Lorna. "Neoconservatism and the Canadian Pro-family Movement." *Canadian Review of Sociology and Anthropology* 30, no. 3 (1993).

Faludi, Susan. *Backlash: The Undeclared War against American Women*. New York: Crown Publishers, 1991.

Finkelhor, David. *Common Features of Family Abuse*. Ottawa: Health & Welfare Canada, National Clearinghouse on Family Violence, 1983.

Glendon, Mary Ann. *Abortion and Divorce in Western Law: American Failures, European Challenges*. Cambridge, MA: Harvard University Press, 1987.

McLaren, Angus, and Arlene Tigar McLaren. *The Bedroom and the State: The Changing Practices and Politics of Contraception and Abortion in Canada, 1880–1980*. Toronto: McClelland & Stewart, 1986.

Mitchell, Alanna. "June Cleaver–style moms back in fashion." *Globe and Mail*, April 20, 1992.

Payne, Julien D. *Payne's Commentaries on the Divorce Act, 1985*. Don Mills, ON: De Boo, 1986.

Phillips, Roderick. *Putting Asunder: A History of Divorce in Western Society*. Cambridge: Cambridge University Press, 1988.

Prentice, Alison, et al. *Canadian Women: A History*. Toronto: HBJ Canada, 1988.

Snell, James G. *In the Shadow of the Law: Divorce in Canada, 1900–1939*. Toronto: University of Toronto Press, 1991)

Statistics Canada. *Labour Force Activity of Women by Presence of Children*. Ottawa: Minister of Industry, Science & Technology, 1993.

———. *Marriage and Conjugal Life in Canada: Current Demographic Analysis*. Ottawa: Minister of Industry, Science & Technology, 1992.

———. *Report on the Demographic Situation in Canada 1992*. Ottawa: Minister of Industry, Science & Technology, 1992.

———. *Report on the Demographic Situation in Canada 1994: Current Demographic Analysis*. Ottawa: Minister of Industry, Science & Technology, 1994.

———. *Women in the Labour Force: 1994 Edition*. Ottawa: Minister of Industry, Science & Technology, 1994.

Statistics Canada, Canadian Centre for Justice Statistics. *Family Violence in Canada*. Ottawa: Minister of Industry, Science & Technology, 1994.

Statistics Canada, Housing, Family and Social Statistics Division. *Women: A Statistical Profile*. 2nd ed. Ottawa: Minister of Supply & Services, 1990.

———. *Lone-Parent Families in Canada*. Ottawa: Minister of Industry, Science & Technology, 1992.

Steuter, Erin. "Women against Feminism: An Examination of Feminist Social Movements and Anti-feminist Countermovements." *Canadian Review of Sociology and Anthropology* 29, no. 3 (1992).

Ursel, Jane. *Private Lives, Public Policy: 100 Years of State Intervention in the Family.* Toronto: Women's Press, 1992.

Walker, Lenore E. *Terrifying Love: Why Battered Women Kill and How Society Responds.* New York: HarperCollins, 1989.

Wilton, Ann, and Judy S. Miyauchi. *Enforcement of Family Law Orders and Agreements: Law and Practice.* Toronto: Carswell, 1989.

York, Geoffrey. "Sexual assault legislation attacked: Bill unfair to men, R.E.A.L. Women say." *Globe and Mail,* May 20, 1992.

———. "Tory politicians form family compact." *Globe and Mail,* June 3, 1992.

Chapter 5: Women and the Law in Canada

Chapter Summary

Chapter 5 describes the law and its effects on Canadian women. We will focus on two aspects of the law: the criminal justice system and the Canadian Charter of Rights and Freedoms. The criminal justice system includes the agencies and institutions that define, detect, and punish criminal behaviour. In this chapter we will look at the Criminal Code of Canada, the police, the courts, and the prisons. The Charter is the part of the Canadian constitution that places limits on the power of the state and specifies the rights and freedoms to which all Canadians are entitled. It also restricts those rights and freedoms under particular circumstances. We will look at the history of the Charter and its effects on the lives of Canadian women.

Chapter Outline

- Gender and Canadian Law
- Justice in Canada

Gender and Canadian Law

It is important to discuss the law's effects on Canadian women, because it helps us to understand women's place in Canadian society. Nowhere is the power of the state over the lives of its citizens more clearly revealed than in the criminal justice system. We will focus here on the attitudes towards women that are reflected in the justice system. These attitudes, although they are present elsewhere, are most evident in the criminal law – particularly the law on sexual assault, which we will discuss in this chapter. Women have worked in recent years to change those attitudes, and to remove their residue from the statute books and justice procedures. But the struggle has been long and hard, and is by no means over.

The Canadian Charter of Rights and Freedoms has become a central part of women's efforts to improve their status and to eliminate discrimination. Many of the women who participated in the drafting of the Charter had high hopes that it would be used by the courts to eradicate discrimination on the basis of gender. Those hopes have not been entirely realized. Nevertheless, there have been a few significant Charter victories. We will discuss those victories, and a few defeats, in this chapter.

Justice in Canada

Origins of the Criminal Law

The Canadian criminal law is based on the British legal tradition.[1] Most of it is statute law, meaning that it has been enacted by Parliament or by a provincial legislature. The major categories of criminal law are collected in the Criminal Code, which is a federal statute. The provinces can also create criminal laws within their areas of jurisdiction (e.g., highway offenses or liquor-related offenses). The Criminal Code has been revised frequently since its introduction in 1892. These revisions have been intended to remove ambiguities in the law, to add new offenses as the need arises, and to keep the criminal law up to date with the realities of Canadian society.

The Police

When a criminal act is committed, the police are usually the first officials on the scene. They have the power to arrest suspected criminals and to interrogate victims and possible witnesses. Because the police deal firsthand with victims of crime, and because they often have the power to determine whether criminal charges will be laid,[2] their attitudes and behaviour are crucial to the way the criminal justice system works. If a police officer believes that a man has a right to hit his wife to "keep her in line," or if he believes that a woman is likely to lie about being raped, this may have an effect on his treatment of both the victims and the perpetrators of these crimes.

The Judicial Process

When the police have investigated a possible crime, and they have decided to lay criminal charges against the perpetrator, they inform the Crown prosecutor. The Crown prosecutor is the official who builds the case against the accused and presents it in court.[3] He or she has the power to stay (cancel) criminal charges laid by the police, if the case looks too weak to convince a judge or jury to convict. The decision to stay or to proceed is generally left to the discretion of the Crown. Thus, the attitudes of Crown prosecutors can have as powerful an impact on a sexual assault case or a wife abuse case as the attitudes of police officers.

If the Crown decides to proceed with criminal charges, the case goes to court. The accused has the right to plead guilty before a judge, or to plead "not guilty" and receive an open trial. Trials on serious criminal charges can be conducted by judge alone or by judge and jury. When the case goes to trial the accused is represented by a defence lawyer, and the Crown is represented by the Crown prosecutor or by one of his or her staff lawyers. Canadian criminal trials operate on the "adversarial" model, which means that the judge is supposed to be an impartial arbitrator between opposing camps. The job of the prosecutor is to present the facts of the case fairly, from the Crown's perspective, and to prove beyond a reasonable doubt that the accused committed the crime with which he or she is charged. The job of the defence is to prove to the judge or to the jury that the accused should be acquitted of the charges.[4] Both sides can present witnesses and physical evidence to support their arguments.

There are many tactics available to the defence.[5] A defence lawyer can challenge the validity of the testimony of Crown witnesses. Where the Crown presents an expert witness, the defence can either attack the credentials of the expert or bring in another expert with a different point of view. The defence can argue that the accused was acting under duress, or acting in self-defence; alternatively, he or she can claim that the accused was insane at the time of the criminal offense, or otherwise incapable of knowing the "nature and consequences" of the act.

In some cases, the defence can argue that the victim consented to the commission of the act. Consent is a valid defence to a charge of assault, including sexual assault. The problem with a consent defence, from the point of view of the plaintiff (victim) and the Crown, is that it reduces the trial to one person's word against another – a contest of credibility. In some situations, a plaintiff may be found by the court to be less credible than the accused, not because the plaintiff is lying, but because she is female or African-Canadian or a prostitute. When a defence of consent is used, or when a defence lawyer chooses to challenge the credibility of the plaintiff's testimony against his or her client, sexist and racist prejudices can have an effect on the outcome of a case.

The trial ends with the verdict, either by the judge in a judge-only trial or by the jury in a jury trial. If the verdict is "guilty," the accused person is convicted of the criminal offence. At that stage he or she can accept the verdict and await sentencing or appeal the conviction to a higher court. Unless an appeal is granted, a person convicted of an indictable offence will probably spend some time in jail. The length of a jail sentence is determined by the trial judge, according to guidelines in the Criminal Code. The judge can take the facts of the case into account in deciding whether the accused should receive a light or a heavy sentence. Another factor in sentencing may be the judge's attitudes towards the crime of which the accused has been convicted. If a judge believes that a man is justified in hitting his wife, he may give a convicted wife abuser a suspended sentence; if he believes that a woman was partly to blame for being sexually assaulted, he may order the man who attacked her to spend only a few months in jail.

The Penal System

Sentences of less than two years' duration can be served in provincial prisons, which usually allows the prisoner to remain fairly close to his or her home and family. Sentences of more than two years must be served in a federal penitentiary. In 1989–90, 3 percent of federal prisoners were female, compared to 8 percent of provincial prisoners.[6] The most serious offenders are sent to maximum-security institutions such as the Kingston Penitentiary. These prisoners are often sent thousands of miles away from their communities. There is only one federal penitentiary for women: the Prison for Women in Kingston, Ontario (P4W). Female offenders from across the country are sent to this decrepit institution, far away from their children and their roots, with little opportunity for training and rehabilitation. Roughly 15 percent of these women are native Canadians, who appear to suffer most harshly from the conditions in the prison.[7] Several have attempted or committed suicide in P4W in recent years. Aboriginal women are appallingly over-represented in Canadian prisons: in 1991 aboriginal peoples accounted for 3 percent of the Canadian population, while aboriginal women made up 20 percent of the female prisoner population.[8]

Most experts believe that the penal system is harsher towards women than it is towards men.[9] In 1981 the Canadian Human Rights Commission found that Corrections Canada discriminated against women on the basis of sex because of the low quality of services for female prisoners.[10] The Royal Commission on the Status of Women raised the issue of correctional services for women in its 1970 report.[11] Fifteen other studies and reports recommended that the P4W be closed, because of the inadequacies of the facility and the unfairness of incarcerating women far from their homes and families.[12] Yet not until 1990 did the solicitor-general finally decide to close the P4W and replace it with five regional centres,[13] one of them a healing lodge in northern Saskatchewan for aboriginal prisoners.

The target date for the completion of the regional facilities was 1994, but construction was delayed by political pressures. The federal government also promised to establish more community services, such as halfway houses, for women prisoners. Budget cuts have made it unlikely that this promise will be kept. In 1994 the country was horrified by a videotape showing female prisoners stripped and restrained by male guards. The tape highlighted the problems for women in the Canadian correctional system, and the need to reform it as quickly as possible.

Women and the Criminal Law

In this section we will explore the effects of the Canadian criminal law on women. We will look at two aspects of the criminal law: the attitudes towards women inherent in its substance, and the ways in which in practice those attitudes affect the operation of the criminal law. These issues have attracted some attention in recent years. A report written by a panel of federal, provincial, and territorial legal officials in 1992 was highly critical of the way the justice system treated Canadian women: "The predominantly male-centered language found in written law and other legal documents reflects a clear gender bias against women."[14] Despite the attention the report received when it was finally released in 1993, there is as yet no evidence that its recommendations to combat the mistreatment of women in the justice system will ever be implemented.

Attitudes towards Women Reflected in Canadian Criminal Law

Despite the efforts to keep the Canadian criminal law *au courant*, old sexist assumptions about women and men persist. The first assumption is that the word of a woman is less reliable than that of a man. Until 1983, for example, a woman's testimony was insufficient to convict a man of sexual assault (or rape, as it was then called); judges would routinely instruct juries that unless the woman's story was corroborated by other witnesses or by physical evidence, they must acquit the accused.[15] This idea is linked to the ancient traditions about women's light regard for the truth, exemplified by the story of Eve. Woman was either inherently false or, because of her sexual and emotional nature, less rational and capable of distinguishing truth from falsehood. Even today, unless a woman appears to be "credible" according to the traditional stereotypes (sexually chaste or married, sober, modestly dressed), she will likely have a more difficult time convincing police and Crown attorneys that she has been sexually assaulted or abused by her partner.

The second assumption is that women are responsible for acts of violence against them: "Supposedly, the battered woman had it coming, the raped woman wanted it, and the harassed woman encouraged it."[16] This "blame the victim" approach is a direct result of the ancient prejudices against the inherent moral corruption of women. As we saw in Chapter 1, women have been feared for centuries as the worm in the core, the source of original sin and temptation. This notion is clearly connected to the distrust of women's truthfulness. In the Western legal tradition, "women are temptresses who arouse men's seething passions only to complain that they cannot control these 'irresistible' forces."[17] Therefore, "when women argue that they do not tempt the men who freely choose to sexually abuse them, they are dismissed as liars. The extent to which the image of woman as lying temptress is woven into the texture of Anglo-American law is remarkable."[18]

This image of women is particularly evident in the laws concerning sexual assault. Until recently it was assumed that rape could not occur within marriage, because the man had a right to sex with his wife whenever he chose. There is still an implicit requirement that a woman must fight back violently against her attacker, risking serious injury, to prove that she did not consent. This requirement is based on the assumption that all women consent to sex all the time, unless proven otherwise. Many observers argue that the law should take the reverse approach: to assume that the sexual act was *not* consensual unless otherwise proven. By putting the onus on the woman to resist, the law effectively places the burden of proof in a rape trial on the woman, not on the man. As a result, the key issue frequently becomes the reputation of the woman, not the guilt of the man. If a woman is believed to have "led him on," she has little chance of seeing her assailant convicted and imprisoned.

The image of the lying temptress is reflected in other areas of law as well. Women who are beaten by their husbands or male partners are less likely to be believed than other victims of assault. Some police officers still ask a woman, when she complains of an assault by her husband, "What did you do to deserve that?"[19] Such attitudes only increase the tendency of most women in abusive relationships to blame themselves, which makes them more likely to remain in the dangerous situation.

Women in Court

We have seen that women are taken less seriously as witnesses and as plaintiffs than men are, because of ancient attitudes that condemn women as liars. These attitudes also colour women's experiences as defendants. The types of crime committed by women are very different from those committed by men. Eighty percent of charges laid against women in Canada are for minor offences: non-violent petty theft, provincial liquor violations, possession of marijuana, breaking bail, prostitution, and mischief. Less than 10 percent of female crime is violent crime,[20] and fewer than 10 percent of all violent crimes are committed by women.[21] Men are seven times more likely than women to commit murder, while women are only four times less likely to be victims of murder.[22]

Feminist legal experts argue that female defendants are unfairly treated by the criminal justice system. The laws governing prostitution only make women more vulnerable to pimps. A charge of contempt of court can be used to force a woman to testify against her husband or partner, even when she knows that her life is in danger as a result.[23] When a woman fights back in self-defence against an abusive partner, she risks a charge of assault or of murder; the defences of self-defence and duress have been so narrowly defined in our law that the courts often refuse to apply them to the battered woman's experience.[24] However, the Supreme Court's decision in *R. v. Lavallée,* which recognized the existence of battered woman syndrome and its relevance to self-defence, is a step in the right direction.

The root of these problems, according to a study for the Canadian Department of Justice, is that the criminal justice system was constructed by men for men: "Many problems arise from applying to women a criminal law which has been devised by male legislators with a view to controlling anti-social acts committed for the very large part by men."[25]

Women have a particular set of values, grounded in their unique experiences, which do not always match those of the men who write the laws, staff the police forces, work for the prosecution or the defence in a criminal case, sit in the jury, or officiate from the bench. This different experience of the world means that women may be treated as criminals for acts that they do not consider wrong, such as killing an abusive husband to protect a child or stealing food to feed a family. The Supreme Court of Canada has taken some steps to redress the problems in the legal system; in 1990 they recognized battered woman syndrome and recommended that it be used to support women's claims of self-defence in the murder of abusive partners.[26] This is an important sign of progress. But as we will see in the next section, Canadian judges cannot always be relied on to protect women from being damaged by the law.

Sexual Assault Law in Canada

Until 1983 the Criminal Code of Canada prohibited "rape." Rape was defined as an act of sexual intercourse between a man and a woman not his wife to which the woman did not consent. There was no recognition that other types of unwanted sexual contact, like a kiss or a "feel," might be injurious to women. In 1983 the Criminal Code was amended, creating a new set of sexual assault offenses and changing the rules of evidence in court trials based on those offenses. In this section we will examine the changes to the law and its effectiveness in meeting its goals. We will also look at some of the problems that women who suffer sexual assault continue to face. We will conclude with a discussion of the type of sexual assault that may affect university students more than any other: "date rape."

The State of the Legislation

As we have seen, the rape law in the Canadian Criminal Code was reformed in 1983. The purpose of the reforms was to bring Canadian criminal law into line with changes in our understanding of the crime of rape. Feminists had argued since the 1970s that rape was a crime of sexual violence, not of violent sex. In other words, rape was an act more akin to assault than to gross indecency or other sex-related offences. Accordingly, Bill C-127 removed rape from the section "Sexual Offences,

Public Morals and Disorderly Conduct" and added it to "Offences Against the Person and Reputation."[27]

In the process, the crime of "rape" was removed and three new offences were created: simple sexual assault; sexual assault involving bodily harm, weapons, or other parties; and aggravated sexual assault. These offences are distinguished by the degree of violence involved. In contrast to the old definition of "rape," which was the penetration of a woman's vagina by a man's penis without her consent, "sexual assault" is a gender-neutral offence. "Theoretically, it can be committed by a male or female assailant upon a male or female victim. Proof of penetration is no longer required to obtain a conviction."[28] A "stolen kiss" or a hand on the knee are now considered to be sexual assault, although the chances of prosecuting and convicting anyone for relatively minor violations of another person's bodily integrity are small. It should also be noted that, despite the gender neutrality of the new offence, virtually all cases of sexual assault involve a male perpetrator and a female victim.

Bill C-127 eliminated some of the most sexist and outdated aspects of the Canadian criminal law, including the idea that sexual assault could not occur within marriage. It also reformed three rules of evidence pertaining to sexual assault trials. First, the bill removed the traditional requirement that a woman's testimony about being raped had to be corroborated before a jury could believe it. Second, the bill created a "rape shield," to protect complainants from being humiliated on the witness stand by cross-examination about their sexual histories or their reputations. The old idea that an "unchaste" woman could not be raped, or that she was likely to lie in court, was rejected categorically. Third, the "recent complaint" doctrine was removed. This doctrine was based on the idea that a woman who reported a rape to police immediately after it happened was more likely to be telling the truth than a woman who took days or weeks to come forward. The "recent complaint" rule failed to take into account the trauma suffered by sexual assault victims, as well as the reluctance of many women to tell their stories to officials for fear of being disbelieved.

The new law was a great improvement over the old law it replaced, but there are still problems. Perhaps the most troublesome is the issue of consent. Sexual assault is unlike other crimes, in two respects: the onus is often on the complainant to prove that she did not consent, and there are rarely any witnesses. Most defences against a charge of sexual assault are based on the issue of consent. The defence may argue that the complainant consented and then changed her mind, or it may argue that the defendant honestly believed that the woman had consented. Even if the woman knows that she was sexually assaulted, a man can be acquitted if he honestly believed that she wanted the sexual contact to occur.

This "honest belief" defence was strengthened by the 1980 Supreme Court of Canada ruling in the case of *R. v. Pappajohn*. The Court ruled that a mistaken belief in consent does not have to be *reasonable*; as long as it was an honestly held belief, it is a valid defence to a charge of sexual assault.[29] Given the prevalence of the rape myths in our culture (see Chapter 6), it is easy to imagine a case in which a woman said "no" to sex and her attacker – honestly believing that "no" means "yes" – could secure an acquittal in a court of law. This scenario is quite common in "date rapes" (see below). And as we have seen, in a consent defence the outcome of the case depends on which person is perceived to be the more credible: the accused or the plaintiff. In a society where women are believed to be less rational and perhaps less truthful than men, and a justice system that may value the protection of the accused more than the protection of the plaintiff,[30] this can put women at a severe disadvantage.

As we will see later in this chapter, the "rape shield" was struck down by the Supreme Court of Canada in 1991. The Court found that it violated the right to a fair trial guaranteed by the Charter. In December 1991 Kim Campbell, then the Minister of Justice, presented a bill to Parliament that replaced the rape shield. It also provided a legal definition of "consent" to sexual activity. The minister had responded quickly to the quashing of the rape shield, meeting with women's groups and victims' rights groups to seek their views on new legislation.[31] The bill received widespread support, and passed easily at second reading in April 1992. It was examined by a legislative committee, which made a few changes in response to the concerns about the original wording, and passed by the House of Commons in June 1992. It passed quickly through the Senate and received royal assent (the last step in becoming law) in the same month.

The bill contained a preamble that set out its objectives, which included the following: to reduce the incidence of sexual violence; to encourage the reporting of sexual assaults and ensure fair trials; and "to promote the full protection of the rights guaranteed under sections 7 and 15 of the *Canadian Charter of Rights and Freedoms*."[32] The preamble concluded with a statement that was clearly designed to remove all traces of the "lying temptress" stereotype from Canadian sexual assault law:

> the Parliament of Canada believes that at trials of sexual offences, evidence of the complainant's sexual history is rarely relevant and that its admission should be subject to particular scrutiny, bearing in mind the inherently prejudicial nature of such evidence.[33]

The bill defined "consent" as "the voluntary agreement of the complainant to engage in the sexual activity in question." It stipulated that consent was *not* present under any of the following circumstances: if someone else agreed to sex on the complainant's behalf; if the complainant was incapable of giving consent; if the accused had abused "trust, power or authority" to obtain consent; if the complainant "expresses, by words or conduct, a lack of agreement to engage in the activity"; or if the complainant changes her mind during the conduct in question.[34]

The bill also eliminated the defence of honest but unreasonable belief in consent endorsed by the Supreme Court of Canada in the *Pappajohn* case, stating that there could be no defence of belief when the accused was drunk, or reckless or "wilfully blind," or when "the accused did not take reasonable steps in the circumstances known to the accused at the time, to ascertain that the complainant was consenting."[35] This section of the bill was referred to during the public debate over the legislation as the "no means no" clause.

Finally, the bill created a new set of rules for the admission of evidence relating to the complainant's sexual history. The bill stated that "evidence that the complainant has engaged in sexual activity, whether with the accused or with any other person, is not admissible to support an inference that, by reason of the sexual nature of that activity, the complainant (a) is more likely to have consented to the sexual activity that forms the subject matter of the charge; or (b) is less worthy of belief."[36] The judge may only admit evidence if it is specific, if it is directly relevant to an issue at trial, and it "has probative value that is not substantially outweighed by the danger of prejudice to the proper administration of justice."

A judge must hold a private hearing to determine the admissibility of such evidence, whose proceedings cannot be published, and must take into account a host of factors: the need to ensure a fair trial for the accused; the need to encourage the reporting of future sexual assault offences; the need to remove "any discriminatory belief or bias" from the process; "the risk that the evidence may unduly arouse sentiments of prejudice, sympathy or hostility in the jury"; and "the potential prejudice to the complainant's personal dignity and right of privacy." This section closely resembles the recommendations of women's groups and feminist lawyers over the years, so their enthusiastic reception of the bill was not surprising.[37]

When she rose in the House of Commons to open debate on the bill, Kim Campbell made an unambiguously feminist statement of its purpose:

> All men, women and children must have authority over their own lives and more specifically, their bodies. They must have the right to make decisions about their lives including their sexual lives without the fear that those decisions will later be subject to unfair scrutiny and misrepresentation.[38]

It is too early to say whether the bill has achieved this goal. Given the opposition that the bill attracted from the Canadian Bar Association, especially criminal lawyers, a Charter challenge is inevitable. It remains to be seen whether the bill will survive a second "rape shield" case before the Supreme Court of Canada.

The Charter's legal-rights guarantees provoked controversy again in early 1994, when the Supreme Court of Canada overturned a sexual assault conviction on the ground that the man was too drunk to be held responsible for his actions.[39] The majority held that under sections 7 and 11(d) of the Charter, the Crown had to establish *mens rea* (the intent to perform a criminal act) beyond a reasonable doubt. In cases of extreme intoxication, when a state of automatism could be said to occur, there would be substantial doubt of the accused's capacity to form a criminal intent. The majority wrote that "to deny that even a very minimal mental element is required for sexual assault offends the Charter in a manner that is so drastic and so contrary to the principles of fundamental justice that it cannot be justified under s.1 of the Charter."[40] The justices predicted that their ruling would apply only to very rare cases of extreme drunkenness. They must have been surprised by the sudden rash of cases in which judges acquitted or stayed charges based on the intoxication of the accused at the time of the offence. In 1995 the federal minister of justice introduced a bill to make extreme drunkenness, leading to criminal behaviour, a new criminal offence. The bill was passed quickly by the House of Commons and the Senate, which reacted to the public outcry against the Supreme Court ruling.

The 'Second Rape'

A woman who has been sexually assaulted will often refuse to report the crime to the police, for fear that they will not believe her. It is difficult to talk about private sexual matters at the best of times; telling a stranger about a sexual assault, when one is in a state of extreme shock, confusion, pain, and self-doubt, can be almost as traumatic as the assault itself (hence the term "second rape"[41]). When the police express skepticism, or ask the victim what she did to "get herself raped," the ordeal becomes even worse. One Canadian study found that 62 percent of women who had been sexually assaulted refused to report the crimes to the police. Many remained silent because they were aware of gender-biased attitudes among law-enforcement officials, and they chose to "'save themselves the revictimization' by police and courts."[42] Other women who have come forward have told researchers that they would not do so again, because of the unsympathetic and careless treatment they received from police and other criminal justice officials.[43] It should be pointed out, however, that reporting rates for sexual assault have risen considerably since the law was changed in 1983; by 1989 the incidence of reports was 127 percent higher than it had been in 1982.[44] Likely reasons include the law itself, the growing number of sexual assault crisis centres where victims can receive help and counselling, and efforts by legislators and activists to remove the prejudices against the testimony of victims.

The federal Justice Department estimates that there were over 72,000 sexual assaults in Canada in 1988, or one every seven minutes.[45] Despite the prevalence of this crime, police and Crown prosecutors do not appear to take it as seriously as other crimes. In 1985, according to Statistics Canada, police categorized 14.2 percent of sexual assault complaints as "unfounded." In other words, they did not consider the victim's story to be sufficiently credible to proceed with charges. Only 6 percent of complaints regarding other criminal offences were declared "unfounded."[46]

In 1988 police in Canada received 29,111 complaints of sexual assault. Of these, 4,225 were declared unfounded (15%) and 24,886 (85%) were deemed to be actual offences. Of the offences, 49% were cleared by charge, 20% were cleared "otherwise," and 31% were not cleared.[47]

These rates have remained more or less constant since the law was changed.[48] There were almost 35,000 reports of sexual assault in 1993, most of them classified at the lowest level. Fewer than half led to actual charges. Over 98 percent of the alleged offenders were male.[49]

Even when charges are laid and an offender is convicted, he generally receives a short jail sentence – when he is sent to jail at all. In some cases, judges suspend sentences so that men convicted of sexual assault can continue in their jobs; or they grant absolute discharges. Law professor Christine Boyle argues that because most judges and legislators are male, they can more easily imagine themselves as men accused of rape than as victims of rape. They are therefore more sympathetic to the man than to the woman.[50] This blinds them to the need to protect women (and children) by imposing stringent enough sentences to reflect the severity of the crime and to deter other potential offenders.

A Manitoba study suggests six further reasons for the disproportionately short sentences for sexual assault, relative to other violent crimes.[51] First, a non-violent sexual assault is likely to be taken less seriously by judges and Crown prosecutors than a violent attack. This attitude trivializes the traumatic impact of any sexual assault on the victim. Second, where the victim did not physically fight back, the criminal justice system takes a more lenient view. No other crime is taken less seriously if the victim fails to resist; indeed, most police officers would advise people *not* to resist a mugging or a holdup. Third, acquaintance rape is not always recognized as a crime: "Convictions are more difficult to secure, and if secured, the sentence will be lower." Fourth, judges often display excessive sympathy for the accused, making comments that "minimize or trivialize the offence; disguise or downplay the severity of the offence; are overly concerned with accused's background and the effect of the charge/sentence on the accused." Fifth, Crown prosecutors often request light sentences, or plea bargain (trading a lighter sentence for a guilty plea) without consulting the victim. Finally, courts do not solicit victim impact statements or expert testimony on rape trauma syndrome, either of which could help the judge to understand the full impact of this crime on its victims.

We have already discussed the importance of personal attitudes in determining the operation of the criminal justice system. The beliefs of police, Crown prosecutors, and judges help to determine the experiences of women with the system. It is therefore discouraging to look at the attitudes expressed by some of these people, most of whom are still male.

Police are less likely to press charges of sexual assault in cases where the victim does not conform to the stereotype of an "innocent" woman. If she wears revealing clothing, if she had one or more drinks before the attack, if she accepted a ride from the alleged offender, if she knew him as an acquaintance or a partner – in all of these cases, police often treat the victim with skepticism.[52] Some Crown prosecutors share those attitudes, choosing to stay charges when they do not believe that they have a strong case – a choice often based on their own personal perceptions of what is "real" rape and what is not.[53]

Perhaps the most disturbing indicators of the attitudes inherent in the Canadian justice system are the remarks made by some judges in their courtrooms. A Manitoba judge made the following statement in 1984, while explaining why he was allowing a man accused of sexual assault to withdraw his guilty plea: "One would have to be completely without worldly experience not to realize that, in sexual encounters, the female party may at first show reluctance or even resistance, but later voluntarily succumb to persuasion at her natural instinct."[54] This is a classic statement of the rape myths that condone, and may help to provoke, violence against women (see Chapter 6).

Another Manitoba judge remarked, while handling the case of a man who had pleaded guilty to hitting his wife, "Sometimes a slap in the face is all she needs."[55] A third Manitoba judge sentenced a man to two years of probation for physically assaulting his girlfriend and holding her hostage at gunpoint, commenting, "Women – can't live with them – can't live without them."[56] This type of remark excuses the physical assault of women by their husbands, and trivializes the whole issue of violence against women. It also reveals that many judges blame the victims for their mistreatment.

The above examples are from Manitoba, but the problem exists everywhere in Canada. Perhaps the most notorious recent remark from the bench was made by a British Columbia judge who gave a man a suspended sentence on a conviction for sexually assaulting a three-year-old girl. The judge found that the toddler had been "sexually aggressive" towards the offender, and he couldn't help himself.[57] That sentence, and the judge's entire ruling, were upheld on appeal. Judicial councils exist at both federal and provincial levels to monitor judges' professional behaviour, and to sanction judges who display "conduct unbecoming a judge." None of these cases has yet been condemned by a judicial council.

It would be a mistake to leave the impression that all judges are similarly prejudiced and unreasonable. Many are sympathetic to women victims and do not allow themselves to be blinded by outdated gender stereotypes. The Supreme Court of Canada has made a number of gender-sensitive rulings in recent years; we will discuss some of them below. We will also discuss the appointment of more female judges in Part 3 of this book.

Date Rape

A "date rape" (also called "acquaintance rape") occurs when a man forces a woman he knows to engage in sexual intercourse against her will. It is the most insidious form of sexual assault, because it often leaves the woman wondering if she is to blame for "turning him on," and because her story is less likely to be believed than if the rapist had been a stranger. Susan Estrich argues that society, and law-enforcement officials in particular, divide reports of sexual assault into two categories: "real" rape, in which a stranger attacks a virginal woman on the street in broad daylight with a knife or a gun and injures her severely as she struggles to escape; and all other reports of sexual assault, including date or acquaintance rape, which are considered less likely to be true or to be convincing to a jury. A man will be found guilty of sexual assault only if a judge or jury believes that the woman did not consent, and it is more difficult for many people to believe that a woman refused sex to a friend or acquaintance than to a violent stranger.[58]

Estimates of date rape are difficult to make with any accuracy, because victims are often reluctant to report their assaults to the police. But a study of American college campuses commissioned by *Ms.* magazine in 1985 found that 25 percent of the female respondents had experienced an attempted or completed sexual assault. Two-thirds had received some unwanted sexual contact in the previous year, ranging from touching to actual penetration. Of those who had been raped, 84 percent knew their attackers; 57 percent of the rapes occurred on dates.[59] According to the authors of the *Ms.* study, based on their findings and on the reports of staff at sexual assault crisis centres, "If you are a woman, your risk of being raped by someone you know is *four times greater* than your risk of being raped by a stranger."[60] In 1993, 82 percent of the sexual assaults reported to Canadian police involved people who knew each other: family members, casual acquaintances, spouses, or ex-spouses.[61]

It is easy to see that if date rape is trivialized as an offence, and if it is by far the most common form of sexual assault, then women are far less well protected in practice than they are on paper. Why is date rape so prevalent among young people (the average age of both victim and attacker is about 18[62])? The most common answer is that young men and women, including those on college campuses, are sufficiently unsure of their own wishes and identities that they fall easily into dangerous sex-role stereotypes. He wants to "score," to make points with the guys in the dorm or at the pub, while she wants to be seen with the most popular guy on campus – but not to be considered a "slut." She may want to wait until a relationship has been established to have sex; he becomes insistent, fearful of losing face in front of his buddies. In many cases, young men actually believe that girls say "no" when they mean "yes." Or they believe that "taking sex" is justified if the woman has "led them on," even when she has had no intention of doing so.[63]

Arrest and conviction rates for date rape are even lower than for other forms of sexual assault. Only 1 percent of date rapes are reported to police.[64] As we have seen, many people do not consider date rape to be "real rape." Sexual assaults by strangers are the most likely to be reported to police, because they are the most likely to be believed.[65] When date rape does lead to a conviction, the sentences are usually less than two years.[66] The gender stereotypes that provoke skepticism in the minds of police, Crown attorneys, judges, juries – even friends of the victim – are the very same stereotypes that can lead to date rape in the first place.

A male college student described dating rituals in a recent book about campus date rape: "the man initiates the date by asking the woman out, with him paying all the expenses or buying the liquor, food, or entertainment. When this happens, the man may expect sexual activity or intercourse."[67] If the man becomes aggressive in his pursuit of sex, "the female enters into a contest with him – either because she really doesn't want to have sex with him or because she feels she must put up some resistance to maintain a good reputation. Dating then becomes a game that each side tries to win. And date rape may be the result."[68]

In other words, if the woman agreed to date the man, and if she accepted the food and drinks and entertainment that he paid for, then in the eyes of many people (often including the man himself and the police), she has led him on. She is implicitly agreeing to "put out" later in the evening. If she decides that she does not want to have sex, or if she never had any attention of having sex, the man may decide to take what he wants anyway. The dating rituals are so ingrained in his mind and behaviour that he really does not believe her when she says "no." Or he may have been taught that "no" means "later," or "maybe," or even "yes," believing that women want sex all the time.

These dehumanizing attitudes, which have little or nothing to do with the actual individual woman accompanying him on the date, can convince a man that "taking sex" is no big deal. After all, he paid for the date, didn't he? Several studies have shown that many men think that if the man paid for the evening, if the woman drinks alcohol, or if she initiates the date, then date rape is justified.[69]

The only ways to combat date rape are to fight the attitudes that provoke and condone it, and to educate all young people about the importance of honest communication concerning sex. Any sexual act should be preceded by an open discussion about what each person wants, and how far they are willing to go. It goes without saying that such a conversation cannot happen if one or both parties are drunk, or if one sees the other as inferior or as somehow less than a fully human individual. (For more discussion of the rape myths, see Chapter 6.)

The Canadian Charter of Rights and Freedoms

Few aspects of the Canadian constitution have received as much public attention as the Canadian Charter of Rights and Freedoms. (For excerpts, see the appendix to this chapter.) The Charter was proclaimed into law in 1982, except for the equality clauses, which came into force in 1985. The Canadian constitution is the special set of laws that guide judges in the interpretation of all regular laws. It describes the division of powers between the federal and provincial governments; it defines the powers and composition of the House of Commons and the Senate; and it protects Canadians against any state action that unjustifiably violates their constitutional rights or freedoms. Any law that conflicts with a provision in the Charter can be struck down by a court, unless it is "saved" by section 1 (see Appendix).

The Origins of the Charter

As we have seen, English Canada inherited its legal theories from the British common law, while French Canada derives much of its law from the *Code Napoléon*. Neither legal tradition has placed much emphasis on individual rights. This is rather surprising, given the English heritage of liberalism, until one remembers that liberalism reached its fullest bloom not in England, but in the United States. The idea of rights took firm root in the American political and legal tradition from the moment of its creation, and is embodied in the Declaration of Independence: "We hold these truths to be self-evident, that all men are created equal, and endowed by their Creator with certain inalienable rights ..." When the language and the ideal of rights finally came to Canada, it came from the United States by way of the United Nations.

Before 1945 Canadians paid little attention to human rights and civil liberties. In the British tradition, parliamentary supremacy was believed to be the best protection for rights and freedoms. But by the end of the Second World War, a number of developments in Canada and elsewhere were pushing human rights and civil liberties onto the public agenda.[70] The Canadian government had used its powers under the War Measures Act to arrest Japanese Canadians and place them in internment camps during the war, without any evidence that they were a threat to Canadian security. Similar violations of individual rights and freedoms occurred in Quebec, as Jehovah's Witnesses and other minorities were persecuted by the Duplessis government. This appalling treatment of innocent Canadians shocked many people, and prompted questions about the effectiveness of parliamentary supremacy in protecting individual rights.

In 1945 the United Nations was formed, and in 1948 it issued its Universal Declaration of Human Rights. This declaration was supported by Canada and heavily influenced by the American doctrine of rights. It placed a responsibility on all member governments to protect human rights in their own countries, and around the world where necessary. The declaration strengthened the calls for constitutional protection of the individual rights of Canadians.

In 1960 the Canadian Bill of Rights was passed into law. The bill was not entrenched in the constitution; it was an ordinary law, which did not have the force to strike down other laws when they conflicted with one or more of its provisions. As a result, the courts could not use it to protect the rights that it supposedly guaranteed. There were a number of cases in which individuals or groups tried to use the bill to strike down discriminatory laws, but almost all of them failed.

In addition, the bill's language reflected a formal notion of "equality," which did not take structural factors into account. Men and women were to be treated equally and given the equal protection of the law, but this did not go far enough. Formal equality means treating like cases alike, based entirely on the facts of the case itself. But this narrow notion of equality overlooks the social context within which we all live our lives, and its effects on individual cases before the courts. If a man and a woman had the same opportunities for employment, for income, for education, and for personal safety, then this formal equality would be appropriate. But often this is not the case, so the formal approach to equality is inadequate for women and for other disadvantaged groups. After a series of disappointing Supreme Court rulings in the 1960s, Canadian feminists gave up on the Bill of Rights and looked for alternative means to break down discrimination.

Women's Participation in the Creation of the Charter

The idea of a constitutional guarantee of equality rights did not originate with the Canadian women's movement. This is in contrast to the American women's movement, which spent much of the 1970s fighting for the Equal Rights Amendment.[71] The Charter of Rights was initiated by former prime minister Pierre Elliott Trudeau in 1980, as part of the constitutional renewal that he promised Quebeckers in return for defeating a provincial referendum on separation from Canada. Trudeau had been a civil liberties expert in Quebec in the 1950s, and he had long been convinced of the need for an entrenched Charter of Rights. After the Quebec referendum failed in the spring of 1980, Trudeau seized the opportunity to renew the constitution.

The Trudeau government put forward a draft charter in the autumn of 1980. Several sections of the draft charter did not differ significantly from the old Bill of Rights. The government held months of public hearings, which gave dozens of interest groups the chance to offer suggestions for improvement.[72] Chief among these groups was the Ad Hoc Committee of Women on the Constitution, a network of feminist lawyers and activists that was brought together by the effort to improve the draft of section 15 (the equality clause). They succeeded in strengthening the wording in order to guarantee the equal benefit of the law to women and to other disadvantaged groups. This meant that in future, any law that discriminated against women in either its substance or its application could be declared unconstitutional. The Ad Hoc Committee also succeeded in inserting section 28 on gender equality into the Charter (see Appendix).

The draft charter was complete by the spring of 1981, but the process of constitutional reform had been stalled.[73] The governments of Quebec, Newfoundland, and Manitoba had asked their Supreme Courts to rule on the legality of the Trudeau government's plan to patriate the constitution unilaterally. The British North America Act of 1867, the constitution of Canada, was actually a British law. It had not been replaced by a Canadian-made (or "patriated") constitution because Canada did not have a formula for amending the constitution. After a meeting of the federal and provincial governments ended in failure in September 1980, Trudeau had decided to proceed without provincial consent; he would present a new constitution to the British Parliament and ask them to pass it into law. This would legally transfer control over the Canadian constitution to the Canadian Parliament. So the three provinces decided to try to stop the Trudeau government's unilateral patriation plan by appealing to the Supreme Court for a ruling on its legality.

The Supreme Court ruled in September 1981 that although the federal government's plan was strictly legal, it violated constitutional convention.[74] It pushed the federal and provincial governments back to the bargaining table, where they struck a deal in November 1981. The premiers wanted to impose limits on the Charter, because they were concerned that it might restrict their powers. The prime minister needed to make concessions after the Supreme Court ruling, so he accepted the amending formula proposed by the premiers and reluctantly accepted section 33 (the "notwithstanding" clause). By the terms of section 33 (see Appendix), Parliament or a provincial legislature can pass a law that conflicts with particular sections of the Charter: section 2 (fundamental freedoms) and sections 7 through 15 (legal and equality rights). The law must contain a declaration that it is adopted "notwithstanding" the Charter, and it can only remain in force for five years before it must be renewed. Despite those limits, section 33 must be regarded as a serious restriction on the rights guaranteed in the Charter.

When Prime Minister Trudeau presented the deal to Parliament a few days after it was signed, he was asked whether the notwithstanding clause applied to section 28. He did not know whether it did or not. Immediately the Ad Hoc Committee swung into action, lobbying MPs and premiers for one intense week. Finally all of the first ministers who had signed the deal (excluding Quebec) agreed to reopen it, in order to make sure that the gender equality clause could not be overridden by Parliament or a provincial legislature. After the intensive effort was over, one of its key organizers reflected on women's gains in the Charter: "[Section] 28 was a helluva lot to lose ... But it was not a helluva lot to win."[75] It should be remembered that despite the victory over section 28, section 15 remains subject to the legislative override.

Alice in Charterland

Before we turn to a discussion of key Charter cases in the courts, it is important to explain how judges use the Charter in their rulings. Imagine a case in which person X is charged with a criminal offence. X's lawyer decides that the section of the Criminal Code under which X has been charged – let's call it section Y – conflicts with a provision in the Charter, and seeks to have the charges dropped on that ground. If the judge agrees, she can declare that section Y of the Criminal Code is null and void, and it ceases to have effect from that moment. The law is effectively removed from the statute books. In that case, the charges against X would be null and void as well. If the judge disagrees, her ruling can be appealed to a higher court, first to the provincial court of appeal and then, if the appeal is rejected, to the Supreme Court of Canada. The Supreme Court has the final word on the case.

Assume that the Supreme Court decides to hear X's appeal from the highest provincial court. It must decide, first, whether the section of the Criminal Code in dispute does conflict with the Charter. If the court decides that there is no conflict, they will reject the appeal. If they find that there *is* a conflict, they will move on to the next step: using section 1, they will determine whether the violation of a Charter right by section Y of the Criminal Code is "a reasonable limitation" of that right, and "demonstrably justified in a free and democratic society." They may also employ other interpretive sections of the Charter, including section 28 where appropriate. If the judges find that the violation is justified, they will dismiss the appeal. But if they find that it is *not* justified, they have the power to strike down section Y and quash the charges against X.

Three of the most important Charter cases for women have arisen from appeals against criminal charges. In two of the three cases, the Supreme Court struck down the law; in the other, the Court found a violation but held that it was justified. A fourth case was sent to the Supreme Court on appeal from the Manitoba Human Rights Commission; it was not explicitly a Charter case, but it reveals the evolution in the Court's thinking about sex discrimination. We will discuss each of these cases briefly.

∾ R. v. Morgentaler

In 1969 the Parliament of Canada enacted a law that declared abortion to be a criminal offence unless performed under certain specific conditions. If a certified doctor performed the abortion in an accredited hospital, after receiving the written approval of a therapeutic abortion committee, the procedure was legal. A therapeutic abortion committee was a panel of three doctors, none of whom could actually perform the abortion under review, who had to determine whether the "life or health" of the pregnant woman would be endangered by the continuation of the pregnancy. If they determined that the pregnancy *was* a threat to the woman, they could declare that an abortion would be "therapeutic" – in other words, necessary in order to remedy a serious physical malady. Any abortion that took place outside a hospital, or that was performed by anyone other than a licensed doctor, or that was not sanctioned by a committee, was a criminal offence. The maximum possible penalty was life in prison for the doctor and a two-year jail sentence for the woman.[76]

As we will see in Chapter 12 of this book, abortion has been a political hot potato in Canada since the passage of that law. The law did not require hospitals to set up therapeutic abortion committees, and the majority did not do so; of those that did, many shut them down after public protests or takeovers of their boards by anti-abortion activists. The committee system itself was riddled with inconsistencies; some boards interpreted the phrase "life or health" very narrowly, requiring evidence of a life-threatening medical condition such as high blood pressure or eclampsia before agreeing to an abortion. Others took a broader view, taking into account the emotional as well as physical health of the pregnant woman and the likely psychological effects of carrying an unwanted pregnancy to term.

Even where the committee was sympathetic to the woman's request for an abortion, the review process could take days or weeks. The delays imposed by the 1969 law worsened the emotional stress of an already extremely difficult situation, and increased the physical risks of terminating a pregnancy. In R. v. Morgentaler[77] the defense argued that the 1969 law,

specifically the section that required the therapeutic abortion committees, violated section 7 of the Charter (see Appendix).

In 1988 the court agreed.[78] Seven judges issued rulings, and five of
them voted to strike down the abortion law. Four of the five were male
judges; Madam Justice Bertha Wilson was the only woman who issued a
ruling. The majority held that the 1969 law did violate women's rights
to "life, liberty and security of the person," due to the lack of access and
the delays inherent in the operation of the committee system.

Madam Justice Wilson went further, declaring that section 2(a) of the
charter (which guarantees everyone freedom of conscience and religion)
gives a woman the right to decide whether or not she will terminate a
pregnancy, without interference from male doctors or judges. She also
argued that to refuse abortion to a woman is to treat her as the means to
an end – the production of a child – rather than as an autonomous individual. Such treatment violates the principles of fundamental justice.
Wilson's declaration of a woman's right to choose is reproduced below.

It is probably impossible for a man to respond, even imaginatively, to
such a dilemma [an unwanted pregnancy] not just because it is outside the
realm of his personal experience (although this is, of course, the case) but
because he can relate to it only by objectifying it, thereby eliminating the
subjective elements of the female psyche which are at the heart of the dilemma.[79]

Since 1988 there has been no national abortion law in Canada, a situation to which we will return in Chapter 12.

∾   *Seaboyer-Gayme*
In 1985 the Supreme Court of Ontario ruled in favour of two men who
sought to nullify the rape shield sections of the Criminal Code.[80] Section
276 of the Code "prohibited as evidence information about the sexual
activity of the complainant with any person other than the accused,"
while section 277 "declared inadmissible evidence of sexual reputation
for the purpose of undermining the credibility of the complainant."[81] In
other words, a woman who had been sexually assaulted would not have
to fear cross-examination on the witness stand about her sexual history,
or accusations of promiscuity from defence counsel.

The lawyers for Seaboyer and Gayme argued that their clients' rights
to a fair trial, enshrined in sections 7 and 11(d) of the Charter, were vio-

lated by the rape shield rules. Their defences were based on mistaken belief, meaning that they honestly thought the victims had consented to sexual activity, and that this honest belief was founded on the previous sexual histories and reputations of the victims. By excluding these histories and reputations from evidence, they argued, the rape shield law made it impossible for them to present their defence, thus denying them a fair trial. In addition, Seaboyer's defence rested on his claim that the victim had had sex with another man just before the alleged rape, which meant that the physical evidence used against him might not have been valid.

The Ontario Supreme Court agreed with the defence and quashed the rape shield provisions in the Criminal Code. The Crown appealed this ruling to the Ontario Court of Appeal, and the Women's Legal Education and Action Fund (LEAF) was granted intervenor status to present the feminist case for the rape shield law. LEAF argued that the victim's past sexual history is irrelevant to the guilt or innocence of the accused; the only thing that matters is the actual sexual encounter on which the criminal charges are based. While the Ontario Court of Appeal agreed with LEAF, they held that section 276 conflicted with sections 7 and 11(d) of the Charter, and that the rape shield could not be saved under section 1. In other words, while they agreed with the objective of the rape shield law, the judges felt that it was not enough to justify the clear violation of the right of an accused to a fair trial. They upheld section 277, arguing that evidence about the victim's sexual reputation does not serve a legitimate purpose in the trial of her accused rapist.

The defence appealed to the Supreme Court of Canada. In 1991 the court upheld the Court of Appeal decision, striking down the rape shield law. Seven of the nine justices held that "section 276 has the potential to exclude otherwise admissible evidence that may be highly relevant to the defence."[82] While the objective of the rape shield law, to protect women from humilation and re-victimization on the witness stand, is an admirable one, the judges felt that the law went too far and violated the rights of the accused. Justices Claire L'Heureux-Dubé and Charles Gonthier dissented from the majority opinion, arguing that "in order to achieve fairness and to conduct trials in accordance with fundamental tenets of criminal law, this provision [the rape shield] must be upheld in all of its vigour."[83] But the other seven justices prevailed, and the rape shield was struck down. (For the subsequent history of the law on sexual assault, see above.)

∾ R. v. Butler

In February 1992 the Supreme Court of Canada ruled on a case involving pornography. Donald Butler opened a store in Winnipeg that sold and rented pornographic videos. He was charged with 250 counts of obscenity, under section 163(8) of the Criminal Code.[84] Obscenity is defined by the Code as "any publication of which a dominant characteristic is the undue exploitation of sex, or sex together with crime, horror, cruelty or violence."[85] There is no Canadian law against pornography as such; the obscenity law is the principal legal mechanism for banning the most degrading and harmful hard-core pornography. (For a discussion of the law on pornography, see Chapter 12.)

The trial judge found Butler innocent on most of the 250 charges, ruling that the obscene materials were protected by the guarantee of freedom of expression (section 2(b) of the Charter). He convicted Butler on eight counts of obscenity. The Crown appealed the 242 acquittals, and the Manitoba Court of Appeal reversed them. The majority of the appellate justices held that the obscene materials were not protected by the Charter, because they unduly exploited sex and were degrading to human sexuality.[86] The Court of Appeal ruling was appealed to the Supreme Court of Canada, which was asked to rule on two constitutional questions: did section 163 of the Criminal Code violate section 2(b) of the Charter; and if so, could section 163 be saved under section 1 of the Charter?

The Supreme Court issued a unanimous ruling, written by Mr. Justice Sopinka. He drew a distinction between three types of pornography: explicit sex with violence; explicit sex that is non-violent but degrading or dehumanizing; and explicit non-violent sex that is neither degrading nor dehumanizing.[87] He then argued that most materials in the first two categories will constitute the undue exploitation of sex, thereby violating the law, and that the only possible defence would be one of artistic expression. This section of the ruling clearly states that the problem with pornography is not that it offends morality, but that it harms vulnerable members of our society – specifically, women and children.

Mr. Justice Sopinka found that section 163 of the Criminal Code does violate the Charter guarantee of freedom of expression, but it can be saved by the "reasonable limitations" clause in section 1. He argued that the violation of section 2(b) is justified by the need to protect women and children from sexual exploitation, and to protect women from the negative effects that may follow from the dissemination of sexualized images of women's suffering and subordination. Pornography is a threat, not just to women's physical safety, but to their social equality as well.

> The burgeoning pornography industry renders the concern even more pressing and substantial than when the impugned sections were first enacted. I would therefore conclude that the objective of avoiding the harm associated with the dissemination of pornography in this case is sufficiently pressing and substantial to warrant some restriction on full exercise of the right to freedom of expression.[88]

The Supreme Court ruling in R. v. Butler is a milestone for Canadian women. The court unanimously ruled against the free distribution of pornography, and it relied heavily on feminist analyses in its judgement. Canada became the first country in the world to officially recognize that hard-core pornography is linked to violence against women.[89]

∾ Janzen-Govereau

Janzen and Govereau were two Manitoba waitresses who were repeatedly sexually harassed by one of the cooks in the restaurant where they worked. They complained to the Manitoba Human Rights Commission, which ruled that their complaints were valid and that the consequences of the harassment had been damaging for the two women. Under the Manitoba Human Rights Code, there was no law against sexual harassment as such; the only way to punish the offender was to declare the sexual harassment to be a prohibited form of sexual discrimination. This is what the Human Rights Commission did.

The employer appealed to the Manitoba Court of Appeal, which ruled that the cook's actions did not constitute sexual discrimination under the terms of the Manitoba Human Rights Act. The court therefore decreed that the employer was not liable for damages. The Court of Appeal ruling was based on classic sexist assumptions about sexual harassment: the cook's actions toward the waitresses were the result of an inevitable attraction of one individual toward two others; and the sexual harassment itself was not serious enough to constitute discrimination.

The case was appealed to the Supreme Court, and LEAF intervened again. LEAF argued that sexual harassment is indeed gender-based harm, a prohibited type of activity under the Manitoba Human Rights Act.

Sexual harassment of the type experienced by Janzen and Govereau happens to women because they are women, and it harms them by poisoning their work environment. It is therefore serious enough to warrant a charge of sexual discrimination. The court agreed, ruling in May 1989 that the sexual harassment had occurred, not because the women were exceptionally attractive, but because they were disadvantaged in society by the fact of their gender. The court held that the two women had been exploited by their employer, and it accordingly upheld the original ruling and sanction imposed by the Manitoba Human Rights Commission.[90]

This ruling established the doctrine of women's subordination *as a group* in Charter jurisprudence. The group doctrine could have profound effects on Canadian women's lives, because it requires courts to treat women as members of a disadvantaged group for the purposes of Charter litigation – not as individuals divorced from their social context. This is a clear breakthrough for feminist jurisprudence.

Is the Charter the Key to Canadian Women's Empowerment?

The women who fought for the gender equality rights in the Charter, and the women who cheered them on, hoped that the Charter would usher in a new era for Canadian women. The legislatures and cabinets had proven to be too slow and unsympathetic; women hoped the courts would be different. There have been some notable successes, but there have also been great disappointments. The voiding of the rape shield is only one example. Men have successfully used the Charter in the courts "to protest against the few protections women enjoyed in law."[91] One review of Charter litigation, undertaken when section 15 had been in force for three years, found that "approximately half of women's sex equality challenges [have] met with success. The success rate for men's challenges is somewhat lower. However, because there are more men's sexual equality challenges (in fact, there were more than three times as many), men's successes have been double those of women."[92]

For example, men have challenged welfare provisions for single mothers that are not available to single fathers. In one such case the Nova Scotia Supreme Court simply shut down the province's social services when it found in favour of the man.[93] How is it possible that a more powerful group can use the Charter to erode the rights of a less powerful group?

Some critics of the Charter have predicted such outcomes since its inception. Michael Mandel, among others, argues that the Charter cannot be an instrument of real social change.[94] The rights that it contains are *negative* rights, meaning that they *restrict* the state from acting instead of *requiring* it to act. In other words, the Charter may give you a guarantee of free speech, with which the state cannot interfere. But the Charter cannot force the state to provide you with adequate housing, or a minimal standard of living. These would be *positive* rights. Therefore, the Charter cannot redress the most basic inequalities in society. Moreover, the Charter is interpreted by judges who are mostly white, male, middle-class, and highly educated. They cannot be expected to empathize with the plight of the powerless; their sympathies lie with those who are already privileged. For Mandel and other radical critics, the Charter is a smokescreen for the growing power of vested economic and political interests. The "legalization of politics" undermines democracy and entrenches the status quo.

To keep matters in perspective, we must remember that the first three or four years of Charter equality litigation were not necessarily a glimpse into the future. The courts were still tentative, trying to feel their way through this new world. The most significant breakthroughs for women have come since 1988, while the number of challenges by men appears to have slowed down.[95] There are no guarantees in Charter litigation. Judges are bound to apply the law as they understand it, and their understanding is almost certainly shaped by their conscious or unconscious beliefs about gender. But the existence of groups like LEAF, and the growing influence of feminist jurisprudence (as shown in the *Morgentaler, Janzen-Govereau* and *Butler* cases) offer some hope for the future. The principal obstacle to future Charter cases is funding. The federal government cancelled the funding for its Charter Challenges program in 1992. This program had made a substantial contribution to some of the crucial Charter cases for women and other groups, and its loss was a severe blow to disadvantaged groups who cannot otherwise afford the high cost of litigation. The Liberals reinstated the program in October 1994.

Conclusion

In this chapter we have discussed the following key points.

1.   The Canadian criminal justice system was designed by men, to
     punish men for violating the property and safety of men. Women
     do not receive fair treatment from this system, whether as defen-
     dants, victims, or witnesses.

2.   The attitudes of judges, police officers, and lawyers can have a sig-
     nificant effect on the outcome of a trial. Women often suffer in-
     justices because of sexism in the justice system.

3.   The Canadian law on sexual assault was reformed in 1983, to
     eliminate some of the worst vestiges of sexism and to encourage
     women to report crimes. The new law is an improvement over
     the old in many ways, but a number of problems in enforcement
     remain. These problems are particularly acute in cases of date rape,
     where the old beliefs about women's dishonesty and promiscuity
     are most clearly evident. The rape shield provisions were struck
     down by the Supreme Court of Canada in 1991, after a Charter
     challenge. A new law was enacted in 1992 to replace it, but its fu-
     ture is uncertain.

4.   The Canadian Charter of Rights and Freedoms was proclaimed in
     1982, after a fierce battle by women's groups to ensure that it
     would protect their rights effectively. Section 15 guarantees equal-
     ity without regard to gender and a host of other criteria. Section
     28 guarantees all Charter rights equally to male and female per-
     sons. The Supreme Court has used the Charter to help eliminate
     sex discrimination in some cases (such as *Morgentaler* and *Butler*)
     and has disappointed women in other cases (*Seaboyer-Gayme,
     Daviault*). Overall, men have used the Charter quite effectively to
     erode the few legal gains that women have made through years of
     intensive lobbying. Critics of the Charter argue that the justice
     system has a built-in bias towards the wealthy and powerful, and
     that women should not be surprised if they are not helped by
     Charter jurisprudence.

In the next chapter we discuss the pervasive mirror of the sexist attitudes discussed in this chapter: the mass media and popular culture in Canada.

Appendix: Key Sections of the Canadian Charter of Rights and Freedoms

1. The *Canadian Charter of Rights and Freedoms* guarantees the rights and freedoms set out in it subject only to such reasonable limits prescribed by law as can be demonstrably justified in a free and democratic society.

2. Everyone has the following fundamental freedoms:
   (a) freedom of conscience and religion;
   (b) freedom of thought, belief, opinion and expression, including freedom of the press and other media of communication;
   (c) freedom of peaceful assembly; and
   (d) freedom of association.

7. Everyone has the right to life, liberty and security of the person and the right not to be deprived thereof except in accordance with the principles of fundamental justice.

11. Any person charged with an offence has the right
    (d) to be presumed innocent until proven guilty according to law in a fair and public hearing by an independent and impartial tribunal.

15. (1) Every individual is equal before and under the law and has the right to the equal protection and equal benefit of the law without discrimination and, in particular, without discrimination based on race, national or ethnic origin, colour, religion, sex, age or mental or physical disability.
    (2) Subsection (1) does not preclude any law, program or activity that has as its object the amelioration of conditions of disadvantaged individuals or groups including those that are disadvantaged because of race, national or ethnic origin, colour, religion, sex, age or mental or physical disability.

24.   (1) Anyone whose rights or freedoms, as guaranteed by this Charter, have been infringed or denied may apply to a court of competent jurisdiction to obtain such remedy as the court considers appropriate and just in the circumstances.

28.   Notwithstanding anything in this Charter, the rights and freedoms referred to in it are guaranteed equally to male and female persons.

32.   This Charter applies
(a) to the Parliament and government of Canada in respect to all matters within the authority of Parliament including all matters relating to the Yukon Territory and Northwest Territories; and
(b) to the legislature and government of each province in respect of all matters within the authority of the legislature of each province.

33.   (1) Parliament or the legislature of a province may expressly declare in an Act of Parliament or of the legislature, as the case may be, that the Act or a provision thereof shall operate notwithstanding a provision included in section 2 or sections 7 to 15 of this Charter.
(3) A declaration made under subsection (1) shall cease to have effect five years after it comes into force or on such earlier date as may be specified in the declaration.

52.   (1) The Constitution of Canada is the supreme law of Canada, and any law that is inconsistent with the provisions of the Constitution is, to the extent of the inconsistency, of no force or effect.

Notes

1   MacIntosh, *Fundamentals of the Criminal Justice System,* chap. 1.
2   Ibid., 137.
3   Ibid., 174–75.
4   Ibid., chap. 13.
5   Ibid., chap. 12.
6   Statistics Canada, Canadian Centre for Justice Statistics, *Juristat Service Bulletin,* December 1990, 1.
7   Ibid., 11.

8   Holly Johnson and Karen Rodgers, "A Statistical Overview of Women and Crime in Canada," in Adelberg and Currie, *In Conflict with the Law,* 109–11.

9   Boyle et al., *A Feminist Review of Criminal Law,* 2.

10 Sheelagh Cooper, "The Evolution of the Federal Women's Prison," in Adelberg and Currie, *In Conflict with the Law,* 45.

11 Royal Commission on the Status of Women in Canada, *Report,* chap. 9. The federal government has announced that the P4W will be shut down and replaced with five regional women's prisons, but this policy has taken years to implement.

12 Cooper, 45.

13 Margaret Shaw, "Reforming Federal Women's Imprisonment," in Adelberg and Currie, *In Conflict with the Law.*

14 Canada, Department of Justice, *Gender Equality in the Canadian Justice System,* quoted in Sallot, "Report links ads."

15 Canada, Department of Justice Research and Statistics Section, *The New Sexual Assault Offences,* 1.

16 Tong, *Women, Sex, and the Law,* 3.

17 Ibid., 3.

18 Ibid., 3.

19 Brown, *Gender Equality in the Courts,* 2-13–2-16.

20 Boyle et al., *A Feminist Review of Criminal Law,* xvii.

21 Statistics Canada, Canadian Centre for Justice Statistics, *Juristat Service Bulletin* 10, no. 10 (October 1990), 5.

22 Statistics Canada, Canadian Centre for Justice Statistics, *Homicide in Canada 1987.*

23 Ibid., 32.

24 The Supreme Court of Canada ruled, in *R. v. Lavallée,* that it was not only fair but proper to hear the testimony of an expert on battered woman syndrome during the trial of a woman who injured or killed an abusive partner. See 1 S.C.R. [1990], 853–54.

25 Ibid., xvii.

26 *R. v. Lavallée,* [1990] 1 S.C.R.

27 *The New Sexual Assault Offences,* 1.

28 Ibid., 1.

29 MacIntosh, *Fundamentals of the Criminal Justice System,* 251.

30 Boyle, *Sexual Assault,* 14: "It might appear on a superficial level, that the law displayed a determination to punish offenders. Judge-made law and enforcement practices, however, ensured a concentration on the need to protect men from false accusations and narrowed the scope of protection to certain women

who had not infringed judicial and societal norms about what was appropriate behaviour and life-style."

31 Paula Bourne, "Women, Law, and the Justice System," in Roach Pierson et al., *Canadian Women's Issues,* 332.

32 Canada, House of Commons, Bill C-49.

33 Ibid.

34 Ibid.

35 Ibid.

36 Ibid.

37 For a discussion of the process, see Sheila McIntyre, "Redefining Reformism: The Consultations that Shaped Bill C-49," in Roberts and Mohr, *Confronting Sexual Assault.*

38 Canada, *House of Commons Debates,* 9505.

39 *R. v. Daviault,* [1994] 3 S.C.R. 63.

40 Ibid.

41 This phrase is taken from Madigan and Gamble, *The Second Rape.*

42 See Brown, *Gender Equality in the Courts,* 5 and 2–32.

43 Ibid., *vi.*

44 Canada, Department of Justice, *Sexual Assault Legislation in Canada, An Evaluation: An Analysis of National Statistics, xii.*

45 Ibid., 2–9.

46 Ibid.

47 Ibid., 6.

48 Canada, Department of Justice Research Section, *Sexual Assault Legislation in Canada, An Evaluation: Overview,* 55.

49 Statistics Canada, Canadian Centre for Justice Statistics, *Canadian Crime Statistics 1993* (Ottawa: Minister of Industy, Science and Technology, 1995).

50 Boyle, Sexual Assault, chap. 1.

51 Ibid., xiii–xiv.

52 Brown, chap. 2.

53 Estrich, Real Rape (Cambridge, MA: Harvard University Press, 1987).

54 Quoted in Brown, 5–18.

55 Brown, 1–22.

56 Ibid.

57 Ibid., 1–24.

58 See Estrich, chap. 2.

59 Warshaw, *I Never Called It Rape,* 11.

60 Ibid., 12.

61 *Canadian Crime Statistics 1993,* 65.

62 Ibid., 24.

63 Ibid., 43.

64 Brown, 2–10.

65 Brown, 5–29.

66 Renate M. Mohr, "Sexual Assault Sentencing: Leaving Justice to Individual Conscience," in Roberts and Mohr, *Confronting Sexual Assault,* 178.

67 Ibid., 38–39.

68 Ibid., 39.

69 Ibid., 42–43.

70 See Williams, "The Changing Nature of Citizen Rights," for a description of these historical events.

71 See Mansbridge, *How We Lost the ERA.*

72 See Hosek, "Women and the Constitutional Process," and Kome, *The Taking of Twenty-Eight,* for a description of this process.

73 For a description of the process of constitutional reform, see Sheppard and Valpy, *The National Deal*; Simeon and Banting, *And No One Cheered*; Romanow, *Canada … Notwithstanding.*

74 See Russell et al., *The Court and the Constitution.*

75 Linda Ryan-Nye, quoted in Kome, *The Taking of Twenty-Eight,* 95.

76 *Criminal Code* R.S.C. 1985, s. 287, quoted in Brodie, Gavigany, and Jenson, *The Politics of Abortion,* 147.

77 Excellent histories of this issue can be found in Morton, *Morgentaler v. Borowski;* Brodie, Gavigan, and Jenson, *The Politics of Abortion;* and Collins, *The Big Evasion.*

78 See Day and Persky, *The Supreme Court of Canada Decision on Abortion.*

79 Ibid., 133.

80 Razack, *Canadian Feminism and the Law,* 109.

81 Ibid., 110.

82 [1991] 2 S.C.R., 581.

83 Ibid., 589.

84 Canada, Library of Parliament Research Branch, *Obscenity,* 2.

85 Ibid.

86 Ibid., 3.

87 Ibid., 4.

88 Ibid., 7. Mr. Justice Sopinka

89 Ibid., 12.

90 Razack, 109.

91 Ibid., 55.

92 Brodsky and Day, *Canadian Charter Equality Rights for Women,* 56.

93   Ibid., 57. It must be noted that recipients of Nova Scotia social assistance benefits did not lose money as a result; see Mandel, *The Charter of Rights and the Legalization of Politics,* 264.

94   Mandel, chaps. 1, 2, 4, 6.

95   Razack, 134.

References and Further Reading

Adelberg, Ellen, and Claudia Currie, eds. *In Conflict with the Law: Women and the Canadian Justice System.* Vancouver: Press Gang, 1993.

Baines, Beverley. "Women and the Law." In Sandra Burt et al., eds., *Changing Patterns: Women in Canada.* Toronto: McClelland & Stewart, 1988.

Boyle, Christine L.M. *Sexual Assault.* Toronto: Carswell, 1984.

Boyle, Christine L.M., et al. *A Feminist Review of Criminal Law.* Ottawa: Minister of Supply & Services, 1985.

Bray, Ruth M. *Sexual Assault in Canada.* Toronto: University of Toronto, 1980.

Brodie, Janine, Shelley A.M. Gavigan, and Jane Jenson. *The Politics of Abortion.* Toronto: Oxford University Press, 1992.

Brodsky, Gwen, and Shelagh Day. *Canadian Charter Equality Rights for Women: One Step Forward or Two Steps Back?* Ottawa: CACSW, 1989.

Brown, Mona G., ed. *Gender Equality in the Courts: Criminal Law.* Winnipeg: Manitoba Association of Women and the Law, 1991.

Cairns, Alan. "Citizens (Outsiders) and Governments (Insiders) in Constitution-Making: The Case of Meech Lake." In Alan C. Cairns (ed. Douglas E. Williams), *Disruptions: Constitutional Struggles, from the Charter to Meech Lake.* Toronto: McClelland & Stewart, 1991.

Canada, Department of Justice Research and Statistics Section. *Sexual Assault Legislation in Canada, An Evaluation: An Analysis of National Statistics.* Ottawa: Minister of Supply & Services, 1990.

———. *Sexual Assault Legislation in Canada, An Evaluation: Overview.* Ottawa: Minister of Supply & Services, 1990.

———. *The New Sexual Assault Offences: Emerging Legal Issues.* Ottawa: Minister of Supply & Services, 1985.

Canada. *House of Commons Debates.* Third Session, 34th Parliament, April 8, 1992.

Canada, House of Commons. Third Session, 39th Parliament, 40–41 Elizabeth II, 1991–92, Bill C-49.

Canada, Library of Parliament Research Branch. *Obscenity: The Decision of the Supreme Court of Canada in R. v. Butler*. Ottawa: Library of Parliament, 1992.

Canadian Advisory Council on the Status of Women. *Sexual Assault and Criminal Justice: Addressing Women's Reality*. Brief presented to the Legislative Committee on Bill C-49, An Act to amend the Criminal Code [Sexual Assault], May 1992.

Collins, Anne. *The Big Evasion: Abortion, the Issue that Won't Go Away*. Toronto: Lester & Orpen Dennys, 1985.

Crean, Susan. *In the Name of the Fathers: The Story behind Child Custody*. Toronto: Amanita, 1988.

Day, Shelagh, and Stan Persky, eds. *The Supreme Court of Canada Decision on Abortion*. Vancouver: New Star Books, 1988.

Eberts, Mary. "The Constitution, the Charter and the Distinct Society Clause: Why Are Women Being Ignored?" In Michael D. Behiels, ed., *The Meech Lake Primer: Conflicting Views of the 1987 Constitutional Accord*. Ottawa: University of Ottawa Press, 1989.

Estrich, Susan. *Real Rape*. Cambridge, MA: Harvard University Press, 1987.

Hosek, Chaviva. "Women and the Constitutional Process." In Richard Simeon and Keith Banting, eds., *And No One Cheered: Federalism, Democracy and the Constitution Act*. Toronto: Methuen, 1983.

Kinnon, Dianne. *Report on Sexual Assault in Canada*. Ottawa: CACSW, 1981.

Kome, Penney. *The Taking of Twenty-Eight: Women Challenge the Constitution*. Toronto: Women's Press, 1983.

MacIntosh, Donald A. *Fundamentals of the Criminal Justice System*. Toronto: Carswell, 1989.

Madigan, Lee, and Nancy C. Gamble. *The Second Rape: Society's Continued Betrayal of the Victim*. New York: Lexington, 1991.

Mandel, Michael. *The Charter of Rights and the Legalization of Politics in Canada*. Toronto: Wall &Thompson, 1989.

Mansbridge, Jane. *How We Lost the ERA*. Chicago: University of Chicago Press, 1986.

Morton, F.L. *Morgentaler v. Borowski: Abortion, the Charter, and the Courts*. Toronto: McClelland & Stewart, 1992.

Razack, Sherene. *Canadian Feminism and the Law*. Toronto: Second Story Press, 1991.

Roach Pierson, Ruth, et al., eds. *Canadian Women's Issues: Twenty-Five Years of Women's Activism in English Canada*. Vol. 1. Toronto: Lorimer, 1993.

Roberts, Julian V., and Renate M. Mohr, eds. *Confronting Sexual Assault: A Decade of Legal and Social Change*. Toronto: University of Toronto Press, 1994.

Robertson, James R. *Obscenity: The Decision of the Supreme Court of Canada in R. v. Butler*. Ottawa: Library of Parliament Research Branch, 1992.

Romanow, Roy, et al. *Canada ... Notwithstanding: The Making of the Constitution 1976–1982*. Toronto: Carswell/Methuen, 1984.

Royal Commission on the Status of Women in Canada. *Report*. Ottawa: Information Canada, 1970.

Russell, Peter, et al. *The Court and the Constitution: Comments On the Supreme Court Reference on Constitutional Amendment*. Kingston: Institute of Intergovernmental Relations, 1982.

Sallot, Jeff, "Report links ads to violence against women." *Globe and Mail,* July 6, 1993.

Sheppard, Robert, and Michael Valpy. *The National Deal: The Fight for a Canadian Constitution*. Toronto: Macmillan Canada, 1982.

Simeon, Richard, and Keith Banting, eds. *And No One Cheered: Federalism, Democracy and the Constitution Act*. Toronto: Methuen, 1983.

Statistics Canada, Canadian Centre for Justice Statistics. *Homicide in Canada 1987: A Statistical Perspective*. Ottawa: Minister of Supply & Services Canada, 1988.

———. *Juristat Service Bulletin*. 1990.

Supreme Court of Canada, *R. v. Daviault*, [1994] 3 S.C.R. 63.

Supreme Court of Canada, *R. v. Lavallee*, [1990] 1 S.C.R.

Tong, Rosemarie. *Women, Sex, and the Law*. Totowa, NJ: Rowman & Allanheld, 1984.

Warshaw, Robin. *I Never Called It Rape: The Ms. Report on Recognizing, Fighting and Surviving Date and Acquaintance Rape*. New York: Harper & Row, 1988.

Williams, Cynthia. "The Changing Nature of Citizen Rights." In Alan C. Cairns and Cynthia Williams, eds., *Constitutionalism, Citizenship and Society in Canada*. Vol. 33 of the collected research studies for the Royal Commission on the Economic Union and Development Prospects for Canada. Toronto: University of Toronto Press, 1985.

Chapter 6: Women, Mass Media and Popular Culture in Canada

Chapter Summary

Chapter 6 examines the images of women that appear in the mainstream Canadian media, and the effects of those images on women's security and self-esteem. Media images can have a powerful influence on our thoughts and assumptions, because they are so pervasive and because, through stereotyping, we tend to see the same images presented over and over. Women are presented as sex objects, whores, housewives, or ugly feminists – always defined by their appearance and by their relationship to men. These stereotypes, including the pernicious images of the rape myths and the beauty myth, help to perpetuate the very gender roles that they so accurately reflect. The chapter concludes with a discussion of the ways in which female politicians and feminists – the only role models for young women that contradict the traditional stereotypes – have been negatively portrayed in the media.

Chapter Outline

- Mediated Reality and the Portrayal of Gender
- Mass Media and Popular Culture in Canadian Politics
  The Structure of the Mass Media and Cultural Industries in Canada
  The Effects of Mass Media and Popular Culture on Political and Social Attitudes
- Images of Women in North American Popular Culture
  The Rape Myths
  The Beauty Myth
  Media Portrayals of Female Politicians and the Women's Movement
  Images of Women and Women's Acceptance of Subordination
- Women as Media Personnel
- Conclusion

Mediated Reality and the Portrayal of Gender

In this chapter we will describe some of the ways in which Canadian women are portrayed in the mass media, and the images of women in popular culture. We will also explore some of the effects of those portrayals and images on women themselves. The influence of media content on the audience is a subject of intense debate, and we may never know exactly how much the images we see on television and in newspapers shape our ideas about the world. But there is evidence that the media and culture do help to determine our opinions about social and political issues, to some extent. This is because much of our knowledge about the world comes to us not from first-hand experience, but from second-hand words and images conveyed to us through mass communication. In simpler times, "most of the world that people needed to know about was close at hand."[1] But in the 1990s, "people are affected by economic and political forces far beyond their own communities. In fact, we could argue that most of the world that matters to us is beyond our direct grasp and must necessarily be mediated."[2]

The media and popular culture influence our attitudes and beliefs, and vice versa. Therefore, we need to understand the ways in which women and the women's movement are depicted on television, in movies, and in print media if we are to understand women's place in Canadian politics and society. We will also look briefly at the women who work in the media and culture industries in Canada.

The political influence of the news media, and the effects of popular culture on peoples' perceptions of the world, are highly complex questions that have received a great deal of scholarly and popular attention.[3] This chapter can offer only a brief sketch of those questions, and a few of the many answers that have been proposed. The interested reader is encouraged to consult the works listed in the References section of this chapter.

Mass Media and Popular Culture in Canadian Politics

The "mass media" include the producers of all print and broadcast, audio and visual material that is aimed at a general audience. The big Hollywood studios, the major television networks, the large record companies, newspaper and magazine publishers are all part of the mass media. In Canada, the principal mass media outlets are the English and French radio and television networks of the CBC; private television undertakings in English and French Canada, such as CTV, Global, and television-Quatre Saisons; the *Globe and Mail,* the *Toronto Star, Le Devoir,* and smaller local newspapers; *Maclean's* and other popular magazines; and, to a lesser extent (because of distribution problems), Canadian film companies (such as Alliance and the National Film Board).

Therefore, the mass media are the private companies and public institutions that produce "popular culture." Popular culture includes any film, television program, book, magazine, newspaper, or music recording that is aimed at a broad general audience. Examples include a movie starring Arnold Schwarzenegger or Mel Gibson; a new CD by Madonna or Michael Jackson; a Danielle Steel romance novel; and a situation comedy like "Roseanne" or "Married with Children." Because most popular culture is produced by large corporations, the mass media in Canada are often referred to as "cultural industries."[4]

The significance of popular culture lies in its huge audiences. Most Canadians own at least one television; we read newspapers and magazines, listen to the radio, rent movies, and watch rock videos on Much-Music. These huge audiences allow mass media companies to sell advertising time or space to other companies, which brings in huge profits. Large corporations like Pepsi, Proctor and Gamble, and McDonald's dominate the airwaves by buying thirty-second or sixty-second time periods during popular television shows. Cosmetic companies buy dozens of pages in popular women's magazines such as *Glamour* and *Flare.*

Those large companies would not pay high fees to advertise their products in the print and broadcast media if they did not believe that media images can affect the behaviour, and in particular the purchasing habits, of their audiences. We turn now to a discussion of those media effects.

The Structure of the Mass Media and Cultural Industries in Canada

In this section we will explore some important aspects of the Canadian mass media. There are many aspects that could be discussed, but we will focus on two. The first is the profit motive in mass cultural production. The second is the degree of American domination of the Canadian media market.

Most Canadian media companies are privately owned and are expected to make a profit. Their profits come from the sale of air time or advertising space to advertisers. As a result, the people who produce the media content – the news and entertainment we read and watch – try to attract the broadest possible audience or readership. They print or air material that appeals to a large number of people, and avoid material that may offend. The power of the advertisers is rarely exerted directly, but it may be felt during the production of a newspaper or a television program.[5]

The second aspect of the Canadian mass media is its domination by American cultural industries. Most Canadians receive American television channels, either off-air or on cable. In English Canada in 1984, three-quarters of audience viewing in prime time (between 7 and 11 p.m.) was devoted to American programming;[6] the proportion has risen since then, with the introduction of new cable channels. (French Canadians watch more Canadian programming, although most of their drama viewing consists of American shows dubbed into French.) Most of the movie screens in Canada are controlled by American companies, which show Hollywood movies; very little screen time is given to Canadian films.[7] Commercial radio is dominated by American music and "foreground" programming. Canadian magazines are forced to compete with American magazines, which consistently sell more copies in the Canadian market.[8]

Why do American cultural products dominate the Canadian market so completely? One reason is the power of advertising. Canadians want to see the movies and television shows about which they have read or heard. American movie studios spend millions of dollars on posters, trailers, television ads, and other devices to build interest in and curiosity about their products. Canadian producers cannot compete. Another reason is the high production values and mass appeal of most American popular culture. Canadians enjoy watching American situation comedies and prime-time dramas as much as Americans do. On average, Canadians spend more than 24 hours per week watching television;[9] they want to see well-known actors and well-produced shows.

A third reason, specific to television, is that it is much less expensive to buy American shows than it is to produce Canadian shows. One episode of a popular American night-time drama program may cost over a million dollars to produce, but it can recoup its costs in the American market from network license fees and advertisers. It can then be sold cheaply to overseas markets to make a profit. This is why broadcasters all over the world show American programs on their television networks: they can buy a show for a few thousand dollars, instead of paying hundreds of thousands or even millions to produce their own programming. To compete with the production values of American programming is prohibitively expensive for most countries, and their viewers will not tolerate anything less once they have become accustomed to the glossy U.S. product. The result is the global dominance of American programming and culture.

The Effects of Mass Media and Culture on Political and Social Attitudes

For decades, beginning with newspapers and continuing with radio and television, people have wondered about the effects of our media consumption on our values and beliefs. Do people change their opinions about an issue because they read a newspaper story? Do people decide to vote for a political candidate because he or she spoke persuasively (or played the saxophone) on a television talk show? There are no clear-cut answers to these questions, largely because it is very difficult to find strong evidence to support a positive or negative answer. Various theories of media effects have been proposed; we will discuss five of them here.

The earliest model of media effects, popular in the 1950s, was the *hypodermic syringe model*. The new medium of television was believed to "inject" ideas directly into the individuals who watched it, who were helpless to fend them off. The model was quickly discredited, because it soon became clear that audiences were not entirely passive; they can "select and reject, make judgements and communicate with each other."[10] The second model, a more subtle approach to media effects, was the *two-step flow model*. "Opinion leaders" watched and read the news regularly, and then talked about it to their friends. This model emphasized the social relationships within the audience, and how they shape an individual's response to media content. It also made a less extreme claim for the effects of media on consumers.[11] The third model is the *uses and gratifications approach,* which assumes that audience members, far from being passive consumers of media content, demand that the media fulfill particular needs. These can include entertainment, information, or companionship.[12]

All of these models focus on individual media consumers, overlooking the influence of media on society as a whole, and the power of social factors (e.g., ethnicity) on people's perceptions of media content. A more wide-ranging model of media effects is the *agenda-setting approach.* According to this model, "the media help to establish an order of priorities in a society about its problems and objectives. They do this, not by initiating or determining, but by publicizing according to an agreed scale of values what is determined elsewhere, usually in the political system."[13]

As the two leading scholars of the agenda-setting school put it, "the mass media may not be successful in telling us what to think, but they are stunningly successful in telling us what to think *about*."[14] If an event or an issue receives wide attention in the media, we may begin to think of it as very important, even though it does not touch us directly. But the media cannot tell us what position we should take on the issue, although there is evidence that the further the issue from our daily experience, the more influential the media can be.[15]

Therefore, it is not yet possible to say with scientific certainty that the mass media *do* affect values and beliefs, or that they do *not* affect values and beliefs. It seems very likely that they do, but we do not yet have the tools to prove it conclusively. Although we lack hard evidence that media can *change* beliefs, we can nonetheless make a plausible argument that media images *reinforce* previously held beliefs among audience members. *Cultural effects* theory focuses on "the slow, cumulative build-up of beliefs and values through which we understand the world."[16] For example, this chapter argues that the stereotypes of women in the media affect our ideas of what women are like and how they should behave. The cultural effects approach asks "how these images are put together or constructed: to ask, for example, how such types as the 'dumb blonde' are created out of styles of dress, speech mannerisms, and the like. To understand this fully we would also need to analyze the plot and the portrayal of characters in a story which used this kind of figure."[17]

These cultural effects arise in part from the media's dependence on *stereotypes*. In the process of turning a chaotic mass of events into a television news program or a daily newspaper, media workers need strategies to simplify reality so that it makes sense to their readers or viewers. One key strategy is to use symbols, or stereotypes, to encapsulate a complex reality in an easily understood simplification: "media personnel, who are short of time and have restricted reportorial space, focus and condense social complexity into a series of colourful typifications. These stereotypes crystallize socially accepted values and expectations, and change over time."[18]

Some people consider the media's use of stereotypes to be an inevitable result of reducing millions of daily events into a manageable set of news stories. Others regard the stereotyping of particular groups as both avoidable and damaging. In particular, feminist critics of the media (especially liberal feminists) have condemned the treatment of women in both news and entertainment content.[19] Five principal themes have emerged. First, "Women are underrepresented in general, and occupy less central roles than men in television programmes."[20] Tuchman refers to this as the "symbolic annihilation" of women.[21] According to media researcher George Gerbner, "Men outnumber women at least 3 to 1. Most women attend to men or home (and appliances) and are younger (and age faster) than the men they meet.[22]" These patterns promote "viewers' acceptance of more limited life chances, a more limited range of activities, and more rigidly stereotyped images than for the dominant and more fully represented social and dramatic types"[23] – that is, men.

The effects of this symbolic annihilation on women in the audience may be far reaching. Some studies have indicated that "television viewing tends to go with stronger prejudices about women and old people."[24] In addition, Canadian women tend to watch more television than do Canadian men: an average of 27 hours and less than 24 hours per week, respectively.[25] Therefore, women have more opportunity to witness their own exclusion from public life. Where women do appear, they are usually subsidiary to men: the pretty young anchorwoman who defers to the middle-aged male anchorman, the "weathergirl," the secretary or assistant on the drama series, the devoted wife in the situation comedy. Most television series have revolved around one or more central male characters, and women have been either absent or firmly in the background. As one feminist critic points out, "The presentation of women always in relation to men, cheerleaders to the male players, is a male vision, the product of a medium in which male creators have predominated."[26]

The second theme in women's media portrayals is directly related to the public-private dichotomy and the gendered division of labour: "Marriage and parenthood are considered more important to women than to men; the traditional division of labour is shown as typical in marriage."[27] The situation comedies of the 1960s and 1970s usually portrayed women as either happy housewives or discontented spinsters.[28] Advertising also tends to show women in the home, with appliances, cleaning products, and children.[29] Women's magazines and popular movies reinforce the message that women are most fulfilled, and their families are happiest, when Mommy stays home.[30]

The third theme is related to the second: "Employed women are shown in traditionally female occupations, as subordinates to men, with little status or power."[31] Their fitness for paid employment may be subtly questioned: "those few working women included in television plots are symbolically denigrated by being portrayed as incompetent or as inferior to male workers."[32] Where they are not incompetent, working women – especially those with children – tend to be portrayed as unfeminine or even villainous.[33]

The fourth theme underlies the previous three: "Women on television are more passive than men."[34] The clearest example of this is the stock character of "the victim" in action series, whether Westerns, medical dramas, or crime shows. Most victims on television have been women. In fact, "Even though dramatic shows presented more than twice as many male as female characters (a seven to three ratio according to most researchers), females were far more likely to be victimized."[35] The fifth and final theme, to which we will return later, is that "television ignores or distorts the women's movement."[36]

Because media industries have to avoid offending readers or viewers, as argued earlier, it is safe to assume that most people accept these stereotypes of women.[37] It is also safe to assume that these stereotypes reinforce traditional attitudes towards women, even as the reality of women's lives changes. Most mothers cannot afford to stay home with their children (and their appliances); according to Statistics Canada, fully 69 percent of women with children at home were in the labour force in 1991.[38] Yet the images they see on television and in women's magazines tell them that they should be at home, that they belong at home, that they have no place in the world of paid work.

There are a growing number of exceptions, of course. Murphy Brown and Roseanne Connor are examples of strong female characters. Unfortunately, they are offset by weaker and more traditional women. It should also be noted that while Murphy is a very beautiful woman, she is often portrayed as sexually unattractive to men because of her outspokenness and drive. Similarly, Roseanne is allowed to be strong and to express her own opinions because she does not fit into the stereotype of conventional attractiveness; because of her weight, she might as well be a man. For every strong, independent female role model there are a host of dumb blondes, dizzy secretaries, and other traditional characters.

There is nothing wrong with showing a happy marriage, a woman caring for her children, or a contented housewife; these are very valuable aspects of women's experience. What is needed is a more balanced and realistic picture of that experience, so that women can see *all* of their choices and possibilities reflected in their popular culture – not just those preferred by the men who dominate the mass media.

Images of Women in North American Popular Culture

As we have seen, the companies that produce popular culture rely on a limited range of stereotypes to represent complex social realities. Women and minorities have been particularly subject to stereotype. There have been few positive images of women, especially older, black, or successful women, to counterbalance the negative effects of these stereotypes. Despite the gap between these media representations and our daily lives, it is the media images that often seem to be more real. It is those stereotypes, and not our own knowledge about the world, which may shape our expectations of other people, of the roles we expect them to play.[39] In this section we will discuss three sets of stereotypes: the rape myths, the beauty myth, and media images of female politicians and feminists.[40]

The Rape Myths

Since the ancient Greeks, women have been associated with sex, sin, and trouble. Women were considered to be naturally lustful, requiring control by fathers and then husbands if they were to be kept in line. These attitudes have persisted to the present day, reflected in the set of related beliefs that many feminists have labelled the "rape myths."[41] Those beliefs include the following:

1. All women say "no" to sex when they mean "yes," or even "maybe" (or "later," "try harder," and so forth).

2. If a woman wears sexy clothing, or goes to a party or a bar alone, or drinks in public, or takes drugs, she is asking for sex; if she gets raped, she deserves it.

3. A woman who charges a man with rape is lying; she just wants to get back at him for something else, or she wants to deny her own willing participation in a sexual act after she gets caught.

4. "Real rape," as we saw in Chapter 5, involves a stranger attacking a chaste, unattractive woman in broad daylight, beating her savagely as she fights back, and using a weapon to force her to submit. Anything else, particularly rape by a husband, a boyfriend, or a less intimate acquaintance, is not real rape; it does not have to be taken seriously by law enforcement, or by anyone else.[42] This is reflected in the term "date rape," which, while it conveys the fact that most women are raped by men they know, trivializes the offence by treating it as a consensual social encounter that just "got out of hand."

5. All women are greedy for sex all the time; they fantasize about rape, and they never really refuse an offer (which brings us back to the first myth).

Stated this baldly, these rape myths are repellent to most of us. But almost everyone believes some or all of them, in their heart of hearts, whether they care to admit it or not. These attitudes were clearly evident in the reactions to the date rape trials of Mike Tyson and William

Kennedy Smith. People asked why the women involved had accepted rides from their attackers, had gone back to the man's home or hotel room, had not resisted more effectively. The victims were blamed, not the men who were charged with the crimes. The rape myths were reflected in the statements of attorneys, in the media coverage of the trials, in the statements of the defendants' supporters who sought to destroy the reputations of the complainants.

Belief in the rape myths is widespread in our society. A 1985 study of 436 Toronto men revealed some particularly disturbing patterns. Thirty-four percent believed that at least a quarter of reported rapes were "merely invented by women who discover they are pregnant and want to protect their own reputation";[43] 45% said that at least 25% of women reporting rapes are lying because they want revenge against the accused; 11% agreed that "many women have an unconscious wish to be raped, and may then unconsciously set up a situation in which they are likely to be attacked."[44]

A recent American study asked male and female undergraduates whether they agreed or disagreed with a series of statements, all of which reflected rape myths prevalent in our society. The men were consistently more likely to agree with the statements than the women, but substantial minorities of the women also agreed with a number of the statements. Perhaps most shocking was the response to the statement "Women provoke rape by their appearance or behaviour." Fifty-nine percent of the men agreed, and 38 percent of the women.[45] There is an important distinction between the idea that women should look out for their own safety and avoid recklessly endangering themselves, which is equally true for men, and the idea that women should be blamed for "provoking" rape if they wear short skirts or drink alcohol. The willingness of so many young people to blame women for their own victimization is chilling. (For the rest of the results in this survey, see Appendix 1 to this chapter.)

What makes the rape myths particularly dangerous, especially to rape complainants, is their effect on the attitudes of many of the powerful men who make and apply the laws. Susan Estrich, in her book *Real Rape,* quotes a 1952 *Yale Law Review* article that relied on Freud to argue that women enjoy sexual aggression: "A woman's need for sexual satisfaction may lead to the unconscious desire for forceful penetration, the coercion serving neatly to avoid the guilt feeling which might arise after willing participation."[46] She also cites a 1966 *Stanford Law Review* article that included the following claim: "Although a woman may desire sexual intercourse, it is customary for her to say 'no, no, no' (although meaning 'yes, yes, yes'), and to expect the male to be the aggressor."[47] These attitudes can still be found in our courts, police stations, and legislatures, as we saw in Chapter 5.

A 1992 report written by Canadian justice officials at all levels of government argued that the images of women in advertising and other media are directly linked to violence against women: "Aggression against women occurs on a spectrum of activity which moves from ... a simple advertisement for automobiles or beer in association with the barely-clad woman, to murder. The state of mind of the aggressor is only a question of degree."[48] Many others agree that the constant treatment of women as sex objects turns the female body into a commodity, and dehumanizes all women. These advertising images are mirrored in tabloid news shows, drama programming, music videos, and even comedy shows. The problem is not confined to television by any means, but because television images come into our homes with little effort on our part, they are of particular concern to women who want to combat sexism in the media.

Where do men and women learn the rape myths? Where do men learn that it is okay to force a woman into having sex against her will, and women learn that if they report a rape they will be blamed? The answer is that men and women are socialized into the prevailing attitudes of our culture by their families, their education system, and their media of mass communication. Popular culture abounds with images of women initially resisting "seduction" and finally swept away with passion. Popular fiction, mainstream movies, and even television drama convey the message to men that women really mean yes when they say no, so a little physical persistence is all that's needed.

Two examples will illustrate the point. The novel and film of *Gone with the Wind* portray the hero, Rhett Butler, seizing his wife Scarlett and carrying her up the stairs to the bedroom, while she struggles and protests all the way. The next morning Scarlett is shown in a blissful state of sexual fulfilment. The popular television series "Moonlighting" revolved around the sexual tension between the two lead characters, David and Maddie. After a few seasons of verbal sparring, they finally consummated their volatile relationship after a violent argument. She slapped him hard in the face; he grabbed her arm, bruising her; and in the twinkling of an eye they were rolling on the floor in ecstasy. This equation of violence with sexual arousal, for both men and women, sends potentially destructive messages to readers and viewers.

These messages can make a particularly powerful impression on children. There is a growing body of evidence that sex-role stereotypes in television programming influence children more profoundly than the reality that they see around them.[49] Several studies have found that "the amount of time children devote to watching television has been found to correlate strongly and positively with their acceptance of traditional gender stereotypes, beginning as early as kindergarten age."[50] The rape myths are absorbed by children along with the rest of the gender stereotypes embodied in our popular culture.

It is little wonder, then, that so many young people have bought into these myths. A study of fourteen-to-eighteen-year-olds at UCLA found that more than half of the boys, and almost as many girls, believed that "it was okay for a man to rape a woman if he was sexually aroused by her."[51] Several studies have found that such attitudes are strongly associated, in young men, with a willingness to actually commit acts of sexual coercion.[52] It is clear that the rape myths are a serious problem in our society, and an ugly flaw in our popular culture.

The Beauty Myth

In her 1991 book *The Beauty Myth,* Naomi Wolf argues that women are prevented from reaching their full human potential by a culture fixated on female appearance. Images of teenaged models, painstakingly made up, posed, airbrushed and trimmed with scissors to look slimmer, are held up to adult women as the standard they must try to emulate. The inevitable failure makes women feel that *they* are failures, which reduces their self-esteem. This, in turn, leads them to regard their disadvantaged social and economic position as their own fault, and to passively accept it instead of fighting to change it. This epidemic of low self-esteem among women is necessary to an economy that depends on acquiescent, low-paid female workers and malleable female consumers; to a male elite that is threatened by self-assured, ambitious, hard-working women; and, in particular, to the industries based on female insecurities, including cosmetics, plastic surgery, fashion, and the diet moguls.

The beauty myth is spread through the mass media, especially the women's magazines that depend on cosmetics companies for their advertising revenues. Women's magazines show women what they must look like in order to be successful, and tell them what they must do in order to look like that. Although the editorial content of the magazines often encourages women to strive for individual achievement, the feminist message is undercut by the pages and pages of glossy advertisements for perfume, makeup, clothing, and skin-care products.[53] The message is that women can only fulfill their ambitions in school or work if they have perfect skin and hair, a fashionable wardrobe, and the type of body constantly portrayed as the ideal. As Wolf observes, "we as women are trained to see ourselves as cheap imitations of fashion photographs, rather than seeing fashion photographs as cheap imitations of women."[54]

This argument sounds suspiciously like a conspiracy theory, but Wolf argues that this is too simplistic an interpretation: "Societies tell themselves necessary fictions in the same way that individuals and families do."[55] The results of those fictions include eating disorders, which afflict millions of women in North America; the growing resort to cosmetic surgery, including facelifts and liposuction, which Wolf condemns as grotesque forms of self-mutilation; and a decline in women's sexual pleasure, related to their extreme self-consciousness in intimate situations.

Wolf's book is provocative and thought-provoking, although some of her conclusions may strike some readers as overdrawn. There is no question that images of women in the mass media are uniformly young, healthy, "beautiful" (according to the prevailing cultural standard), slender, and mostly white. It is clear that such images can have a damaging effect on the self-esteem of women who compare themselves to the glossy picture. The real question is *why* women compare themselves to the cultural ideal of beauty, when most men appear to be immune from such anxieties.

Wolf's answer is that because men have controlled the economy, advertising, and popular culture, and because men like to look at women, images of women have dominated. In turn, women have been susceptible to these images because they have no other role models to emulate in the public sphere, and no other mass culture of their own; in addition, women (especially middle-class women) have been isolated from each other and given no other goal to achieve except that of "beauty."[56] But these cultural factors have changed dramatically in the past thirty years, with more women leaving the suburbs and going to the office, and with more women becoming role models in politics and other fields. How then do we explain the continuing (and, Wolf argues, the growing) impact of "beauty" images on women, if not by a conspiracy theory?

Despite its problems, Wolf's book makes a major contribution to our thinking about the effects of popular culture on women's self-esteem. Her argument also draws our attention to the absence of other images of women – something other than the young, perfect, self-absorbed, artificial "beauties" who dominate the magazines and the television. Other feminist critics agree that "it is not only how we are portrayed, but also how we are *not* portrayed which is significant."[57] They point to the lack of positive images of women: "Images of women being strong and powerful; demanding their rights; forming close, loving relationships with one another; images of women in all our diversity, each as beautiful and important as the next."[58]

Media Portrayals of Female Politicians and the Women's Movement

Women who have entered the public sphere in recent years have had a paradoxical relationship with the mass media. On the one hand, they have often attracted a great deal of news coverage because of their novelty. It is possible, for example, that the six women running for the United States Senate in 1992 earned as much coverage as all of the male candidates put together. It is also more newsworthy when a woman achieves a high position in business, in culture, or in the media itself than when a man does the same. The media also helped to give the women's movement a boost in the late 1960s and early 1970s, especially in Canada. By reporting on the public hearings of the Royal Commission on the Status of Women, the media turned the commission into a three-year consciousness-raising exercise. Women read the papers and watched television, and discovered that other women felt the same as they did. The women's movement was assisted immeasurably as a result.

On the other hand, the character of that intense coverage is often harmful. Women find themselves reflected in the media in different ways from men. Their appearance, their private lives, their qualifications, their personalities – all of these attract much closer scrutiny from the media than do the equivalent features of men in the public eye. There have been a host of examples: the controversy over Hillary Rodham Clinton; the exposure of the dubious financial dealings of the husband of U.S. vice-presidential candidate Geraldine Ferraro in 1984; the description of what Audrey McLaughlin wore to give her first speech in the Commons as NDP leader. Women are still framed within gender-based narratives that glorify traditional roles (particularly the housewife and mother), and subtly derogate women in non-traditional roles. In particular, women who are publicly identified as feminists face caricature at best and open hostility at worst. Finally, the character of the women's movement itself has been distorted to some extent by the media coverage it has received.

A recent Canadian study examines the coverage of Canadian female politicians in the news media. It points out that women are largely invisible on television, both in drama and on news programs; in Canadian television in 1989, "77% of news readers, 91% of experts and 70% of voice-overs [were] male."[59] This invisibility extends to news content, even where high-profile female politicians are concerned. Where women politicians do appear in news coverage, they are confined to a limited set of narrative frames; they are portrayed in stereotypical ways, which emphasize their gender over other characteristics.

Those stereotypes have changed in the past quarter-century. Before 1970 news reporters portrayed female politicians as oddities. They emphasized the women's gender-related qualities, forcing them into traditional female roles such as "wife" and "spinster," to downplay the fact that these women were directly challenging the public-private dichotomy and the gendered division of labour. This was also the period when the homemaker was glorified in prime-time television comedy and drama, and single career women were treated as either dangerous or pitiable.[60] After 1970 the emphasis shifted from women's traditional social roles to an emphasis on power: from "spinster" to "superwoman," from "wife of" to "one of the boys." But the traditional attitudes towards women persisted in news coverage, despite the growing influence of feminist ideas.[61]

Despite the shift in stereotypes, "the existing stereotypical narrative conventions treat political women and men very differently."[62] In particular, the media's narrative frames for female politicians "tend to ignore the substance of a female incumbent's speeches in favour of her personal characteristics (looks, dress, hair)"[63] and "use 'feminism' to denote a negative personal characteristic, and thus erase the group dimensions of this diversified social movement."[64] The disapproval of women who flout the traditional roles is more subtle now than it was in the 1960s, but it continues nonetheless; indeed, there is evidence of a growing media backlash against feminism (see Chapter 4).

In addition, the performance of male and female politicians is judged differently by the media: "Women have to live up to a considerably higher standard of excellence than do men."[65] In addition, "Women politicians have to live up to a moral code of sexual abstention not imposed on men."[66]

We have seen that the appearance of public women is emphasized, often to the detriment of their competence. A related issue is the media stereotype of feminists as unattractive, even dangerous women who have no social or sexual credibility. Wolf argues that "the caricature of the Ugly Feminist was resurrected to dog the steps of the women's movement ... That resurrected caricature, which sought to punish women for their public acts by going after their private sense of self, became the paradigm for new limits placed on aspiring women everywhere."[67] As Wolf points out, "If the public woman is stigmatized as too 'pretty', she's a threat, a rival — or simply not serious; if derided as too 'ugly', one risks tarring oneself with the same brush by identifying oneself with her agenda."[68]

According to some critics, the media's portrayal of the women's movement is more than just a reflection of the beauty myth. It is "less a reflection of, than a counterattack on, the women's movement as a social force for structural change."[69] Instead of reflecting and celebrating the changes in women's lives, these critics argue, "the media appear to be cultivating resistance and preparing for a last-ditch defense. And the gap between actual social reality and what is portrayed in the media is widening."[70]

In a less direct way, the women's movement as a whole has suffered from its media image. Media critic Todd Gitlin has argued that protest movements are often transformed by their efforts to attain news coverage of their activities and goals. He believes that in the television age, "political movements feel called upon to rely on large-scale communications in order to *matter*, to say who they are and what they intend to publics they want to sway."[71] But by trying to use the media to get out their messages, social movements "become 'newsworthy' only by submitting to the implicit rules of newsmaking, by conforming to journalistic notions ... of what a 'story' is, what an 'event' is, what a 'protest' is."[72]

In the process, protest movements may change their tactics; they may find themselves vilified because of a media image that bears little resemblance to the truth; and they often find their power structures altered beyond recognition. The media often seize on a particularly photogenic or articulate member of the movement and designate him or her as the spokesperson, thus creating a powerful celebrity within a formerly egalitarian movement. According to Gitlin, "what defines a movement as 'good copy' is often flamboyance, the presence of a media-certified celebrity-leader, and usually a certain fit with whatever frame the newsmakers have construed to be 'the story' at a given time; but these qualities of the image are not what movements intend to be their projects, their identities, their goals."[73]

Although Gitlin was describing the experiences of the American student movement in the 1960s, his analysis applies equally well to the women's movement. The media seized on a few high-profile events, such as the picket of the 1970 Miss America pageant, and created a stereotype of "bra-burning" angry feminists. They also seized on a few personalities, and made them the embodiment of a much more broadly based movement. In particular, the media made stars of Gloria Steinem and Germaine Greer, both young, good-looking, and witty. The celebrity status of these two women caused great dissension within the American women's movement, and provoked splits that damaged the credibility and effectiveness of the movement's leadership.[74] Feminist process, as we saw in Chapter 2, rejects the hierarchy of leaders and "stars." But in the 1990s a movement without a single, readily identifiable television star is often a movement that fails to get off the ground.

Images of Women and Women's Acceptance of Patriarchy

We have discussed negative media images of women, including the rape myths, the beauty myth, and the stereotyped treatment of women in public life. We will conclude this section by discussing the cumulative effects of these media images on Canadian women. These effects include: women's reluctance to publicly associate themselves with feminism and the women's movement; guilt among women who work outside the home over the glorification of the housewife image; and low self-esteem arising from the rape myths and the beauty myth.

The first effect is the tendency of many women to shy away from the women's movement. Many young women, in particular, belong to the "I'm not a feminist, but ..." category. They do not wish to associate themselves with the image of feminists that the media has given them — loud, ugly, man-hating, freakish — despite their acceptance of many of the central ideas and goals of feminism. They are afraid that if they publicly avow an attachment to feminism, they will be seen in the same way as the caricatures of the women's movement on television. Older women perceive the women's movement as too radical, too angry, to represent them. They have been told that feminists hate marriage and families, that feminists believe that all housewives are lazy parasites. It is no wonder that they reject feminism, even though what they are rejecting is an extreme and misleading caricature and not feminism itself.

The guilt experienced by many working mothers is a second problem caused by media images. A 1992 newspaper story described how "a rosy celebration of the 1950s-style mom who polished floors, kissed scraped knees and had a pot roast on the table by 6 p.m. is surfacing on several fronts across Canada, spurred by shifting social attitudes, advertising campaigns and some government policies."[75] The result of this media nostalgia was "a guilt so intense it has wrapped many working mothers in a winding sheet of anxiety."[76] Forget the fact that the images weren't real, or that they represented only the minority of women who could afford to stay home and still maintain their middle-class lifestyle. The power of the media is such that its most misleading images can become the standard against which we measure ourselves, and we punish ourselves for failing to live up to them.

Working mothers are caught between the economic pressure to earn money and the social and emotional pressure to stay home with the children. Such anachronistic and unrealistic images in the media, whether in advertising, entertainment, or news, impose even greater strains on women. It is interesting that despite women's massive entry into the public sphere in recent years, the gendered division of labour remains firmly intact. Women, not men, are portrayed in the rosy new scenes of domestic bliss; women, not men, are seeking professional help to deal with the guilt of spending their days away from their children.[77]

The third damaging effect of media images on women is low self-esteem. As we have seen, women who fail to measure up to the prevailing cultural standard of physical attractiveness may feel unworthy of a better life and alienated from other women. Even worse, we have seen that many women, even young women born during the second wave of feminism, believe the rape myths. They believe that sexual attacks on women are their own fault, not the fault of insensitive men or misleading media messages about women's sexuality.

When we compare the rape myths and the beauty myth, we can see the bind in which today's young women are trapped. On the one hand, they are pressured to fit a specific standard of beauty; if they fail, they will be considered sexually unattractive. On the other hand, if they encounter unwanted sexual attention, it is their own fault for trying to look attractive. Catharine MacKinnon has discussed this dilemma in the context of workplace sexual harassment, noting that women in many jobs are forced to "ask for it" – required to look attractive as a condition of employment – and then punished if they refuse to submit to the "natural" sexual aggression of their male employers.[78] But the dilemma traps all women, young or old, "beautiful" or not. It forces us to make a choice between beauty and brains, sexual identity or an image of competence. It crams women, in all their human variety, into a tiny set of accepted images and punishes those who cannot or will not fit; those who do fit are vulnerable to even worse types of punishment.

Women as Media Personnel

As we have seen in the chapter on women in the economy, women are under-paid and concentrated in powerless jobs. This pattern holds true for women in the cultural industries. One overview of the research on women workers in the mass media reached the following conclusions:

1. "Men are more likely than women to be media managers."

2. "Men in media have higher salaries than women."

3. "Men in media are more likely than women to receive promotions."

4. "Desirable assignments are primarily given to men."

5. "Sexist beliefs of male managers work against the acceptance of women in the media."[79]

In this section we will briefly discuss these issues.

The number of women in media management has grown rapidly in recent years, but women are still under-represented in key decision-making positions.[80] In Canada in 1991, "women made up only 9 percent of editors-in-chief and 6 percent of managing editors in the Canadian Daily Newspapers Publishers Association."[81] Thirty-three people were promoted to senior management jobs on newspapers in 1989, none of them female. "The situation is no better in television and film production, where, according to an American study by the National Commission on Working Women, 'women made up 15 percent of producers, 25 percent of writers and 9 percent of directors of shows aired in 1990."[82]

It is sometimes suggested that women's exclusion from these higher-level positions contributes to the negative portrayal of women in media content. Studies of influences on media content have found no evidence that journalists bring their own personal backgrounds to bear on their work: "although women and minorities are gaining ground in communication careers, many people believe that the media's practices and routines effectively suppress effects on content due to gender or ethnicity."[83] There may be a greater impact made by women in entertainment programming, but the evidence here is primarily anecdotal. It should be noted that the two strong female characters mentioned earlier, Murphy Brown and Roseanne Connor, were both created by women: producer Diane English and comedian Roseanne, respectively. Women also created the shows "Designing Women" and "Golden Girls," which focused on strong female characters.

The second point, the wage gap between men and women in media, is hardly surprising given the wage gap in all other occupations. There is evidence that the gap is narrowing, but it remains significant.[84] The third claim, the greater likelihood of promotions for male journalists, is borne out by the discrepancy between the proportion of women at lower levels of journalism – roughly one-third by 1990[85] – and the smaller proportion of women at higher levels, as discussed above. The fourth claim, that men are given the best assignments in news coverage, follows naturally from the previous three points, as does the fifth claim, that women in media face open sexism from male media managers.

The conclusion must be that women in the media face the same problems as women everywhere else in the workforce. There are a growing number of women who have broken through the barriers, and been rewarded with considerable commercial success; in the early 1990s "Roseanne" and "Murphy Brown" were two of the most successful series on television. Although we lack firm proof that the exclusion of women from positions of power in the media has led to the negative reflections of women discussed earlier in the chapter, we can only hope that as more women rise to the top, we will see a more accurate and inspiring reflection of women's experience in our popular culture.

Conclusion

This chapter has provided a brief overview of some issues concerning women in the Canadian mass media and popular culture. Its purpose has been to underline the importance of media and culture in shaping women's self-image and in portraying women's lives. We have discussed the following key points:

1.   Canadian women are not well served by their media, or by the media products that flood in from the United States. Our popular culture is full of inaccurate and potentially harmful images of women, with few positive images to counterbalance them.

2.   The most dangerous of the stereotypes that populate our mass media and popular culture are the rape myths and the beauty myth. Given the constant messages that all women are sexually available, and that all women must be slender and beautiful in order to succeed, we should not be surprised that rape and eating disorders are endemic to our society.

3.   Women who work in the media are subject to the same barriers and injustices faced by other women in the workplace, with the added pressure to present a glamorous, youthful image.

4.   Women in the public sphere, particularly women who challenge the patriarchal status quo, are vilified or ridiculed by the mass media.

The political implications of these issues have been touched on at various points in the chapter. Two Canadian feminist scholars have argued that "the veracity and accuracy with which the media represent women politicians are inextricably linked to the effectiveness with which political women can shape their society."[86] Readers should bear this point in mind as we turn to Part III of this book, "Women in Canadian Political Institutions."

Appendix: Results of the Barnett/Feild Study of Rape-Related Attitudes

Statement	% Men Agreed	% Women Agreed
In most cases, when a woman was raped, she was asking for it.	17	4
If a woman is going to be raped, she might as well relax and enjoy it.	17	7
Women provoke rape by their appearance or behaviour.	59	38
A woman should be responsible for preventing her victimization in a rape.	41	27
The degree of a woman's resistance should be the major factor in determining if a rape has occurred.	40	18
In order to protect the male, it should be difficult to prove that a rape has occurred.	40	15
It would do some women some good to get raped.	32	8

Source: Warshaw, 46.

Notes

1   Shoemaker and Reese, *Mediating the Message,* 29.

2   Ibid., 29.

3   For an introduction to these issues, see Graber, *Media Power in Politics.*

4   See Vipond, *The Mass Media in Canada,* 71.

5   Ibid., 90.

6   Ibid., 53.

7   Ibid., 59.

8   Ibid., 60.

9   Ibid., 53.

10   Glover, *The Sociology of the Mass Media,* 4.

11   Ibid., 5–7.

12   Ibid., 8.

13   Denis McQuail, "The Influence and Effects of Mass Media," in Graber, *Media Power in Politics,* 28.

14   Maxwell E. McCombs and Donald L. Shaw, "The Agenda-Setting Function of the Press" in Graber, *Media Power in Politics,* 75.

15   McQuail, 28.

16   Glover, 10.

17   Ibid.

18   Robinson and Saint-Jean, "Women Politicians and Their Media Coverage," 136.

19   Liesbet van Zoonen, "Feminist Perspectives on the Media," 35.

20   Gallagher, *Unequal Opportunities,* 38.

21   Gaye Tuchman, "Introduction: The Symbolic Annihilation of Women by the Mass Media," in Tuchman, Daniels, and Benet, *Hearth and Home,* 7.

22   Gerbner et al., "Charting the Mainstream: TV's Contributions to Political Orientations," in Graber, *Media Power in Politics,* 139.

23   Ibid.

24   Ibid., 138.

25   Vipond, 53.

26   Meehan, *Ladies of the Evening,* 113.

27   Gallagher, 39.

28   See Meehan, chap. 4.

29   Butler and Paisley, *Women and the Mass Media,* 93.

30   Glover, 30; Weibel, *Mirror, Mirror,* Introduction.

31   Gallagher, 39.

32   Tuchman, 13.

33   Ibid.

34   Gallagher, 40.

35   Meehan, 64.

36   Gallagher, 41.

37   Sochen, *Enduring Values, xv.*

38   Alanna Mitchell, "Working women gaining equality," *Globe and Mail,* March 3, 1993.

39   See Butler and Paisley, 306; Graber; Meehan, chap. 13.

40   There are a host of other media stereotypes that may harm women, including ageism and racism, but those have not been included here, not because they are less important, but because they are beyond the scope of this chapter.

41   See Warshaw, *I Never Called It Rape;* Scully, *Understanding Sexual Violence.*

42   See Estrich, *Real Rape.*

43   Marshall and Barrett, *Criminal Neglect,* 110.

44   Ibid.

45   Warshaw, 46.

46   Estrich, 39.

47   Ibid., 38.

48   Canada, Department of Justice, *Gender Equality in the Canadian Justice System,* quoted in Sallot, "Report links ads to violence against women."

49   Kath Davies, Julienne Dickey, and Teresa Stratford, "Introduction," in Davies, Dickey, and Stratford, *Out of Focus,* 4.

50   B.W. Robinson and E.D. Salamon, "Gender Role Socialization: A Review of the Literature," in Salamon and Robinson, *Gender Roles,* 127.

51   Wolf, *The Beauty Myth,* 167.

52   Scully, 50–53.

53   Wolf, 69.

54   Ibid., 105.

55   Ibid., 17.

56   Ibid., chap. 2.

57   Davies, Dickey, and Stratford, 5.

58   Ibid.

59   Robinson and Saint-Jean, 133.

60   See Meehan; Butler and Paisley; Tuchman, Daniels, and Benet.

61   Robinson and Saint-Jean, 131.

62   Ibid., 151.

63   Ibid.

64   Ibid., 152.

65   Ibid.

66   Ibid.

67   Wolf, 18–19.

68   Ibid., 69.

69   George Gerbner, "The Dynamics of Cultural Resistance," in Tuchman, Daniels, and Benet, 50.

70   Ibid.

71   Todd Gitlin, "Making Protest Movements Newsworthy," in Graber, *Media Power in Politics*, 276.

72   Ibid.

73   Ibid., 277.

74   See Cohen, *The Sisterhood*.

75   Mitchell, "June Cleaver–style moms."

76   Ibid.

77   Ibid.

78   MacKinnon, *Sexual Harassment of Working Women*, 21–22.

79   Butler and Paisley, 230.

80   Gallagher, 105.

81   Robinson and Saint-Jean, 142.

82   Ibid.

83   Shoemaker and Reese, 80.

84   Ibid., 56.

85   Ibid.

86   Robinson and Saint-Jean, 152.

References and Further Reading

Barthel, Diane. *Putting on Appearances: Gender and Advertising.* Philadelphia: Temple University Press, 1988.

Butler, Matilda, and William Paisley. *Women and the Mass Media: Sourcebook for Research and Action.* New York: Human Sciences Press, 1980.

Cantor, Muriel G. "The Politics of Culture: Feminism and the Media." In Arthur Asa Berger, ed., *Political Culture and Public Opinion.* New Brunswick, NJ: Transaction, 1989.

Chrisman, Robert, and Robert L. Allen, eds. *Court of Appeal: The Black Community Speaks Out on the Racial and Sexual Politics of Clarence Thomas vs. Anita Hill.* New York: Ballantine, 1992.

Cohen, Marcia. *The Sisterhood: The Inside Story of the Women's Movement and the Leaders Who Made It Happen.* New York: Fawcett Columbine, 1988.

Cole, Susan G. "Gender, Sex, Image, and Transformation in Popular Music." In Geraldine Finn, ed., *Limited Edition: Voices of Women, Voices of Feminism.* Halifax: Fernwood, 1993.

Cole, Susan G. *Pornography and the Sex Crisis.* Toronto: Amanita, 1989.

Coverdale Sumrall, Amber, and Dena Taylor, eds. *Sexual Harassment: Women Speak Out.* Freedom, CA: Crossing Press, 1992.

Creedon, Pamela J., ed. *Women in Mass Communication: Challenging Gender Values.* Newbury Park: Sage, 1989.

Davies, Kath, Julienne Dickey, and Teresa Stratford, eds. *Out of Focus: Writings on Women and the Media.* London: Women's Press, 1987.

Estrich, Susan. *Real Rape.* Cambridge, MA: Harvard University Press, 1987.

Gallagher, Margaret. *Unequal Opportunities: The Case of Women and the Media.* New York: UNESCO, 1981.

Glover, David. *The Sociology of the Mass Media.* Ormskirk, UK: Causeway Press, 1984.

Graber, Doris A., ed. *Media Power in Politics.* 2nd ed. Washington, DC: CQ Press, 1988.

Ingham, John N., ed. *Sex 'n' Drugs 'n' Rock 'n' Roll: American Popular Culture since 1945.* Toronto: Canadian Scholars' Press, 1988.

Lewis, Lisa A. *Gender Politics and MTV: Voicing the Difference.* Philadelphia: Temple University Press, 1990.

MacKinnon, Catharine A. *Sexual Harassment of Working Women.* New Haven: Yale University Press, 1979.

Marshall, William, and Sylvia Barrett. *Criminal Neglect: Why Sex Offenders Go Free.* Toronto: McClelland–Bantam, 1992.

Marshment, Margaret. "The Picture is Political: Representation of Women in Contemporary Popular Culture." In Diane Richardson and Victoria Robinson, eds., *Thinking Feminist: Key Concepts in Women's Studies.* New York: Guilford, 1993.

Meehan, Diana M. *Ladies of the Evening: Women Characters of Prime-Time Television.* London: Scarecrow Press, 1983.

Mills, Kay. *A Place in the News: From the Women's Pages to the Front Page.* Rev. ed. New York: Columbia University Press, 1990.

Mitchell, Alanna. "June Cleaver–style moms back in fashion." *Globe and Mail,* April 20, 1992.

———. "Working women gaining equality: Labour force total hits 45%." *Globe and Mail,* March 3, 1993.

Robinson, Gertrude, and Armande Saint-Jean. "Women Politicians and Their Media Coverage: A Generational Analysis." In Kathy Megyery, ed.,

Women in Canadian Politics: Toward Equity in Representation. Vol. 6 of the collected research studies for the Royal Commission on Electoral Reform and Party Financing (Toronto: Dundurn, 1991).

Salamon, E.D., and B.W. Robinson, eds. *Gender Roles: Doing What Comes Naturally?* Scarborough: Nelson Canada, 1991.

Sallot, Jeff. "Report links ads to violence against women." *Globe and Mail,* July 6, 1993.

Scully, Diana. *Understanding Sexual Violence: A Study of Convicted Rapists.* Boston: Unwin Hyman, 1990.

Shoemaker, Pamela J., and Stephen D. Reese. *Mediating the Message: Theories of Influences on Mass Media Content.* New York: Longman, 1991.

Sochen, June. *Enduring Values: Women in Popular Culture.* New York: Praeger, 1987.

Tuchman, Gaye, et al., eds. *Hearth and Home: Images of Women in the Mass Media.* New York: Oxford University Press, 1978.

van Zoonen, Liesbet. "Feminist Perspectives on the Media." In James Curran and Michael Gurevitch, eds., *Mass Media and Society.* New York: Edward Arnold, 1991.

Vipond, Mary. *The Mass Media in Canada.* Toronto: Lorimer, 1989.

Warshaw, Robin. *I Never Called It Rape: The Ms. Report on Recognizing, Fighting and Surviving Date and Acquaintance Rape.* New York: Harper & Row, 1988.

Weibel, Kathryn. *Mirror, Mirror: Images of Women Reflected in Popular Culture.* New York: Anchor, 1977.

Wolf, Naomi. *The Beauty Myth.* Toronto: Vintage, 1991.

Part 3: Women in the Canadian

Political System

EVERY WESTERN COUNTRY IS CONFRONTED BY A POLITI-cal paradox. On the one hand, women constitute a small majority of the electorate. In theory, therefore, women should control the political system through their votes. After all, the idea of democracy rests on the will of the majority. On the other hand, women constitute less than half—in most cases, less than a quarter—of all MPS and a smaller minority in national executives.

How do we explain the paradox of a politically disadvantaged majority? In a country such as South Africa, where a majority of the population was (until recently) forbidden to vote or run for office, the answer is easy. But at present, no such legal obstacles confront the women of Western countries (see Appendix 1, Chapter 8). The barriers to women in politics are unofficial and often invisible. They lie both inside and outside the political system: in the political parties, in the structures and traditions of the political institutions, in the ideologies of the public-private dichotomy and the gendered division of labour, and in the socio-economic disadvantages and family structures that flow from those ideologies.

Part 3 describes the place of women in the Canadian political system and explains their under-representation in the political system that so powerfully affects their lives. A "political system" is defined as the set of distinct institutions that work together to govern a specific territory—also called "the state"—and those institutions that link the government to the people.

The state consists of the Parliament of Canada, the Cabinet, the federal public service, the judiciary, the military, and the police. It is linked to the Canadian people by the national political parties, interest groups, and the media. All of these entities collectively make up the Canadian political system. We use the word "system" to suggest that while each is a separate and distinct entity, it must work interdependently with the others like the organs of the digestive system. The Parliament depends on political parties for its election and its organization. The Cabinet depends on the House of Commons to pass legislation, and on the media (and public opinion polling) to tell it whether its legislation is popular. In this book we will focus on the national level of government. This does not mean that the provinces and territories are unimportant. It simply means that one cannot cover all levels of government in a single book of this nature.

For those not majoring in political science, a brief introduction to Canadian government may be helpful. There are three branches in the Canadian federal state: legislative, executive, and judicial. The national legislature is made up of the House of Commons, which is elected by Canadian citizens at least once every five years, and the Senate, which is appointed by the prime minister. The prime minister is the leader of the largest party in the House of Commons; the second largest party is the Official Opposition. To become law, a bill must pass through several stages, including intensive scrutiny by a committee made up of Members of Parliament (MPs). Both houses of Parliament must approve a bill before it can take effect.

Most laws are proposed by a member of the Cabinet, which straddles the legislative and executive branches. All Cabinet ministers must also be legislators; most are MPs, with one or two senators. The members of the

Cabinet are all from the governing party, and all are appointed by the prime minister. Each Cabinet minister is responsible for an individual department of the federal government: Justice, Finance, Agriculture, and so forth. The Cabinet is a very powerful collective unit; it controls the executive and, because of party discipline in the Commons, it controls the legislative branch as well.

The judicial branch includes the Canadian courts, the most senior of which is the Supreme Court of Canada. It is the final court of appeal. Since the proclamation of the Canadian Charter of Rights and Freedoms in 1982, the Supreme Court of Canada has become a major player in the making of Canadian public policy (see Chapter 5). It has the power to strike down any laws that conflict with the constitution, either by violating a Charter right (e.g., the *Morgentaler* case) or by infringing on the division of powers between the federal and provincial governments (e.g., the striking down of the Nova Scotia Medical Services Act in 1993).

We will begin Part 3 with a discussion of women's patterns of political participation. Chapter 7 examines the ways in which women are socialized into the political culture and the political system, and the ways in which women's grassroots political participation differs from that of men. Chapter 8 discusses the barriers women face when they try to advance from the mass level to the elite level of politics, via the political parties. Chapter 9 looks at the experiences of women when they reach the elite levels of politics, and at the reasons why so few actually make it.

Chapter 7: Women's Participation in Politics

Chapter Summary

Chapter 7 is an introduction to the study of women's political participation. It discusses the ways in which women's patterns of political involvement differ from those of men. The two patterns are similar in many ways. While most Canadians vote in elections, few pursue other activities such as joining a political party or running for office. Women are even less likely than men to become involved in the "conventional" politics of parties and interest groups. They are more likely to participate in "unconventional" politics, such as local neighbourhood groups or single-issue protest movements. As a result, feminist scholars have argued that the traditional conception of "politics" does not accurately reflect women's experiences. A broader definition of "politics" is needed to capture women's orientation to the political system. Women also differ from men in many political attitudes, and face greater barriers to their participation in the higher levels of political life. We will discuss those barriers in this chapter.

Chapter Outline

- Major Themes in Women's Political Participation
- Women and Unconventional Politics
- The Political Beliefs of Women
- From Mass to Elite Politics: The Barriers for Women
  The Gendered Division of Labour in the Home
  The Gendered Division of Labour in the Workplace
  The Public-Private Dichotomy
  The Parties as Gatekeepers
  The Old Boys' Club
- Conclusion

Major Themes in Women's Political Participation

In this chapter we will discuss some broad themes relating to the political participation of women. In many ways the pattern of women's participation resembles that of men's, but there are some significant differences. We will focus on three principal themes:

1. Women participate less in "conventional" politics than men do, but they are more likely to participate in "unconventional" political activity. Many women are more comfortable in informal interest organizations than in large, institutionalized structures such as labour unions and political parties.

2. Women have a tendency to be less interested in politics than men, and to display lower levels of political efficacy (self-confidence). This is due partly to role socialization and partly to the conflicting demands of work and family.

3. Women participate equally with men at the mass level of politics, but they are dramatically under-represented at the elite level of politics.

In this chapter we will try to explain these differences in women's political activity. We will also discuss what they tell us about the Canadian political system and its treatment of women. The next two chapters discuss women's under-representation in elite politics in some depth;

this chapter begins that discussion with a broad overview of the reasons why women cannot, or will not, participate in elite politics as much as men do.

Women and Unconventional Politics

Studies around the world have shown that women who participate in political activity often choose unconventional forms of politics: local neighbourhood pressure groups, ad hoc issue movements, peace and environmental movements, protest activities, and the women's movement.[1] Black women and university-educated white women are the most likely to participate in such political activities.[2] Men, by contrast, are more likely to participate in conventional political organizations such as political parties, interest groups, and unions. This section will describe this pattern and try to find explanations for it.

It is impossible to find exact statistics for the ephemeral and informal groups in which women operate. Traditional political science has not considered this participation to be "political," because our understanding of "politics" has been confined to the conventional institutions and practices of the state (see Chapter 1). But if we are to understand women's political activity, we must recognize the importance of local volunteer associations, from the Junior League to the neighbourhood recycling pressure group. Students of such groups divide them into two categories, based on the purpose of their formation. *Instrumental* groups seek to influence public officials, while the purpose of *expressive* groups is more social than political. Women tend to be more numerous and more prominent in expressive groups,[3] but have played a leading role in both types of activity.

Unconventional political groups can also be distinguished on the basis of their organization, and their relationship to the state. The two principal categories are *ad hoc* groups and *protest* groups. Vicky Randall defines ad hoc politics as follows: "participation in political campaigns that are relatively short-lived, throwing up makeshift organizations and tending to rely on direct tactics such as pickets, squats [sit-ins] and self-help projects. Typically, too, they focus on issues of local and community concern."[4] Other tactics include letter-writing campaigns and media stunts to attract attention. Examples of ad hoc activities include picketing an abortion clinic, organizing a group of women to set up a women's shelter or a rape crisis centre, a Take Back the Night march, or a vigil on a university campus to commemorate December 6.

Women's ad hoc political activity can be traced back several centuries. If political science had not defined "politics" so narrowly, women would have been highly visible participants in politics from the beginnings of the discipline. In the United States, Canada, and Britain, volunteer women's groups created the social welfare agencies that were later taken over by the state. Women were active in the union movement, despite opposition from some male labour leaders. Women were instrumental in the anti-slavery and temperance movements in Britain and the United States, which laid the foundations for the suffrage movement of the late nineteenth and early twentieth centuries. The popular myth that women are "apolitical" reveals both the limits of our understanding of political activity and our tendency to equate politics with masculine activity. By including women's ad hoc groups under the rubric of "politics," we can see clearly that politics can and does go on without any men in the room.

Both men and women became increasingly involved in ad hoc political activity in the 1960s, as opposition to the Vietnam war grew in the United States, Canada, and Britain. In the 1970s ad hoc politics spread to Western Europe, via the peace, environmental, and anti-nuclear movements. It is often argued that the boom in ad hoc political activity is partly the result of the rise in education levels in the West after the Second World War, coupled with a long period of peace and prosperity that shifted the concern of the younger generations from physical and material security to the quality of life.[5] Whatever the reasons, ad hoc political activity has become commonplace in all Western societies.

At least one feature of ad hoc politics has remained constant: the preponderance of women in local and community-based groups. American and British studies of these groups reveal the characteristics of the women who participated in the 1970s and 1980s.[6] Typically, they were over forty years of age, married, with children of high-school age or older. They did not identify with feminism. They were involved in local child-care initiatives, movements for school reform, and local groups fighting a declining quality of life in their neighbourhoods. They were motivated by concern for their communities and their children.

It is worth noting that most of the women involved in ad hoc activities did not work for pay, so that they had the time to become involved in local community projects. Given the massive shift of women into the paid workforce in recent years, it is probable that these local groups are suffering a loss of "woman-power." It is also interesting that these women were working not on their own behalf, but for the benefit of their neighbourhoods and their children. It is sometimes suggested that women view such volunteer activity not as a movement away from their domestic responsibilities, but as an extension of them.[7] It may be equally accurate to suggest that just as many women and men are attracted to political parties by the social milieu, women join ad hoc groups partly to make friends. Those friendships can develop into personal networks that, in time, can boost women into positions of prominence in the community.

The other type of unconventional political activity is *protest* activity. The distinguishing feature of protest movements is that they are directed against the political authorities. They may be violent, and they are usually against the law.[8] Whereas an ad hoc movement may try to work with the local authorities to get resources to build a women's shelter, a protest movement might try to embarrass the government for its refusal to give money. Tactics include demonstrations, such as the picketing of the Toronto Morgentaler clinic; illegal sit-ins, like the occupation of Greenham Common air base by British women; and terrorism, exemplified by the IRA.

Women have been well represented in protest movements over the years, although usually in less violent activities.[9] Women were particularly active in the protests that preceded the American Revolution, and popular notions of women's gentleness and frailty were shattered by the direct action tactics adopted by British suffragettes. In this chapter we will focus on the ad hoc activities of women, rather than the protest movements.

Why do women tend to participate in unconventional rather than conventional political activity? There are several possible answers. The first is that many women are more comfortable in less formal groups. Women who have been ignored, excluded, or otherwise mistreated in formal political structures, or who have not had experience in such structures, may find a warmer welcome in a more loosely structured political forum. Some feminists argue that formal structures – rules of procedure, membership criteria, a hierarchical chain of authority – are inherently masculine, and that women should refuse to conform to them. Whether or not one agrees with this analysis, it is clear that many women find participation in ad hoc groups more rewarding than participation in political parties or institutionalized interest groups.

A second possible explanation is that ad hoc activities are more easily combined with child care and other responsibilities than more structured forms of political participation, like parties. We have already noted the localized character of much ad hoc political activity. It is considerably easier for women with small children to spend a few hours at a meeting a few blocks from home than to spend days or weeks at a time in the national or provincial capital. In addition, the hours required by ad hoc activity, though often considerable, may be more flexible than those demanded of participants in formal political activity.

A third possible explanation is that women participate in unconventional politics because they reject the option of joining political parties. A fourth, related, explanation is that women have been rejected *by* the political parties, and they find that ad hoc groups are a useful outlet for their political energies and ambitions. Why would women have such a conflicted relationship with political parties? We will examine some of the specific reasons in this chapter and the next. One general explanation offered by many feminists is that women experience the political system differently from men.[10] Whereas men have been welcomed by conventional political organizations, particularly political parties, women have been regarded with suspicion if they try to leave their "proper sphere." Parties have not welcomed them, or have shunted them off into auxiliaries with little influence on political events. As a result, "less formal, community-based political activity has offered a more attractive and promising venue."[11] We will return to this "dual cultures" analysis in the next section.

Women's participation in unconventional political activity is often the first step towards a career in conventional politics, especially at the municipal level. Brodie's study of female politicians found that "volunteerism channels women to municipal candidacy,[12]" especially those women who have been group leaders or executive members. Many women first develop an interest in politics during their involvement with an ad hoc group, while many female politicians report that they were first encouraged to run for municipal office by the members of their voluntary organizations.[13]

None of this is meant to suggest that conventional politics is somehow better than unconventional politics. The point is that women have different political recruitment patterns from those of men, and that we should be careful to avoid analyses that treat women as defective because they do not conform to the standard (male) models of political behaviour. We will return to this point in the next section.

The Political Beliefs of Women

Political scientists often try to discover and to explain the political beliefs and values held by citizens. The term *"political culture"* refers to the sum total of orientations to the political system of a country held by the individuals who live there. These orientations are acquired by individuals through a process called "political socialization." A child learns about politics by overhearing discussions at home, which shape her or his political ideas and values. Later, when a child goes to school, she or he acquires information about politics. The peer group is also a source of political ideas, particularly as the child grows older. University is often a time when political orientations change quite dramatically, although these changes are not always permanent. Finally, there is evidence that adults continue to adjust their political orientations throughout their lives, in response to events.

The concept of political culture is usually applied to a particular territorial area. We speak of the political culture of Germany, or the political culture of Canada. When we do so, we often speak of "political culture" as both a cause and an effect of political events. We explain the political culture of a country as the product of its history, its immigration patterns, its economic development, or its political institutions. We also use the concept of political culture to explain why countries with similar institutions operate in different ways. For example, some people argue that the German Weimar Republic, which was founded in 1919 with a democratic constitution similar to those in other Western countries, fell to Hitler in 1933 because the Germans were not prepared to accept the compromises necessary for liberal democracy. The concept of political culture is also used to explain individual political behaviour and beliefs.

Feminist scholars argue that in addition to national political cultures, there are also distinct political cultures that cut across territorial boundaries. In particular, they point to a distinct female political culture, which differs sufficiently from the masculine "norm" to have important effects on women's political attitudes and behaviour. It is generally agreed that boys and girls are socialized differently.[14] They acquire political ideas while simultaneously learning what it means to be "boys" or "girls." It is not entirely clear how boys and girls develop different attitudes to politics, and it is dangerous to press this point too far; studies of childhood political socialization are among the most notorious examples of sexism in political science.[15] It is clear that not all women are successfully socialized away from politics. Nevertheless, if we accept that children are socialized into their gender roles, it makes sense to assume a link between gender socialization and political socialization. Boys are taught that politics is an aggressive, masculine endeavour; girls are taught that politics is a man's world and that they are ill equipped to understand or participate in it.[16]

Feminists now emphasize adult learning in their explanations of women's attitudes towards the political system.[17] They argue that male dominance of political institutions makes them uninviting to women, and that women's unwillingness to become involved with them is the product of a rational choice rather than the result of women's failings. Instead of blaming women for their inadequacies, whether as the result of their socialization or their domestic responsibilities, feminists point to alienating features of the political system itself: "the exclusionary behaviour of male politicians who undermine women's motivation to participate and who are inhospitable to women with political aspirations."[18] It is clear, therefore, that we cannot ignore adult experiences in our account of women's political socialization.

The differences between men's and women's attitudes to political issues, feelings towards the political system, and political participation are summed up under the label "the gender gap." We will discuss differences in mass-level political participation in the next section; here we concentrate on the gender gap in attitudes towards political issues and the political system.

Numerous American and Canadian studies have found that men and women tend to hold different attitudes on some political issues: war and peace, nuclear power, capital punishment, and social welfare spending.[19] These differences in issue attitudes, which are particularly pronounced among younger voters, sometimes translate into different partisan attachments. It would be foolish to overstate the case: not all women think alike, and there is a great deal of variance within as well as between the sexes. Political parties are also internally divided, both ideologically and along gender lines.[20] For a gender gap to translate into voting behaviour, there must be a clear division between parties or candidates over those issues where the gender differences are clearest. The 1980

American presidential election was the first in which the gender gap became a major factor in the vote, because of the strong perception of a major split between Ronald Reagan and Jimmy Carter on issues of war and peace.[21] The gender gap also favoured the Democratic candidate, Bill Clinton, in 1992, and helped to elect a number of women to the U.S. Congress.

In Canada, women have always tended to vote for the Liberal Party more than for the Progressive Conservatives or the New Democrats. It is not entirely clear why.[22] There are some significant differences among the three major parties on issues of particular concern to women, including child care and abortion, which might be expected to translate into a gender gap. But the NDP has only recently overcome a historic disadvantage among female voters, which flies in the face of that expectation.[23] And there is evidence that among the Canadian electorate as a whole, men and women do not differ significantly over issues of particular concern to women.[24] These findings should cause us to wonder about the importance of the gender gap in political attitudes in Canadian politics.

Women's feelings towards the political system as a whole are also somewhat different from men's, as the "dual cultures" approach would predict. In particular, women display lower levels of both political interest and political efficacy.[25] The expression "political efficacy" refers to a sense of political self-esteem and a feeling of trust in the political system. A person with a strong sense of political efficacy believes that he or she can make a difference in the political system, and that he or she is capable of understanding political events. Women, on average, report lower levels of political efficacy than men do.

There are a few interesting points to be made about the survey findings on political efficacy. First, while women show lower levels of efficacy than men, this does not always apply to women with university educations.[26] Second, an American study has found that while politically active women have higher efficacy measures overall than women who are not involved, women who have been involved in political parties show lower average levels of efficacy than those who are involved with non-partisan organizations.[27] This suggests that women who have been involved with parties come away from the experience less sure that their participation in politics can really make a difference. Such a finding is highly suggestive of women's mistreatment in party structures.

Third, women differ significantly from men on only *one* standard measure of efficacy: "Politics is too complicated to understand." This is the only measure that reflects a person's opinion of herself or himself vis-à-vis the political system; the others are more general statements such as "People have no say about government" and "Public opinion is unimportant to elected officials."[28] This suggests that the real difference between women and men is that women have a lower sense of self-esteem regarding politics.[29] Such an interpretation is backed up by Canadian survey data that show women are significantly more likely than men to answer "don't know" to survey questions on political matters.[30] It is clear that more women than men feel intimidated by and alienated from the political system. As Sandra Burt argues, "women are less involved psychologically and are more likely to find politics complicated."[31] This finding supports the idea that there are two political cultures, one male and one female.

If women are brought up to consider politics none of their business, how do we explain the growing number of female politicians? Brodie's study of female candidates indicates that many were born into political families with weak gender-role norms. Some women married politically active men, or were encouraged to enter politics by friends and colleagues. As we have seen, participation in voluntary organizations politicizes many women. There are a host of factors that can socialize a woman "against the norms" and free her to enter politics. Brodie concludes that the adult factors are more important in this regard than childhood socialization.[32]

From Mass to Elite Politics: The Barriers for Women

Mass politics includes all political activities that require little time, effort, or money: voting, keeping up with political events through the media, discussing politics with friends, going to the occasional political meeting or trying to persuade someone to support a particular candidate or party. *Elite politics* includes the more time-consuming and higher-status activities: donating money to a party, taking an executive position in a party, running for office, sitting in a legislature. In this book we will focus on the last three items in the list of elite politics.

Neither men nor women participate very much in mass politics, apart from voting. Over two-thirds of Canadians turn out to vote in federal elections. Women vote at about the same rate as men, a pattern that has been constant since the first National Election Study in 1965.[33] Women are almost as likely as men to attend political meetings, contact public officials about an issue, or work for a party. On other measures of mass political activity, significant gender differences are apparent. Women are less likely to pay attention to politics, to take an interest in an election, to claim a good knowledge of politics, to follow political news on television or in the newspapers, to discuss politics, or to try to convince others to vote a certain way.[34] These differences are not huge, but they are clear and they are consistent across time. The principal reason for them, as we will see, is the constraints on women's time and energy imposed by children. Women without children are as involved in mass politics as men with children or men without children.

The differences in men's and women's mass political participation are not enough to explain the extreme under-representation of women in elite politics. How, then, do we explain this discrepancy? The traditional recruitment literature in political science predicts that anyone can rise from the mass to the elite level of politics, given the will to do so. But this is clearly untrue for most women.[35] What factors prevent a disproportionate number of women from entering elite politics?

There are a host of reasons why the numbers of women in Canadian elite politics are so low.[36] Some of them also explain why the vast majority of men stay out of politics: the cost of campaigning, the difficulty of combining politics with a more permanent career, a simple lack of interest, a preference for other activities. But there are also gender-specific reasons why women are disproportionately scarce in elite politics. These include the following:

- The gendered division of labour in the home
- The gendered division of labour in the workplace
- The public-private dichotomy
- The "gatekeeping" role of the political parties
- The structure of the political system itself

We will briefly discuss each of these factors in turn.

The Gendered Division of Labour in the Home

One popular explanation of women's under-representation in elite politics focuses on the "role constraints" that affect women more than men. All of us have personal responsibilities that may prevent us from becoming deeply involved in political activity. The gender role constraints approach argues that women bear a disproportionate burden of those personal responsibilities, because of the gendered division of labour inside the home. As we saw in Chapter 4, women are generally responsible for most or all of the cleaning, cooking, and child care within the family. These tasks require time and energy, especially the care of young children. It is therefore plausible that women with children would face gender role constraints that would reduce their opportunities for political involvement.

This explanation of women's lower political involvement is substantiated by evidence in both Canada and the United States.[37] In 1984 the Canadian National Election Study included, for the first time, a question about the number and age of children in the respondent's household. The results showed a clear pattern of gender role constraints: "The participation figures for men are altered little by the responsibilities of fatherhood ... For women, quite the contrary, there is an almost uniformly negative association between political activity and the presence of children, a pattern that is frequently significant."[38]

Across the whole spectrum of lower-level political activity, from voting to political interest, from attending meetings to donating money, women with children were less likely to participate than men. They were also less politically involved than were women without children, whose participation rates were much closer to those of men.[39] This pattern is even stronger for the elite levels of politics. If this study is accurate, it means that gender role constraints are both persistent and powerful.

We must be careful, however, not to take the gender role constraints approach too far. As Brodie points out, not all women are married, and not all women have children. Among those women who do have family responsibilities, those in the upper-income brackets – the ones most likely to seek entry to political elites – can afford to hire household help. Given these variations among women, and the lack of gender-role constraints for some, Cynthia Fuchs Epstein argues that "emphasis on women's limitations because of their sex-role-associated statuses is an exclusionary mechanism – an ideological ploy to keep women out of the running for high-ranking activity"[40] – and not necessarily a reflection of reality.

We must also be careful not to suggest that women *always* have to choose between marriage and children on the one hand and a political career on the other. Brodie's survey of Canadian female politicians found that their gender roles imposed some limits on their political careers, but they did not rule out elite political participation altogether: "Mothers and homemakers more often delayed their entry into the electoral field and more often confined their political ambitions to the local level of government."[41] Brodie concludes that gender role constraints do place women at a competitive disadvantage in politics, and argues that "as long as women are assigned primary responsibility for homemaking and child-rearing, their political activism will likely be constrained."[42]

The Gendered Division of Labour in the Workplace

A second explanation of women's lower levels of political participation focuses on women's experiences in the workplace. As we have seen in the second part of this book, women are concentrated in low-status, low-paying jobs. Even women who work in traditionally male fields are often paid less than men. The pattern of women's employment has a number of implications for their political participation. *First,* the members of political elites tend to be drawn from a small number of high-status, high-paying jobs that require extensive formal qualifications: law, medicine, business, journalism, and finance (see the appendix to this chapter).[43] Women have, until recently, made up only a small percentage of workers in those fields. This is changing, as more and more women enter law school, medical school, and business programs. By the 1989–1990 academic year, women accounted for 45 percent of medical students, 50 percent of law students, and 45 percent of business and management students.[44] Despite these hopeful signs for the future, it will take years for those young women to rise to the elite levels from which political leaders are recruited.

The educational and occupational backgrounds of Canada's MPs are clearly unrepresentative of the Canadian population as a whole (see Appendix). In 1995 the largest single group of MPs listed their sole or principal occupation as teaching (including university professors and school principals). The second largest group were businesspeople (including finance, real estate, and accounting). Lawyers were the third largest group, followed by a number of smaller categories. With the exception of teaching, these fields have traditionally been dominated by men. The jobs where women have been most numerous, including nursing and social work, account for only a tiny handful of MPs. These numbers suggest that the pink-collar ghetto is still a barrier to women's participation in elite politics. At the same time, they show that MPs are a highly un-representative sample of the electorate. Lawyers account for less than 1 percent of Canadian workers, according to the 1991 census, while teachers make up 4.4 percent (6.3 percent of women).[45]

Though the 1993 election brought more women into the House, it did not really change the occupational pattern of women's repre-sentation. Women were over-represented (relative to their numbers in the Commons as a whole) among teachers, municipal or provincial poli-ticians, and public servants, medical workers (two nurses and a doctor), the economist/consultant category, and administrators. The major de-viation from previous patterns is that women are now under-repre-sented in the "business" category, where they were substantially over-represented in the 1980s. Women who are prepared to enter traditionally male-dominated fields are most numerous in the Com-mons, with the important exception of teachers.

It is risky to rely on women's lack of formal qualifications to explain their exclusion from political elites. This approach "blames the victim," implying that if only women would exert themselves more the political elites would welcome them with open arms. It also overlooks the rea-sons *why* women have tended to acquire fewer or lower-status qualifica-tions than men. Finally, this approach suggests that political parties and other political institutions are "equal-opportunity employers," who re-cruit and promote members without regard to their sex. In other words, "Women consistently perform the menial tasks within political party or-ganizations not because of any deeply rooted biases against women in leadership positions, but simply because few are 'qualified' to do other-wise."[46] But as we will see later in this chapter, and in the next chapter, it is simply wrong to place all the blame on women for their own exclu-sion and to overlook the sexism inherent in the political system.

Second, few women have had access to the informal occupational networks on which political careers are built. Male lawyers and business-men can go to their clubs to make political contacts, or lobby party re-cruiters on the golf course. Women have been excluded from this mas-culine camaraderie, to their cost. As Epstein notes, "There is a direct relationship between acquisition of formal statuses and participation in informal networks."[47]

Women's exclusion from high-status jobs and from crucial informal networks combines to produce the third problem: women tend to lack *social capital*. The concept of social capital has been used to explain why women's power in the private sphere – as mothers and wives – has not been transferable to the public sphere. Social capital is defined as "social knowledge, contacts, privileged access to culturally valued qualifications, and social skills as embodied in the various strategies employed by competitors in a social field – a network of power relations characterized by its own rules of competition, conflicts and strategies, and interests and profits."[48] Social capital is acquired through informal contacts with elite members, as well as by acquisition of elite skills and attitudes through formal channels (e.g., work in a law firm or a brokerage house). Only those people with social capital can rise through the ranks to elite levels, because it is the currency needed to purchase greater status and power. Only those people who are acceptable to the present elites will be given the opportunity to amass social capital. "Elites tend if at all possible to reproduce themselves, to recruit in their own image. Hence, a history of male-dominated elites has been more than enough to ensure a future of male-dominated elites."[49]

The fourth employment-related barrier to women's political participation is lack of money. Not only are women paid less than men on average, which limits their ability to fund their own political efforts, but their exclusion from elite networks denies them access to rich sources of political funds. It is much easier for a respected lawyer or financier to raise the thousands of dollars needed for a contested nomination than it is for a teacher or a nurse. The risks of running for office are much greater for a woman, who may find herself deeply in debt after losing a nomination battle.

The Public-Private Dichotomy

As we have already seen, the public-private dichotomy defines women as belonging to the home and family and men as belonging to the world of power and competition. Women have been defined out of politics, and kept in their homes. This has had a number of implications for women's political participation.

First, women who stay at home are somewhat less likely to participate in politics than women who work outside the home.[50]

Second, women (and men) have been socialized to associate politics with men and with masculine values, not with women and their values. This has discouraged women from taking an interest in political matters – they were afraid of being considered less "feminine" – and it may also have led to the evolution of the political system as a more competitive, aggressive sphere of activity than it would otherwise have been (see below).

Third, the public-private dichotomy has led political scientists to misinterpret the political ideas and acts of women. As we saw in the first chapter, political scientists have assumed that women were either more apathetic about politics than men or were more conservative in their policy preferences and voting choices. The belief that women were less engaged with politics than men appears to have some basis in fact, as we have seen, although the conventional explanation of this phenomenon – which attributed political apathy to women's biological and mental weakness – has now been completely discredited. The idea that women were more conservative also appears to have been true earlier in this century, but it is no longer true.[51] Nonetheless, the old ideas die hard. Women are still being interpreted according to old prejudices, not current realities.

The Parties as Gatekeepers

As we will see in the following chapter, women have been less successful than men at securing party nominations in winnable ridings. The gatekeeping role of the parties is a crucial barrier to women's representation in elite politics. If parties deny women a realistic chance to run for office, numerical under-representation is inevitable. Fortunately, there are signs that the parties – especially the Liberals and the NDP – are beginning to accept their responsibility for both nominating and electing more women. But the process has been slow, and it will continue to encounter resistance from entrenched male power-holders in the parties.

Epstein suggests that women can make dramatic gains in representation in institutions whose power is eroding: "When political parties lose power and need new members to bolster their resources and do the work (or need work done cheaply, e.g., as volunteers), women are welcomed."[52] There is reason to believe that Canadian parties are presently losing much of their legitimacy in the eyes of the Canadian public: the appeal of direct democracy and referenda, the rise of protest parties and new social movements, and criticism of the parties' monopoly over such processes as nominating candidates for office and selecting the people who compete for the prime ministership. If this is true, it may help to explain why parties are opening their arms to women. It also suggests that this process of women's integration into the parties will continue, and even accelerate, in the near future. As Epstein points out, however, "There is no doubt that women benefit in such cases, but the institutions to which they are thus admitted are no longer the same, and it is often questionable whether the prize has the value originally attributed to it."[53]

The Old Boys' Club

Ever since Canadian women received the right to vote, they have been torn between two opposing approaches to the party system. According to Sylvia Bashevkin, "on the one hand, early women's groups were attracted towards a position of political independence, which could guarantee both organizational autonomy and purity; on the other hand, they were drawn towards conventional partisanship, which might better ensure their political influence and legislative success."[54] In this section we will consider the appeal of political independence for women – or, in other words, the features of conventional partisanship that have discouraged many women from participating. (See also the discussion of the "strategic practice" approach in Chapter 2.)

The first such feature of conventional partisanship is the dominance of values and practices that feminists characterize as "masculine."[55] These include competition, hierarchy, rigid rules and processes, strict membership criteria, and an emphasis on majority rule rather than consensus. Underlying the feminist critique of traditional politics is a rejection of traditional notions of power. Radical feminists perceive the purpose of traditional political structures and procedures to be the exercise of X's *power over Y*. This notion of "power over," which is inherently coercive and exercised for its own sake, is contrasted with the feminist conception of *power to*. This is a more cooperative, consensual, and egalitarian concept of organizational procedure. All participants, not just those in the majority, are allowed to have a genuine voice in the deliberations and an influence over the final outcome. Power is shared, and dedicated to the creation of a greater good, not concentrated in one leader or executive committee and used for their personal aggrandizement.

Long before this feminist critique of politics emerged in the late 1960s, women had been expressing discomfort with the conventional political system. Many suffragists in the early part of this century believed that women were morally superior to men and should not pollute themselves by actively participating in the rough-and-tumble world of party politics.[56] As we have seen, politics has always been defined as a male activity. But it was not until the second wave of the women's movement that women began to try to change that definition instead of maintaining their purity on the sidelines. The tension between independence and partisanship, identified by Bashevkin, remained. But some women, mostly liberal feminists, began to try to remake political process in a female image. As we saw in Chapter 2, two different models of strategic practice emerged: "Institutionalized feminism retained many of the structures and processes of traditional organizations, but modified them to meet its own needs. Grass-roots feminism, on the other hand, initially rejected traditional organizational forms altogether and set out to build a new alternative."[57]

By and large, the political system has not been responsive to the reform efforts of feminists, and most of them have remained outside it.[58] Those women who have participated have tended to eschew feminism, both in their policy positions and in their approach to political activity: "The evidence is that many women politicians are surrogate men, that they have no interest in pursuing women's rights or questions of particular concern to their women electors."[59] This is changing slowly, as we will see in the next section. But party politics is still shunned by most feminists, largely because of its macho atmosphere and the "old boys" values that permeate the entire structure.[60] Even worse, it is clear that in many instances women are still unwelcome in the boys' club.[61] Explanations of women's under-representation that focus entirely on women's supposed deficiencies (e.g., lack of formal qualifications) overlook "the exclusionary behaviour of male politicians who undermine women's motivation to participate and who are inhospitable to women with political aspirations."[62]

A second reason why conventional politics has not been inviting to women is that it demands a great deal of time, much of it spent away from home. Provincial and federal legislators must work in the capital, and most of them leave their families in their home ridings. This does not appear to impose serious constraints on male legislators, but – given the gendered division of labour – it does impose severe constraints on female legislators. Women who seek political office have tended to wait until their children were old enough to look after themselves, with the help of a spouse or a babysitter. This places them at a competitive disadvantage relative to politicians who begin to build their careers in their twenties.[63] Almost all of these career politicians are male – including former Progressive Conservative Cabinet ministers Perrin Beatty and Joe Clark – although an increasing number of women are approaching politics as a lifelong career (including Liberal Deputy Prime Minister Sheila Copps).

Women who decide to run for political office at a younger age tend to be more single-minded in their approach to politics. Their experience suggests that although the choice between family and politics is not always as black and white as has sometimes been implied, some female politicians do end up sacrificing whatever family life they might otherwise have had. Joni Lovenduski points out that "women who succeed in the world of men are exceptions when compared to women at large ... Women politicians sacrifice more for their position. They are less often married, have fewer children and are better trained than other women."[64] While the careers of male politicians are helped by marriage, "being unattached increases a woman's chances of success in terms of career and public life. Data from country after country confirm such patterns."[65] We have only to look at childless, twice-divorced Kim Campbell to recognize the truth of Lovenduski's analysis.

Conclusion

In this chapter we have discussed the following key points:

1. Women participate equally with men at the level of voting, but above that level they are more constrained by domestic responsibilities (especially the presence of children).

2. Women share a different political culture from that of men, with lower levels of political efficacy. This is consistent with the idea that women have been defined out of politics, which has always been seen as a male activity.

3. There are a host of barriers to women who want to pursue elite politics: the gendered division of labour at home and at work, the public-private dichotomy, sexism in the political parties, and the nature of conventional politics itself.

The purpose of this chapter has been to outline the pattern of women's participation in the Canadian political system. In order to understand that pattern, we have had to abandon two widely held ideas. First, we have had to broaden our idea of politics to include local community groups, child-care cooperatives, and other structures that have traditionally been seen as non-political. Politics has long been defined in ways that exclude women, as we saw in Chapter 1. To bring women back in, we must recognize that politics goes on outside the House of Commons, the political parties, and the formal structures of public policy-making.

Many political scientists are reluctant to define politics so broadly, because they do not want to blur the lines between their discipline and other social sciences. But this type of interdisciplinary work is precisely what women's studies is all about. If we are ever to understand the lives of women, we must break the bounds of academic disciplines and put all the pieces together. Women's political situation cannot be understood without first understanding their economic, social, legal, and cultural situation, because political power is intertwined with all of those other power structures – hence the plan of this book.

Second, we have had to stop looking at women as if they were politically defective. Instead of blaming women for their own exclusion from politics, we have to ask why women have not been welcome, why women have chosen not to participate, and why women have come to believe that politics is too complicated for them to understand. The blame lies with the gendered structures of power in our society, and with the male-dominated political system, not with women themselves. An accurate analysis of women's political activity reveals that the Canadian political system is sexist, exclusionary, and geared towards people without constant and pressing family responsibilities. As we will see in the next two chapters, there are signs of improvement, especially within the political parties. But despite the anomalous success of women like Audrey McLaughlin and Kim Campbell, we are a long way from the day when a qualified woman has the same chance of political success as an equally qualified man. We will go on now to a discussion of women's place in Canada's national political parties, and in the national political institutions.

Appendix: Occupational Backgrounds of Canadian MPs (March 1995)

Occupation	% of All MPs	% of Female MPs	Women as % of Occupational Group in the Commons
EDUCATOR	22.0	30.2	24.6
BUSINESS/FINANCE	18.9	16.9	16.1
LAWYER	16.6	15.1	16.3
FARMER	5.4	1.9	6.7
POLITICS/POLICY/ PUBLIC SERVICE	5.4	7.5	33.3
MEDICINE/NURSING/ VETERINARIAN	3.4	5.7	30.0
ENGINEERING/MANUAL	2.4	0	0
SOCIAL WORKER/CLERGY	1.4	0	0
JOURNALISM/BROADCASTING	5.1	3.8	13.3
ECONOMIST/CONSULTANT	6.4	7.5	26.7
ADMINISTRATION	6.8	9.4	25.0
UNION	0.7	1.9	50.0
FORCES/POLICE/CORRECTIONS	1.7	0	0
HOMEMAKER	0	1.9	100.0
NONE LISTED	1.4	0	0

Source: John Bejermi, *Canadian Parliamentary Handbook* (Ottawa: Borealis, 1994).

Notes

1. Randall, *Women and Politics,* 58–64; Lovenduski, *Women and European Politics,* 126.
2. Beckwith, *American Women and Political Participation.*
3. Brodie, *Women and Politics in Canada,* 45–46.
4. Randall, 58.
5. Ronald Inglehart, *The Silent Revolution* and *Culture Shift in Advanced Industrial Society.*
6. Randall, 59.
7. Brodie, *Women and Politics,* 44.
8. Randall, 60.
9. Ibid.
10. See, for example, Thelma McCormack, "Toward a Nonsexist Perspective on Social and Political Change," in Millman and Moss Kanter, *Another Voice,* 24–27.
11. Bashevkin, *Toeing the Lines,* 44.
12. Brodie, *Women and Politics,* 51.
13. Ibid., 102.
14. See Brodie, *Women and Politics,* 7, 25; Epstein, *Deceptive Distinctions,* chap. 8; Sapiro, *The Political Integration of Women,* chap. 3; Maccoby and Jacklin, *The Psychology of Sex Differences,* chaps. 8, 9.
15. Susan Bourque and Jean Grossholtz, "Politics an Unnatural Practice: Political Science Looks at Female Participation," in Siltanen and Stanworth, *Women and the Public Sphere,* 113–15.
16. Sapiro, chap. 3.
17. Randall, 92–94; Epstein, *Deceptive Distinctions,* 167; Bashevkin, 44.
18. Epstein, *Deceptive Distinctions,* 167.
19. See Baxter and Lansing, 57–59; Poole and Harmon Zeigler, *Women, Public Opinion, and Politics;* Mueller, *The Politics of the Gender Gap.*
20. Brodie, "The Gender Factor and National Leadership Conventions in Canada."
21. Baxter and Lansing, chap. 9.
22. Wearing and Wearing, "Does Gender Make a Difference?"
23. Bashevkin, chap. 2.
24. Brodie, "The Gender Factor," 181.
25. See Bashevkin, *Toeing the Lines,* chap. 2; Beckwith, chap. 2.
26. Baxter and Lansing found that women with higher education display levels of efficacy equal to those of men; see *Women and Politics,* 51. More recent studies have found that education does not make a difference in women's

low levels of efficacy; there is no consensus on the interpretation of these data.

27. Ibid., 142.

28. Beckwith, 21.

29. Gloria Steinem reports studies of teenaged girls in math courses that reinforce the idea that women answer "I don't know" because they lack faith in their own intelligence, not because they are really uninformed. See Steinem, *Revolution from Within: A Book of Self-Esteem,* 121–22.

30. Bashevkin, 51.

31. Sandra Burt, "Women's Issues and the Women's Movement in Canada," 126.

32. Brodie, 39.

33. Kay et al., "Feminist Consciousness and the Canadian Electorate," 7.

34. Ibid.

35. Brodie, *Women and Politics,* 3.

36. For discussions of these various explanations, see Brodie, *Women and Politics,* 7–8; Sapiro; Epstein, "Women and Elites."

37. See Black and McGlen; McGlen, "The Impact of Parenthood on Political Participation"; Sapiro.

38. Kay et al., 10–12. However, an American study has found little or no correlation between family responsibilities and women's political activity at the mass level, except where there are four or more children.

39. Ibid., 12.

40. Epstein, *Deceptive Distinctions,* 12.

41. Brodie, *Women and Politics,* 93.

42. Ibid., 94.

43. See Norris, *Politics and Sexual Equality,* 121.

44. Statistics Canada, *Education in Canada.*

45. Statistics Canada, *The 1991 Census.*

46. Brodie, *Women and Politics,* 60.

47. Epstein, *Deceptive Distinctions,* 11.

48. Nowotny, "Women in Public Life in Austria," 147–48.

49. Lovenduski, 210.

50. See Randall, 127.

51. Wearing and Wearing, "Does Gender Make a Difference?"

52. Epstein, *Deceptive Distinctions,* 13.

53. Ibid.

54. Bashevkin, 1–2.

55. See Adamson, Briskin, and McPhail, *Feminist Organizing for Change,* chap. 7; Carroll, "Feminist Scholarship on Political Leadership"; French, *Beyond Power.*

56. Bashevkin, *Toeing the Lines,* chap. 1; Adamson et al., chap. 1.

57. Adamson, Briskin, and McPhail, 233.

58. Lovenduski, 160.

59. Ibid., 243.

60. Randall, 92–94.

61. See, for example, Randall's argument, p. 131, that "given men's competitive edge in any current leadership contest and their dominance of the existing selection processes, women who seek political power are operating within an entirely different political context than when they simply join in grass-roots political activity."

62. Epstein, *Deceptive Distinctions,* 167.

63. Randall, 126.

64. Lovenduski, 240–41.

65. Ibid., 241.

References and Further Reading

Adamson, Nancy, Linda Briskin, and Margaret McPhail. *Feminist Organizing for Change: The Contemporary Women's Movement in Canada.* Toronto: Oxford University Press, 1988.

Bashevkin, Sylvia B. *Toeing the Lines: Women and Party Politics in English Canada.* 2nd ed. Toronto: Oxford University Press, 1993.

Baxter, Sandra, and Marjorie Lansing. *Women and Politics: The Visible Majority.* Rev. ed. Ann Arbor: University of Michigan Press, 1983.

Beckwith, Karen. *American Women and Political Participation: The Impacts of Work, Generation, and Feminism.* New York: Greenwood, 1986.

Bejermi, John. *Canadian Parliamentary Handbook.* Ottawa: Borealis, 1994.

Black, J.H., and N.E. McGlen. "Male-Female Political Involvement Differentials in Canada, 1965–1974." *Canadian Journal of Political Science* 12 (1979).

Brodie, Janine. "The Gender Factor and National Leadership Conventions in Canada." In George C. Perlin, ed., *Party Democracy in Canada: The Politics of National Party Conventions.* Scarborough: Prentice-Hall Canada, 1988.

———. *Women and Politics in Canada.* Toronto: McGraw-Hill Ryerson, 1985.

Burt, Sandra. "Women's Issues and the Women's Movement in Canada Since 1970." In Alan Cairns and Cynthia Williams, eds., *The Politics of Gender, Ethnicity and Language in Canada.* Vol. 34 of the collected research studies for the Royal Commission on the Economic Union and Development Prospects for Canada. Toronto: University of Toronto Press, 1986.

Carroll, Susan J. "Feminist Scholarship on Political Leadership." In Barbara Kellerman, ed., *Leadership: Multidisciplinary Perspectives.* Englewood Cliffs, NJ: Prentice-Hall, 1984.

———. *Women as Candidates in American Politics.* Bloomington: Indiana University Press, 1985.

Christy, Carol. *Sex Differences in Political Participation: Processes of Change in Fourteen Nations.* New York: Praeger, 1987.

Epstein, Cynthia Fuchs. *Deceptive Distinctions: Sex, Gender, and the Social Order.* New Haven: Yale University Press, 1988.

———. "Women and Elites: A Cross-National Perspective." In Cynthia Fuchs Epstein and Rose Laub Coser, eds., *Access to Power: Cross-National Studies of Women and Elites.* Boston: George Allen & Unwin, 1981.

French, Marilyn. *Beyond Power: On Women, Men, and Morals.* New York: Ballantine, 1985.

Inglehart, Ronald *Culture Shift in Advanced Industrial Society*. Princeton: Princeton University Press, 1990.

———. *The Silent Revolution: Changing Values and Political Styles among Western Publics*. Princeton: Princeton University Press, 1977.

Kay, Barry J., et al. "Feminist Consciousness and the Canadian Electorate: A Review of National Election Studies 1965–1984." *Women and Politics* 8, no. 2 (1988).

Kealey, Linda, and Joan Sangster, eds. *Beyond the Vote: Canadian Women and Politics*. Toronto: University of Toronto Press, 1989.

Lovenduski, Joni. *Women and European Politics: Contemporary Feminism and Public Policy*. Brighton: Wheatsheaf, 1986.

Lovenduski, Joni, and Jill Hills, eds. *The Politics of the Second Electorate: Women and Public Participation*. London: Routledge and Kegan Paul, 1981.

Maccoby, Eleanor Emmons, and Carol Nagy Jacklin. *The Psychology of Sex Differences*. Stanford: Stanford University Press, 1974.

Maillé, Chantal. *Primed for Power: Women in Canadian Politics*. Ottawa: CACSW, 1990.

McGlen, N.E. "The Impact of Parenthood on Political Participation." *Western Political Quarterly* 33 (1980).

Millman, Marcia, and Rosabeth Moss Kanter, eds. *Another Voice: Feminist Perspectives on Social Life and Social Science*. New York: Anchor, 1975.

Mishler, William, and Harold D. Clarke. "Political Participation in Canada." In Michael S. Whittington and Glen Williams, eds., *Canadian Politics in the 1990s*. 3rd ed. Scarborough: Nelson Canada, 1990.

Mueller, Carol M., ed. *The Politics of the Gender Gap: The Social Construction of Political Influence*. Beverly Hills: Sage, 1988.

Norris, Pippa. *Politics and Sexual Equality: The Comparative Position of Women in Western Democracies*. Boulder, CO: Lynne Rienner, 1987.

Nowotny, Helga. "Women in Public Life in Austria." in Cynthia Fuchs Epstein and Rose Laub Coser, eds., *Access to Power: Cross-National Studies of Women and Elites*. Boston: George Allen & Unwin, 1981.

Poole, Keith T., and L. Harmon Zeigler. *Women, Public Opinion, and Politics: The Changing Political Attitudes of American Women*. New York: Longman, 1985.

Randall, Vicky. *Women and Politics: An International Perspective*. 2nd ed. Chicago: University of Chicago Press, 1987.

Sapiro, Virginia. *The Political Integration of Women: Roles, Socialization and Politics*. Chicago: University of Illinois Press, 1984.

Siltanen, Janet, and Michelle Stanworth, eds. *Women and the Public Sphere.* London: Hutchinson, 1984.

Statistics Canada. *Education in Canada.* Ottawa: Minister of Industry, Science & Technology, 1991.

———. *The 1991 Census: Occupations.* Ottawa: Minister of Industry, Science & Technology, 1992.

Steinem, Gloria. *Revolution from Within: A Book of Self-Esteem.* Boston: Little, Brown, 1992.

Wearing, Peter, and Joseph Wearing, "Does Gender Make a Difference in Voting Behaviour?" In Joseph Wearing, ed., *The Ballot and Its Message: Voting in Canada.* Toronto: Copp Clark Pitman, 1991.

Chapter 8: Women in Canadian Political Parties

Chapter Summary

Chapter 8 examines the status of women inside Canada's major national political parties. It discusses the roles played by the parties in the political system, and their treatment of their female membership. The chapter argues that women have been denied access to positions of real power within the parties, and that a gendered division of labour operates within party structures: men make policy, women make coffee. Women are more numerous at the bottom levels of the party structures than at the top. This is expressed in the phrase "the higher, the fewer." In addition, women are less likely to succeed in competitive races for any position, whether on a party executive or for a party nomination. These patterns are beginning to break down, mostly as a result of pressures from outside the parties, but there remains a core of resistance to gender equality within Canada's national party organizations.

Chapter Outline

- Parties and Political Power
- Women in the Parties
  Women's Auxiliaries and the Gendered Division of Labour
  The Higher, the Fewer
  Parties as Gatekeepers
  Women as Sacrificial Candidates in Hopeless Ridings
- Conclusion: What Is To Be Done?

Parties and Political Power

Every society includes groups whose members are, on average, less powerful than the members of other groups. Such groups include women, ethnic or cultural minorities, the disadvantaged, and those with physical or mental disabilities. They have little access to the political and economic resources that they need to catch up. In theory, political parties are the best vehicle for the political aspirations of powerless groups. For example, the British Labour Party was founded in 1906 to secure the election of working men to Parliament. But in practice, party politics in Canada has tended to reinforce – not to overcome – the inherited privilege of wealthy white males.[1]

In particular, parties have failed to bring women into Western political systems in proportionate numbers. Women constitute 51 per cent of the adult population of Western countries, but in most countries they make up less than one-third of elected officials. (See Appendix 5.) The parties' failure has denied women the opportunity to reshape politics and public policy. In this chapter we examine and explain the status of women in Canada's major national parties.

Women in the Parties

In this chapter we will focus on the extra-parliamentary (i.e., "outside Parliament") sections of political parties. We will examine the roles played by women in the local riding associations and at the executive level. We will then discuss the problems women face when they seek their party's nomination for the House of Commons. The parliamentary arena will be discussed in Chapter 9.

As we saw in Chapter 2, Canadian women won the right to vote in federal elections in 1918. Instead of using their new-found voting rights to change the way the political system worked, or to secure policies beneficial to women, women were integrated into the existing parties "in such a way as to reinforce an ideology of sexual difference and political inequality."[2] The Liberal and Conservative[3] parties set up women's auxiliaries, which were separate from the main party organizations. The Women's Liberal Federation was set up in 1928;[4] there were Conservative women's clubs in the major cities by 1920.[5]

The women in these auxiliaries did menial chores: providing refreshments at meetings, taking minutes, answering telephones, stuffing envelopes, updating membership lists. Meanwhile, the men continued to run for office, make party policy, raise campaign funds, and manage campaigns. The gendered division of labour, characteristic of the home and family, was reproduced in the political parties.

It is not entirely clear why women accepted the status quo instead of fighting the entrenched male power of the political system, a power they had clearly identified in their suffrage campaigns. One reason is that the women who joined the auxiliaries did not want to rise to the elite levels of the parties. They were satisfied to work for the election of male candidates. Another reason is that many of the women in the auxiliaries genuinely believed in the gendered division of labour, which both justified the existence of a separate women's organization and allowed women to claim a special role in party affairs. Both men and women in the parties believed women possessed "special qualities" that fitted them for particular party tasks and for particular policy areas.

In the long run, the auxiliaries simply reinforced the pink-collar ghetto. "Maintaining that women performed certain duties better than men because of certain common qualities [damaged] women's case for equal participation ... This attitude limited women to participating only in areas where those qualities were applicable and deemed as assets, and helped to prevent expansion beyond these clearly defined areas."[6]

Even after a party had agreed to give its female members a small share of the political spoils as a reward for their work, including a few token female candidates and Cabinet ministers, "It could very easily be argued, and was, that women would be suited for only certain types of appointments in specific fields, or that women were carbon copies of one another, making the appointment of more than one unnecessary."[7]

Defenders of the auxiliaries claimed that they provided a springboard for women who aspired to run for office. They argued that women did not feel comfortable in the smoky backrooms dominated by the "old boys," so they needed their own organizations where they could acquire the contacts and organizational skills necessary to rise to higher levels within the party. Despite these claims, the parties never really considered the women's auxiliaries as a pool of prospective candidates or leaders. That pool is limited to the people who run the constituency associations, manage the campaigns, raise the money, and devise the policy platforms; it does not include the people who make coffee and clean up after meetings. Because most of the former group are male and most of the latter group are female, it is easy to see why so few women have broken through to the highest levels of party structures.

The auxiliaries are still in place, despite calls for their abolition from the Royal Commission on the Status of Women and from feminist political scientists. But they have changed significantly in recent years. The Women's Liberal Federation was amalgamated with the mainstream party organization in 1969, and the Women's Liberal Commission was set up in 1973. The mandate of the commission was not to hive off Liberal women into their own groups, but to integrate them into "all levels of the Party."[8] This proved easier said than done, largely because of the tensions between younger, more activist women and older women who remained more comfortable with the auxiliary model.

The same tensions arose in the Progressive Conservative Party of Canada, which replaced its PC Women's Association with the PC Women's Federation in 1981.[9] Its goal, like that of its Liberal counterpart, is to work on behalf of women within the party instead of devoting all of its efforts to the election of male party members. "Although a few traditional women's clubs remain, especially in rural ridings, most now function as active lobby groups concerned with recruiting more women candidates, sponsoring political-skills seminars and generally promoting the position of women within their party organizations."[10] In 1995 the party's restructuring committee recommended that the PCWF be abolished and women be integrated into the mainstream of the party through caucuses that would be explicitly designed to train women to run for office.[11]

The CCF-NDP has never had a separate women's organization; women have been direct members of the party since its founding in 1933. But in recent years the party has become concerned about the small numbers of women who have joined it and voted for it. The party's response has been to adopt policies that actively promote the advancement of women within the party – as members of party executives and committees, as candidates for public office, and even as national party leadership contenders. In 1969 the Participation of Women (POW) committee was set up to ensure the recruitment and advancement of women within NDP structures.[12] Women have always been integrated into the party mainstream, but few were comfortable there until the initiatives of the 1970s and 1980s, which we will describe in a later section.

One contribution of the new women's organizations in the older parties, and of the NDP POW committee, has been the establishment of special party funds for female candidates. The single greatest obstacle to women who seek public office is their lack of money for campaigning.[13] Each of the three main parties has set up a fund, named in honour of a pioneering woman, from which female candidates can draw funds during campaigns for office (see below). Although raising money for these funds has become a priority for women within the parties, they remain too small to make a major difference – especially in light of the parties' efforts to nominate more women, who will have to share the pie.[14] But they will doubtless grow in the future, as the women within the parties become increasingly skilled, assertive, and dedicated to promoting their own interests within the Canadian political system.

The Higher, the Fewer

According to Sylvia Bashevkin, there are two consistent patterns of women's participation within Canadian parties.[15] The first is "the higher, the fewer": as we move from the lowest echelons of party activity to the highest, we see fewer and fewer women. Women are most common in the relatively powerless positions within party organizations; they are still quite rare in the powerful senior positions, although this is changing. The second pattern is "the more competitive, the fewer": any position that is coveted by more than one person is a position a woman is less likely to get. In other words, women tend to get the party jobs – from membership secretary to leader – that no man is willing to take.

Bashevkin has documented the "higher and fewer" pattern within the parties at the level of the riding associations: "In both the federal and Ontario provincial systems, the numbers and percentages of women who held local president and treasurer/chief financial officer (CFO) positions were far lower than the numbers and percentages for constituency secretary."[16] The constituency secretary is the lowest level of party official; she takes minutes at meetings, maintains membership and telephone lists, and generally keeps everyone in touch. The riding association presidents and CFOs are much more powerful. The riding presidents run the meetings and sometimes influence the nomination of candidates, and the CFO's control the campaign budgets.

Women have also been drastically under-represented at the provincial and federal levels of party activity, including the election of delegates to party conferences and the election of members to party executives. At the 1967 PC leadership convention, 19 per cent of the delegates were female; a year later, 18 per cent of the delegates to the Liberal leadership convention were female.[17]

The pattern of "the higher, the fewer" has shown some signs of change over the past two decades, but the change has not been consistent. In 1990 two-thirds of riding association secretaries were female; in the 1980s the figure was 70 per cent.[18] The numbers of women elected to delegate positions have grown, partly owing to affirmative action rules (see below), but the *ex officio* delegates[19] are still overwhelmingly male. By 1989, 46 per cent of PC delegates were female, as were 47 per cent of Liberal delegates the following year.[20] In the federal PC party and the NDP, the numbers of women on the national executives grew substantially during the 1980s. In 1983 women made up half the NDP federal executive and almost a quarter of the PC national executive; in 1990 women constituted 58 per cent and 43 per cent respectively. It should be noted, however, that the number of women on the executive of the Liberal Party of Canada shrank over the same period: from 43 per cent in 1983 to 38 per cent in 1990.[21]

Both the Liberal Party of Canada and the New Democratic Party of Canada have had woman presidents (the NDP has had four female presidents; see below), and Audrey McLaughlin was elected leader of the federal NDP in 1989. Kim Campbell won the leadership of the Progressive Conservative Party of Canada in 1993.[22] There have also been a number of female party leaders at the provincial level, including Alexa McDonough of the Nova Scotia NDP, Sharon Carstairs of the Manitoba

Liberals, Lyn McLeod of the Ontario Liberals, and Rita Johnston of the Social Credit Party (who briefly became the first female premier in Canadian history). The Prince Edward Island election of 1993 was noteworthy because the leaders of the two largest parties, Catherine Callbeck and Pat Mella, were both women. Callbeck's Liberals won a smashing majority, making her the first woman premier elected by the voters.

The extraordinary achievement of these women should not be underestimated in any way. However, we cannot overlook the fact that most of them won the leaderships of dispirited, uncompetitive parties over a field of uninspiring male candidates. This brings us to the second pattern described by Bashevkin, "the more competitive, the fewer."

Before the mid-1980s, most women who rose above the lowest levels in the parties did so by taking jobs men did not want. For example, the female riding association presidents were concentrated in ridings that their parties could not win. According to Bashevkin, these women "seemed to hold symbolic power only, since they had little opportunity to elect members to their legislative caucus."[23] Women were given these positions not as a mark of respect or as a reward for their party service, but because they were the only people who could be prevailed on to take these jobs, which nobody really wanted. The "more competitive, the fewer" rule has been breaking down in recent years, at least with regard to internal party positions: "In general, the distribution of women appears less skewed than in the past, since there is no longer the very clear concentration of females in president and CFO positions in marginal constituencies."[24]

It must be pointed out, however, that the concept of a "marginal constituency" is less useful now than it was in the early 1980s. The electoral earthquake of 1984 and the redrawing of electoral boundaries in 1987 have thrown the parties into confusion, and it is difficult to distinguish a marginal seat from a safe seat. The result is that it is more difficult for parties to reserve "hopeless" ridings for women, whether as party officials or as candidates for election (see below).

There are two principal reasons why these patterns have started to break down. The first reason is that women's groups, both inside and outside the parties, have been pressuring the parties to put more women in senior positions. As we have seen, since the second wave of the women's movement the party women's organizations and the NDP POW Committee have worked hard to convince party elites to respond to women's demands for more meaningful participation. Their efforts have been reinforced by a host of groups outside the parties, including the Voice of Women, the Royal Commission on the Status of Women, NAC, the Canadian Action Committee on the Status of Women, the Committee for '94, and Canadian Women for Political Representation.[25] Much of the inspiration for this extra-party activity has come from the United States, where fund-raising and political action groups like the Fund for the Feminist Majority and EMILY's List have made a substantial difference to women's chances of success in recent elections.

The second reason for the diminishing resistance to women within the parties is the changing political landscape. The 1992 election in the United States demonstrated the depth of voters' disillusionment with the political status quo, symbolized by men in suits. The same feelings were clearly reflected in Canadians' reactions to the Meech Lake Accord, the Charlottetown Accord, and other recent political developments. Political parties everywhere are scrambling to present an image of change, renewal, and caring. What better way than to put women in highly visible positions, as candidates and as party leaders? This is one reason why Kim Campbell was the early front-runner in the race to succeed Brian Mulroney as Progressive Conservative leader and prime minister: the party wanted a woman leader, because it believed that a woman would be more appealing to the electorate than a man. This belief was not borne out by the results of the 1993 federal election, although it would be foolish to blame the PC defeat on the gender of the leader.

In response to these external pressures, Canada's major national parties have made commitments to advance women within their own structures. The NDP led the way in creating affirmative action policies, the effects of which can be seen in the numbers of women on the NDP's federal executive (see above). In 1983 the party adopted new rules requiring that 50 per cent of executive members, as well as members of all critical party committees, be female. The results have been impressive: within a few years, women held seven of the twelve vice-president positions within the party. As we saw earlier, the party has also elected four female presidents in the past twelve years.[26] More recently the PC and Liberal parties have recognized the importance of a distinct "women's vote," and have begun to court that vote by promoting women to powerful and visible positions within their structures.[27] The PC's have rejected formal affirmative action policies, preferring to recruit and encourage the most promising women without the use of quotas.[28]

The pattern of "the higher, the fewer" applies to nominations for elected office, not just to internal party positions. Women find it very difficult to win their party's nomination for the House of Commons or a provincial legislature. Appendix 2 shows the percentage of female candidates for the House of Commons in the decades since women received the right to vote in federal elections. Women accounted for 19.2 per cent of candidates in 1988. This figure is lower than the most recent percentages of female candidates in many provinces: 25 per cent in Saskatchewan and Prince Edward Island, 23 per cent in Ontario, and 21 per cent in British Columbia, Manitoba, and Nova Scotia.[29] There were significant variations among the three main federal parties in 1988: women made up 28 per cent of NDP candidates, 18 per cent of Liberal candidates, and only 13 per cent of PC candidates.[30]

The 1993 election reshaped the Canadian party system in many ways, including the participation of women. The highest proportion of women in history ran for office: 21.7 per cent of candidates were female. Almost 60 per cent of the women ran as candidates for the five major parties. For the first time, women were less likely than men to run hopeless candidacies: 41.6 per cent of women ran as minor-party candidates, as unaffiliated candidates,[31] or as independent candidates, compared to 47 per cent of men.[32] Women made up 23 per cent of PC candidates, 21 per cent of Liberal candidates, 37 per cent of NDP candidates, 11 per cent of Reform candidates, and 13 per cent of Bloc Québécois candidates. Women also accounted for 21 per cent of minor-party and unaffiliated candidates and 2 per cent of independent candidates. Therefore, female candidates were more numerous among the PCs, the NDP, and the minor parties than in the Liberal, Reform, and BQ ranks. The problem, of course, is that PC, NDP, and minor-party candidates were destroyed in the 1993 election; we will return to this issue later on.

How do we explain the small proportion of female candidates for the House of Commons? The answer becomes clearer when we look at the process of becoming a parliamentary candidate. Until recently, nominations were given to preferred candidates by party "gatekeepers" – local power-brokers who judged the potential candidates to determine who could win and who could not. Many gatekeepers believed women could not win, and they did not want to risk losing the riding by nominating a woman.[33] Although the nomination process has recently become more open and democratic, some of those who gather to elect candidates still believe that nominating a woman is a risky proposition.[34] As a result, local party gatekeepers are a serious barrier to women seeking elected office. Female candidates in the 1988 federal election ranked a lack of support from their party as the third biggest obstacle to their success.[35]

The shift to open and democratic nomination meetings has helped many ethnic groups in Canada to secure the nomination of their preferred candidates.[36] But it has not been a great help to women. When the incumbent MP or candidate retires, leaving a winnable seat up for grabs, there is often a highly competitive contest for the party nomination. Such contests can last for months, cost thousands of dollars, and require huge outlays of time and effort by the potential candidate and his or her campaign team. Unlike federal election campaigns, there are no legal limits on the amount that an individual or organization can spend in a nomination campaign. Nor are there public reimbursements for candidate races, as there are in general elections.

Many women are at a disadvantage in this type of race: they have less money, they are more likely to have jobs that do not allow them the time to contest a nomination, and they often lack the high-status social and occupational networks that are the foundation of a campaign staff.[37] Money is the greatest tangible barrier for women in nomination races; the persistence of outdated assumptions about women's proper sphere is the greatest intangible barrier.

Incidentally, there is no evidence to support the belief that voters will not vote for women. In fact, some observers now believe that women have a slight electoral advantage, because they represent a change from the old boys who have always run Western political systems. So the real problem is not an aversion to voting for women. The real problem, according to one political professional, is "the general misperception of the appropriate public roles for women."[38] Party power-brokers believe that a woman in a non-traditional position will alienate voters, even where there is no proof that this is true.

The old attitudes are not confined to the senior power-brokers in the ridings. The volunteers who staff party campaigns may also be reluctant to associate themselves with an apparent "lost cause." The most experienced organizers and fundraisers, usually males, often refuse to work for a female candidate.[39] There is evidence that female candidates have more difficulty finding official agents who have done the job previously;[40] this difficulty could compromise the effectiveness of the entire campaign organization, and even pose a risk of later prosecution under the Election Expenses Act. The lack of support from key party figures often means that women without substantial financial resources of their own cannot compete with the well-connected men who usually win nomination battles.

The parties have come up with two solutions to the problem of female candidacy. The first is an affirmative action plan for women. This can involve a quota of female candidates in winnable ridings (the NDP approach) or special powers for the leader to appoint female candidates over the heads of the local riding associations (the Liberal approach). Because Canadian parties leave nomination in the hands of local party associations, affirmative action policies are very difficult to implement. The Ontario and federal NDP programs aim for 50 per cent female candidates *and* female winners. The latter target means that women must be nominated in winnable ridings, not just in hopeless ridings (see below).

These programs have not yet been completely successful. In the 1990 Ontario election only 30 per cent of the NDP candidates were women.[41] At the federal level there has been intense controversy over the policy, both because of the restrictions on the autonomy of local riding associations and because of discomfort with a quota system. The target was not reached in the 1993 federal election; as we have seen, the actual proportion of women was 37 per cent. No such policies have been seriously discussed by the other two major parties. However, the Liberal Party did pass a resolution in 1992 that permitted the leader to personally select candidates in ridings where the local association had failed to nominate a woman or a visible minority person. Jean Chrétien hand-picked a few women, some of them women of colour, to run in the 1993 election. This move caused controversy within the party, because it violated the strong tradition of local control over nominations; but Chrétien claimed that he had no choice if the party was to present a more modern and inclusive face to the voters. Most of his hand-picked candidates subsequently won election to the House of Commons.

A second approach to the problem, one that may prove equally effective in the long run, is to level the playing field for female candidates. All three parties have established special campaign funds for women: the Ellen Fairclough Fund for the PCs, the Judy LaMarsh Fund for the Liberals, and the Agnes Macphail Fund for the NDP.[42] The amounts of money available to female candidates are still limited, but the very existence of the funds has helped to persuade some women that the parties are serious about encouraging female candidates. Another promising idea was offered by the Royal Commission on Electoral Reform and Party Financing in its 1991 report. The commission called for spending limits on nomination contests. Each would-be candidate would be permitted to spend only 10 per cent of the maximum allowed in an election campaign, and this spending would be regulated and monitored as it would in a real election.[43]

The commission also offered a third approach to the problem. It recommended financial incentives to parties to nominate more women in winnable ridings. At the present time, a registered party that wins a minimum percentage of the vote in an election, and that spends a certain amount of money in its campaign, is entitled to a partial reimbursement of its expenses from public funds. Parties with between 20 and 40 per cent female MPs would receive subsidy bonuses equivalent to the percentage of women in their caucuses. In other words, a party with 25 per cent female MPs would receive its normal post-election reimbursement plus a 25 per cent bonus. A party with 40 per cent female MPs would receive a 40 per cent bonus. Above 40 per cent, the incentives would no longer apply.[44]

Had this system been in place in 1988, and had the PC party elected 25 per cent women, it would have received $850,000 as a reward.[45] The PCs had only 13 per cent female candidates in 1988 without incentives. There was a high number of incumbent candidates in that election, which would have made it very difficult to nominate more women.[46] Nevertheless, it is likely that there would have been significantly more female PC candidates in winnable ridings had there been such an incentive for the party. As yet, the government has not adopted any of the commission's recommendations in this area.

Women as Sacrificial Candidates in Hopeless Ridings

The "more competitive, the fewer" pattern shows up most clearly in the nomination of women to run for elected office. We referred earlier to the fact that while national parties are expected to run candidates in every federal riding, this is sometimes difficult for them to do. Some ridings will be so hopeless for a party that no one wants to waste their time and energy as its candidate. In those cases, the party has to beat the bushes and twist arms and make promises – in short, to do everything short of blackmail to persuade someone to run under its banner. Women make up a disproportionately large number of these "sacrificial lambs" (see Appendix 4). Women also make up a surprisingly large percentage of minor-party candidates and those who run for Parliament without party backing ("independent" candidates).

Appendix 3 shows the lower rate of success for female candidates in recent Canadian general elections. Women nearly closed the gap in 1993, mostly because of the unusually low success rate of male candidates. It might be tempting to conclude from those figures that Canadians do not wish to elect women to office. In reality, as we have seen, there is no evidence of such an attitude. The real reason for women's relative lack of electoral success is that most female candidates are doomed before they even start. A female NDP candidate running in Quebec in 1988, or a Green party candidate running anywhere in the country, has no chance of winning the seat. Neither does a woman running on her own, without the financial and organizational backing of a political party. She may be the most talented candidate in the race, or the least talented. But the end result will always be the same: she cannot win. Historically, the majority of major-party candidates in winnable ridings have been men (see Appendix 4). This explains why one out of every five men in the 1988 election won his seat, while only one out of seven women did the same. One senior party organizer states the problem succinctly: "Obtaining the nomination of a mainstream party in a riding where they have a realistic chance of being elected is the biggest obstacle to increasing the number of women in public office."[47]

Because of the extraordinary changes in the party system during the 1993 election, women (and men) who ran for the Progressive Conservative and New Democratic parties faced almost impossible odds. While 58 per cent of Liberal women won election, compared to 35 per cent for the Reform Party and 70 per cent for the Bloc Québécois, only 1 of the 67 female candidates for the PCs and 1 of the NDP's 110 female candidates were successful. Liberal and BQ women were almost as successful as their male colleagues, while Reform women were considerably more successful than male Reform candidates. All of these figures suggest that women have finally begun to break out of the sacrificial lamb stereotype, at least in some cases.

Among the minor parties, the proportion of female candidates varies. The more right-wing parties, including Reform, Christian Heritage, and the Confederation of Regions, had roughly 10 per cent female candidates in 1988. Left-wing or progressive parties had more women: 22 per cent of Green candidates and 38 per cent of Communist candidates were female. The tendency for left-wing parties to nominate more women than right-wing parties also characterizes the three major parties, and is consistent with patterns found elsewhere in the Western world.[48] For that reason, countries where left-wing parties are more popular tend to have more women in elected office; the Scandinavian countries are the best examples of this phenomenon.[49]

However, there is another factor to be considered when we try to explain why women candidates are more successful in some Western European countries than they are in Canada (see Appendix 5). That factor is the electoral system, or the set of rules and practices by which voters choose their elected officials. There are several different types of electoral systems, of which only two will be described here. The first type, which is present in Canada, the United Kingdom and the United States, is called the single-member-plurality (SMP) system. The country is divided into territorial constituencies, each of which elects one MP; the winner is the candidate who takes more votes than any other. He or she need not have won a majority of the vote (50 per cent plus 1). In a close three-way race a candidate can win with as little as 35 per cent of the vote. In this example, 65 per cent of the voters in that riding would have cast their votes in vain; they did not elect an MP in that riding, and they cannot be transferred to another riding.

The second type of electoral system, which exists in most Western European countries and in Israel, is proportional representation by lists (list-PR). In this type of system the voters cast their ballots for lists of candidates drawn up by the parties, and each party is awarded a proportion of seats equal to its proportion of votes. For example, if the Dutch PvdA (Labour) party wins 30 per cent of the vote – that is, if 30 per cent of voters cast their ballots for the PvdA list – then it is awarded 30 per cent of the seats in the lower house of the Dutch parliament. There are 150 seats, so a 30 per cent share would equal forty-five seats. The top forty-five people on the PvdA list would be declared elected. If a substantial proportion of those 45 people are female, there will be a large contingent of women in the PvdA caucus. Therefore, women within many Western European parties – particularly the socialist and ecological parties – have campaigned for quotas on the party lists.[50] The result has been a much higher proportion of women in many Western European legislatures than in the Canadian and British House of Commons or the American House of Representatives (see Appendix 5).

The principal advantage of a list-PR system is that it facilitates a national quota for female candidates. By contrast, SMP systems allow local party notables with traditional attitudes towards women to resist any type of quota system. There is little likelihood of Canada adopting a list-PR system in the foreseeable future, so the local party gatekeepers will remain in place for the time being. But the proposals put forward by the Royal Commission on Electoral Reform and Party Financing may point the way to an alternative solution, within the framework of the existing electoral system.

It is not completely clear why so many women – between three and four hundred in 1993 alone – agree to run as sacrificial lambs, or what benefits they receive from the process. Many seem to feel a sense of duty to the party, while others are looking to gain political experience and perhaps to win a shot at a better seat in the next election. Another explanation focuses on the role strains for women who try to combine elite politics with raising children. One way to experience electoral politics without sacrificing family responsibilities is to run in a lost-cause riding. Any role strain is short term, yet the woman has the opportunity to build her political skills and perhaps to make valuable contacts for a future full-time political career.[51] Whatever the reasons, the "more competitive, the fewer" pattern is still in place at the level of party nominations. Sometimes this can lead to unexpected results. For example, before the 1984 federal election the prospects for the PC party in Quebec looked grim. A large number of women were nominated in the hopeless ridings, only to be swept into office in the electoral earthquake of that year. The result was that the new federal government had the largest proportion of women in Canadian history, at that time, purely by accident.

Conclusion: What Is to Be Done?

In this chapter we have discussed the following key points.

1. In some countries, political parties have been the vehicle for large but powerless groups to secure political influence. In Canada the opposite has been the case: the parties have kept women out of

positions of power. This is due mostly to traditional attitudes and partly to the electoral system.

2.   Women have been disadvantaged in party competitions by a lack of money and organizational contacts. They have also been taken less seriously as potential candidates, a situation reflected (and reinforced) by the establishment of women's auxiliaries in the Liberal and Progressive Conservative parties.

3.   There have been some changes in recent years: policies to encourage female candidates, women winning party leaderships, women taking senior positions in party organizations. These changes have been provoked by women's pressure from outside the parties, and by the parties' realization that voters in the 1990s may be *more* likely to vote for a woman than for a man.

How can women overcome the barriers we have identified in this chapter? The top priority must be to change the attitudes of many men in the parties, who cannot or will not come to terms with gender equality. One research finding from the mid-1980s suggests that this attitude change will not be easy. When a national sample of voters was asked in 1984 whether "more should be done for women's equality," 85 per cent of women and 80 per cent of men agreed. When delegates to the 1983 PC leadership convention were asked the same question, only 46 per cent of women and 28 per cent of men agreed. The following year, 63 per cent of female Liberal leadership delegates agreed; the figure for male delegates was 38 per cent.[52] It is clear that the most active members of the PC and Liberal parties, the people who nominate the candidates, run the campaigns, and eventually run for office themselves, are out of touch with the Canadian electorate regarding issues of particular concern to women.

    The leaders of the parties, and their key advisors, are aware that "the parties could suffer, among women voters, from a public image of insensitivity to the concerns of women";[53] as a result, they have attempted to increase the numbers of women in visible party positions. But they are encountering stiff resistance, both from the entrenched local gatekeepers and from more traditional women who were comfortable with the old auxiliary system. Until the election of more women becomes a matter of conviction for the two older parties, not just a question of electoral strategy, Canadian women will not be able to look to the parties as vehicles for their proportionate representation in the political system.

How can women use the party system more effectively? There are a few possibilities, none of which is completely satisfactory. First, women can form their own party. This tactic was tried in 1918 with the foundation of the Woman's Party, and again in 1979 when the Feminist Party was set up. Both groups were short lived, and neither had any electoral success.[54] Under the SMP electoral system, fringe parties have almost no hope of winning seats unless they are concentrated in a few ridings; a gender-based party could not meet this criterion.

Second, women can continue to pressure the parties to respond to women's demands for participation, from both inside and outside. The women on the inside can use their experience and contacts to make changes in the system; the women on the outside can use publicity and other protest tactics to force the parties to listen to the feminist activists in their own ranks. This strategy appears to have been effective so far, but the pace of change has been more gradual than many women would like.

Perhaps, in the end, we must accept incremental change if we wish to minimize backlash and to create permanent alterations in party structures and women's representation. One Canadian party professional argues that "the chance of some dramatic breakthrough in the next few years, resulting in equal legislative representation for women, is highly unlikely. What is more likely is a gradual increase in the number of women directly involved in the power processes, more women seeking direct political power, and more women and men being elected who will promote gender parity."[55]

Appendix 1: The Date of Women's Suffrage in Selected Countries

Country	Date of Women's Suffrage
AUSTRALIA	1902
AUSTRIA	1919
BELGIUM	1948
CANADA	*1920* ★
COLOMBIA	1957
DENMARK	1915
DOMINICAN REPUBLIC	1954
FINLAND	1906
FRANCE	1944
WEST GERMANY (PRE-1990)	1919
GREECE	1952
INDIA	1919
IRELAND	1918
ISRAEL	1948
ITALY	1946
JAPAN	1946
NETHERLANDS	1922
NEW ZEALAND	1893
NORWAY	1909
PORTUGAL	1975
SPAIN	1977
SRI LANKA	1949
SWEDEN	1918
SWITZERLAND	1971
TURKEY	1934
UNITED KINGDOM	1918
UNITED STATES	1919
VENEZUELA	1946

★**Note:** This date does not refer to all Canadian women. Chinese and East Asian women did not receive full Canadian citizenship (including the right to vote) until 1947, while aboriginal women living on reserves could not vote in federal elections until 1960.

Source: Crotty, *Comparative Political Parties,* 5–10.

Appendix 2: Women as a Percentage of Candidates and MPs in Canadian General Elections

Year	% Candidates	% Elected
1921 1967	2.4	0.8
1968	3.5	0.4
1972	6.4	1.8
1974	9.4	3.4
1979	13.8	3.6
1980	14.4	5.0
1984	14.5	9.6
1988	19.2	13.5
1993	21.7	18.3

Source: Brodie, "Women and the Electoral Process in Canada," 4; Canada, *Report of the Chief Electoral Officer,* table 13.

Appendix 3: Success Rates for Male and Female Candidates, Canadian General Elections, 1972–1988

Year	% Women Elected	% Men Elected
1972	7.6	25.6
1974	7.2	20.4
1979	5.1	22.1
1980	6.4	20.0
1984	12.8	20.6
1988	12.9	20.1
1993	11.4	14.4

Source: Brodie, "Women and the Electoral Process in Canada," 7; Canada, *Report of the Chief Electoral Officer,* table 13.

Appendix 4: Women and Nominations in Competitive Seats, 1988 (Based on Actual Result of Election)

	Sex of Candidate (%)	
Competitiveness of Local Party	Male	Female
SAFE SEAT	12	25
GOOD CHANCE	18	26
UNLIKELY	14	12
HOPELESS	56	38
	100	100

Source: Erickson, "Women and Candidacies for the House of Commons," 108.

Appendix 5: Percentages of Women in National Legislatures

Country	% Women	Year
NORWAY	34.9	1987
FINLAND	30.5	1986
SWEDEN	28.9	1986
DENMARK	25.7	1986
WEST GERMANY	15.0	1987
NEW ZEALAND	14.4	1987
CANADA	18.3	1993
UNITED STATES	11.0	1992
SWITZERLAND	10.2	1986
BELGIUM	7.5	1986
UNITED KINGDOM	6.3	1987
AUSTRALIA	6.1	1987
FRANCE	4.4	1987

Source: Brodie, "Women and the Electoral Process in Canada," 8; Canada, *Report of the Chief Electoral Officer,* table 10.

Notes

1   Brodie, "Women and the Electoral Process in Canada," 9.

2   Gotell and Brodie, "Women and Parties," 56.

3   The name "Progressive Conservative" was adopted in 1942.

4   Myers, "'A Noble Effort,'" 39.

5   Bashevkin, *Toeing the Lines,* 104.

6   Myers, 42.

7   Ibid., 45.

8   Bashevkin, *Toeing the Lines,* 115.

9   Ibid., 116.

10 Brodie, "Women and the Electoral Process," 28.

11 Progressive Conservative Party of Canada, *Report.*

12 Bashevkin, *Toeing the Lines,* 113.

13 See, for example, Brodie, "Women and the Electoral Process," 45.

14 Chantal Maillé, *Primed for Power: Women in Canadian Politics* (Ottawa: CACSW, 1990), 23.

15 Bashevkin, "Women's Participation," 61.

16 Ibid., 62.

17 Ibid., 66.

18 Ibid., 62; Bashevkin, "Political Parties and the Representation of Women," 453.

19 These include federal and provincial legislators, members of party executives, defeated or recently nominated candidates for office, and provincial party leaders.

20 Bashevkin, "Women's Participation," 66.

21 Ibid., 67.

22 It is interesting to note that Campbell's principal opponent, Jean Charest, appointed a woman – Jodi White – to run his leadership campaign, while Campbell had no women above the bottom rank of her organization. This suggests that Campbell did not consider herself to be responsible for promoting other women within the party, as Audrey McLaughlin did within the NDP.

23 Bashevkin, "Women's Participation," 65.

24 Ibid.

25 Brodie, "Women and the Electoral Process," 38–39.

26 Ibid., 31.

27 Erickson, "Women and Candidacies for the House of Commons," 103.

28 Brodie, "Women and the Electoral Process," 31.

29 Ibid., 6.

30 Erickson, 106.

31 "Unaffiliated" candidates are those who belong to a party that has not met the conditions for registration with Elections Canada. In 1993 such parties included the Communist Party of Canada, the Rhinoceros Party, and the Confederation of Regions (Western) Party. See Canada, *Report of the Chief Electoral Officer,* for details.

32 These data are taken from table 13 of the 1993 *Report of the Chief Electoral Officer,* ibid.

33 Brook, *Getting Elected in Canada* (Stratford, ON: Mercury Press, 1991), 76.

34 Laschinger and Stevens, *Leaders and Lesser Mortals,* 15.

35 Brodie, "Women and the Electoral Process," 45.

36 See Stasiulis and Abu-Laban, "The House the Parties Built."

37 Laschinger and Stevens, 15.

38 Brook, 81.

39 Ibid., 79.

40 See Carty, "Official Agents in Canadian Elections."

41 Brodie, "Women and the Electoral Process," 37–38.

42 Bashevkin, *Toeing the Lines,* 107.

43 Laschinger and Stevens, 236.

44 Ibid.

45 Ibid., 237.

46 Erickson, 104.

47 Laschinger and Stevens, 15.

48 Erickson, 106.

49 See Norris, *Politics and Sexual Equality.*

50 Brodie, "Women and the Electoral Process," 35.

51 Brodie, *Women and Politics in Canada,* 83.

52 Ibid., 29.

53 Erickson, 103.

54 Bashevkin, *Toeing the Lines,* 13, 30–31.

55 Brook, 86.

References and Further Reading

Bashevkin, Sylvia. "Political Parties and the Representation of Women." In Alain G. Gagnon and A. Brian Tanguay, eds., *Canadian Parties in Transition: Discourse/Organization/ Representation.* Scarborough: Nelson, 1989.
———. *Toeing the Lines: Women and Party Politics in English Canada.* Toronto: University of Toronto Press, 1985.

————. "Women's Participation in Political Parties." In Kathy Megyery, ed., *Women in Canadian Politics: Toward Equity in Representation.* Vol. 6 of the collected research studies for the Royal Commission on Electoral Reform and Party Financing. Toronto: Dundurn, 1991.

Brodie, Janine. *Women and Politics in Canada.* Toronto: McClelland & Stewart, 1985.

————. "Women and the Electoral Process in Canada." In Kathy Megyery, ed., *Women in Canadian Politics: Toward Equity in Representation.* Vol. 6 of the collected research studies for the Royal Commission on Electoral Reform and Party Financing. Toronto: Dundurn, 1991.

Brook, Tom. *Getting Elected in Canada.* Stratford, ON: Mercury, 1991.

Canada. *Report of the Chief Electoral Officer: 35th General Election.* Ottawa: Elections Canada, 1993.

Carty, R. K. "Official Agents in Canadian Elections: The Case of the 1988 General Election." In F. Leslie Seidle, ed., *Issues in Party and Election Finance in Canada.* Vol. 5 of the collected research studies for the Royal Commission on Electoral Reform and Party Financing. Toronto: Dundurn, 1991.

Crotty, William. *Comparative Political Parties.* Washington, DC: American Political Science Association, 1985.

Erickson, Lynda. "Women and Candidacies for the House of Commons." In Kathy Megyery, ed., *Women in Canadian Politics: Toward Equity in Representation.* Vol. 6 of the collected research studies for the Royal Commission on Electoral Reform and Party Financing. Toronto: Dundurn, 1991.

Gotell, , Lise, and Janine Brodie. "Women and Parties: More than an Issue of Numbers." In Hugh G. Thorburn, ed., *Party Politics in Canada.* 6th ed. Scarborough: Prentice-Hall Canada, 1991.

Laschinger, John, and Geoffrey Stevens. *Leaders and Lesser Mortals: Backroom Politics in Canada.* Toronto: Key Porter, 1992.

Lovenduski, Joni, and Pippa Norris, eds. *Gender and Party Politics.* London: SAGE, 1993.

Myers, Patricia A. "'A Noble Effort': The National Federation of Liberal Women of Canada, 1928–1973." In Linda Kealey and Joan Sangster, eds., *Beyond the Vote: Canadian Women and Politics.* Toronto: University of Toronto Press, 1989.

Norris, Pippa. *Politics and Sexual Equality.* Boulder, CO: Wheatsheaf Books, 1987.

Progressive Conservative Party of Canada. *Report of the Restructuring Committee.* Ottawa: Progressive Conservative Party of Canada, 1995.

Stasiulis, Daiva, and Yasmeen Abu-Laban. "The House the Parties Built: (Re)constructing Ethnic Representation in Canadian Politics." In Kathy Megyery, ed., *Ethno-Cultural Groups and Visible Minorities in Canadian Politics: The Question of Access.* Vol. 7 of the collected research studies for the Royal Commission on Electoral Reform and Party Financing. Toronto: Dundurn, 1991.

Vickers, Jill, and Janine Brodie. "Canada." In Joni Lovenduski and Jill Hills, eds., *The Politics of the Second Electorate.* London: Croom Helm, 1981.

Chapter 9: Women in Canadian Legislatures, Executives and Judiciaries

Chapter Summary

Chapter 9 completes Part 3 by examining the status of women in Canada's national political institutions. We will discuss the place of women in the House of Commons, the Senate, the federal public service, and the judiciary. The same patterns that we identified in the political parties characterize our national institutions as well: "the higher, the fewer" and the gendered division of labour. Despite the recent breakthroughs by Audrey McLaughlin, Alexa McDonough, and Kim Campbell, the road for female politicians in Canada is a rough one. This chapter will explain how the exclusion of women from elite politics, described in the two previous chapters, affects the few women who do make it into politics, and in turn how the small numbers of women at the top may affect Canadian women as a whole.

Chapter Outline

- The Representation of Women in Canadian Politics
- Women MPs and Senators
- Women in Canadian Cabinets
- Women in the Federal Public Service
- Women in the Canadian Judiciary
- Why Are Some Countries More Representative than Others?
- The Consequences for Women
  Role Models
  The Public Treatment of Female Politicians
- Would Electing More Female Politicians Really Make a Difference?
- Conclusion

The Representation of Women in Canadian Politics

Women constitute over half of the Canadian electorate, yet they account for less than one-quarter of Canadian legislators, Cabinet ministers, senior government officials, and judges. This dramatic under-representation is one of the most striking facts about Canadian government and politics. Canada is hardly unique in this respect; women's numerical under-representation is a fact of life all over the world, although it varies widely even among Western countries (see Appendix 5 in the previous chapter). In this chapter we will describe the status of women in Parliament, the Cabinet, the national public service, and the judiciary. In Chapter 7 we discussed the reasons why there are so few women at the elite levels of Canadian politics. In this chapter we will seek to answer two further questions:

1. How can we explain the wide variation in women's numerical representation among Western states?

2. What are the consequences of this numerical under-representation for Canadian women as a whole?

Before we go further, three key terms in this chapter must be defined. The first is "numerical under-representation." This phrase describes a situation in which the composition of the national political institutions does not reflect the social make-up of the electorate as a whole. In particular, it refers to a legislature in which women make up fewer than 52 per cent of the membership. Ideally, in representative theory, the composition of a society should be reflected in the composition of its political institutions. If the population is 52 per cent female and one-quarter francophone, the national parliament would be numerically representative if it included 25 per cent francophones and 75 per cent anglophones, *and* if 52 per cent of each group were female and the rest male. This ideal becomes very difficult to realize when there are a large number of different social groups to be accommodated. Nevertheless, given the primacy of the gender division in society, it is impossible to justify the numerical under-representation of women in national legislatures, executives, and judiciaries. The word "representation" has other meanings, apart from its numerical aspect; we will discuss those in the following chapter.

Elite political activity, as we have seen, is open only to a select few. This level of activity includes seeking a party nomination, running for public office, or holding a party executive position. At this level, politics demands a huge commitment of time, energy, and other resources. Most people do not want to participate in elite-level politics, nor do they have the means to participate even if they chose to do so. A problem arises when those who do wish to participate are barred from elite politics because of discrimination or lack of resources. Most of this chapter will be concerned with elite politics; but when we turn to the explanations for women's under-representation at elite levels we will explore women's citizen-level activities.

In the standard political science literature on political participation and recruitment, it is assumed that citizen politics is the only prerequisite to elite politics. Anyone who votes or discusses politics can, if they so choose, advance up the ladder to the elite level. It follows, therefore, that because women are under-represented at the elite levels, they must be derelict in their performance of citizen-level political duties. But as Janine Brodie has argued, this model does not apply to women. In the last twenty years "women have achieved parity with men at the level of citizen politics in Canada."[1] Yet women are still under-represented at the elite levels of political activity. It is obvious that women who wish to move from citizen to elite participation face unique barriers, which we will discuss later in this chapter. We begin with a description of women's elite-level political participation in Canada.

Women MPs and Senators

As we saw in the last chapter, women constituted 18.3 per cent of Canadian MPs after 1993. This is the largest proportion of women in the history of the Canadian House of Commons (see Chapter 8, Appendix 2). In December 1994 there was one female Progressive Conservative MP, thirty-six in the governing Liberal caucus, one female NDP MP, seven Reform MPs, and eight Bloc Québecois MPs (see Appendix 1 to this chapter). The total number of women is fifty-three, most of whom were first elected in 1993.

The first woman elected to the House of Commons was Agnes Macphail, who won a seat in Ontario for the Progressive United Farmers of Ontario in 1921 (the first election in which women were allowed to run). Macphail remained in the Commons until 1940. She was joined or succeeded there by sixty-nine women in the following seventy years. Of those sixty-nine, eight were either elected at by-elections or appointed by the party leader to fill seats vacated by the death or retirement of their husbands.[2] The rest were elected in their own right, although many only served one or two terms. This pattern is in keeping with other Western democracies: "Most available evidence shows the rate of *turnover* of women legislators to be proportionately higher than for their male counterparts."[3]

Another pattern that characterizes Western governments is the concentration of women in particular areas of policy. Vicky Randall describes this as "the tendency to relegate [women] to those fields considered to be the logical extension of traditional feminine concerns – health, welfare, education, culture, the family, consumer affairs."[4] There is no consensus about why women tend to be clustered in those policy areas. One study of Scandinavian women legislators concludes that women *prefer* to work in these policy fields: "female legislators indeed have different priorities from men, since the former generally focus upon issues which represent extensions of the conventional feminine sphere – notably health, education, child care, family law, and social welfare defined more generally."[5] Critics of this interpretation argue that "women's apparent specialization in feminine areas of policy-making largely reflects the roles assigned to them by male-dominated political institutions."[6]

Whatever the reason, this stereotyping of female legislators has had both positive and negative effects for women in politics. On the positive side, the gender-associated portfolios – "the 'soft' ministries of family, welfare, culture, and, except where this is considered to be an important post, education"[7] – have given a number of women the opportunity to influence public policy. There has been room for women on legislative committees and as parliamentary secretaries where they otherwise might not have been welcomed by their male colleagues. On the negative side, as Joni Lovenduski argues, "such posts tend not to lead to further promotion in that they do not provide the experience of high-level management of economic or foreign affairs considered to be important in top leadership selection."[8] There are exceptions to this rule; Margaret Thatcher was elected leader of the British Conservative Party despite the fact that her highest Cabinet post had been as the junior minister for education – a typical "feminine" portfolio.[9] But for the most part, the feminine portfolios have been a dead end for female legislators.

Of course, it would be wrong to suggest that all female legislators are hungry for leadership positions and resent their assignment to pink-collar portfolios. Most female MPs, like most male MPs, are content to serve as backbenchers and to make a contribution in areas of policy that particularly interest them. In addition, we must remember that many female politicians are not feminists. Particularly in conservative parties, female MPs are comfortable with the status quo, or are reluctant to take feminist positions publicly for fear of losing the respect and support of their male colleagues.[10] For all of these reasons, it is reasonable to assume that many female MPs will find family, education, and other related fields the most interesting. What is *not* reasonable is to assume that *all* female MPs think policy begins and ends with home and children.

What is the pattern of committee assignments in the Canadian House of Commons? A 1981 study of Canadian female MPs found "few similarities in women's apparent patterns of interest or legislative behaviour." The authors argued that "most women have actively participated in the legislative committee system but the issue areas are as diverse as agriculture, prison reform, transportation and human rights. While some have shown interest in women's issues and rights, most have pursued the interests of their electoral districts. In fact, some have vigorously rejected a specific women's orientation to legislative work."[11]

But this conclusion is contradicted by the distribution of women on Canadian parliamentary committees, shown in Appendix 4. As of March 1995, female MPs were under-represented on the powerful finance, government operations, and public accounts committees. Women were also under-represented on the traditionally masculine committees of natural resources, agriculture and agri-food, foreign affairs, industry, national defense, fisheries and oceans, and transport.

Women were adequately represented, in proportion to their numbers in the Commons as a whole, on the human rights and environment committees. Women are over-represented on the remaining committees, most of them traditionally feminine: health, Canadian heritage, human resources development, and citizenship and immigration. The exception was the justice and legal affairs committee, which is traditionally viewed as a masculine portfolio.

Despite the conclusions of the 1981 study, we must conclude that the pattern in other Western legislatures also exists in Canada: women are scarce or even absent on the stereotypically masculine committees and plentiful on the pink-collar committees. It is also important to note that most of the female committee chairs or vice-chairs were found in the feminine fields (see Appendix 4).

In addition to their responsibilities as constituency representatives and supporters of the Cabinet, many MPs on the government side are appointed as parliamentary secretaries (Appendix 3). These people assist particular Cabinet ministers, by standing in for them at committee meetings, delivering speeches, meeting with interest groups, and so forth. In March 1995, out of a total of twenty-three parliamentary secretaries, five, or 22 per cent, were women (see Appendix 3). Thus women were slightly over-represented in the ranks of parliamentary secretaries. But despite their numerical strength, none of the female parliamentary secretaries was attached to the powerful and traditionally male portfolios of finance, justice, external relations, energy, or trade. Instead, they were assigned to the ministers of Canadian heritage, health, and citizenship and immigration. The exceptions were Jean Augustine, who was assigned to the prime minister, and Susan Whelan, assigned to the minister of national revenue.

Female senators make up a slightly larger percentage of their House than their colleagues in the Commons. Women accounted for 19 per cent of the Senate in April 1995 (see Appendix 5). The first woman was appointed to the Senate in 1930. In the 1920s, as we saw in Chapter 2, five women took the federal government to court because it refused to nominate women to the Senate. The Supreme Court of Canada ruled in 1927 that the section of the constitution that described eligibility for the Senate did not apply to women; it referred to "persons," and women were not "persons" in the legal sense. The decision was overruled by the

Judicial Committee of the Privy Council in London in 1929, clearing the way for women to be appointed to the Senate. The first female senator, Cairine Wilson, was not one of the five progressive women who had brought the "persons" case; rather, she had been the president of the National Liberal Women's Federation.[12]

The first appointment set a precedent for future female senators: they tended to be chosen not as a reward for their contribution to Canadian life or to the cause of women's equality, but because they had served the governing party. (There have been notable exceptions, including senators Thérèse Casgrain, a Quebec suffragist and former leader of the CCF in that province, and Florence Bird, who was recognized for her service as chair of the Royal Commission on the Status of Women.[13])

Women in Canadian Cabinets

The first woman was appointed to the Canadian Cabinet in 1957. She was Ellen Fairclough, appointed secretary of state in the first Cabinet of Prime Minister John Diefenbaker.[14] She remained in the Cabinet until 1963, when the Liberals returned to power under Lester Pearson. Pearson appointed Judy LaMarsh as minister of national health and welfare in 1963.[15] LaMarsh was deeply involved in the negotiations to create medicare, and moved to the secretary of state position to oversee the plans for the Canadian centennial in 1967.[16]

Despite LaMarsh's strong performance in these key portfolios, she was regarded by Prime Minister Pearson as a token woman. Before Pauline Jewett was elected to the House of Commons in 1965, she asked Pearson if she could serve in his Cabinet. Pearson replied that while she was certainly qualified, he already had a woman in the Cabinet and he didn't think LaMarsh wanted to be replaced. As LaMarsh later wrote about the incident, "It simply never occurred to Pearson that there could be more than one woman in the same Cabinet."[17] This attitude was gone by the 1970s and early 1980s, when such women as Iona Campagnolo, Judy Erola, and Monique Bégin served simultaneously in Pierre Trudeau's Cabinet. By that time it was clear that women were not just tokens; many of them were highly capable and qualified, and they did not all share the same views about policy – just like men.

In March 1995 there were twenty-four senior Cabinet ministers, five of whom (21 per cent) were female (see Appendix 2). Women were thus slightly over-represented in the Cabinet according to their proportion of the House of Commons, and their proportion of the government caucus. However, they were under-represented among the more senior and powerful ministers. All of the women except one, Senate Government Leader Joyce Fairbairn, were in the bottom half of the order of precedence. Even Sheila Copps, the deputy prime minister, is only thirteenth out of twenty-four. Three of the eight secretaries of state, the junior ministers without full Cabinet status, are women. The total proportion of women in the ministry is 24 per cent.

There are two reasons for the low rankings of the female Cabinet ministers. First, many of their male colleagues had greater seniority in Cabinet. Some had served under Prime Minister Trudeau before 1984. The women were all elected for the first time in 1988 or 1993, except for Sheila Copps and Sheila Finestone (who entered the Commons in 1984). Joyce Fairbairn was appointed to the Senate in 1984. Second, most of the women hold less powerful portfolios. The combination of shorter Cabinet service and less powerful positions placed most of the women in the lower half of the precedence order.

None of the junior ministers belong to the "inner Cabinet," which has the final say on government policy. Nor do they have a major voice on the powerful Cabinet committees. So while Canada officially has seven female Cabinet ministers, there are only two whose participation really matters in the overall political system. Meanwhile, the other top positions – prime minister, deputy prime minister, minister of finance, minister of international trade, minister of national health and welfare, minister of transport, minister responsible for constitutional affairs – are held by men.

We have seen that women in legislatures tend to be concentrated in a pink-collar policy ghetto. The same is true at the Cabinet level. Despite the existence of high-profile exceptions like Copps and AnneMcLellan, and their predecessors such as Flora MacDonald (the first female secretary of state for external affairs), women in Canadian cabinets "continue to hold conventional health, education, human resource, and social development portfolios, as well as newer status of women responsibilities ... at the same time as men's specialization in the more prestigious fields of finance, justice, treasury, and industry and trade is further entrenched."[18] At both the federal and provincial levels, women in Cabinet tend to be given responsibility for health and welfare, education, and culture and recreation.[19] Some of these departments are very large and important in the overall scheme of government; but their ministers do not always hold a proportionate amount of power in Cabinet.

Women in the Federal Public Service

Women make up a disproportionately large number of lower-level public servants, principally clerical staff. As of 1990, 44 per cent of women in the federal public service held clerical jobs; another 15 per cent held secretarial jobs. A further 17 per cent were accounted for by program administration and administrative services.[20] Over three-quarters of female public servants are in low-paying, usually dead-end jobs. In the professional and technical categories, women are significantly under-represented relative to their proportions in the overall labour force. For example, although 36 per cent of actuarial scientists (insurance assessors) in the Canadian labour force are female, there were no women in the federal public service in that job category in 1990. Only 9 per cent of defense scientists were women, compared to 33 per cent in the labour force overall; only 30 per cent of psychologists were female, compared to 60 per cent outside the public service; 40 per cent of social workers were female, compared to 71 per cent; and 7 per cent of foresters were female, compared to 31 per cent.[21] The higher-paying jobs are all but closed to women. In the highest echelon of the public service, the management sector, only 12 per cent of employees were women.[22] Similar patterns apply to the provincial public services as well; women make up the majority of clerical employees, nurses, primary-school teachers, and other lower-level workers, while men dominate the managerial fields (from school principals to deputy ministers).

In 1990, 29 per cent of appointments to federal boards and tribunals were women. Women were particularly numerous on the boards of the Bank of Canada (36.3 per cent), the National Farm Products Marketing Board (33.3 per cent), and the CBC (30.7 per cent). Women were also prominent on the CRTC (26.6 per cent).[23] Between 1984 and 1990 the proportion of female managers in the federal public service rose from 12 per cent to 20 per cent.[24] The federal government announced in 1985 that 30 per cent of its future order-in-council appointments would go to women, double the number in that year, and the results have been striking. The first woman deputy minister was only appointed in 1972, but by 1990 women made up 13 per cent of deputy ministers and 16 per cent of equivalent-ranking officials.[25]

It is clear that when the Cabinet decides to appoint more women, it has little difficulty in finding suitable candidates. The problem is not a lack of women, but a lack of will. It is time for similar initiatives at the lower, and less visible, levels of the public service, both federally and in the provinces.

Women in the Canadian Judiciary

Because the attitudes of judges can have such an impact on court proceedings, many women's groups have argued for a greater female presence on the bench. The most famous advocate of appointing more female judges is Madam Justice Bertha Wilson, now retired from the Supreme Court of Canada. She has argued that if the law and the justice system are to fairly reflect the needs of Canadian women, there must be more women in the judiciary.[26] Evidence from other Western democracies bears her out: "Women lawyers and judges have been responsible for changing the administration of justice in dealing with women victims of physical abuse (including rape) and of employment discrimination. They have also been responsible for review of outdated and inequitable views about women in the courts."[27]

Ironically, Madam Justice Wilson's retirement led to a retrograde step for women in this respect. Before she left the court, three of the nine justices were female: Wilson, Claire L'Heureux-Dubé, and Beverly McLachlin. Women's groups expected that Wilson would be replaced by a female judge. Instead, Prime Minister Mulroney appointed a male judge to fill her vacant seat. He responded to criticism by stating that no one pressure group should feel that it has a claim on a certain number of Supreme Court seats. This is a strange position to take, given that each region traditionally holds a certain number of seats (two for Ontario, two for the West, and two for the Atlantic), and that Quebec has demanded legal recognition of its claim to three judges from its civil bar. Perhaps the former prime minister meant that no *non-territorial* pressure group has a claim to a certain number of seats.

Whatever the reason, Mulroney's refusal to replace Wilson with another female judge reduced the number of women from three to two out of nine. In 1990, less than 10 per cent of federally appointed judges (in the national and provincial courts) were women; but it is expected that this percentage will increase as more women enter law school.[28]

This pattern is also consistent with the situation in the United States and Western Europe.[29]

Why Are Some Countries More Representative than Others?

As we have seen, although the pattern of women's under-representation is consistent throughout the Western world, its extent varies from country to country. It is important to try to explain this variation, and in particular the success of some countries, if we are to improve women's representation in Canada. British political scientist Pippa Norris has conducted a statistical analysis of women's political representation in several countries, to determine the relative importance of cultural, socio-economic, and political factors.[30] The primary cultural factor in the study is attitudes towards social equality, and gender equality more specifically. The chief socio-economic factor is "the proportion of women in a country who are eligible for office by virtue of their economic and educational experience."[31] The most important political factors are the gatekeeping roles played by parties and the effect of the electoral system on women's chances of nomination and election.

The results of Norris's statistical analysis are striking. Norris found that "right-wing parties tend to act as the major barrier to female representation."[32] This finding suggests that "the small number of women in political elites is due less to the shortage of women qualified to stand as candidates than to the party selectorate failing to nominate women for office."[33] This was not the only factor that explained variances in women's political representation; the electoral system, public attitudes towards women in politics, and women's educational status also played a part. In contrast, the study found that "socio-economic factors, the position of women in the workforce, in the professions and in college, did not have a major influence on the number of women in office."[34] Norris pointed to countries such as Canada and the United States, where women are increasingly going to university and holding powerful jobs and are still drastically under-represented in political elites. She argues that "even if women are making breakthroughs in other areas ... this does not imply that there will be similar progress in politics. As the 'gatekeepers' to public power, unless party selectorates are willing to nominate female candidates, placing them in winnable positions on party lists or in individual constituencies, then political inequalities will continue irrespective of other socio-economic trends."[35]

If Norris's analysis is correct, the explanations of women's minority presence in political elites that blame women themselves are clearly wrong. We should focus instead on the political parties in our efforts to redress the gender imbalance in our political institutions.

The Consequences for Women

What are the effects of this numerical under-representation of women? Is this simply an abstract question of mathematics, or do the majority of women somehow suffer from the lack of female representation in political institutions? We will conclude this chapter by arguing that the majority of women *do* pay a price for men's domination of the political system. We will list four particular problems; the last two will be considered here and the first two left to the next section of the book.

1. When policy issues of great import to all Canadians are discussed, little is heard about the specific interests of women, which may differ substantially from those of men.

2. Issues of particular concern to women are taken less seriously than those that are identified with male interests.

3. Women lack role models in the political system.

4. Women in politics are, for the most part, either ignored or treated less seriously than their male colleagues.

Role Models

Many people believe that by putting a member of a disadvantaged group in a position of power, no matter what their own personal beliefs may be, we can inspire other members of that group. A female professor, an African-Canadian high-school principal, or an Asian-Canadian television reporter is visible proof that anyone in this society can make it to the top if they work hard enough.

There are obvious risks of tokenism inherent in this argument, and it is clear that a single role model cannot break down all of the gender and racial barriers to achievement in this society. There is also evidence to suggest that role models have not been particularly influential for older generations of female politicians.[36] But there probably is something to be said for giving young women, and young people from visible minority backgrounds, a role model to try to emulate. If nothing else, a female Cabinet minister or party leader may inspire other young women to enter politics, which might not have occurred to them as a career option had they not seen that earlier example. Therefore, the greater the number of role models, the greater the chance of emulation.

The Public Treatment of Female Politicians

Any Canadian who watches the television news has seen clips of Question Period in the House of Commons. Every so often, those clips show a confrontation between a male Cabinet minister and a female opposition MP. All too often, the man is using sexist or demeaning language in an attempt to silence the woman. One particularly notable example is Progressive Conservative John Crosbie's admonition to Liberal MP Sheila Copps to "Quiet down, baby!" On another occasion he referred to her as a "slut." A third occasion was the notorious 1982 episode when NDP MP Margaret Mitchell was interrupted during a speech about wife battering by heckling and loud laughter from male MPs. The House is not a place for the sensitive, but female MPs seem to face particularly hurtful verbal abuse.[37] This is clearly the result of sexist attitudes, but it is probably also related to the small number of women in the House. Women are still regarded as interlopers – or, in Audrey McLaughlin's phrase, as freaks. Until women become more numerous in the Commons, they can expect to be treated as second-class – if not third-class – citizens by many of their male colleagues.

Nor do female politicians have a much easier time outside the Commons chamber. As we have seen in the chapter on women and the mass media, Canadian news reporters often concentrate on the appearance of female politicians, not on the substance of their policies. On her first day in the House as NDP leader, Audrey McLaughlin's clothing received more attention than her remarks. When she was asked by a reporter outside the chamber if her knees had been shaking when she rose to address the House, a female reporter responded, "Give me a break. Do you think that will be the first question to Paul Martin if he becomes Liberal leader?"[38] McLaughlin herself responded to this type of coverage in her 1992 book, asking, "How often have you read a newspaper report about a male politician that began like this? 'Brian Mulroney, wearing a dark blue suit tailored by Armani, a cream coloured shirt by Dior and a silk tie from Pierre Cardin, visited Calgary today.'"[39] In an even more blatant example, Kim Campbell's campaign for the leadership of the national Progressive Conservative party was nearly hijacked right at the beginning by the intense media interest – in Canada and elsewhere – in a 1992 photograph of her as justice minister, bare-shouldered, coyly holding up her lawyer's robes to hide her apparently naked body. The British tabloids compared her not to her male competitors in the race, but to Madonna – hardly a comparison one would make to a politician whom one took seriously as a potential prime minister.

The reason for this mistreatment of women by the media appears to be that women are still regarded as a novelty. They are also regarded primarily as sexual beings, not as politicians with differing beliefs, abilities, and ambitions, as male politicians are. Perhaps with more women in the House of Commons and elsewhere, they can weaken the existing stereotypes. But the stereotypes will persist until all sexism has been eliminated from Canadian society – a project well beyond the scope of this book.

There is no consensus about the effects of these two problems – a lack of role models and the trivialization of female politicians – on Canadian women. But given the evidence that women are alienated from and intimidated by the political system, which we saw in Chapter 7, one can argue that the scarcity of female politicians and their treatment by the media are sending a very strong message to Canadian women: "Stay out of politics, this is no place for you; if you do try to challenge the men who were here first, we will ridicule your appearance and ignore the substance of your remarks." It is little wonder, after years of these media stereotypes, and the relegation of most female politicians to supporting roles, that most women see politics as something with which they would rather not get involved. The Canadian polity is all the poorer as a result.

Would Electing More Female Politicians Really Make a Difference?

After devoting an entire chapter to the problem of female under-representation, it may seem strange to pose the question of whether the number of women really matters. If the number of women didn't matter, why would we take the trouble to complain about it? But as strange as it seems, this is a central issue in the study of women in Western political systems. It is often argued that one of the keys to improving women's status in Canadian society is to put more women in the Commons, the Cabinet, the federal public service, and the judiciary. It is assumed that once this is accomplished, public policy will inevitably become more attuned to the problems and the needs of women and children. This is the real reason behind the liberal feminist campaign to increase women's representation in politics: to make life better for the rest of us. But this approach has come under attack from a number of perspectives in recent years. It is therefore appropriate to question it in this chapter.

Part of the skepticism about putting more women into political elites arises from the experience of those who have already gotten there. As we saw earlier, women have been streamed into pink-collar ghettoes in the parties, in the Commons, and in Cabinet. If more women enter the political elite, but they end up in the same policy fields, the gain for women as a whole will be slight.

Fortunately, there is reason to believe that past experience is not a reliable guide to future performance. Younger generations of female politicians appear to be more interested in traditionally male policy fields, and less willing to accept mistreatment based on gender.[40] And many observers argue that as more women enter Canadian politics, a "critical mass" will develop. A critical mass of women is a large enough proportion of the legislature – estimates vary from 15 to 50 per cent – to ensure that women's voices are heard and their input is influential in the making of public policy.

One study of women in Norwegian politics concluded that "the relatively high number of women in public office in Norway, in addition to bringing the country closer to obtaining sex equality in governance, has also served to create a change in the content of the political agenda and legislation."[41] The Norwegian case proves that "the strategy of getting more women into public offices can make a difference provided their numbers are substantial enough (at least 15 per cent of the total) and that the women entering public politics have an alternative agenda to offer."[42]

Some Canadian observers have expressed doubts about the critical mass argument. But one recent study suggests that if women MPs work together across party lines, they can make a significant difference. In 1990 women MPs formed the Association of Women Parliamentarians (AWP), a group that resembles the American women's caucuses.[43] Its purpose is "to create a sense of solidarity in the face of negative aspects of political life for women."[44] The members of the group have suffered from sexism, harassment, loneliness, and other problems confronting women on Parliament Hill. The AWP was a support group, not a policy forum. Still, its existence suggests the possibility of more cross-party co-operation on policy issues, like the free vote on abortion in the House of Commons in 1988 (see Chapter 12).

Another arena for cross-party cooperation in the Commons was the sub-committee on the status of women, an offshoot of the standing committee on health and welfare, social affairs, seniors and the status of women.[45] The sub-committee was set up in 1990 and received considerable public attention in 1991 when it issued a strongly feminist report on violence against women. Its title, *The War Against Women,* provoked strong hostility in the government caucus and in the standing committee. Despite the reaction, many of the report's recommendations have been implemented. The sub-committee suffered from the same constraints that affect all legislative committees, namely party discipline, insufficient resources, and a lack of power to ensure the adoption of its recommendations. Nevertheless, research suggests that the sub-committee was an unusual and promising policy arena for women in the Canadian parliamentary system.[46]

Neither the AWP nor the sub-committee survived the 1993 federal election. The Reform and BQ women showed little interest in cross-party cooperation with the Liberals,[47] and the committee system was streamlined. But while they lasted, the AWP and the sub-committee allowed female parliamentarians to make a difference for Canadian women. Putting more women in the Commons could mean a greater scope and success for these two organizations. But we should remember that even if the institutional constraints in the Commons itself can be partially offset by women's cooperation, there are a host of other forces in the political system that can render women's representation ineffective. We will examine some of those forces in Chapter 11.

Another source of skepticism about putting more women in the Commons and Cabinet is the fact that female politicians are not necessarily feminists. As we saw earlier, many women in politics are either unsympathetic to feminism or reluctant to express feminist views. A study by Susan Carroll found that roughly a third of female legislators in the United States were "closet feminists."[48] They shared the goals and values of the women's movement, but they did not act on behalf of women or identify themselves as representatives of women. Their wariness of feminism was largely the result of fear. They were afraid of losing the hard-won respect of male colleagues if they were stereotyped as "women's libbers."[49] Carroll argues that these women constitute a "vast reservoir of latent feminist attitudinal support among women officials,"[50] which the women's movement should try to mobilize. But it is worth asking whether these closet feminists are really an asset to the women's movement. Will a critical mass enable these women to come out of the closet? Or would it be more constructive to focus on electing openly feminist candidates to office?

Not all female politicians are concealing feminist convictions. Some are strongly opposed to feminism. One example is Deborah Grey, the first Reform Party MP in the House of Commons (first elected in 1989). Another is Baroness Thatcher, formerly prime minister of the United Kingdom. Many of these women see their sex as irrelevant to their political careers, while others see themselves as MPs first and women second.[51] They see themselves as representatives of their ridings and their parties, not of their gender. Such women may come around to a feminist way of thinking after some years in politics. One former policy adviser to Brian Mulroney has said, "Give them a few months on the Hill. It's amazing how immersion in that male world educates women who start off wincing at the feminist label."[52] Some women will never understand the appeal of feminism, and their choice should be respected. However, for those women who believe that all female MPs should work on behalf of women, a non-feminist woman MP is hard to accept. As younger women enter politics, it is likely that the proportion of declared feminists in political life will rise dramatically. This prediction is borne out by Sue Thomas's study of female state legislators in the United States.[53]

Third, some critics have argued that putting more women into power is merely a symbolic measure. Gotell and Brodie contend that political parties may seek to increase their numbers of female MPs, to improve their image of representativeness, while simultaneously adopting policies that threaten the interests of Canadian women.[54] Because most of the women who are elected are cooperative, and therefore acceptable to the party elites, Gotell and Brodie do not see them as an asset to the women's movement. They expect to see more such women elected in the future, "because it enables mainstream parties to respond to women without any commitments to costly or interventionist social programmes."[55] In other words, as long as the parties in power remain opposed to measures that would bring substantive improvements to the lives of Canadian women, they will continue to throw them the bone of more women – though certainly not more feminist women – in Parliament.

Gotell and Brodie paint a gloomy picture, and one that is not altogether accurate. The number of feminist women in the House of Commons has certainly increased in the three elections since 1984. Instead of sitting back passively and accepting the dictates of the male elites, women MPs and senators have rebelled against a new abortion law and repeatedly drawn public attention to issues like child care and violence against women. It is true that public policy has not done enough to help women in recent years, but this is not the fault of the female MPs on the government side of the House. Gotell and Brodie are correct in their assertion that the numbers of women have been increasing in recent years, at the same time as a neo-conservative social and political agenda has threatened the few gains made by women in previous decades. However, they go too far when they assert that spineless female MPs are somehow to blame. The value of their argument lies in their analysis of why female MPs have not transformed politics. But that does not mean that an increase in the numbers of women in Parliament is necessarily useless.

In the end, we cannot simply assume that putting more women in Parliament and the Cabinet will automatically lead to more woman-sensitive policy. There are missing links in this argument, which the critiques discussed here have helped us to identify. First, the women elected to Parliament must be actual or potential feminists. Second, they must be willing to work together to overcome party discipline and other parliamentary constraints. Third, there must be enough of them to support each other and to present feminism as a legitimate perspective on politics and public policy. Fourth, there must be a strong women's movement outside Parliament, to push for better policies and to keep the female MPs mobilized and motivated. Given the present conditions, it is no wonder that the women in the Canadian political elite have been unable to transform Canadian politics. What is surprising is not that so *little* has been done, but that so *much* has been done. We will take a look at some of the successes of women in the Canadian policy process in Chapters 11 and 12.

Conclusion

In this chapter we have discussed the following key points:

1.   In Canada, like other Western countries, women are drastically under-represented in political institutions. Women made up 18.3

per cent of the House of Commons in 1993, and a slightly greater percentage of senators.

2.   Women in the Commons and the Cabinet are concentrated in a few policy fields, most of them traditionally feminine. These fields do not command the kind of respect that leads to higher office.

3.   The rule "the higher, the fewer" applies to the federal public service, as does the gendered division of labour.

4.   Only 10 per cent of Canada's federal judges are women. There are now two women on the Supreme Court of Canada, down from a high of three.

5.   Analyses of women's representation in Western countries reveal that the greatest barrier to women's election is the sexism of the political parties, followed by the electoral system and public attitudes. Socio-economic factors were not strongly influential.

6.   The lack of women politicians means that young women have few role models in the public sphere. The media treatment of female politicians is often sexist and degrading.

7.   It is incorrect to assume that electing more women to office will necessarily lead to better public policies for women; but under the right circumstances, more female MPs and Cabinet ministers could make a real difference.

   In Part 3 we have described the ways in which women participate in Canadian politics, and have examined the reasons why so few women choose to participate. We will now look at the ways in which the political system treats the women of Canada. How is public policy made? How does it affect women's lives? How have women tried to influence the policy process? We will discuss those questions in the next section.

Appendix 1: Female MPs in the Canadian House of Commons (March 1995)

Name	Province/Territory	Party
Diane Ablonczy	Alberta	Reform★
Jean Augustine	Ontario	Liberal★
Eleni Bakopanos	Quebec	Liberal★
Sue Barnes	Ontario	Liberal★
Colleen Beaumier	Ontario	Liberal★
Judy Bethel	Alberta	Liberal★
Ethel Blondin-Andrew	Northwest Territories	Liberal
Margaret Bridgman	British Columbia	Reform★
Bonnie Brown	Ontario	Liberal★
Jan Brown	Alberta	Reform★
Dianne Brushett	Nova Scotia	Liberal★
Marlene Catterall	Ontario	Liberal
Brenda Chamberlain	Ontario	Liberal★
Mary Clancy	Nova Scotia	Liberal
Shaughnessy Cohen	Ontario	Liberal★
Sheila Copps	Ontario	Liberal
Marlene Cowling	Manitoba	Liberal★
Madeleine Dalphond-Guiral	Quebec	BQ★
Maud Debien	Quebec	BQ★
Sheila Finestone	Quebec	Liberal
Hedy Fry	British Columbia	Liberal★
Beryl Gaffney	Ontario	Liberal
Christiane Gagnon	Quebec	BQ★
Deborah Grey	Alberta	Reform
Albina Guarnieri	Ontario	Liberal
Monique Guay	Quebec	BQ★
Sharon Hayes	British Columbia	Reform★
Bonnie Hickey	Newfoundland	Liberal★
Daphne Jennings	British Columbia	Reform★
Karen Kraft Sloan	Ontario	Liberal★
Francine Lalonde	Quebec	BQ★
Shirley Maheu★★	Quebec	Liberal
Diane Marleau	Ontario	Liberal

Audrey McLaughlin***	Yukon	NDP
Anne McLellan	Alberta	Liberal*
Val Meredith	British Columbia	Reform*
Maria Minna	Ontario	Liberal*
Carolyn Parrish	Ontario	Liberal*
Jean Payne	Newfoundland	Liberal*
Beth Phinney	Ontario	Liberal
Pauline Picard	Quebec	BQ*
Pierrette Ringuette-Maltais	New Brunswick	Liberal*
Georgette Sheridan	Saskatchewan	Liberal*
Roseanne Skoke	Nova Scotia	Liberal*
Christine Stewart	Ontario	Liberal
Jane Stewart	Ontario	Liberal*
Anna Terrana	British Columbia	Liberal*
Paddy Torsney	Ontario	Liberal*
Suzanne Tremblay	Quebec	BQ*
Rose-Marie Ur	Ontario	Liberal*
Pierrette Venne	Quebec	BQ
Elsie Wayne	New Brunswick	PC*
Susan Whelan	Ontario	Liberal*

* First elected to the House of Commons in 1993. ** Deputy chair of Committees of the Whole House (i.e., assistant deputy speaker). *** Former leader of the New Democratic Party of Canada.

Appendix 2: Female Ministers in the Canadian Cabinet by Order of Precedence in the Ministry* (March 1995)

Name	Order of Precedence	Portfolio(s)
Joyce Fairbairn	12	Government Leader in the Senate
Sheila Copps	13	Deputy Prime Minister, Minister of the Environment
Diane Marleau	16	Minister of Health
Anne McLellan	22	Minister of Natural Resources
Lucienne Robillard	24	Minister of Labour
Sheila Finestone	25	Secretary of State (Multiculturalism, Status of Women)
Ethel Blondin-Andrew	27	Secretary of State (Training and Youth)
Christine Stewart	29	Secretary of State (Latin America and Africa)

* Order of precedence is determined by the seniority of the minister's portfolio, and the length of his or her service in the ministry, relative to the rest of the cabinet. Thus Sheila Copps was only thirteenth out of the twenty-four senior ministers, despite holding the powerful deputy prime minister portfolio, because she had been in the House of Commons only since 1984. In 1993 Jean Chrétien appointed a two-tier Cabinet. In addition to the twenty-four senior cabinet ministers, he appointed several junior ministers. These are the secretaries of state, who have some of the powers but not all of the perks accorded to real ministers. Women account for five of the twenty-four senior ministers (21 per cent) and 38 per cent of the secretaries of state. Women make up 24 per cent of the entire ministry.

Appendix 3: Female Parliamentary Secretaries (March 1995) (in Order of Precedence)

Jean Augustine	Parliamentary Secretary to the Prime Minister
Susan Whelan	Parliamentary Secretary to the Minister of National Revenue
Mary Clancy	Parliamentary Secretary to the Minister of Citizenshi and Immigration
Hedy Fry	Parliamentary Secretary to the Minister of Health
Albina Guarnieri	Parliamentary Secretary to the Minister of Canadian Heritage

There were twenty-three parliamentary secretaries in March 1995, five of them women. That is roughly 22 per cent, which means that women are slightly over-represented among parliamentary secretaries.

Source: House of Commons Debates, April 5, 1995.

Appendix 4: Committee Assignments of Female MPs (March 1995)

Committee	Female Members	Female Associates
Aboriginal Affairs and Northern Development	0/11	2/4
Sub-Committee on Aboriginal Education	0/5	____
Agriculture and Agri-Food	1/15	0/5
Sub-Committee on Grain Transportation	1/5	____
Canadian Heritage★	5/11	0/4
Citizenship and Immigration★	5/11	3/6
Sub-Committee on Immigration Consultants	1/4	____
Sub-Committee on Witnesses★	1/5	____
Environment and Sustainable Development★	2/11	0/6
Sub-Committee on Environmental Awareness★	2/6	____
Finance	2/15	2/13
Fisheries and Oceans	0/11	1/6
Foreign Affairs and International Trade	1/15	2/13
Government Operations	1/11	1/7
Health★	4/11	1/8
Sub-Committee on the Controlled Drugs and Substances Act	3/6	____
Sub-Committee on HIV/AIDS	3/8	____
Human Resources Development★	5/15	3/8
Human Rights and Status of Disabled Persons	2/11	0/5
Industry	1/15	2/19
Justice and Legal Affairs★	5/15	4/13
Sub-Committee on National Security★	2/6	____
National Defence and Veterans Affairs 1/11	1/10	

Natural Resources	1/15	0/5
Procedure and House Affairs★	2/14	0/7
Sub-Committee on Electronic Voting	0/4	____
Sub-Committee on Members' Travel★	1/3	____
Sub-Committee on Private Members' Business	0/4	____
Public Accounts	2/12	1/4
Transport	1/11	1/7
Sub-Committee on the St. Lawrence Seaway	0/5	____

Note: The committees on which female MPs are over-represented (i.e., they account for more than 18.3 per cent of the membership, not including associates) are printed in boldface. The committees on which women are proportionately represented are in *italics*. All the others, on which women are under-represented or absent, are in normal type. An asterisk (★) denotes a committee with a female chair or one or more female vice-chairs. Suzanne Tremblay is a vice-chair of the Canadian Heritage Committee. Eleni Bakopanos is chair of the Citizenship and Immigration Committee. Judy Bethel is chair of the Sub-Committee on Witnesses (Citizenship Act). Monique Guay and Karen Kraft Sloan are the two vice-chairs of the Committee on Environment and Sustainable Development. Karen Kraft Sloan also chairs the Sub-Committee on Environmental Awareness for Sustainability. Pauline Picard is a vice-chair of the Health Committee. Francine Lalonde and Maria Minna are the two vice-chairs of the Human Resources Development Committee. Sue Barnes and Pierrette Venne are the two vice-chairs of the Justice and Legal Affairs Committee. Shaughnessy Cohen chairs the Sub-Committee on National Security. Marlene Catterall is a vice-chair of the Committee on Procedure and House Affairs.

Appendix 5: Women in the Canadian Senate (December 1992)

The total number of senators in April 1995 was 102; there were 19 women senators, constituting 19 per cent of the membership.

Name	Province	Party
Raynell Andreychuk	Saskatchewan	PC
Lise Bacon	Quebec	Liberal
Patricia Carney	B.C.	PC
Sharon Carstairs	Manitoba	Liberal
Ethel Cochrane	Newfoundland	PC
Erminie Cohen	New Brunswick	PC
Anne Cools	Ontario	Liberal
Mabel DeWare	N.B.	PC
Joyce Fairbairn	Alberta	Liberal
Céline Hervieux-Payette	Quebec	Liberal
Janis Johnson	Manitoba	PC
Thérèse Lavoie-Roux	Quebec	PC
Marjory LeBreton	Ontario	PC
Rose-Marie Losier-Cool	N.B.	Liberal
Joan Neiman	Ontario	PC
Landon Pearson	Ontario	Liberal
Brenda Robertson	N.B.	PC
Eileen Rossiter	P.E.I.	PC
Mira Spivak	Manitoba	PC
Dalia Wood	Quebec	Liberal

Notes

1   Brodie, *Women and Politics in Canada,* 2.

2   Kome, *Women of Influence,* 202–3.

3   Randall, *Women and Politics,* 104.

4   Ibid., 112.

5   Ingunn Norderval, "Party and Legislative Participation among Scandinavian Women," in Bashevkin, *Women and Politics in Western Europe,* 84–86 passim.

6   Lovenduski, *Women and European Politics,* 156.

7   Ibid., 241.

8   Ibid.

9   Jenkins, *Mrs. Thatcher's Revolution,* 87.

10 See Epstein, *Deceptive Distinctions,* chap. 8; Carroll, *Women as Candidates;* Randall, chap. 3.

11 Jill McCalla Vickers and Janine Brodie, "Canada," in Lovenduski and Hills, *The Politics of the Second Electorate,* 73.

12 Myers, "'A Noble Effort,'" 40.

13 Kome, 204–5.

14 Ibid., 71.

15 Ibid., 83.

16 Bashevkin, *Toeing the Lines,* 78–79.

17 Judy LaMarsh, quoted in Myers, 45.

18 Bashevkin, 79.

19 Ibid., 192, n. 38.

20 Task Force on Barriers to Women in the Public Service, *Beneath the Veneer,* 25.

21 Ibid., 19.

22 Ibid., 17.

23 Maillé, *Primed for Power,* 20–21.

24 Ibid., 21.

25 *Beneath the Veneer,* 99.

26 Maillé, 18.

27 Epstein, 184–85.

28 Ibid., 18.

29 Randall, 118–19.

30 *Politics and Sexual Equality: The Comparative Position of Women in Western Democracies* (Boulder, CO: Lynne Rienner, 1987).

31 Ibid., 120.

32 Ibid., 126.

33 Ibid., 129.

34 Ibid., 131.

35 Ibid.

36 Brodie, 33.

37 See McLaughlin and Archbold, *A Woman's Place*, 28.

38 Quoted in Robinson and Saint-Jean, "Women Politicians and Their Media Coverage," 149.

39 McLaughlin and Archbold, 92.

40 Randall, 152.

41 Jill M. Bystydzienski, "Influence of Women's Culture on Public Politics in Norway," in Bystydzienski, *Women Transforming Politics,* 22.

42 Ibid.

43 Young, "Fulfilling the Mandate of Difference," 8.

44 Ibid., 9.

45 Ibid., 11.

46 See Young.

47 Shaughnessy Cohen, Liberal MP for Windsor-St. Clair, personal communication, January 30, 1995.

48 Carroll, *Women as Candidates,* 152–54.

49 Randall, 155.

50 Carroll, *Women as Candidates,* 155.

51 Randall, 154.

52 Jocelyne Coté-O'Hara, quoted in Luinenberg and Osborne, *The Little Pink Book,* 14.

53 Thomas, *How Women Legislate.*

54 Gotell and Brodie, "Women and Parties," 55.

55 Ibid.

References and Further Reading

Adamson, Nancy, Linda Briskin, and Margaret McPhail. *Feminist Organizing for Change: The Contemporary Women's Movement in Canada.* Toronto: Oxford University Press, 1988.

Bashevkin, Sylvia. *Toeing the Lines: Women and Party Politics in English Canada.* 2nd ed. Toronto: Oxford University Press, 1993.

———, ed. *Women and Politics in Western Europe.* London: Frank Cass, 1985.

Brodie, Janine. *Women and Politics in Canada.* Toronto: McGraw-Hill Ryerson, 1985.

Bystydzienski, Jill M., ed. *Women Transforming Politics: Worldwide Strategies for Empowerment.* Bloomington: Indiana University Press, 1992.

Carroll, Susan J. "Feminist Scholarship on Political Leadership." In Barbara
   Kellerman, ed., *Leadership: Multidisciplinary Perspectives.* Englewood Cliffs,
   NJ: Prentice-Hall, 1984.
———. *Women as Candidates in American Politics.* Bloomington: Indiana
   University Press, 1985.
Christy, Carol. *Sex Differences in Political Participation: Processes of Change in
   Fourteen Nations.* New York: Praeger, 1987.
Epstein, Cynthia Fuchs. *Deceptive Distinctions: Sex, Gender, and the Social Order.*
   New Haven: Yale University Press, 1988.
Gotell, Lise, and Janine Brodie. "Women and Parties: More than an Issue of
   Numbers." In Hugh G. Thorburn, ed., *Party Politics in Canada.* 6th ed.
   Scarborough: Prentice-Hall, 1991.
Jenkins, Peter. *Mrs. Thatcher's Revolution: The Ending of the Socialist Era.*
   London: Pan Books, 1989.
Kay, Barry J., et al. "Feminist Consciousness and the Canadian Electorate: A
   Review of National Election Studies 1965–1984." *Women and Politics* 8, no.
   2 (1988).
Kome, Penney. *Women of Influence: Canadian Women and Politics.* Toronto:
   Doubleday, 1985.
Lovenduski, Joni. *Women and European Politics: Contemporary Feminism and
   Public Policy.* Brighton: Wheatsheaf, 1986.
Lovenduski, Joni, and Jill Hills, eds., *The Politics of the Second Electorate.*
   London: Routledge & Kegan Paul, 1981.
Luinenberg, Oline, and Stephen Osborne, eds. *The Little Pink Book: Quotations
   on Women.* Vancouver: Pulp Press, 1990.
Maillé, Chantal. *Primed for Power: Women in Canadian Politics.* Ottawa: CACSW,
   1990.
McGlen, N.E. "The Impact of Parenthood on Political Participation." *Western
   Political Quarterly* 33 (1980).
McLaughlin, Audrey, and Rick Archbold. *A Woman's Place: My Life and
   Politics.* Toronto: Macfarlane Walter & Ross, 1992.
Myers, Patricia A. "'A Noble Effort': The National Federation of Liberal
   Women of Canada, 1928–1973." In Linda Kealey and Joan Sangster, eds.,
   Beyond the Vote: Canadian Women and Politics. Toronto: University of
   Toronto Press, 1989.
Randall, Vicky. *Women and Politics: An International Perspective.* 2nd ed.
   London: Macmillan, 1987.
Robinson, Gertrude J., and Armande Saint-Jean. "Women Politicians and
   Their Media Coverage: A Generational Analysis." In Kathy Megyery, ed.,

Women in Canadian Politics: Toward Equity in Representation. Vol. 6 of the collected research studies for the Royal Commission on Electoral Reform and Party Financing. Toronto: Dundurn, 1991.

Sapiro, Virginia. *The Political Integration of Women: Roles, Socialization, and Politics*. Chicago: University of Illinois Press, 1983.

Sallot, Jeff. "Report links ads to violence against women." *Globe and Mail,* July 6, 1993.

Sharpe, Sydney. *The Gilded Ghetto: Women and Political Power in Canada*. Toronto: HarperCollins, 1994.

Task Force on Barriers to Women in the Public Service. *Beneath the Veneer,* Vol. 1: *Report and Recommendations*. Ottawa: Minister of Supply & Services, 1990.

Thomas, Sue. *How Women Legislate*. New York: Oxford University Press, 1994.

Young, Lisa. "Fulfilling the Mandate of Difference: Cross-Party Cooperation among Women in the Canadian House of Commons." Paper presented at the annual meeting of the Canadian Political Science Association, Carleton University, June 1993.

Part 4: Women and Canadian Public Policy

IN PART 3 WE DISCUSSED THE STRUCTURE AND OPERATION of the Canadian political system. In this section we look at the *output* of the political system, and its effects on women's lives. By "public policy" we mean more than the laws and regulations created by governments. We mean "the broad framework of ideas and values within which decisions are taken and action, or inaction, is pursued by governments in relation to some issue or problem."[1] The study of public policy goes beyond an analysis of the laws and regulations themselves. It is impossible to understand why a government passes a law, or does not pass a law, without examining the context in which policy is made: the social, economic, and political context within which the political system operates.

The state and its public policy profoundly affect the lives of all Canadians. When you work you pay taxes, contribute to the Unemployment

Insurance program and the Canada Pension Plan, and go on Worker's Compensation if you are injured. When you are sick you go to publicly funded hospitals. Most children go to public schools. When you go to college or university you may receive student loans to help finance your education—the majority of which is already paid for by the federal and provincial governments. When you look for work you may go to a Canada Employment Centre, and if unsuccessful you may receive UI benefits if you have been previously employed. The state, both federal and provincial, is a constant presence in our lives.

In most discussions of public policy, one important fact is over-looked: women are especially dependent on, and affected by, the state and its policies. As we have seen, women make up the majority of state employees: teachers, nurses, clerical staff, social workers. Women also account for the majority of health care costs, largely because of pregnancy and childbirth but also because women live longer, on average, and thus require more geriatric care. Women are more likely to be un-employed or on social assistance, and single women with children are particularly likely to depend on the state. Because more women than men are likely to depend on the state for a job or some material help, state cutbacks affect women disproportionately. This is a central issue for Canadian women in the 1990s.

But women's relationship with the state is more than just a matter of financial dependence. Historically, Western governments have taken a strong interest in the supposedly private details of women's lives: their sexuality and reproduction, their relation to their husbands and children, their economic status, and their opportunities for employment or education outside the home. Chapter 10 discusses that interest; it then describes some of the public policies that have resulted from it, and their effects on women's lives. Chapter 11 examines the other side of the coin: the ways in which women have attempted to influence public policy on their own behalf. Chapter 12 describes five case studies of "women's issues" in the Canadian political system, and their treatment by the public policy process.

Note

1   Stephen Brooks, *Public Policy in Canada: An Introduction,* 1st ed. (Toronto: McClelland & Stewart, 1989), 16.

Chapter 10: Public Policy-Making in Canada and Its Effects on Women's Lives

Chapter Summary

Chapter 10 examines the treatment of women by public policy-makers, in Canada and other Western countries. The chapter discusses six specific areas of women's lives and the ways in which governments have dealt with them. It concludes with a discussion of how public policy is divided into "women's issues" and really important issues, a division based largely on the traditional attitudes towards women discussed in Chapter 1.

Chapter Outline

- Women and the State
  The Effects of Public Policy on Women's Lives
  Powers within Marriage
  Control of Sexuality and Fertility

Rights and Duties as Mothers
Control of Wealth and Income
Employment
Education
- 'Serious Issues' versus 'Women's Issues'
- Conclusion

Women and the State

As we saw in the previous section of the book, women have traditionally been excluded from the Canadian political system. We argued at the
end of Chapter 9 that women have paid a price for men's domination of
the Canadian political system. The problem goes far beyond abstract
considerations of numerical representation. Women have suffered as a
result of public policies made by men who could not, or would not, understand the realities of women's daily lives. This is an important issue
because, as Joni Lovenduski observes, "most areas of women's lives are
affected by public policy of one kind or another."[1] We put forward two
claims at the end of Chapter 9:

1.   When policy issues of great import to all Canadians are discussed,
     little is heard about the specific interests of women, which may
     differ from those of men.

2.   Issues of particular concern to women are taken less seriously than
     those that are identified with general (i.e., male) interests.

In this chapter we will discuss these claims, in the context of a
broader discussion of the policy-making process. We will also examine
six major areas of public policy pertaining specifically to women, and
their effects on women's lives.

The Effects of Public Policy on Women's Lives

Vicky Randall has identified six areas of women's lives in which all
Western states have taken a particular interest: "powers within marriage,
control of sexuality and fertility, rights and duties as mothers, control of
wealth and income, employment, and education."[2] Most of these areas
impinge directly on the most private areas of human experience: sex,

childbirth, intimate family relationships. According to the ideology of the public-private dichotomy (see Chapter 1), such state interference in the family should be unusual, if not impossible. But in fact, the family has been a highly political institution for a very long time (see Chapter 4). Governments and churches have consistently tried to regulate the behaviour of individuals within the supposedly sacred bosoms of their families. In this section we will examine the overall patterns of these efforts to regulate women, the reasons for them, and their effects on women's lives.

Policies based on traditional gender stereotypes have hurt all women, even those not directly affected by a particular policy. Policies that reflect the attitudes of bygone days may "help to prolong them beyond what would otherwise have been their 'natural' lifespan."[3] The *absence* of policy has also threatened women's interests; the clearest example is the refusal of police authorities to intervene in cases of wife battering.

Until quite recently, all policy-makers were men, who were ignorant of the realities of women's lives. They were blinded by misleading ideologies about women, particularly the public-private dichotomy and the gendered division of labour (see Chapter 1). The public-private dichotomy led to public policies that ignored women. The images of women as lying, irrational temptresses resulted in public policies that treated them as inferior beings who could not be trusted to control their own money, fertility, or children. Until less than a century ago most women lost their separate legal identities upon marriage, lost any right to own property, "had little control over their own fertility and virtually no redress against rape, were severely discriminated against in employment and pay, were denied access to higher education and were deprived of all rights to participate politically."[4]

Some great strides have been made in this century. Married women are now able to keep their names, their legal identities, and their property, and are usually awarded custody of children upon divorce. But there is no room for complacency. Women's control of their own fertility is still hotly contested. Redress against rape is still far from guaranteed. Discrimination in employment and pay persists (see Chapter 3). Higher education is still male dominated, despite the numerical majority of female undergraduates (see Chapter 1). Women are still barred from political participation, though not by law (see Chapter 7). How is it possible for these problems to persist, in a time when we look to the state to redress social injustices? The answer lies in the traditional attitudes of the people (still mostly men) who make, interpret, and enforce the laws.

Powers within Marriage

Since at least the eighteenth century, the British common law has assumed that a man and a woman became one person upon marriage, and that person is the man.[5] The woman lost the right to own property, to make decisions about her children, even her own separate legal identity, along with her name. The origins of this assumption are clearly visible in the Greek and Roman law, under which the woman and her property passed from her father's ownership to her husband's or brother's ownership (see Chapter 1). It persisted until very recently, reflected in such policies as the single tax return for married couples.

Until early in this century women had no right to the custody of their children if their husbands deserted them. In one famous case, when the novelist Charles Dickens forced his wife to leave their home in 1858, he forbade his children to leave with her or even visit her.[6] The children were the man's property, a fact reflected in the habit of assigning children their father's name. Even worse, in many ways, the law regarded the man's home as his castle. The police would rarely intervene in a private dispute. This policy of non-interference is eroding under the pressure of feminist criticism (see Chapter 5), but it still persists among some police officers.

Control of Sexuality and Fertility

The state has long taken a close interest in women's sexuality and fertility, both in Western society and elsewhere. By the beginning of recorded history, "authoritarian societies had already discovered that by disciplining sexual relationships it was possible to exercise a control over the family that contributed usefully to the stability of the state. Even so, they interfered in sexual matters mainly insofar as they related to areas of public concern – legitimacy, inheritance, and population control."[7]

The issues of legitimacy and inheritance are closely linked. We have already discussed the problem of paternity in Chapter 1: while the mother of a child was never in doubt, the identity of the father could not be known for certain until this century. The only way for a husband to ensure that his wife did not conceive a child by another man – a child who could inherit the husband's property – was to physically prevent her from illicit intercourse, either by keeping her in isolation, by ensuring that she was never left unguarded, or by locking her in a chastity belt or similar device. The state, backed up by religion, assisted the husband with a battery of laws against independent female activity and powerful social pressures for female chastity.

The issue of population control has varied over time and in different cultures. Some states have tried to encourage fertility, others to restrict it. In states where a high birth rate is a matter of national policy, such as the former East Bloc state of Romania, birth control and abortion are outlawed. Every act of sexual intercourse between a man and a woman carries with it the chance of pregnancy, and every pregnancy must end either in miscarriage or in childbirth. Until 1969 birth control and abortion were illegal in Canada,[8] although both were available if one knew where to look and could pay. Other states prohibit birth control and abortion for purely religious reasons. Ireland, which has a hard time supporting its existing population financially, nevertheless bans birth control and abortion because of the powerful influence of the Roman Catholic church. Other measures to increase fertility, such as state services to help parents combine family and work responsibilities, will be discussed below.

States that have tried to restrict fertility have not only *permitted* birth control and abortion, they have *encouraged* people to use them. India and China are two countries with exploding populations whose governments have encouraged people to keep their families small. In India the government encourages men and women to undergo sterilization after one or two children. In China couples are only permitted by law to have one child. Such state policies are uncommon, but they have a long history. In ancient Greece and Rome the population was controlled by leaving weaker babies in the marketplace or exposing them on the nearby hillsides.

Women's sexual orientation has not been a matter of great state concern, unlike that of men, although other aspects of their sexuality have attracted considerable attention. There is no mention of lesbianism in the English common or criminal law; the story goes that when a law banning sexual activity between women was presented to Queen Victoria for approval, she refused to believe that women could engage in such acts and instructed her ministers to remove that section. Canadian law is similarly silent on lesbianism. But this does not mean that lesbians are free from legal discrimination. For example, some judges have been reluctant to grant custody of children to lesbian mothers.[9] Women's sexuality has been regarded as a delicate flower, to be protected from every man except her husband; there are laws against men having sex, even consensual sex, with young girls, and as we have seen in Chapter 5, there have long been harsh laws against rape.

Rights and Duties as Mothers

Throughout the history of Western states, laws and public policies have been based on "the assumption of women's primary responsibility for housekeeping and childrearing."[10] Public policy in the nineteenth century was largely silent on the subject of motherhood. Married women were the responsibility of their husbands, and women who had children out of wedlock were generally condemned (the "fallen women" of Victorian melodrama). This was also an era when limited government was thought to be the best government, so the lack of state action concerning motherhood is consistent with other policy areas at the time.[11]

In the twentieth century the state began to take an active interest in motherhood. The middle-class ideology of motherhood had triumphed over the working-class reality of most women's lives. Women who failed to live up to the ideology, by working outside the home or engaging in "immoral" conduct of any kind, risked losing their children. The federal state also began, grudgingly and ineffectively, to provide a little help to women who had been deserted or widowed with children to bring up.[12] These measures were extended to war widows after the First World War, and at the same time some of the provincial governments (Ontario and the western provinces) began to assist women with dependent children.[13] The Great Depression of the 1930s forced hundreds of thousands of people onto municipal and provincial welfare rolls, and prompted the first large-scale federal-provincial cooperation in the field of social assistance. The unemployment insurance scheme was set up in 1941. After 1945 the size and complexity of the "welfare state" grew geometrically, with the introduction of family allowances and a host of other programs to ensure a basic standard of living to all Canadians. Between 1945 and 1960 federal and provincial governments entered "areas of legislation such as employment and income security, which formerly had been regarded as outside the scope of public policy."[14]

For much of Canadian history, therefore, policy-makers only dealt with women in their capacity as mothers. Women did not exist in any other politically meaningful way, as long as they had a father or a husband to look after them. Even after the state began to take an interest in the welfare of mothers and their children, the programs available were inadequate. Most of the "relief" for women in poverty, especially in the cities, was provided by the charitable efforts of middle-class women. These charitable organizations supplied the nucleus of the suffrage movement. After the First World War the state increasingly took over these volunteer social services, squeezing out the women and replacing them with male bureaucrats and policy-makers. But the volunteers had succeeded in persuading the state that women and their children needed help, which was an important achievement. The veil of the public–private dichotomy was beginning to fall from the eyes of powerful men.

Despite these signs of progress, the Canadian state still refuses to give parents adequate assistance with their work and family responsibilities. As we have seen, the majority of women with young children are in the labour force. They have to juggle the demands of child care with those of paid work. But the Canadian state does not recognize these facts, and continues to assume that women either are, or should be, full-time mothers. At the same time, it stigmatizes women who have to resolve this dilemma by leaving work and going on welfare.

Control of Wealth and Income

Perhaps the greatest single influence on women's income, at least in the past two centuries, has been the idea of the family wage. As we saw in Chapter 4, the state and employers assumed that women were not the primary wage-earners in their families, and that they could rely on their husbands to help them provide for their children. At the same time, men were supposedly paid a wage that would enable them to support their wives and children by themselves.

The truth, of course, was often quite different. The family wage was sometimes inadequate, and there were many husbands who put their earnings to uses other than feeding and clothing their dependents. The assumptions on which the family wage system rested – that all men and women were married, and that all men took financial responsibility for their children —were no more true in the nineteenth and early twentieth centuries than they are today. But the idea of the family wage continues to depress women's earnings, and to deny them access to high-paying "men's jobs." It also penalizes single mothers on welfare, and it led to tax laws that, until recently, treated the husband as the sole wage-earner.

As we have seen, the Canadian state has greatly expanded its income support policies in this century. Underlying these changes in Canadian social policy is one consistent theme: women are still assumed to be the dependents of male breadwinners, who remain with them and support them financially for life. This assumption is clearly reflected in tax law, pension law, and welfare law. The details are too complicated to present here. Overall, their effect is to ensure that women in the real world – a world where a substantial proportion of parents are divorced, where too many fathers fail to pay child support, where child-care services for single mothers are grossly insufficient, where women are paid less than men (therefore earning fewer pension, UI, and tax benefits), and where women tend to outlive men – are frequently poor. Poverty is a particular problem of elderly women and single mothers, in large measure because these women do not live up to the breadwinner model assumed by federal and provincial policy-makers.[15]

Employment

The lack of public policies relating to women's employment has perpetuated the wage gap, the pink-collar ghetto, and other types of sex discrimination. The labour market has proven to be inadequate at self-regulation where women are concerned, and the only recourse has been government intervention. In addition, women have had difficulty balancing the need to earn money and the need to look after their children – particularly in recent years, when the extended child-care networks of relatives and friends on which women have traditionally depended began to fall apart. Therefore, until the state's recent and reluctant consideration of pay and employment equity policies, and the adoption of child-care programs in some European countries, its failure to act has kept women poor and without opportunities for advancement.

Women have also been deliberately excluded from law, medicine, and other professions. Those policies officially ended in this century. Women have also been barred from higher-paying industrial jobs because of "protective laws," which supposedly shielded their delicate reproductive systems from the effects of "men's jobs." Their real effect was to keep women segregated in clerical and other low-paying jobs. Ironically, as we saw in Chapter 4, microcomputers are creating concerns about the effects of radiation from video display terminals on the gynaecological and obstetrical health of women who work in offices. It may turn out that "women's work" is as dangerous in the long run as the more physically demanding jobs from which women's delicate biology had to be "protected."

Education

State-run education has long been a barrier to women's efforts to break out of traditional gender roles. Indeed, the fact that so few women made such efforts can also be partly blamed on the education system. Numerous studies of primary and secondary schools have shown that girls are called on less often than boys, are taken less seriously by both teachers and fellow students, and have been discouraged (subtly or otherwise) from pursuing "masculine" subjects like science and math.[16] The role of the schools in reducing girls' self-esteem is one of the root causes of women's lack of progress in employment and income. The education system has also encouraged girls to enter traditionally "feminine" fields like home economics and secretarial and clerical work instead of higher-paying "masculine" fields like science, engineering, and medicine.[17]

'Serious Issues' versus 'Women's Issues'

We will now return to the two claims reiterated at the beginning of this chapter. The first claim is that when policy issues of great import to all Canadians are discussed, little is heard about the specific interests of women, which may differ substantially from those of men. The second claim is that issues of particular concern to women are taken less seriously than those that are identified with male interests. Both of these claims are related to an underlying assumption: that there is a category of "women's issues" on the policy agenda, separate and distinct from other issues like defense spending or deficit reduction.

I would argue that there *are* areas of policy where most women differ to some degree from most men. This argument is supported by survey evidence. The existence of a gender gap on issues is a principal reason why women have claimed a place in political life in recent years. These differences do *not* mean that policy-makers should treat issues of greater concern to women as less important than those of greater concern to men. But this is what has happened, in Canada and elsewhere in the Western world. Many issues identified with women's "special sphere" have been defined out of politics, so that no policy change has taken place. Others have been marginalized in the political system. As a result, state actions that could benefit millions of Canadian women *and men,* such as the creation of a national child-care program, have not been taken.

Canadian policy-makers only pay genuine attention to women's groups when they lobby on "women's issues": abortion, child care, the feminization of poverty, pay and employment equity. They are likely to ignore women's concerns about other types of issues, though these may affect women as much as men. Former United States Congresswoman (now Senator) Barbara Mikulski challenged the idea of women's issues as a separate category in 1981: "Every issue is a women's issue. We have too long been identified with single issues. A budget that gets balanced by cutting foodstamps is a budget balanced on the backs of women."[18] Even foreign aid is a women's issue, because women and children bear the brunt of civilian casualties in war, and constitute the majority of the world's refugees.

Why are issues such as child care and poverty marginalized as "women's issues," when they clearly affect children and men as well as women? Why are issues like national defense and deficit reduction considered to be men's issues, in which women have little or nothing to contribute, when they affect every Canadian equally?

It is clear to anyone who has been inside the policy process that most politicians and bureaucrats relegate women's issues to a separate category for two reasons (usually implicit rather than explicit). First, by creating a distinct category of women's issues they can keep such controversial and expensive matters as child care and pay equity off the primary policy agenda. To redress the economic and social injustices suffered by Canadian women, especially women of colour and native women, would cost billions of dollars. No government is presently willing to face the fiscal implications of a genuine effort to solve these problems. Therefore, they are labelled as women's issues, not quite serious issues, and of interest only to a minority of feminists. Any issue that is not a women's issue is, by definition, not something with which a proper woman would concern herself.

Second, the designation "women's issues" not only marginalizes, but trivializes, issues that most policy-makers would rather not bother with. Abortion, employment and pay equity, and child care are potentially explosive issues. If a government can play them down by associating them with a less powerful, politically marginal group like women, then it can justify keeping them off the public agenda in favour of "serious issues." There are still a lot of men (and some women) who say the words "women's issues" with a sneer, to imply that problems like child care are frivolous diversions from the serious business of running a country.

Therefore, the first claim can be explained as follows. The voices of women may be heard on "women's issues," but not on other issues that are just as important to women's daily lives. As a result, women's distinct interests are ignored in the making of policy on issues such as state cutbacks and the end of universal medicare. This leads to the creation of policies that may appear to be gender neutral, but whose effects threaten women's interest more than those of most men. For example, the re-introduction of user fees for health care would disproportionately burden women having babies, women caring for sick children, women caring for aged relatives, and elderly women. Any cutbacks to health services would also mean that nurses, physiotherapists, nurses' aides, and other hospital support staff would lose their jobs. These job cuts would affect many more women than men.

Another reason why women's interests are overlooked in policy-making, which will come as no surprise after Chapter 9, is the lack of women in decision-making positions. As we have seen, even those women who do reach elite levels in politics are not necessarily feminists, so their power is not used to benefit other women. A woman who plays by the boys' rules to advance her own career is an unlikely champion of other, less privileged women. As we saw earlier, putting more women in decision-making positions will lead to changes in policy *only* if the women are feminists, if there is a critical mass of them (however large that proportion may be), if the women are willing to work together across political boundaries, and if there is a strong women's movement outside the political elite to keep the insiders mobilized.

The second claim is also related to the division of issues into those relevant to women and those relevant to men. "Women's issues" are considered to be less important and less serious than other policy issues. A particularly clear example occurred in early 1993, when the Mulroney government announced the purchase of five billion dollars' worth of military helicopters. This announcement came less than a year after the cancellation of a promised national child-care program, partly because of its "excessive" cost (see Chapter 12). Other examples can be found in the demeanour of some legislators when discussing women's issues. One notorious example, discussed in Chapter 9, is the laughter among male MPs during a speech about wife battering by a female MP in 1982. This is beginning to change, largely because the division between "women's issues" and others is no longer as universally accepted as it was ten years ago. But old habits die hard.

In fact, the idea that old habits die hard is the dominant theme of this chapter. Traditional ideas about women, derived from ancient Greek and Hebrew prejudices, have continued to shape legislators' attitudes about women into the twentieth century. In the next chapter, we will examine some of the efforts made by women to overcome these old prejudices, and the policies that enshrined and perpetuated them. One central theme will emerge: that women have had to fight hard to overcome the assumption that they are wives, daughters, mothers, temptresses, or irrational beings. Women have struggled for recognition as mature, grown-up people struggling to do the best they can with heavy work and family responsibilities. It should now be clear why women (and men) have been left to try to juggle those responsibilities on their own, without assistance from the Canadian state.

Conclusion

We have discussed the following key points in this chapter:

1. Women may be just as profoundly affected by public issues as men, but women's representations are unlikely to be taken seriously except on "women's issues" (and not always then).

2. The trivialization of some issues as women's issues reflects the sexism inherent in the political system, and the continued influence of the gendered division of labour and the public-private dichotomy in Canadian policy-making.

3. Women's groups and the economic changes of the past three decades have succeeded in forcing many policy-makers to recognize the new realities of women's lives. But pockets of resistance re-

main, and some policies have been very slow to change. One reason for the slowness is the high cost of programs such as child care and pay equity.

The pattern of Western public policy is clear: it not only reflects the existence of patriarchy, it actively discourages women from attempting to challenge it.[19] Women are assumed to be wives and homemakers, and are treated as such in public policy, despite the clear evidence (which we examined in Part 2) that this is no longer the case for most women. This evidence has begun to make a difference to the attitudes of public policy-makers, as has the growing – but still minuscule – number of women in their ranks (see Chapter 9). But despite the changes, "policies which treat women as autonomous individuals or regard couples as consisting of equal partners have been slow to develop."[20]

In addition to the growing weight of evidence against the traditional attitudes, women's groups have forced governments to realize that most women have needs and interests separate from those of home and family. Women share some of those interests with men, but others are distinct. Their distinct interests arise from women's different experience of the world: as victims of male violence, as underpaid workers with a "second shift" at home, as intelligent people assessed on the basis of their looks rather than their brains. While some policies still assume that women are, or should be, wives and mothers exclusively, others are more congruent with the realities of women's lives in the 1990s. We will look at some individual policies in Chapter 12.

Notes

1   Lovenduski, *Women and European Politics*, 246.
2   Randall, *Women and Politics*, 157.
3   Ibid.
4   Ibid., 158.
5   See Jo Freeman, "Women and Public Policy: An Overview," in Boneparth, *Women, Power and Policy*, 47.
6   Rose, *Parallel Lives*, 181–82.
7   Tannahill, *Sex in History*, 434.
8   Burt, "Legislators, Women, and Public Policy"; McLaren and McLaren, *The Bedroom and the State*.
9   Crean, *In the Name of the Fathers*, 31–34.

10   Randall, 162.

11   Burt, 130.

12   Ibid., 10–11.

13   Eichler, *Families in Canada Today,* 381.

14   Ibid., 137.

15   For a more complete discussion of these issues, see Eichler.

16   For an excellent summary of this research, see Istance, *Girls and Women in Education.*

17   See Russell, "The Hidden Curriculum of School."

18   Quoted in Ellen parth, ed., *Women, Power and Policy,* xi.

19   Randall, 194–95.

20   Lovenduski, 247.

References and Further Reading

Atkinson, Michael, ed. *Governing Canada: Institutions and Public Policy.* Toronto: Harcourt Brace Jovanovich Canada, 1993.

Boneparth, Ellen, ed. *Women, Power and Policy.* Oxford: Pergamon, 1982.

Brooks, Stephen. "Public Policy and Policy-Making in Canada." In Robert M. Krause and Ronald H. Wagenberg, eds., *Introductory Readings in Canadian Government and Politics.* Toronto: Copp Clark Pitman, 1991.

———. *Public Policy in Canada: An Introduction.* Toronto: McClelland & Stewart, 1989.

Burt, Sandra. "Legislators, Women, and Public Policy." In Sandra Burt, Lorraine Code, and Lindsay Dorney, eds., *Changing Patterns: Women in Canada.* Toronto: McClelland & Stewart, 1988.

Bystydzienski, Jill M., ed. *Women Transforming Politics: Worldwide Strategies for Empowerment.* Bloomington: Indiana University Press, 1992.

Carroll, Susan J. *Women as Candidates in American Politics.* Bloomington: Indiana University Press, 1985.

Crean, Susan. *In the Name of the Fathers: The Story behind Child Custody.* Toronto: Amanita, 1988.

Doern, G. Bruce, and Richard W. Phidd. *Canadian Public Policy: Ideas, Structure, Process.* 2nd ed. Scarborough: Nelson Canada, 1992.

Eichler, Margrit. *Families in Canada Today: Recent Changes and Their Policy Consequences.* 2nd ed. Toronto: Gage, 1988.

Epstein, Cynthia Fuchs. *Deceptive Distinctions: Sex, Gender, and the Social Order.* Hew Haven: Yale University Press, 1988.

Gelb, Joyce. *Feminism and Politics: A Comparative Perspective*. Berkeley: University of California Press, 1989.

Istance, David. *Girls and Women in Education: A Cross-National Study of Sex Inequalities in Upbringing and in Schools and Colleges*. Paris: OECD, 1986.

Lewis, Jane. "Feminism and Welfare." In Juliet Mitchell and Ann Oakley, eds., *What is Feminism?* New York: Pantheon, 1986.

Lovenduski, Joni. *Women and European Politics: Contemporary Feminism and Public Policy*. Brighton: Wheatsheaf, 1986.

McCormack, Thelma. *Politics and the Hidden Injuries of Gender: Feminism and the Making of the Welfare State*. Ottawa: CRIAW, 1991.

McLaren, Angus, and Arlene Tigar McLaren. *The Bedroom and the State: The Changing Practices and Politics of Contraception and Abortion in Canada, 1880–1980*. Toronto: McClelland & Stewart, 1986.

Randall, Vicky. *Women and Politics: An International Perspective*. 2nd ed. Chicago: University of Chicago Press, 1988.

Rose, Phyllis. *Parallel Lives: Five Victorian Marriages*. New York: Vintage, 1983.

Russell, Susan. "The Hidden Curriculum of School: Reproducing Gender and Class Hierarchies." In Heather Jon Maroney and Meg Luxton, eds., *Feminism and Political Economy: Women's Work, Women's Struggles*. Toronto: Methuen, 1987.

Sapiro, Virginia. *The Political Integration of Women: Roles, Socialization, and Politics*. Urbana: University of Illinois Press, 1983.

Tannahill, Reay. *Sex in History*. 2nd ed. London: Sphere Books, 1989.

Ursel, Jane. *Private Lives, Public Policy: 100 Years of State Intervention in the Family*. Toronto: Women's Press, 1992.

Chapter 11: Women's Effects on Public Policy

Chapter Summary

Chapter 11 discusses the ways in which the Canadian women's movement has campaigned for changes in national public policies, and the factors that have influenced the success of those campaigns. A model of women's influence in the Canadian policy process is used to identify the reasons for success or failure. The chapter concludes with an example to illustrate the model: the success of the Canadian women's movement in inserting section 28 into the Canadian Charter of Rights and Freedoms, compared to the failure of the American women's movement in securing the passage of the Equal Rights Amendment.

Chapter Outline

- Grassroots and Institutionalized Feminism
- Women's Groups and the Policy Process
  Institutionalized Feminism
  Grassroots Feminism

Grassroots and Institutionalized Feminism

In the previous chapter we discussed some of the principal patterns in public policy relating to women. In this chapter we will discuss the efforts of the women's movement to change those patterns. There were a few breakthroughs during the "first wave," including an expansion of state policies to help deserted or widowed mothers and their children, but not enough to satisfy many of the women activists involved in the campaign for family welfare. So, as we saw in Chapter 2, women decided to fight for the vote. They believed that female suffrage would lead to changes in public policy. As we saw in Part 3, those changes did not happen automatically, because women did not use their voting power as a cohesive bloc. Other methods of influencing public policy had to be found.

In the 1960s and 1970s, the "second wave" of the women's movement borrowed many of the tactics of the American civil rights and anti-war movements: sit-ins, marches, and other public confrontations with representatives of the political system. This approach was a strategy of outsiders, hostile to conventional politics and contemptuous of bureaucratic organization. As we saw in Chapter 2, in the discussion of strategic practice, this is the *grassroots feminist* strategy for change.[1] At the same time, more traditional women's groups (such as the Canadian Federation of University Women and the YWCA) developed a second approach: operating *inside* the political system as an organized interest group, lobbying policy-makers to demand specific changes in the state's treatment of women. This is the *institutionalized feminist* strategy for change.

Of the two strategies, the grassroots strategy has tended to attract more media attention (much of it negative or tending to ridicule), while institutionalized feminists have worked for change within the established system.[2] Institutionalized feminism is dominated by white, middle-class, heterosexual feminists to a greater degree than the various grassroots groups, many of which have been established by women of colour, lesbians, disabled women, and other groups who have felt excluded from the mainstream of feminism.[3]

The coexistence of the two strategies has caused considerable difficulty for the Canadian women's movement.[4] Conflicts have arisen that have, at times, threatened the survival of umbrella groups like the National Action Committee on the Status of Women (NAC) and the Fédération des femmes du Québec (FFQ). The effectiveness of the institutionalized wing has been somewhat compromised by demands for widespread consultation and feminist process from the grassroots wing. As we saw in Chapter 2, women in the movement have been torn between *mainstreaming* (the politic of institutionalized feminism) and *disengagement* (the politic of grassroots feminism), and have been partially paralyzed as a result.

Despite the tensions, some observers argue that the only effective feminist strategy for change is one that combines elements of both approaches. Too much mainstreaming risks co-optation; too much disengagement risks marginalization.[5] In practical terms, feminists who work for change within the political system face pressures to assimilate, and they need a strong movement outside the system to remind them of their purpose. Feminists outside the system need allies on the inside, both to provide access to resources (i.e., funding and decision-making power) and to provide the kind of information necessary for effective strategy and organization.[6]

In practice, public policy in Canada, like elsewhere in the Western world, has been more directly affected by institutionalized feminism. But this does not mean that grassroots feminism has been powerless. Institutionalized feminists in Canada have built strong coalitions with grassroots feminists, thus affording them some influence within the policy process. According to Jill Vickers, "small-group collectives organized along radical feminist norms have operated in state politics under the umbrella of coalition organizations such as NAC."[7] As a result, "it is possible in Canada for such groups to play a role within the overall women's movement."[8]

In the United States, by contrast, small radical groups reject state involvement. They are essentially marginalized and powerless to change the larger social structures that oppress them. The "radical liberalism" of the institutionalized Canadian women's groups allows them to operate within the political system, while simultaneously preserving some degree of autonomy within which to construct a feminist critique of the state.[9]

The next section of this chapter will focus on women's groups in the Canadian policy process. We will begin by looking at some key institutionalized feminist organizations, and then briefly turn to the role of grassroots feminism in the policy process. The next part will return to the model of Canadian policy-making presented in the previous chapter, and discuss the access points for women's groups within that model. The chapter concludes with a discussion of the various factors that determine the effectiveness of women's intervention in the policy process: environmental factors, systemic factors, political factors, and the characteristics of the policies themselves.

Women's Groups and the Policy Process

Institutionalized Feminism

By "institutionalized feminism" we mean those groups that, whatever their origin, have come to occupy a position within the policy communities of the state. These are the groups whose views are sought by parliamentary committees, by royal commissions and other public inquiries, and by the media. There are multi-issue groups at the national and provincial levels, including Status of Women councils, as well as single-issue groups like the Canadian Abortion Rights Action League and the Canadian Day Care Advocacy Association. For the sake of brevity, this section will focus on three national groups. One is organizationally independent of government, although it has relied on government funding. Another was an offshoot of the federal government, created to advise it on "women's issues." The third is the most recently established, and perhaps the most independent of the state. They are, respectively, the National Action Committee on the Status of Women, the Canadian Advisory Council on the Status of Women (CACSW), and the Women's Legal Education and Action Fund (LEAF). Unlike the weaker and less developed groups, these organizations are capable of direct participation in policy-making rather than advocating changes from the sidelines.[10]

NAC is a unique organization. It is the most inclusive national women's organization in the world. It seeks to represent the views of liberal, radical, and socialist feminists, as well as more traditional women's groups like the YWCA and the Canadian Federation of University Women, and women's associations in the major national parties. As of 1988 NAC claimed 570 affiliated groups.[11] Its size, its longevity, and its focus on lobbying the state has transformed NAC from a watchdog group into a "parliament of women,"[12] an alternative policy structure for feminists.

NAC was founded in 1972 as a permanent interest and watchdog group. Its initial purpose was to monitor the federal government's progress on the recommendations of the Royal Commission on the Status of Women. Its present purpose is to emphasize the interests of women within the existing political system. Its most important roles are to speak for women in the media and the policy process, and to keep member groups informed about events in Ottawa. NAC can mobilize its membership quickly when it needs to, and it is an invaluable clearing-house of knowledge and expertise for its members.

NAC is a multi-issue organization; it focuses on whichever topics are most relevant to its members at a given time. In recent years the organization has focused on employment and economic issues, although many of its member groups would prefer a stronger emphasis on violence against women and sexual issues.[13] This gap between the leadership and the membership is created by NAC's need to respond to government initiatives such as free trade, and by the ad hoc structure of the NAC committee system. If a woman with expertise in a particular policy area wishes to chair a NAC policy committee, she can become NAC's spokesperson on these issues.[14]

NAC has been dependent on federal government funding for most of its history. The Mulroney government repeatedly cut the funding for the Women's Program of the Secretary of State's Department, which subsidized NAC and hundreds of other federal and provincial women's groups (see below). NAC lost an estimated 70 per cent of its government funding between 1987 and the 1993–94 fiscal year.[15] In recent years the organization has raised funds in the private sector and from its member organizations.

The public profile of NAC has depended in large measure on its various presidents. When the president has been able and willing to use the media effectively, as Chaviva Hosek did from 1984 to 1986, NAC has attracted membership and money.[16] The presidency of Judy Rebick, which spanned the years 1991 to 1993, saw the finances of NAC placed on a firmer and more reliable footing outside the government. Rebick also made NAC more visible in public debates over "real issues," such as the constitution, and pursued an aggressive policy of promoting previously excluded groups of women within the organization. In 1994 she stepped down and was replaced by Sunera Thobani.[17]

The structure of NAC is a balance between the grassroots and mainstream strategies. As an umbrella structure for hundreds of diverse groups, NAC has a great deal of internal differentiation. Vickers lists seven types of affiliated groups: (1) national, chapter-based groups; (2) national groups with individual memberships; (3) provincial umbrella groups representing varying organizations (e.g., the FFQ); (4) national federations of local groups; (5) networks of service groups (e.g., women's shelters); (6) single-issue coalitions (e.g., the Canadian Abortion Rights Action League); and (7) local groups, collectives, centres, and services.[18]

To impose some order on this potential chaos, NAC has evolved some traditional representative structures. There is an executive board and a series of policy committees. The membership is based on groups, not individuals. Delegates from the member groups attend the annual general meeting (AGM) and vote on issues of strategy and policy. But beneath the formal structures lies a profound ambivalence about representation. Feminist process requires that individuals speak for themselves, and rejects representation and hierarchy as elitist and oppressive. However, the realities of running a large national organization require that delegates attend on behalf of member groups.

Because of the unease with representative forms, there are no provisions in NAC's rules for accountability or for keeping leaders in line. In addition, many of the member groups adhere to feminist ideas of "rotating" leadership positions among their participants, to avoid creating a permanent power clique within the organization. As a result, they send different delegates to the AGM every year. This means that an experienced and knowledgeable executive board is annually confronted, not by an equally experienced and knowledgeable group of delegates, but by a large number of people attending their first AGM, with little knowledge of traditional process (NAC operates by Robert's Rules of Order) or of the issues on the agenda.[19]

NAC has become the recognized voice of women in English Canada, and its Quebec counterpart, the Fédération des femmes du Québec (FFQ), has become the voice of Québécois women. NAC is invited to present briefs to government hearings on matters considered to be within its purview, and it has demanded to be heard on other issues where it believes women's interests are at stake (the constitution, free trade). Because NAC does not have the budget to employ a staff of professional researchers, as CACSW did (see below), the NAC delegation at a hearing usually consists of the president, perhaps a vice-president, and the chair of the relevant policy committee. There is little in the way of membership consultation before the brief is presented – although the committee and the executive board are usually canvassed – because of a lack of time and money. But there is little evidence that the membership has strongly disagreed with official NAC positions. Instead, the issues that have divided NAC are issues of process, of "identity" politics (the exclusion of non-white, disabled women), and of strategy.[20]

The Canadian Advisory Council on the Status of Women was set up by the Trudeau government in 1973. Its official purpose was to advise the government on issues pertaining to women. It commissioned research on such matters as reproduction, women and poverty, domestic violence, women in sport, and women's activity in Canadian public life. It presented briefs to parliamentary committees and other bodies of enquiry, building on its research to construct credible critiques of proposed legislation and of the status quo. The council also organized conferences at which feminist academics and activists shared information and prepared strategies for action.

The research conducted by the CACSW has had an impact on policy debates in Canada. Anyone who is familiar with its work will be struck by the frequency with which it is referred to in other government publications. For example, the National Clearinghouse on Domestic Violence, a branch of the Department of National Health and Welfare that collects and distributes information on family abuse, relies almost entirely on the CACSW report *Battered but Not Beaten*[21] in its publications on wife abuse. The CACSW was not an isolated think tank producing reports that were read only by other feminists; it was regarded within the federal bureaucracy as an authoritative voice on matters pertaining to women. It should be noted, however, that the effectiveness and influence of the

CACSW fluctuated with the political independence of its chair. A chair who wished to curry favour with the governing party toed the line, while a more independent and authoritative chair could strengthen the autonomy and legitimacy of the council and its work.[22] The CACSW was eliminated in the 1995 federal budget.

The nucleus of LEAF was the Ad Hoc Committee of Women on the Constitution, which was formed in 1980–1982 to fight for improvements to the Charter of Rights (see Chapter 5). After the Charter was proclaimed in 1982, with the equality provisions scheduled to come into effect three years later, many of the women who had lobbied for sections 15 and 28 decided to form a permanent organization to monitor the use of these sections in the courts. LEAF was officially established in April 1985, with a war chest to support legal action and an agenda of issues to pursue.[23]

LEAF's original intention was to be pro-active, to initiate litigation to ensure that the Charter was applied in ways that would help women. Instead, the organization has been forced to be reactive, to respond (often with insufficient time and resources) to court cases that threaten women's equality rights. As men have challenged women's "privileges" under the law, LEAF's resources have been consumed by damage control.[24] Whenever possible, LEAF consults with groups of feminists who work in areas relevant to particular cases. But given the strict time limits imposed on groups who wish to intervene in court proceedings, LEAF's ability to build networks with other feminist groups has been limited. The organization's agenda for Charter jurisprudence has been scrapped, and a piecemeal strategy of defending turf already won has evolved in its place.

We have seen in Chapter 5 (and we will see in Chapter 12) that LEAF has had an impact on judicial reasoning in some cases. We have also seen that a great deal remains to be done. LEAF can only intervene in a Charter case with a judge's permission, and not all judges have been willing to hear LEAF or to give credence to its arguments. The cancellation of the Charter Challenges Program in 1992 (see Chapter 5) reduced LEAF's ability to litigate on behalf of disadvantaged women. LEAF has also presented briefs to parliamentary committees and other inquiries, describing women's experience of a particular law or criticizing draft legislation, but the group's analyses only carry weight when the committee is already predisposed to accept feminist reasoning. For example, LEAF's intervention in the parliamentary committee hearings on the Meech Lake

Accord in 1987 was all but ignored by the committee, despite the widespread concern about the accord among Canadian women's groups.[25] Like NAC and the CACSW, LEAF cannot effect changes in policy by itself. There are a host of factors that determine the effectiveness of women's groups in the policy process. We will consider those factors in the next section.

Grassroots Feminism

We have seen that grassroots feminist groups can participate in the Canadian policy process, if they so choose, through their membership in national and provincial umbrella groups. These groups can be multi-issue organizations like NAC and the FFQ, or single-issue movements like CARAL or the CDCAA. Many grassroots groups also provide services, instead of or in addition to advocating policy change. This grassroots access to the political system differs somewhat from the American situation. Many grassroots groups do not choose to engage directly with the state; they do not believe that a patriarchal state can really help women, or they reject the hierarchy and bureaucracy that characterize state organization. Those groups tend to focus on small-scale endeavours such as consciousness-raising, operating small collectives (bookstores, cafes, baby-sitting groups), or just supporting each other as individual women.

For these small groups, financial survival is often a serious problem. We have seen that institutionalized feminist groups receive funding from the federal government, through the Women's Program of the Department of the Secretary of State. Most grassroots groups are profoundly uneasy about taking government money, because they do not want to be dependent on (or co-opted by) a patriarchal state, and because they are afraid that any funds will have strings attached. One solution to this problem is to set up a core organization that represents several smaller groups, and channel any funding through that core. Then the member groups can negotiate for funding among themselves, rather than taking it directly from the government.[26]

The role of these grassroots groups in the policy process is less formalized than that of the institutionalized groups, but this should not be taken to mean that the grassroots are irrelevant. Grassroots groups can help to put issues on the public agenda, especially at the local level. They can hold rallies, protest marches, and other public events to attract attention to their cause. They can set up women's shelters, rape crisis hotlines, and other services, often combining government assistance with funding from the private sector, thus filling the gaps left by state policy. They can act as the conscience of the institutionalized feminist groups, reminding women within the policy process what their goals are and why they are working on behalf of women. Because they remain outside the political system, away from the temptations of power, they can sustain an autonomous critique of the state that may be lost when women enter the policy-making process.

Some grassroots groups have tried to engage directly with the state, and the experience has changed them significantly. A good example is the grassroots campaign for child care, which lobbied the federal and provincial governments in the 1970s and 1980s. After child care became part of the public agenda, government agencies began to integrate the child-care lobbyists into its own structures. The issue became one of mainstream social policy, instead of a grassroots campaign for parent-run child-care collectives that would transform social relations.[27]

At the same time, the character of the movement changed from a non-hierarchical collection of activists to a few national and provincial, government-funded, bureaucratically organized interest groups: the Ontario Coalition for Better Day Care and the Canadian Day Care Advocacy Association. The critique of gender and class relations that sparked the grassroots movement has shifted to a less threatening agenda of equal opportunities for women in the workplace and the needs of families. As one observer of this process observes, "while coalitions offer an important opportunity for different groups to work together in solidarity, they also frequently require a moderation of political demands to maintain this solidarity."[28] Instead of a mass-based network of community-organized child-care services, the focus of the child-care movement is now a national child-care program jointly funded by the federal and provincial governments, with some flexibility for parents, and no demand for a shift in the balance of power in Canadian society.

This example explains why many grassroots groups prefer to remain outside the political system, retaining their procedural and ideological integrity. They pay a price in terms of policy influence. However, it must be remembered that not all women's groups exist for the purpose of influencing the state. Many serve a host of other purposes: consciousness-raising, providing services, or an alternative space for women seeking to minimize the effects of patriarchy on their lives. But by their existence and their numbers, they constitute a visible demand for change in gender relations, whether by state policy or by other means.

The Women's Program

In 1974 the federal government established a separate program to distribute money to women's advocacy groups. There had been similar programs administered by the Citizenship Branch of the Secretary of State's Department since the late 1960s. The impetus for the separate Women's Program came from the United Nations designation of 1975 as International Women's Year.[29] The objectives of the program were as follows: "to help in establishment of community-based Women's Centres; to provide women's services; to assist in investigation of areas where women's participation was restricted (e.g., the media); to assist in formation of new women's groups; to help mount projects addressing the status of women; and to assist in co-ordinating activities through conferences, workshops, and newsletters."[30] The program gives money to women's groups to support particular projects, and it gives operating grants to most of the key women's advocacy groups in Canada. According to Pal's study of the Secretary of State's Department, "this funding usually accounts for between 50 per cent and 80 per cent of [each] organization's budget."[31] (For the overall budget of the Women's Program, see Appendix 2 to this chapter.)

The Women's Program has been a major factor in the success of the women's movement in changing Canadian public policy. LEAF, the CDCAA, NAC, the Canadian Research Institute for the Advancement of Women (CRIAW), and other key groups have been sustained or assisted by the Women's Program. The benefits of the program have been tempered by concerns about dependence on state funding by groups that seek to change the status quo, as we have seen. For example, Burt argues that women's advocacy groups are "fragmented, diverse in their goals and organizationally weak, partly as a consequence of their continued reliance on government funding."[32] Burt also notes that "the government controls the groups' agenda by setting a priority list for funding."[33] These criticisms are justified, though we have to ask whether any of these groups would have survived, let alone had an impact, if the Women's Program had not been set up.

By the late 1980s the program faced political and economic threats. The Conservative government was less enthusiastic about funding advocacy groups than the Trudeau Liberals had been, partly because it regarded many of these groups as enemies. The PCs were particularly angry at NAC, which opposed the Meech Lake Accord and the Free Trade Agreement with the United States. Under the circumstances, and given the government's emphasis on fiscal restraint, it was not surprising that the program sustained major cuts in the 1990s. In addition, the objectives of the program became controversial in the 1980s because of the efforts of R.E.A.L. Women (see Chapter 4) to obtain project grants and operational funding. They were repeatedly refused money because they did not support the goal of gender equality as defined by the federal government and by the United Nations.[34] They complained to the media and to their supporters in the government caucus, and in late 1986 the House of Commons Standing Committee on the Secretary of State began to review the program's objectives and funding criteria. The committee reported in May 1987, and recommended that the criteria and objectives be left unchanged, stating that "funding should be directed to women's groups whose main purpose is to improve the status of women in the home, the workplace, the community or the world at large [and] whose principles, objectives and activities support the attainment of equality for women as stated in the Canadian Charter of Rights and Freedoms [and other legal documents]."[35] The report was a clear victory for feminist groups and a defeat for R.E.A.L. Women. However, the latter group did receive a $21,000 grant to hold a conference in 1989.[36] The cuts to the program in the 1990s suggest that feminist groups who welcomed the committee's recommendations may have celebrated too soon.

In 1993 Kim Campbell reorganized the federal government (see Chapter 9). She eliminated the Secretary of State's Department and divided its responsibilities between the new departments of Canadian Heritage and Human Resources Development. The Women's Program, along with the rest of the "Social Development" branch, was transferred to Human Resources Development. In 1995 the program was shuffled yet again, to the much smaller Status of Women Department. Status of Women Canada has never been a strong or effective department within the federal government.[37] It no longer has a full-fledged Cabinet minister, and its future appears somewhat precarious in light of the 1995 federal budget and the elimination of the CACSW.

Women's Access to the Canadian Policy Process

We have seen, in the previous chapter, that there are a number of access points for interest groups in the policy-making process in Canada. Women's groups have sometimes exploited them very effectively. In this section we will briefly discuss some of those access points, and their use by the women's movement.

The first access point is the bureaucracy. The Women's Bureau in the federal Department of Labour was set up in 1956, and there are now several other bureaucratic niches where the women's movement can count on support: the Status of Women office, the Women's Program, the Canadian Advisory Council on the Status of Women (see p.331), and its provincial equivalents. In addition, as we saw in Chapter 9, there are female MPs, senators, and Cabinet ministers. Most of them, whatever their attitude towards feminism, can be mobilized to support women's causes in an emergency, such as the lobby to save section 28 (see Chapter 5) or the House vote on abortion (see Chapter 12).

The second access point is *lobbying*. Women's groups outside the bureaucracy can make contacts with civil servants, ministers, MPs, and other participants in policy-making, and use those contacts to try to influence the outcome of the process. Lobbying tactics include letter writing, visits to the offices of MPs and bureaucrats, and regular telephone calls. Women's groups have been less effective in this respect than they might have been, largely owing to a lack of funds and some lack of legitimacy among the wider public.

The third access point is the *media*. Women's groups can use print and broadcast news coverage to draw attention to their causes and put pressure on governments to respond to them. Effective use of the media is crucial to the success of an interest group, as we saw in Chapter 5. Paid advertising is very expensive, so only the wealthiest organizations – the National Citizens' Coalition or the Business Council on National Issues – can rely on it. Other groups have to attract news cameras and reporters by holding media events, like marches or pickets. Women's organizations have had some success in this regard. Some NAC presidents have made regular appearances on television to speak on behalf of Canadian women on particular issues, like the constitution or free trade.

The fourth access point is *public inquiries*. Task forces, royal commissions, and other inquiries are set up to advise governments that are either uncertain of what to do about a particular issue or hoping to postpone action on it.

The Canadian women's movement was galvanized by the Royal Commission on the Status of Women in the late 1960s (see Chapter 2), and since then they have taken advantage of public inquiries to represent the interests of women. All public inquiries whose subjects touch on women's interests – from child care and employment equity to reproductive technologies and unemployment insurance – have heard from NAC, and usually from the CACSW as well. The constitutional hearings of recent years have hosted NAC, the CACSW, LEAF, the National Association of Women and the Law (NAWL), the FFQ, and other women's groups. Sometimes these appearances generate policy change; sometimes they do not. If an inquiry has already decided which position it will take, or if its members are unsympathetic to the feminist position, the women will be heard more or less politely and their views ignored. This is particularly likely when the subject of the inquiry has not been defined as a women's issue. In other cases, women's groups do influence the recommendations of the inquiry. The 1984 Commission on Employment Equity and the 1986 Task Force on Child Care are two examples. Finally, by appearing before an inquiry, women's groups can make an impact on the public debate over the issue, even if their immediate policy goals are ignored.

The fifth access point is *parliamentary committees.* Under the rules of the House of Commons, all legislation must go before a parliamentary committee for clause-by-clause debate and possible amendment. Committees can hold public hearings, call for briefs, and invite witnesses to testify about bills. NAC, the CACSW, LEAF, and NAWL, among other groups, have made numerous appearances before parliamentary committees. Sometimes party discipline prevails, and the women are ignored; this happened with the Special Joint Committee on the Meech Lake Accord in 1987. On other occasions, women's concerns can influence the committee's report, and their suggested amendments can be put before the Commons at report stage.

The sixth access point is *the Charter.* Since its passage, LEAF has used the Charter and the rules for intervenors to put the feminist case before the courts on a number of occasions (see Chapter 5). Sometimes LEAF's arguments have influenced the outcome, and at other times they have not. Much depends upon the opinions of the judge or judges presiding. Sometimes they may deny LEAF intervenor status, arguing that the issue at stake is not a women's issue; at other times they may simply disagree with LEAF's analysis. But the fact that the Charter is in place does give women another crucial access point into the policy process. There is no telling how long it would have taken to liberalize the abortion law without the *Morgentaler* case, or whether the feminist analysis of pornography would have been adopted as completely by the Cabinet as it was by the Supreme Court (see Chapter 12).

The points of access to the policy process differ in each political system. The United Kingdom does not have a written Charter of Rights, although the European Court has reinforced women's gender equality rights in Britain and elsewhere in the European Community. The United States offers more access points for lobbying, because party discipline is weaker and an individual representative or senator – especially on a powerful committee – can make a difference to legislation. Access points also differ across time and according to the issue under consideration. In the next section we will examine the factors that determine how effectively Canadian women's groups have taken advantage of the access points available to them.

Conditions Determining the Effectiveness of Women in Public Policy

In this section we will look at the factors that determine the success or failure of the women's movement in its efforts to influence public policy.[38] There are two sets of factors. The first are *long-range factors,* which determine the prospects for policy change in general: the environment within which the policy process operates (society, the economy, politics), and the character of the political system itself (concentration of power, access to interest groups). The second are *short-range factors,* which influence the outcome of particular policy battles: the strength of the women's movement on that particular issue (lobbying, coalitions, and leadership), and the nature of the policy itself (e.g., controversial and broad in scope, versus low-profile and affecting only a small range of interests). We will begin the analysis with a look at the long-range factors.

The Long-Range Factors

∞ *The Environmental Variables.*
The policy process does not operate in a vacuum. It operates within a *social and economic environment,* which affects the way the policy process operates and the types of policies it tends to create. The first environmental factor to be considered is the *social climate.* In the 1960s the social climate

in North America favoured an extension of rights and resources, whether to blacks in the United States or to Québecois and natives in Canada. In such a progressive and optimistic period, women's campaigns for greater equality of opportunity met with greater acceptance than they had during the "first wave."

In the 1970s and 1980s social acceptance of feminism grew, as Canadians became more comfortable with the idea of "rights" (see Chapter 5). This acceptance can be measured in polling data, and in general attitudes towards equality. More recently, there has been a growing skepticism about the state and its ability to solve social problems.[39] The optimism about the state and social progress that marked the 1960s is gone, replaced by a growing distrust of representative institutions. At the same time, there is a backlash against women and other groups who benefited from the state expansion of the 1960s and 1970s. In this social climate, policy changes that would benefit women (and many that would also benefit men) are difficult to secure.

The second environmental variable is the *economic climate*. The optimism of the 1960s was fuelled by economic growth, a growth that stopped in the early 1970s as the OPEC oil price shocks rocked the industrial economies. The 1980s and 1990s have brought a "fiscal crisis of the state," in which governments have stopped introducing new social programs and have been forced to cut existing programs. Many of the policies demanded by the Canadian women's movement – a national childcare program, better training and pension coverage for women, adjustment programs for workers harmed by free trade with the United States and Mexico – would cost a lot of money, and are almost impossible to attain in a climate of economic restraint. Many of the most significant victories of the Canadian women's movement – including the attainment of suffrage and the gender equality clause in the Charter – have been the least expensive to implement.

The third environmental factor is the *political climate*. Governments can choose which interest-group demands they wish to respond to. Those choices are often based on "the extent to which a social movement's goals are recognized as legitimate and deserving of a political response."[40] The political legitimacy of the Canadian women's movement was largely created by the Royal Commission on the Status of Women (see Chapter 2). Women who were active in the women's movement at that time have argued that women did not constitute a politically relevant constituency before the commission was established in 1967.[41] But after the commission's hearings raised the consciousness of women across the country, and its report was published in 1970, women became legitimate claimants for state resources. In addition, it has been argued that NAC was considered to be more legitimate by the Liberal government than by the Progressive Conservative government that succeeded it in 1984.[42]

In addition, the institutionalized women's movement in Canada has largely operated within a political ideology – which Vickers calls "radical liberalism" – that is congruent with Canadian political culture as a whole. Its values include "a commitment to the ordinary political process"; a faith in the state, and in change; "a belief that dialogue with those who differ may be useful"; and an acceptance of the importance of service to others.[43]

This radical liberalism differs from the ideology of the American women's movement, which rejected cooperation with the state and alienated some potential supporters by its intransigence towards those who disagreed with its analysis and aims. Vickers argues that this ideology allowed the Canadian women's movement (particularly its institutionalized wing) to balance mainstreaming and disengagement, to compromise ideological purity for political efficacy, and to build coalitions among groups that disagreed on many important aspects of doctrine. It also made the Canadian movement more legitimate in the eyes of the political system than its counterpart in the United States.

Political legitimacy also enhances the ability of a group to redefine an issue according to its own perception. As we will see in the case of abortion (Chapter 12), the power to redefine the terms of an issue is a crucial step towards winning a new policy. The tendency of Canadian policymakers to divide the universe of public policy into "women's issues" and real issues demonstrates its unwillingness to listen to women speaking about matters that are not directly related to family and reproduction. In recent years this division of policy areas has broken down to some extent; NAC is now asked to comment on issues relating to employment and the economy, as well as child care and reproductive technology. And women's groups have been successful in redefining a few crucial issues, thus gaining some measure of control over the debate: abortion, child care, employment equity, pornography, reproductive technology, and sexual harassment (see Chapter 12).

The legitimacy of the women's movement has come under attack in recent years, mostly from the right wing. The anti-feminist group

R.E.A.L. Women has argued that NAC does not speak for Canadian women, as have members of the Mulroney government (see Chapter 4). Former prime minister Mulroney condemned women's groups for opposing the Meech Lake and Charlottetown Accords, attacking their supposed lack of patriotism and accusing them of being "anti-Quebec." That government also tried to weaken the women's movement by cutting funds to the Women's Program. However, the visibility and media skill of recent NAC presidents has reinforced the claims of the Canadian women's movement to political legitimacy, as has the introduction of the Charter.

∾ *The Systemic Variables.*

The systemic variables that affect policy-making are the specific characteristics of the political system that determine the distribution of power among various individuals or groups. The first such systemic variable in Canada is the *federal system*. Canada is divided into ten provinces and two (soon to be three) territories. Each of the provinces has a government similar in structure to the national government in Ottawa. The Constitution Act, 1867 divides the various subject areas of public policy between the federal and provincial governments. The provinces are responsible for health care, social welfare, education, the solemnization of marriage, municipal governments, and provincial taxes, among other matters.

A provincial government is technically sovereign in its designated areas of policy: Ottawa cannot tell it what laws to pass.[44] The province has the power to pass the laws and to implement them. The federal government is responsible for all other policy fields, including most taxation, marriage and divorce, and the criminal law. The federal government also has the "residual power," which means that any policy field not mentioned in the constitution automatically comes under federal jurisdiction (telecommunication is a good example). A few policy fields – agriculture and immigration – are assigned to both levels of government.

In practice, despite the "watertight compartments" into which policy fields are divided, the federal and provincial governments often work together. Because the provincial governments have much less revenue-raising capacity than Ottawa, yet are responsible for such expensive areas of policy as health, education, and welfare, they have come to depend on federal payments. Ottawa has used its spending power to influence provincial policy in particular fields of provincial jurisdiction. For example, the 1984 Canada Health Act imposed strict conditions on federal transfer payments to provincial Ministries of Health. Any province that permitted doctors to charge user fees would suffer financial penalties. Most of the time, such open conflicts are avoided. Thousands of meetings of bureaucrats from different governments take place every year, mostly in secret, as well as dozens of meetings of provincial and federal cabinet ministers, and at least one First Ministers' Meeting. In theory, the power to make policy in Canada is neatly divided among eleven federal and provincial capitals; in practice, there is constant collaboration among them in the policy-making process.

The Canadian federal system has a number of implications for policy-making. First, because it divides jurisdictions, it decentralizes power. Unlike the United Kingdom or Sweden, where only one national government must be lobbied for a particular policy change, Canada poses a challenge for interest groups who want a policy change requiring intergovernmental cooperation. A classic example is the women's lobby for section 28 in the Charter (see Chapter 5). Second, it is often argued that the division of jurisdictions retards policy innovation, particularly in the field of social welfare.[45] Because many of the reforms demanded by the women's movement, notably child care, require intergovernmental co-operation, this has been a major obstacle to reform (see Chapter 12).

The decentralization of power inherent in federalism also affects the implementation of policy. When the Canadian abortion law was struck down in 1988, women's groups thought that they had won a crucial victory. But some provincial governments started to legislate against abortion, using their power over health care budgets (see Chapter 12). If a federal law is counteracted at the provincial level, there is often little that the federal government can do about it. This is particularly true in recent years, when federal governments have moved to cap transfer payments to the provinces as a way to reduce the federal deficit. Now a province will receive a flat sum of money, without any strings attached. In a time of increasing provincial demands for autonomy, it is impossible for Ottawa to impose uniform national standards in any effective way. Therefore, it is possible to win the legislative battle in Ottawa and lose the implementation war in the provinces.

The second systemic variable is *party/parliamentary government*. Canada's system of responsible party government concentrates power in the hands of a small group of people in the Cabinet. Individual members of Parliament are virtually powerless in the policy process, stifled by executive dominance and strong party discipline. Unlike in the United States, where interest groups can lobby representatives or senators for small concessions, Canadian interest groups must win the support of the Cabinet. If they fail, there is little point in going to the House of Commons or the Senate. In a few cases, groups have won some improvements in proposed legislation by going before a Commons committee (see Chapter 10). But the present committee system has only been in place since 1986, and party discipline is nearly as strong in committee rooms as it is on the Commons floor. In the end, if you don't have the support of the Cabinet, or at least of a few key ministers, you won't get the policy you want.

The third systemic variable is the most recent. Canada has been a federal state since 1867; the utter dominance of Cabinet, backed by intense party loyalty, has been in place since the late nineteenth century; but *the Charter of Rights and Freedoms* has been a feature of Canadian politics for just over a decade. Since its proclamation in 1982 the Charter has dramatically changed Canadian law and politics (see Chapter 5). The decades that preceded the Charter saw a new awareness of rights discourse in Canadian politics, and a growing acceptance of the ideal of substantive equality for all Canadians. This change in political values was accelerated by the women's movement and other campaigns for reform, and in turn it reinforced the legitimacy of their demands.

In practice, the Charter has been a mixed blessing for women (see Chapter 5). But as we have seen, there have been cases in which the Supreme Court of Canada ruled according to the arguments of the women's groups that intervened: *Morgentaler, Janzen-Govereau,* and *Butler.* The court did not have to compromise among fiercely opposed groups; it simply applied its own interpretation of the law, upholding some statutes and striking down others. Finally, the Charter created a new access point for women's groups, particularly LEAF. Interest groups can now apply for intervenor status in Charter cases, to present their interpretations of the relevant laws, and can hope to influence the judges' rulings.

The Short-Range Factors

The first set of short-range factors are the *political variables*. These variables refer to the political complexion of the incumbent government and the effectiveness of the women's movement at a particular time. The *political complexion of government* is determined partly by the ideology of the governing party. A governing party with a left-wing ideology, all other things being equal, is more likely to respond favourably to the demands of the women's movement than a more right-wing government. For example, a government that believes in and tries to preserve the traditional gender roles will be much less likely to introduce a national child-care program than a government that is not so attached to the old gender ideologies (see Chapter 3).

In addition, different governments will have made promises to *different constituencies* in order to win or retain power. A government that depends politically on labour unions and progressive social activists is likely to have different priorities than one that relies on big business and financial interests (except when the economy is in a state of collapse, as with the Ontario NDP government elected in 1990). A government that believes women's votes will increase its chances of election is more likely to agree to the requests of women's groups; a case in point was the 1917 "khaki" election, when the Unionist Government of Robert Borden promised Canadian women the right to vote if re-elected. In addition, the emergence of a gender gap in the United States and Canada has led some politicians to direct specific electoral appeals to women (see Chapter 7); the 1984 "women's debate" among Canada's major national party leaders is an example.

There are other political factors that determine a government's policy agenda. One is the proximity of the next election. Canadian governments have the power to decide when an election will be called, although there are some constraints; the constitution requires that a federal election be held every five years. Towards the end of the fourth year, governments begin to feel the pressure to appeal to the voters. A government nearing the end of its mandate, and feeling nervous about its chances of re-election, will be more likely to make promises to previously ignored groups, seeking to win their support.

The effectiveness of the women's movement depends on a number of factors. The first is *lobbying*. The access points available to the women's movement are meaningless if the movement is incapable of using them by effective lobbying. Both the multi-issue groups like NAC and single-issue groups like CARAL and the CDCAA have a place in the effort to secure a new policy. They can use the media, they can mobilize telephone and letter-writing campaigns, they can approach bureaucrats, and they can work with sympathetic opposition MPs to get their interests raised in the House of Commons (Question Period is a good time to embarrass the government for failing to act on an important issue). Groups with the resources to hire researchers and consultants can use their appearances before public inquiries and Commons committees to full advantage, arriving with high-quality briefs including pre-drafted bills or legislative amendments. These make it easier for the members of the inquiry or committee to adopt the group's position; no extra work is required on their part to turn the group's ideas into legislative language.

The second factor determining the effectiveness of the women's movement is its success in building *political coalitions* and a *strong organization*. Rarely does one interest group have the clout to move a government towards a new policy. Any major policy innovation requires interests to build a strong coalition, both inside and outside the political system. Women's groups have to link up with each other – a process made much easier by the presence of NAC and the FFQ – and with other groups whose members could benefit from progressive policies, such as trade unions, civil libertarians (on some issues), ethnic organizations, the disabled, and gay/lesbian groups. The key is to build a coalition whose members agree on the overall goal but can tolerate differences in tactics or approaches. These coalitions need not be permanent; indeed, it is difficult to imagine the interests of different groups overlapping on more than one or two issues.

Women's, aboriginal, and multicultural groups can work together to campaign for employment equity policies, but they may have different approaches to the issues of violence against women and child care. Women may be able to link up with unions to fight for flex-time and better maternity leaves, but there may be differences of interest on some features of employment and pay equity. As long as the coalition remains intact for the duration of the lobby on the principal shared issue, it will have served its purpose.

It is also important to include people inside the system in the coalition. When women mobilized to lobby federal and provincial governments to remove section 28 of the Charter from the section 33 override (see below), the support of female legislators, bureaucrats, and Cabinet ministers was critical to their success. It is important to remember, however, that not all women within the political system are feminists. As we have seen, most female MPs can be mobilized on the most crucial issues for women, particularly when party lines are loosened; this happened in the 1981 campaign to save section 28 of the Charter (see below) and in the 1988 free vote on abortion in the House of Commons (see Chapter 12). But many women in politics and the bureaucracy have been reluctant to embrace "women's issues." Therefore, as we argued in Chapter 9, it is not enough just to put more *women* in office; we cannot assume that a woman in positions of power will choose to actively represent the interests of other women. Instead, the focus of the women's movement should be on putting more *feminists* into office, *and* on building and maintaining links with the women already in the political system to ensure their mobilization when necessary.

Political scientists often refer to "policy communities": groups of experts on particular issues who work together on drafting policy. Some members of the policy community are inside the state, working in government departments and affiliated agencies; others are outside the state, working in non-governmental organizations, building contacts with the client groups in society and amassing expertise in the area. These two groups of policy experts must work together in order to create policies that are both technically viable and likely to be acceptable to the client groups.

In the case of women, the key inside members of the policy community are bureaucrats and ministers in the federal and provincial departments of Health and Welfare, Labour, Employment, Education and Training, and Status of Women, as well as MPs. The outside members are women's groups, occupational organizations such as nurses' unions and associations of women teachers, and groups advocating reforms that would benefit women substantially but not exclusively (employment equity, child care). The women's movement has built strong links with people and agencies inside the political system, which they can use as a resource in the policy process.

The *organization of women's groups* themselves is a key determinant of their success and effectiveness. As we have seen, the issue of process is a crucial one for the women's movement. Feminist process is non-hierarchical and anti-bureaucratic; the process of the political system is exactly the opposite. To engage effectively with policy-makers, women's groups have to compromise their process goals to some extent. A group that is bureaucratically organized, with a permanent staff and a designated executive in a central location, can respond fairly quickly to changing circumstances. A group that is dispersed and has no permanent source of expertise and leadership is likely to be less effective in responding to state initiatives and in exploiting opportunities for influence.

The third factor is the *quality of the leadership of the women's movement.* We have seen that leaders who are skilled in their use of media, who possess experience and skill in institutional settings, and who can build and maintain coalitions of allied groups can contribute to the success of women's efforts to change public policy. A related issue is the degree of *sympathy for feminism among political elites.* The women's movements in the United States, Germany, Britain, and Canada experienced frustrating setbacks in the 1980s and early 1990s, under conservative governments. Political elites that oppose feminism, or that do not see the need for a women's movement, are unlikely to allow women much influence in policy-making.

The *characteristics of a policy* also help to determine its chances of success. The first set of characteristics relate to the political "sellability" of a policy: its *visibility, degree of controversy,* and *scope.* If an issue is highly visible, the women's lobby to secure favourable policy is more likely to attract an organized and effective opposition. Abortion is a classic example. The abortion issue also illustrates the second point: the greater the degree of controversy surrounding an issue, the greater the difficulty in creating the consensus on which policy is based. In addition, the broader the scope of a policy, the more people will be affected by it, and the greater the chance that some groups will perceive it as a threat. An issue that affects a majority or a large minority of people also implies that a new policy will be extremely costly to implement. In a climate of economic constraint (see above), this factor alone can eliminate any chance of policy change or innovation.

Secondly, there are three different *policy types,* each of which carries different implications for policy-making. These types are: *distributive* policy, which gives "benefits to individuals or groups, essentially in the form of a governmental subsidy";[46] *regulatory* policy, which means "governmental regulation of practices by individuals or groups, most frequently in the private sector";[47] and *redistributive* policy, or "the redistribution of benefits, tangible or intangible, from one broad group to another."[48] Distributive policies are the easiest to pass, especially if the public believes that there is an element of fairness or redress to the policy. Regulatory policies can be difficult, if there is already a lot of regulation in the area, or if it is an area traditionally left unregulated or the client group is fiercely independent and well organized (like the Canadian Medical Association). Redistributive policies are the most difficult to pass, especially if the issue has high visibility; those who will lose in the redistribution can resist strongly (such as white men who fear that they will suffer from employment equity).

A third set of policy characteristics relates to the effect of the potential policy on gender roles. Some policies would promote *role equity,* while others could lead to *role change.* Role equity means equal opportunity for men and women in the same roles; equal pay legislation is an example of a role equity policy. Gender roles are left intact, and there is little controversy about the introduction of the policy. Role change opens up *new* opportunities for women and implicitly challenges male roles. It threatens the status quo, and those who benefit from it may oppose the change as strongly as they can. According to Ellen Boneparth, "Equity issues address the distribution of power in society but do not disturb basic sex-role definitions. In contrast, role change challenges traditional sex-role ideology."[49] Policies entailing role change require "the redefinition of sex roles in some areas, [and] the elimination of sex roles in others."[50] In other words, they require that *both* men and women change their gender roles. No wonder the resistance is so intense.

Sandra Burt applies Boneparth's analysis to Canadian public policy: "Canadian policy-makers have become increasingly sympathetic to the feminist claim that women should have equal access with men to the competitive spheres of politics and work. But they have consistently resisted demands for a fundamental restructuring of relations among both women and men to reflect the feminist values of participation, nurturing, caring, and peace."[51] So demands for role equity, like the inclusion of section 28 in the Charter, are much more likely to meet with success than demands for role change, such as a national child-care program.

A Case Study of the Model: The Charter versus the ERA

To clarify this discussion of the factors that determine women's success in the policy process, we will briefly examine the fight for section 28 of the Charter between 1980 and 1982 (see Chapter 5 for background and context), and contrast it with the unsuccessful campaign for the Equal Rights Amendment in the United States.

The *environmental variables* surrounding the Charter were largely positive. The social climate favoured the extension of equality rights to disadvantaged groups. The economic climate was constrained by a recession, but the economic implications of the Charter did not concern many people at the time. The political climate was favourable, because the Canadian population was increasingly enthusiastic about the Charter, and section 28 seemed fair to most people. In addition, the demand for section 28 had some political legitimacy, because it conformed to the requirements of the United Nations Declaration on Elimination of All Forms of Discrimination Against Women, to which Canada is a signatory.[52]

The *systemic variables* posed greater difficulties. The main problem was federalism. The federal government wanted the Charter, and the provinces wanted a new amending formula. The two levels of government had to strike a deal. Some provincial governments were suspicious of the Charter, afraid that it would excessively restrict provincial powers. Despite these barriers, a deal was struck in November 1981. The crucial trade-off was the federal government's acceptance of section 33, which allowed any government to "override" certain Charter rights for a maximum of five years at a time. As we have seen, women's groups were able to put pressure on the first ministers to exempt section 28 from the override.

The other two systemic variables did not enter the picture: the Charter, for obvious reasons, and the party/parliamentary system because constitutional negotiations take place between governments, not between parties. It is important to note that the process of amending the Canadian constitution in 1981 was much simpler than the American ratification process that killed the Equal Rights Amendment. We will return to this issue later.

The short-term *political variables* were more promising for section 28. The federal government needed to build public support for the Charter section of its patriation package, because it faced stiff opposition from eight provincial governments and their allies in London. The women's lobby was well organized, quick to respond to changes in the political climate, and highly effective. The coalition included NAC, the CACSW (which had been radicalized by the politically motivated firing of its former president, Doris Anderson), the Ad Hoc Committee of Women on the Constitution, provincial Status of Women councils, a number of women MPs, the federal Minister Responsible for the Status of Women, and bureaucrats throughout the federal and provincial governments.

In addition, the campaign to strengthen the Charter mobilized native groups, multicultural groups, the disabled, gays and lesbians, and others who saw the Charter as a chance for stronger legal rights and political legitimacy. Some groups, notably gays and lesbians, did not succeed in their attempts to achieve recognition in the Charter; their political legitimacy was not yet sufficient to overcome the resistance of policy-makers. But the more legitimate groups formed a strong, though loose, coalition, which secured some of their desired changes.

Many women in the Ad Hoc Committee were respected lawyers, whose knowledge and status allowed them to deal with officials on a basis of equality. They managed to get section 28 inserted in the Charter, and then saw it threatened by the November 1981 deal among the first ministers. They went back to the phones, mobilized their people nationally and provincially, and launched an intense campaign to remove section 28 from the "notwithstanding clause." In the end, they succeeded in forcing the first ministers to reopen the deal and protect section 28 from legislative override. Without the combined efforts of thousands of women, together with the face-to-face lobbying of female MPs and Status of Women Council members, section 28 could have been eviscerated by section 33.[53]

By contrast, the American women's movement lost its major fight for legal rights: the passage of an Equal Rights Amendment to the American Constitution. (See the appendix to this chapter for the text of section 28 and of the 1972 ERA.) The origins of section 28 and the ERA were very different. The Canadian Charter of Rights was a government initiative, and women's groups worked with the government to draft section 28; in contrast, the ERA was drafted in 1923 by activist Alice Paul and faced stiff resistance from the political system.[54] It was not passed by the American Congress until 1972. It also needed the approval of the legislatures of two-thirds of the states before ratification, an exceedingly difficult process given the conservative political culture of many American states. In 1982 the ERA reached the deadline for ratification – three states short of a victory. It died, and will have to be reintroduced into Congress if the process is to start again.

Apart from the systemic factor of the complex ratification procedure for constitutional amendment in the United States – which contrasts strongly with the elite accommodation that created section 28 – there were environmental and political factors at work in the American case. There was an organized anti-ERA campaign, led by Republican Phyllis Schafly, which mobilized a religious and free-enterprise coalition against the aims of the feminists. This "pro-family" coalition was strongly integrated into the Republican Party and received a lot of support from the Reagan White House. While there are similar groups in Canada, notably the anti-feminist organization R.E.A.L. Women, their strength is nowhere near comparable to the clout of Schafly and her group south of the border. Nor has R.E.A.L. Women ever received the publicly avowed support of a Canadian government (although there was a great deal of private agreement with the group's goals within the Progressive Conservative caucus).

The terms of the political debate were quickly taken away from the ERA supporters. Instead of the role equity they expected the ERA to provide, the debate focused on the role changes prophesied by the anti-ERA coalition. They warned legislators about the horrors of women in combat, unisex public washrooms, children abandoned in the streets, and other catastrophes that would inevitably follow upon ratification of a constitutional amendment that would essentially "turn women into men." ERA supporters ridiculed and tried to counter these jeremiads, but in vain. The American women's movement, partly because of its greater radicalism and marginalization (see above), did not have the political legitimacy (at least in parts of the country) to achieve a profoundly symbolic policy breakthrough like the ERA. In contrast, the debate over section 28 was brief and mostly positive. To the extent that anti-feminist groups were involved in the Charter debate, they focused on section 7, trying to ensure that the Charter would protect the rights of the unborn (which it does not do).

Conclusion

In this chapter we have discussed the following key points:

1. The Canadian women's movement has been divided between the institutionalized and grassroots strategies for change. Despite this profound division, NAC in its role as a national umbrella group has managed to bridge many of the differences. NAC's success as a "parliament of women" has given the women's movement a more

influential voice in Canadian politics than that enjoyed by American feminists.

2.   Women's groups have a number of access points to the Canadian policy process: women in the bureaucracy, lobbying, the media, public inquiries, parliamentary committees, the Charter, and political parties. Some of these points are more effective than others, and each will vary in importance depending on the particular issue of concern.

3.   A set of long-range and short-range factors help to determine a social movement's chances for policy success on any given issue. We have seen that the principal long-range variables in Canada are the environmental variables (the social, economic, and political climate) and the systemic variables (federalism, party/parliamentary government, and the Charter). The short-range variables include political factors (e.g., the party in power), the effectiveness of the women's movement on a particular issue, and the characteristics of the policy itself.

How successful has the Canadian women's movement been in securing its policy goals? The material in the next chapter will help us to answer that question. For the moment, the answer is: very successful on some issues, not so successful on others. The laws on sexual harassment, pornography, and domestic violence are still inadequate, and often badly enforced. There is no national child-care program. There are no guarantees of reproductive rights. Women are still underpaid and overrepresented in low-level jobs. The list goes on and on.

At this point, we should ask how many of these problems the state should be expected to solve. There are areas of life into which the state should not intervene, although there is no consensus about what those areas are. The women's movement is rather ambivalent about the state, seeing it as the bulwark of patriarchy and capitalism on the one hand, and the most effective means of redressing social and economic inequalities on the other hand. For the foreseeable future, the Canadian women's movement will continue to direct much of its effort towards influencing the policy process. In the next chapter we will look at some crucial issues on the feminist agenda for this century and the next.

Appendix 1: The Charter versus the ERA

The text of the Equal Rights Amendment, as adopted by the Congress of the United States in 1972:

> Equality of rights under the law shall not be denied or abridged by the United States or any State on account of sex.

The text of section 28 of the Canadian Charter of Rights and Freedoms, proclaimed in 1982:

> Notwithstanding anything in this Charter, the rights and freedoms referred to in it are guaranteed equally to male and female persons.

Source: Naomi Black, "Ripples in the Second Wave: Comparing the Contemporary Women's Movement in Canada and the United States," in Backhouse and Flaherty, *Challenging Times,* 94.

Appendix 2: The Budget of the Women's Program, 1973–1995

Fiscal Year	Budget ($)
1973–74	223,2000
1974–75	2,500,000*
1975–76	406,2000
1976–77	955,2000
1977–78	800,2000
1978–79	726,2000
1979–80	876,2000
1980–81	1,286,500
1981–82	2,780,300
1982–83	2,967,200
1093–84	4,245,000
1984–85	9,300,500
1985–86	12,538,000
1986–87	12,426,900
1987–88	12,467,996
1988–89	12,758,000
1989–90	10,599,200
1990–91	10,582,000
1991–92	10,068,000
1992–93	11,068,000
1993–94	8,929,000
1994–95	8,599,000**

* International Women's Year. ** Projected.

Sources: Pal, *Interests of State,* 221; Government of Canada, *Estimates:* Department of the Secretary of State (1988–93), Department of Human Resources Development (1994–95), Status of Women Canada (1995–96).

Notes

1   Adamson, Briskin, and McPhail, *Feminist Organizing for Change.*

2   Irene Tinker, "Introduction: Two Decades of Influence," in Tinker, *Women in Washington,* 9.

3   Jeri Dawn Wine and Janice L. Ristock, "Introduction: Feminist Activism in Canada," in Wine and Ristock, *Women and Social Change,* 3.

4   An earlier analogue is the tension between partisanship and independence in the first-wave feminists of English Canada, as documented by Sylvia Bashevkin. See her *Toeing the Lines.*

5   See Adamson, Briskin, and McPhail; Linda Briskin, "Feminist Practice: A New Approach To Evaluating Feminist Strategy," in Wine and Ristock, *Women and Social Change.*

6   Sometimes the links are even stronger than this analysis suggests. The National Organization of Women (NOW) in the United States was formed in 1966, largely in response to the efforts of feminists working within the Equal Employment Opportunities Commission (EEOC). They saw that the new federal laws against sex discrimination in employment would never be fully implemented unless there was "some sort of NAACP for women" to fight discrimination in the courts. See Jo Freeman, "Women and Public Policy: An Overview," in Boneparth, *Women, Power and Policy,* 53.

7   Jill Vickers, "Bending the Iron Law of Oligarchy: Debates on the Feminization of Organization and Political Process in the English Canadian Women's Movement, 1970–1988," in Wine and Ristock, 85.

8   Ibid., 85.

9   See Jill Vickers, "The Intellectual Origins of the Women's Movements in Canada," in Backhouse and Flaherty, *Challenging Times.*

10   Burt, "Organized Women's Groups and the State," 192.

11   Vickers, "Bending the Iron Law of Oligarchy," 88.

12   Vickers, Rankin, and Appelle, *Politics As If Women Mattered,* 11–12.

13   Lorraine Greaves, "Reorganizing the National Action Committee on the Status of Women 1986–1988," in Wine and Ristock, 113.

14   Ibid., 105–6.

15   National Action Committee on the Status of Women, *Action Now!,* January 1993.

16   Hosek organized a televised debate on women's issues during the 1984 federal election campaign. This debate, among other events, raised the profile of NAC and led to an influx of new member groups. See Greaves, "Reorganizing the National Action Committee," 102.

17 Thobani faced an unprecedented racist attack when her presidency was announced. A Progressive Conservative MP questioned her appointment in the House of Commons, claiming that Thobani (an Indian woman born in Tanzania) was an illegal immigrant. Thobani is in fact a legal landed immigrant, so the real motivation behind the attack appears to have been a belief that she wasn't a "real" Canadian, and thus could not speak on behalf of Canadian women. See Deborah Wilson, "Heir to NAC stung by attack," *Globe and Mail,* May 10, 1993. For the record, Judy Rebick was born in the United States, yet no one has ever questioned her Canadian credentials.

18 Vickers, "Bending the Iron Law of Oligarchy," 88.

19 Ibid., 92–93.

20 Ibid.

21 MacLeod, *Battered but Not Beaten.*

22 See Sweet and Findlay, "Canadian Advisory Council on the Status of Women."

23 Razack, *Canadian Feminism and the Law,* 46–48.

24 Beth Symes, founding president of LEAF, quoted in Razack, 61.

25 See Baines, "Gender and the Meech Lake Committee."

26 Vickers, "Bending the Iron Law of Oligarchy," 85.

27 Susan Prentice, "The 'Mainstreaming' of Daycare."

28 Ibid.

29 Pal, *Interests of State,* 117.

30 Ibid.

31 Ibid., 8.

32 Burt, "Organized Women's Groups and the State," 193.

33 Ibid., 199.

34 Ibid., 144.

35 Standing Committee on Secretary of State, *Fairness in Funding: Report on the Women's Program* (Ottawa: Minister of Supply & Services, 1987), 15–16.

36 Pal, 147.

37 Burt, "Organized Women's Groups and the State," 208–9.

38 This analysis is based on the factors set out in Ellen Boneparth, "Chapter One: A Framework for Policy Analysis," in Boneparth, *Women, Power and Policy,* and in Gelb, *Feminism and Politics.*

39 Boneparth, 3.

40 Ibid., 4.

41 Monique Bégin, "The Royal Commission on the Status of Women in Canada: Twenty Years Later," in Backhouse and Flaherty, *Challenging Times,* 26.

42 Vickers, Rankin, and Appelle, chap. 4.

43　Vickers, "Bending the Iron Law of Oligarchy," 79–80.

44　Technically, the federal government can instruct the lieutenant governor of a province to veto or delay a provincial law with which it disagrees; but these powers have not been used for decades.

45　Banting, *The Welfare State and Canadian Federalism.*

46　Boneparth, 11.

47　Ibid.

48　Ibid.

49　Ibid., 13.

50　Ibid.

51　Burt, "Organized Women's Groups and the State," 192.

52　Kome, *The Taking of Twenty-Eight,* 84.

53　The best account of this process is in Kome.

54　Naomi Black, "Ripples in the Second Wave: Comparing the Contemporary Women's Movement in Canada and the United States," in Backhouse and Flaherty, 101.

References and Further Reading

Adamson, Nancy, Linda Briskin, and Margaret McPhail. *Women Organizing for Change: The Contemporary Women's Movement in Canada.* Toronto: Oxford University Press, 1988.

Anderson, Doris. *The Unfinished Revolution: The Status of Women in Twelve Countries.* Toronto: Doubleday Canada, 1991.

Backhouse, Constance, and David H. Flaherty, eds. *Challenging Times: The Women's Movement in Canada and the United States.* Montreal/Kingston: McGill-Queen's University Press, 1992.

Baines, Beverley. "Gender and the Meech Lake Committee." In Clive Thomson, ed., *Navigating Meech Lake: The 1987 Constitutional Accord.* Kingston: Queen's Quarterly/Institute of Intergovernmental Relations, 1988.

Banting, Keith G. *The Welfare State and Canadian Federalism.* 2nd ed. Kingston/Montreal: McGill-Queen's University Press, 1987.

Bashevkin, Sylvia. *Toeing the Lines: Women and Party Politics in English Canada.* 2nd ed. Toronto: Oxford University Press, 1993.

Boneparth, Ellen, ed. *Women, Power and Policy.* Oxford: Pergamon, 1982.

Brodie, Janine, ed. *Women and Canadian Public Policy.* Toronto: Harcourt Brace, 1995.

Brooks, Stephen. *Canadian Democracy: An Introduction*. Toronto: McClelland &Stewart, 1993.

Burt, Sandra. "Canadian Women's Groups in the 1980s: Organizational Development and Policy Influence." *Canadian Public Policy* 16, no. 1 (1990).

———. "Organized Women's Groups and the State." In William D. Coleman and Grace Skogstad, eds., *Policy Communities and Public Policy in Canada: A Structural Approach*. Mississauga: Copp Clark Pitman, 1990.

Burt, Sandra, Lorraine Code, and Lindsay Dorney, eds. *Changing Patterns: Women in Canada*. 2nd edition. Toronto: McClelland & Stewart, 1993.

Bystydzienski, Jill M., ed. *Women Transforming Politics: Worldwide Strategies for Empowerment*. Bloomington: Indiana University Press, 1992.

Canada, House of Commons Standing Committee on Secretary of State. *Fairness in Funding: Report on the Women's Program*. Ottawa: Minister of Supply & Services, 1987.

Carroll, Susan J. *Women as Candidates in American Politics*. Bloomington: Indiana University Press, 1985.

Dahlerup, Drude, ed. *The New Women's Movement: Feminism and Political Power in Europe and the USA*. Beverly Hills: Sage, 1986.

Gelb, Joyce. *Feminism and Politics: A Comparative Perspective*. Berkeley: University of California Press, 1989.

Hartmann, Susan M. *From Margin to Mainstream: American Women and Politics since 1960*. Philadelphia: Temple University Press, 1989.

Iglitzin, Lynne B., and Ruth Ross, eds. *Women in the World, 1975–1985: The Women's Decade*. 2nd rev. ed. Oxford: Clio, 1986.

Kome, Penney. *The Taking of Twenty-Eight: Women Challenge the Constitution*. Toronto: Women's Press, 1983.

Lovenduski, Joni. *Women and European Politics: Contemporary Feminism and Public Policy*. Brighton: Wheatsheaf, 1986.

MacLeod, Linda. *Battered but Not Beaten: Preventing Wife Battering in Canada*. Ottawa: CACSW, 1987.

Pal, Leslie A. *Interests of State: The Politics of Language, Multiculturalism, and Feminism in Canada*. Montreal/Kingston: McGill-Queen's University Press, 1993.

Prentice, Susan. "The 'Mainstreaming' of Daycare." *Resources for Feminist Research* 17, no. 3 (September 1988).

Randall, Vicky. *Women and Politics: An International Perspective*. 2nd ed. Chicago: University of Chicago Press, 1987.

Razack, Sherene. *Canadian Feminism and the Law: The Women's Legal Education and Action Fund and the Pursuit of Equality*. Toronto: Second Story, 1991.

Rendel, Margherita, ed. *Women, Power and Political Systems*. London: Croom Helm, 1981.

Sweet, Lois, and Sue Findlay. "Canadian Advisory Council on the Status of Women: Contradictions and Conflicts." In *Feminist Perspectives on the Canadian State,* special issue of *Resources for Feminist Research*. Toronto: OISE, September 1988.

Tinker, Irene, ed. *Women in Washington: Advocates for Public Policy*. Beverly Hills: Sage, 1983.

Vickers, Jill, Pauline Rankin, and Christine Appelle. *Politics As If Women Mattered: A Political Analysis of the National Action Committee on the Status of Women*. Toronto: University of Toronto Press, 1993.

Wine, Jeri Dawn, and Janice L. Ristock, eds. *Women and Social Change: Feminist Activism in Canada*. Toronto: James Lorimer, 1991.

Chapter 12: 'Women's Issues' and the Canadian Political System

Chapter Summary

Chapter 12 presents five brief case studies of Canadian public policy in areas of particular concern to women. Each case study is described, and then evaluated according to the model of women's policy influence set out in Chapter 11. The chapter ends with a critique of the concept of "women's issues."

Chapter Outline

- Women and the Canadian Public Policy Process
- Abortion
- Child Care
- Pornography
- Sexual Harassment
- New Reproductive Technologies
- Conclusion

Women and the Canadian Public Policy Process

In the two preceding chapters we have looked at how public policy is made in Canada. We have studied the effects of that process on women, and vice versa. Table 12.1 summarizes the model of policy-making presented in Chapter 11.

Table 12.1:

Factors Influencing the Success of the Women's Movement in Policy-Making

Long-range factors

Environmental	The social climate
	The economic climate
	The political climate
Systemic	Federalism
	Party/parliamentary government
	The Charter

Short-range factors

Political Variables	The political complexion of the government
The Women's Movement	Effectiveness in lobbying
	Organization and coalition building
	Leadership
Policy Characteristics	Controversy/visibility/scope
	Distributive, regulatory or redistributive
	Role equity versus role change

Women's access points to the political system include:

1. The bureaucracy and the political elite

2. Lobbying

3. The media

4. Public inquiries

5. Parliamentary committees

6. The Charter

In this chapter we will conclude our discussion of public policy by examining a number of issues that are of particular – but not exclusive – relevance to women. We have seen that the phrase "women's issues" is often used to belittle or ghettoize issues that actually affect most Canadians directly or indirectly, such as abortion and child care. This chapter will describe five such issues and their treatment by the Canadian policy-making process.

Abortion

In 1969 the Parliament of Canada enacted a law that made abortion a criminal offence except under certain specific conditions (see Chapter 5). The Supreme Court of Canada's ruling in *Morgentaler* struck down that law in 1988, sending the issue of abortion back to the politicians. Abortion is an extremely difficult issue for governments to deal with, so they prefer to leave it alone.[1] On occasion they are forced to respond, when a court strikes down an existing law or when the prevailing social consensus has shifted, making the old laws impossible to enforce. The Canadian government has been particularly reluctant to deal with the issue of abortion, preferring to wait until an individual challenges the law before acting.[2]

The years since the *Morgentaler* ruling have been particularly stormy for people on both sides of the abortion issue. The January 1988 ruling was greeted with joy and relief by pro-choice groups, particularly the Canadian Abortion Rights Action League (CARAL) which had contributed money to Morgentaler's fight against the 1969 law. The decision was also welcomed by individual men and women who believe that a woman has the right to choose whether to end a pregnancy. Anti-abortion groups were angered and saddened by the court's ruling, which struck down the only national law regulating access to abortion. Without a new law, there would be no criminal sanctions against abortions performed in free-standing clinics. Anti-abortion groups foresaw a future of rapidly expanding abortion services all over Canada, permitting abortion on demand.

The battle over abortion shifted from the courts, where it had been centred for the previous two decades, to the streets, the provincial governments, and the federal Parliament. Almost immediately, anti-abortion activists stepped up the intensity of their protests against clinics and hospitals where abortions were performed. At the same time, they began to lobby provincial governments for laws and regulations that would restrict women's access to abortion services. The government of British Columbia responded by cutting medical insurance funding for abortion, unless the procedure was performed in a hospital and was necessary to save the life or physical health of the woman.[3] Nova Scotia passed laws that made it difficult to establish abortion clinics, and denied insurance coverage to medical services performed outside hospitals. Pro-choice groups resisted these policies fiercely, and Dr. Morgentaler challenged the Nova Scotia law in the courts. The Supreme Court of Canada struck it down in 1993, finding that the law was *ultra vires* (outside the power of) the provincial government.[4]

At the same time, rulings by lower courts forced pro-choice activists to recognize that the elimination of abortion from the Criminal Code had not removed all legal restrictions on women's ability to choose. In July 1989 lower courts in Quebec and Ontario granted injunctions to two men who wanted to stop their girlfriends from having abortions. In Quebec, Chantal Daigle had to take her case all the way to the Supreme Court of Canada after the Quebec Superior Court and the Quebec Court of Appeal upheld the injunction. The Superior Court ruled that the original injunction was valid because the Quebec Charter of Rights protects the rights of the fetus. The delays multiplied both the risks of an abortion and the tremendous emotional stress of her situation; Daigle had decided to have an abortion after breaking up with her boyfriend because he had physically abused her. Finally, five months pregnant, and just before the Supreme Court quashed the injunction, Daigle travelled to the United States and had an abortion.

The Ontario case was similar in many respects: Barbara Dodd also had an abortion, after the Supreme Court of Ontario overturned a lower court injunction obtained by her ex-boyfriend. But the Dodd case had a bizarre twist: soon after the abortion Barbara Dodd held a news conference to announce that she had been converted to the anti-abortion cause, and she greatly regretted what she had done. She had also reunited with the man who had sought to prevent her from ending the pregnancy.

A few months after the intense publicity surrounding the Daigle and Dodd cases, the federal government introduced a new law to regulate abortion. The Progressive Conservative caucus had been badly split over the issue of abortion, as had the other parties in the House of Commons. In July 1988 the government had held a free vote in the Commons on a series of proposals for a new abortion law. The results were ambiguous.[5] The three pro-choice amendments were defeated by huge majorities. The strongest pro-choice amendment was defeated by a vote of 198 to 20. The strongest pro-life amendment, which would only have allowed an abortion if two doctors believed that the woman's life was in danger without it, nearly passed. The final vote was 105 in favour and 118 against. The results of this vote were disturbing enough by themselves, to those people who believe a woman should have the right to choose. But there was a further chilling aspect. Every one of the female MPs present voted against the pro-life amendment. Had there been seven fewer women in the House, the amendment would have passed and the "sense of the House" might have led to a restrictive anti-abortion law.[6]

In November 1989 the federal government introduced a new abortion law into the House of Commons. Bill C-43 would have replaced the section of the Criminal Code that had been struck down in the *Morgentaler* decision. In many ways it resembled the 1969 law that the Supreme Court of Canada had found to be unconstitutional. It declared abortion to be a criminal offence, except when performed under strictly limited conditions to avoid threatening "the health or life of the female person."[7] But there were two important differences. The first difference was the removal of the therapeutic abortion committees. The decision to abort or not to abort would now rest with the woman's doctor. The second difference was the definition of "health" as "physical, mental and psychological health." This broader interpretation of the woman's well-being made it clear that doctors should take the woman's emotional state into account, and not just the presence or absence of a life-threatening physical condition.

The bill had been intended as a compromise between the two sides on the abortion issue. But by 1989 any chance of a compromise was remote. The pro-choice lobby condemned the power given to the doctor, the restrictions on women's freedom of choice, and the fact that abortion was being recriminalized. The anti-abortion lobby criticized the bill for being too lax, arguing that it would permit free-standing clinics and would essentially allow abortion on demand. On third reading in the House of Commons, a strange alliance of forces took shape behind the bill. MPs who thought it was not restrictive enough, but preferred it to having no law at all, joined forces with MPs who thought it was too restrictive but that it at least guaranteed some access to abortion. Some pro-choice MPs also believed that Parliament had a duty to legislate on the issue of abortion, to keep the provincial governments from taking matters entirely into their own hands.

In the end, Bill C-43 was passed by the House of Commons in May 1990. The vote was unusually close: 140 in favour, 131 against. The Cabinet was required to support the bill, but backbench MPs from all parties voted according to their consciences. The bill went to the Senate, which was tied up with the goods and services tax (GST) for the next several months. When Bill C-43 finally came to a vote in the Senate in January 1991, the result was extraordinary. There was a tie, 43 in favour and 43 against. Under Senate rules a tie means an automatic defeat. Bill C-43 was dead. The federal government quickly announced that it would make no further attempt to legislate on abortion.[8]

As of 1995 there was no national law on abortion, and it was not a criminal offence to terminate a pregnancy. Nevertheless, provincial governments and anti-abortion protesters are doing their best to restrict access to abortion services, with considerable success. Some provincial governments are still fighting attempts by Dr. Morgentaler and others to establish clinics. Hospital boards have been taken over by anti-abortion activists, and abortion services shut down as a result. Doctors are harassed at home and at work. The shooting of a doctor in Vancouver in 1994 was the most extreme case, but far from the only one. Even some of the most dedicated physicians eventually decide that it is not worth the bother and quit performing abortions.

The abortion issue reveals some interesting aspects of the Canadian political system and its treatment of morally difficult issues of special relevance to women. First, abortion is a divisive issue with which all Canadian governments try to avoid associating themselves. No political party was willing to impose a particular policy on its MPs. The votes in the House of Commons in 1988 and 1990 were entirely or partially free votes, and most of the resolutions debated in 1988 were private members' amendments to government-sponsored legislation. These manoeuvres are characteristic of the abortion issue in all Western countries.[9]

Second, the abortion issue highlights the fact that public policies must be properly implemented if they are to be effective. European studies have shown that the single most important factor in determining access to abortion is not the permissiveness of the law, but "the independent existence of a network of good medical facilities organized either by the state or the private sector."[10] Without such facilities, laws are irrelevant. If doctors can be pressured to stop performing abortions, as they have been in the United States and Italy; if hospitals can be taken over by anti-abortion activists and their abortion facilities shut down, as has occurred in Canada and the U.K.; if governments can use their control of health-care budgets to deny funding for abortion, as has occurred in both Canada and the U.S. – then the absence of a criminal law against abortion is meaningless.

Third, the debate over abortion illustrates the tendency of the political system to respond to strongly organized minorities rather than to silent majorities. By the 1980s public opinion surveys revealed that the majority of Canadians held moderate pro-choice views.[11] Yet the small but intensely vocal anti-abortion movement was given much more attention by politicians. There are two reasons for this. The first is that, from a politician's point of view, any organized group with which he or she disagrees can campaign against him or her in the next election. This is a rather frightening prospect, especially in the case of the anti-abortion movement, which regularly floods MPs' offices with mail. MPs are justifiably worried about an organization that appears to have so much support, despite its minority status within the electorate as a whole. This perception is reinforced by the news media, which tends to cover the anti-abortion movement in a way that exaggerates its strength and influence.[12]

The second reason for the influence of the anti-abortion movement in the recent abortion debates is the high incidence of similar views among Canadian parliamentarians. The results of the 1988 free votes are instructive. As we have seen, all of the female MPs voted as a bloc on the pro-choice side, but strong anti-abortion sentiment was expressed by a substantial proportion of male Progressive Conservative and Liberal MPs.[13]

Fourth, the history of the abortion issue in Canada reminds us that the power to define the terms of the debate – to determine the discourse – is critical to the success of a campaign. The 1969 law recognized abortion as a medical issue, not as a moral issue or as an issue of women's rights. Before 1969 abortion was a criminal offence in Canada under any circumstances, and doctors who did perform abortions feared prosecution. In 1966 the CMA passed a resolution at its annual meeting calling for a law permitting therapeutic abortions if approved by a committee of doctors. This resolution was enacted into law almost word-for-word three years later.[14]

When the law was changed the CMA abruptly lost control of the discourse, as the anti-abortion movement crystallized in opposition to the new law. They campaigned successfully to make abortion a moral and, to a lesser extent, a religious issue. At the same time the women's movement seized on the issue of abortion. It both defended the new law against its attackers and criticized it on the grounds that the committee system denied access to abortion. The women's movement redefined abortion as an issue of women's reproductive rights. By the mid-1970s, when Dr. Morgentaler went to prison, the "pro-choice" and "pro-life" positions had already taken shape and hardened into implacable opposition. The battle to define the issue has raged ever since. The Supreme Court of Canada took the pro-choice position in 1988 and refused to hear the pro-life arguments of Joe Borowski in 1989. But the pro-life discourse has been influential in the legislative and executive arenas of Canadian politics, despite the greater appeal of the pro-choice position among all Canadians.

Finally, the post-1988 debate over abortion has demonstrated that women's reproductive choices are still limited by the power of male doctors and policy-makers. Whether on hospital boards, in provincial governments, or in lower courts, men still have the power to tell women that they cannot terminate unwanted pregnancies. Indeed, the two individuals who came to personify the pro-choice and pro-life camps, Dr. Henry Morgentaler and Joe Borowski respectively, are both men. Most people are justifiably troubled by the issue of abortion, and it would be wrong to suggest that it is anything other than a dreadful experience that no one would choose unless the alternatives were even worse. It would also be wrong to suggest that all women, or even that all feminists, are pro-choice. But for most women (and many men), the fact that an elected official or a bureaucrat or a judge can tell a woman she cannot have an abortion remains galling and frustrating. The pro-choice side may have won the court battle, but it is losing the implementation war.

We will conclude this section by applying the model of Canadian policy-making and the list of access points to the issue of abortion. Of all the access points, the two most important were the *political elite* and the *Charter*. The political elite was crucial because the female MPs swung the Commons vote in 1988 away from the pro-life amendments. Female senators also ensured that Bill C-43 did not survive third reading in the upper chamber. The Charter was crucial because of the Supreme Court of Canada ruling in 1988, which returned the abortion issue to the policy-makers.

The *environmental variables* were clearly important in the abortion controversy. The *social climate* was largely favourable to a liberal abortion law. A Gallup poll in June 1991 found that 24 per cent of Canadians thought abortion should be legal under any circumstances, and 60 per cent thought it should be legal under particular circumstances.[15] Those circumstances included danger to the woman's health (80 per cent), rape or incest (70 per cent), a strong chance of birth defects (65 per cent), agreement between the woman and her doctor (47 per cent), during the first three months of pregnancy (41 per cent), and severe poverty (34 per cent). Only 14 per cent of Canadians believed that abortion should be illegal in all circumstances. Those figures have been very consistent for the past fifteen years. So a total of 84 per cent were in favour of the pro-choice position, although most of those did not want to see completely unrestricted access to abortion.

Despite this pro-choice social climate, the *political climate* was not entirely favourable to the pro-choice approach to the issue. (The *economic climate* is not directly relevant to abortion policy, though it is certainly a factor in many women's decisions about terminating pregnancies.) The pro-life movement, although small and unrepresentative of the Canadian population as a whole, has been very successful in lobbying policy-makers. In particular, the pro-life movement has targeted sympathetic MPs and worked hard to keep them on side. Most of those MPs were in the governing Progressive Conservative caucus. They imposed limits on the freedom of the more liberal Cabinet to legislate (or not to legislate) on abortion. The Cabinet had to walk a fine line between the majority of the electorate and the demands of their parliamentary supporters.

The *systemic variables* are also crucial to any resolution of the abortion issue. The *federal system* assigns responsibility for criminal law to the national Parliament and the power to regulate health care to the provincial governments. Once the abortion law was struck down, the key decision-makers on the issue were no longer the Supreme Court judges and the federal Cabinet; the locus of power switched to the provinces and the lower courts. This meant that national standards were gone. The implementation battle had always been fought at the local level, but now the policy battle was decentralized as well. The influence of the *party/parliamentary system* was reduced by the resort to a free vote in 1988 and by the central role played by the courts. The *Charter*, as we have seen, was the most important systemic variable. Without the Charter, and a Supreme Court prepared to use it to strike down legislation, the 1969 abortion law would probably still be in place.

The *political variables* were important, insofar as they paralyzed the federal government and eventually doomed the new abortion law. The *women's movement* had been effective in keeping the pressure on governments to ensure abortion services, and in supporting Dr. Morgentaler's legal battles over the years. But in the climactic court battles they found themselves shut out because of the central role played by Dr. Morgentaler. The women's movement did play a role in redefining the issue of abortion as one of reproductive freedom, and in pressuring the women in the Commons and the Senate to prevent any new law from being passed.

The *nature of the policy* itself was critical to the outcome. Abortion is one of the most *controversial* and *visible* political issues facing governments. As we have seen, they try to wash their hands of it whenever possible. The result was the court case, the free vote, the government's inability (or unwillingness) to ensure passage of Bill C-43 despite a Commons and Senate majority, and the present unsettled state of policy. Bill C-43 was clearly *regulatory* in nature, which added to the ire of the pro-choice supporters for whom any government regulation of a woman's right to choose is unbearable. Finally, access to abortion is clearly a *role equity* issue. A woman's ability to control her own fertility is a prerequisite to gender equality. But despite the fact that role equity is-

sues are generally less controversial than role change issues, abortion remains a political hot potato because of the moral chords it strikes in most
of us. This is why governments fumbled it so badly in 1988–91, and why
the issue continues to simmer quietly on the back burner. It is unlikely
that any new government will reverse the decision of the Mulroney
government not to introduce any new legislation on abortion, but the
issue will not go away for a long time to come.

Child Care

Child care is one of the central issues on the agenda of both the women's
movement and most Canadian families. In 1970 the Royal Commission
on the Status of Women identified a crisis in child care and called for a
national child-care program.[16] Judge Rosalie Abella echoed the call in
1984, in her Royal Commission report on Canadian employment equity: "For women who are mothers, a major barrier to equality in the
workplace is the absence of affordable childcare of adequate quality."[17]
The National Council on Welfare argued in 1988 that "the lack of adequate child care is a major obstacle to single mothers on social assistance,
preventing them from returning to the work force or taking the training
or upgrading courses they need to get a job."[18]

Despite these warnings, and clear evidence of a pressing problem
with severe potential consequences for the future of Canadian society,
the issue of child care has received little serious attention from the federal government. That issue can tell us a great deal about the priorities of
successive Canadian governments. It also demonstrates the resistance
against the changes in the family and the economy described in Part 2 of
this book.

According to a 1992 study issued by Statistics Canada, over two and a
half million Canadian children need some form of non-parental care for
at least one hour during an average week.[19] Roughly one in ten of these
children can be accommodated in a licensed child-care centre or family
home. Most children are left with babysitters, with relatives, or on their
own.[20] Such arrangements are sometimes ad hoc and unreliable, which
adds to the stress of parents who must leave their children in the care of
other people. Inadequate care is sometimes a last resort. Parents suffer
from the emotional stress, and employers suffer from reduced productivity as a result. The children suffer most of all from inadequate care: from
a lack of mental stimulation and individual attention, and even from

poor nutrition and hygiene. The staff-child ratios are particularly high in profit-making centres, which constitute the fastest-growing category of child care in Canada.

The costs of care can be prohibitive for many families. An unsubsidized toddler-care space costs an average of $792.00 per month in Ontario, $438.00 in British Columbia, and $370.00 in New Brunswick.[21] That adds up to over $9,000, over $5,000, and $4,440 per year respectively. The cost for an older pre-school child is lower: $6,216 in Ontario per year, $4,488 in B.C., and $3,924 in New Brunswick. Not surprisingly, many parents cannot afford these high prices. They may be forced to quit work, or to work fewer hours than they would prefer, in order to look after the children themselves.[22] There are three federal programs that help parents with the cost of child care. The first is a set of tax benefits for parents, to help offset the costs of care. The second is the Canada Assistance Program (CAP), through which the federal government shares with the provinces and territories the costs of child care for low-income families. CAP was set up in 1966 to help the provinces pay for social welfare programs. It is a means-tested program, available only to the working poor or the long-term unemployed. The third is a set of special initiatives to subsidize child care for particular groups, including parents on Canada Employment and Immigration Commission (CEIC) training programs and natives living on reserves.

These programs are often touted by the federal government as a solution to the problems of paying for child care. But the truth is very different. First, the tax measures provide significant benefits to only a small minority of parents: middle- and upper-income families whose children are in formal types of care, such as licensed centres.[23] There are two types of tax benefit: the child care expense deduction and the new child tax credit. Tax deductions are regressive, meaning that they benefit the wealthy more than the poor. The value of the tax savings increases with taxable income, so that a family earning $100,000 a year would benefit a great deal more than a family earning $40,000 a year. Only parents whose children are in formal care can claim tax benefits, because they must attach receipts to their income tax forms. Most babysitters and ad hoc caregivers do not provide tax receipts. Even with deductible income and tax receipts, for families with high taxable income the 1992 program pays less than half the cost of care.[24]

The refundable child tax credit, which replaced family allowances in 1993, pays parents $1,020 per year per child under 18. The entire amount of the benefit goes only to parents in the low-to-middle-income range; those families earning over $25,000 receive lower benefits. And even the maximum benefit of $1,020 would not cover the average cost of care, let alone the other expenses of raising a child. This measure is not regressive, because its value does not depend on the amount of taxable income: families that have no taxable income are still eligible for the full benefit.

The CAP child-care benefits are available only to parents on welfare and to the working poor. CAP subsidizes child care, but only care in licensed child-care centres. The supply of subsidized spaces is completely inadequate to meet the demand, because there are no government funds for the creation of new spaces. In some cities, the waiting lists for subsidized spaces are measured in years, not weeks. And those parents lucky enough to find a subsidized space must often pay hundreds of dollars in fees, over and above the subsidy. Because of all of these problems, fewer than one-third of eligible children in 1987 actually received any benefits from CAP-subsidized child care.[25] The special initiatives are available only on native reserves and in other specific situations. In 1986–87 government support for child-care programs added up to $682 million. The breakdown among programs, federal and provincial, can be seen in Appendix 1.

There is an unfortunate tendency in North America to blame or stigmatize parents for putting their children in care. Most parents have to earn a living, and it is very difficult to combine family responsibilities with full-time work or study. Over 60 per cent of women with pre-school-aged children are in the work force, and many others study full time. Instead of making it difficult for parents to combine work and family responsibilities, Canadians should begin to treat children as a social responsibility instead of a private luxury. Many European states, some considerably less wealthy than Canada, have established extensive state-run child care systems.[26] Others provide generous assistance to parents to subsidize the costs of care. Most Western countries (with the United States as a significant exception) also allow female workers to take some time off, with some level of pay for at least part of the leave period, to care for newborn or newly adopted children. Sweden also provides a further period of subsidized parental leave, to give fathers a chance to share in the care of infants.[27]

The European services were not provided in response to feminist demands. They were created because governments saw the need to ensure a supply of healthy children in the long run, and a need for women in the paid workforce in the short run. The same needs are present in Canada; yet there is no national child-care program, and as we have seen, the supply of licensed services provided by the provinces and the private sector is inadequate. There are maternal leave policies in Canada, but they are not as generous or as well enforced as those in many European states. Child-care and maternal leave policies are not only in the national interest; they are also required by such international organizations as the United Nations and the International Labour Organization, of which Canada is a member.

According to Judge Abella, the United Nations Convention on the Elimination of All Forms of Discrimination Against Women, which Canada ratified in 1981, requires that:

> in order to prevent discrimination against women on the grounds of marriage or maternity and to ensure their effective right to work," countries take measures "to encourage the provision of the necessary supporting social services to enable parents to combine family obligations with work responsibilities and participation in public life, in particular through promoting the establishment and development of a network of childcare facilities.[28]

How do we explain Canada's failure to meet international standards of child-care services?

We can partly explain this failure if we look at the history of child care as a policy issue in Canada. At both the federal and the provincial levels, governments have been reluctant to take responsibility for Canadian children, preferring to leave it entirely to families. As we saw in Chapter 4, the only real exception occurred during the Second World War, when day nurseries were set up in Ontario and Quebec for the children of female munitions workers. The nurseries were shut down immediately after the war, as part of the campaign to send women back to the home as men returned from the war demanding employment.[29]

When CAP was set up, it reinforced the idea that child care is "a welfare service and not a program to which all children should have access."[30] All of the governments involved with the issue have justified their "intrusion" into the mother's proper sphere by referring to exceptional situations, such as wartime or welfare. There was profound resistance among policy-makers to the growing reality of the 1970s and

1980s: families who needed child care were no longer the exception, but the rule.

Another reason for the lack of action on child care has been the division of responsibilities between the federal and provincial governments. It has often been argued that Canada's division of powers leads to inaction in the area of social policy.[31] The provinces are responsible for setting and enforcing standards for the quality of care. Most provincial governments also provide some financial assistance to non-profit child-care centres, in the form of operating grants or start-up grants. They may also subsidize care for children with special needs.[32] Because there has not been a national child-care program, each province has set different standards, and some have had very little money to contribute to child care.

In the 1984 election campaign the Progressive Conservative party promised a national child-care program. This promise followed years of intensive lobbying by the Canadian Day Care Advocacy Association (CDCAA), by NAC, and by other advocates of public-funded, licensed child care. In 1986 the government received the report of the Federal Task Force on Child Care (the Cooke Report), which called for a national program to be funded jointly by all levels of government. By that time the federal deficit had become the overriding concern of the government, and the report was shelved because its recommendations were considered to be too expensive. The Cooke Report was sent to a special parliamentary committee chaired by Conservative MP Shirley Martin. The committee was deeply split, and in the end the Liberal and NDP members issued dissenting minority reports. The Conservative majority thought that the focus should be on giving money to parents to pay for child care; the Liberals and NDP wanted governments to invest in the building and operation of more child-care spaces.

The opposition members on the parliamentary committee were more in tune with public opinion: in 1989 Gallup reported that 41 per cent of Canadians believed the mother or family should take responsibility for child care, while 54 per cent thought the government should share the responsibility.[33] Men and women differed considerably on this issue: 44 per cent of men and 38 per cent of women were pro-family, while 51 per cent of men and 57 per cent of women wanted the government to take a larger role. The biggest differences, however, were based not on gender but on political party preference – which may explain the willingness of the Liberals and NDP to distance themselves from the PC position.

In early 1988 the government finally released its National Strategy on Child Care. The strategy was not a new national government program. Instead, it was a package of existing tax measures with some additional funding to create and operate new child-care spaces. The funding was seriously inadequate: it was targeted to create 200,000 new spaces over seven years, when the actual present need is over a million spaces. At the time the strategy was released, Gallup found that 57 per cent of Canadians were in favour of paying higher taxes to support government-funded day care for preschoolers, and 38 per cent were opposed;[34] but the PC government knew that its own supporters were the most strongly opposed to higher taxes, so it constructed the new policy to appeal to them.

Advocates of non-profit care criticized the strategy for promising operating grants to profit-making centres. Most child-care advocates were unhappy with the overall thrust of the program: to give a little more money to parents to pay for services that did not exist. There were no measures to provide better-qualified staff or to increase their wages (which are the lowest in Canada). Child-care centres, particularly those run for profit, have high staff turnover rates and require few qualifications. This means that children cannot form bonds with particular caregivers and that the overall quality of care is compromised.

The strategy was delayed because it had to be negotiated with the provinces. When the 1988 election was called, the strategy died in the Senate. The government promised to revive it, but it took no action after winning the 1988 election. Finally, in the 1992 federal budget, then-Finance Minister Don Mazankowski announced that there would be no new national program on child care. The announcement did not come as a great surprise, after almost four years of inaction, but it was still greeted with anger and disappointment by parents and child-care experts.

Who killed the child-care program? There appear to be a number of culprits. By the spring of 1992 the Reform Party, a neo-conservative party opposed to government social spending and changes to women's traditional roles, had attracted 100,000 members and a lot of attention from the media. The Progressive Conservative government had to try to fend off the threat from Reform, and cancelling the national child-care plan was an obvious way to do this. Another likely reason was the influence of the "family caucus" within the PC ranks. After the program was cancelled, this group of right-wing MPs publicly claimed credit for the decision.[35] Some critics argued that the decision to kill the program was part of an overall anti-feminist agenda within the PC government, a concerted effort to send women back into the home.[36] (See Chapter 4 for a discussion of this argument.)

Whatever the reason for its decision, the government sent a strong signal that the issue of child care was not one of its priorities. The only national party that has taken a stand in favour of a national program is the New Democratic Party. The Liberal Party shares the belief of Progressive Conservatives that the deficit is the biggest problem facing Canadians, although it is more sympathetic than the Conservatives to publicly funded care. As long as the bottom line continues to preoccupy Canada's policy-makers, parents and children will continue to muddle along as best they can in a very imperfect system.

How does the child-care issue fit with the model outlined in Chapter 11? The most important *access points* for the women's movement appear to have been public inquiries and the special parliamentary committee, but these were stymied by the government's reluctance to undertake new social programs and party discipline on the Martin Committee. The *social climate* was changing in response to a growing need. The public resistance to child care was diminishing as more and more mothers went out to work, and a greater acceptance of the need to invest in children was developing. But these changes in the social climate, which were favourable to an increased government role in child care, were offset by the negative *economic climate*. All Western governments are paralyzed by deficits and unwilling (or unable) to undertake expensive new social programs. This is probably the single greatest reason for the government's failure to introduce a child-care program that would likely bring an electoral windfall. The *political climate* was also unfavourable, both because of the government's stated commitment to fiscal restraint and because of the hostility to child care among many PC supporters and MPs.

Systemic factors also contributed to the cancellation of the proposed national child-care program. *Federalism,* as we have seen, required the national government to work out the details of a child-care program with the provincial governments. Any sort of intergovernmental bargaining adds considerable complexity to the policy-making process. *Parliamentary government* added another obstacle, splitting the Martin Committee along party lines and reducing its effectiveness in building a constituency for child care within the government. The *Charter* was not a factor in the child-care issue.

The *political variables* were unfavourable to a national child-care program. The government was split over the issue of public funding for child care. The *women's movement* was fairly united, and had built strong coalitions between the CDCAA, the NAC Child Care Committee, and the Ontario Coalition for Better Daycare. The fact that the government promised a program at all was due to the effectiveness of the united lobbying effort. The *policy* itself was fairly *controversial*, with a *broad scope*. Although there was a narrow majority in favour of more government participation in child care, there was also substantial opposition. A new child-care program would be a *redistributive* policy, in the sense that it would use the taxes of the wealthy to pay for child care for everyone, including the less wealthy. It would promote *role equity*, because it would lighten some of the burden carried by women who juggle work and family responsibilities. However, it also promised some *role change*, because it could help to equalize the division of family responsibilities between men and women.

In the end, as we have seen, the principal reason why the policy was not put into practice was expense, followed by the ambivalence of the Mulroney government towards child care. The Liberal Party promised, in the 1993 election campaign, that it would set up a national child-care program as soon as economic growth topped 3 per cent per year; this promise will probably not be fulfilled during the government's current mandate. Given the constant business and media emphasis on fiscal restraint it is doubtful that any government will be able to introduce a national child-care policy in the foreseeable future.

Pornography

Pornography has been a central issue for the women's movement since the 1960s. There is not sufficient room in this section to discuss the feminist debate over pornography in any depth. What we will try to do is to explain why pornography has been such an important issue for Canadian feminists, and to describe the efforts by successive federal governments to respond to public concerns. Despite repeated attempts to change the existing laws, which date from the 1950s, no government has been able to build a consensus around a single approach to pornography that would permit them to legislate on the issue.

As in the case of abortion, a central part of the debate over pornography has been the struggle to define it. Some people frame the issue as one of freedom. They believe that pornography should be freely available, because any attempt to ban it or to censor it is a violation of the right to free speech protected by the Charter (see Chapter 5). These people may not like pornography; indeed, they may be profoundly disturbed by it. But they do not want to impose their standards of taste or morality on the community. Other people see pornography as a moral issue. They are revolted by the explicit depiction of sex, even the consensual lovemaking of two adults. They want to see pornography banned, to get rid of the "filth" that disgusts them and, they fear, corrupts their children. Both of these positions are deeply held and passionately argued.

The feminist definition of pornography is quite different. This is because many feminists perceive the harms caused by pornography to be physical and psychological rather than moral. As we saw in Chapter 6, many feminists believe that women are damaged and endangered by the prevalence of the rape myths in our society. Nowhere are the rape myths more strongly portrayed than in pornography. Many feminists believe that the images of women presented in pornographic films, videos, magazines, and books encourage men to believe that all women want sex all the time, and that "no" really means "yes." By reducing women and children to sexual objects, instead of human beings with free will and the right to control their bodies, pornography threatens the physical security and self-esteem of all women and children – especially the ones involved in the creation of pornographic materials. Therefore, a feminist definition of pornography incorporates concepts of power and coercion. Pornography is "a presentation ... of sexual behaviour in which one or more participants are coerced overtly or implicitly, into participation; or are injured or abused physically or psychologically; or in which an imbalance of power is obvious, or implied ... and in which such behaviour can be taken to be advocated or endorsed."[37]

By the early 1980s it had become obvious that the existing laws did not satisfy anyone. There was no law against pornography as such. There were two laws against obscenity, one applied by judges and the other by Customs officials. The first law was a section of the Criminal Code that forbade the selling or distribution of obscene materials. "Obscenity" was defined as "any publication a dominant characteristic of which is the undue exploitation of sex, or of sex and any one more of the following subjects, namely, crime, horror, cruelty and violence."[38] The second law is the Customs Act, which allows Customs officers to seize "indecent" or "immoral" materials entering Canada. There are no precise rules about what may be allowed in and what may not, although there are some broad guidelines and a list of prohibited materials that Customs agents may use in making their decisions.[39] The role played by Customs is crucial, because over 95 per cent of all pornographic materials in Canada are imported (mostly from the United States).[40]

The laws applied by judges and Customs agents are over thirty years old, and the pornography situation in Canada has changed radically during that time. Sexually explicit material is now available in corner stores, much of it involving children. "Hard-core" pornography, extremely graphic presentations of sex (usually involving violence, coercion, or degradation of various kinds), is increasingly accessible and popular. The newsstand sales of *Penthouse* exceed those of *Time* and *Newsweek* put together. Pornographic videos, magazines, and books are a multi-billion-dollar industry in Canada.[41] At the same time, public reaction to pornography has become increasingly divided. On the one hand, hundreds of thousands of Canadians are buying these materials. This implies a high level of tolerance. On the other hand, there is growing concern about the effects of pornography on the attitudes of teenage boys towards women and sex, and about possible links between exposure to pornography and sexual violence. Finally, the women's movement, although divided over pornography itself, has redefined the issue as one of harm to women and children. This approach has reinforced the arguments of the moralists in favour of restrictions on the distribution of pornographic materials.

Successive governments have made several attempts to update the laws relating to pornography. The Liberal government of Pierre Elliott Trudeau made three such attempts. Each of these was part of an omnibus bill, a huge collection of diverse amendments to the Criminal Code. None of these bills passed the House of Commons. In August 1984, during the federal election campaign that brought the Progressive Conservatives to power, a federal committee on sexual offenses against children issued its final report. It recommended that child pornography be specifically prohibited in the Criminal Code. The following year the Fraser Committee issued its report on pornography, with recommendations for new legislation. The Mulroney government was eager to bring in tougher laws against pornography, but it did not find the assistance it needed in either of these reports.

The Fraser Committee recommended that pornography be divided into three "tiers" for the purposes of the criminal law.[42] The first tier would include child pornography and pornographic materials whose production causes "actual physical harm" to the participants – such as "snuff films," in which real women are murdered on camera for the purpose of titillating male audiences. The stiffest penalties would attach to the sale or production of these materials, and there would be no possibility of defence against these charges based on the artistic merit of the material. The second tier would include depictions or descriptions of sexual violence and "deviant" sexual behaviour; a defence of merit would be available, and the penalties would be less harsh. The third tier would include materials that are generally known as "erotica": nonviolent sexual activity between two consenting adults. No criminal penalties would attach to the sale or production of these materials unless they were "displayed to the public without a warning as to their nature or made accessible to people under age 18."[43]

The Fraser Committee had tried valiantly to find a balance between the moral, liberal, and feminist viewpoints on pornography. Feminists had long argued that a ban on all sexual depictions was excessive. Erotica should be decriminalized – that is, made legal – while pornography that degraded women and children should be subject to harsher penalties. This distinction was adopted by the Fraser Committee, but it did not find a sympathetic audience in the Mulroney Cabinet. This became evident in June 1986, when Justice Minister John Crosbie introduced Bill C-114. The bill not only tightened criminal penalties for hard-core pornography; it would have made the sale or display of any type of erotica illegal as well. The bill created four categories of pornography: pornography that shows physical harm; degrading pornography; violent pornography; and a residual category of pornography that included "any visual matter showing vaginal, anal or oral intercourse," and a list of other acts that concluded with the words "or other sexual activity."[44]

Critics of the bill were horrified at this Victorian approach, and attacked the blanket prohibition of sexual depictions. Feminists were particularly upset with the bill's denial of the difference between pornography and erotica.[45] The bill had a few defenders, including some religious groups, who tried to push the government forward. But it was clear that despite its huge parliamentary majority, the Mulroney government did not have the will to impose the legislation on the divided country. The storm of outrage ended when Parliament was dissolved at the end of the year and Bill C-114 died on the order paper.

In May 1987 the government tried again. The new justice minister, Ray Hnatyshyn, introduced Bill C-54. It was very similar to C-114, except that it omitted the words "or other sexual activity." The new bill also recognized pornography as hate literature against women, which feminists had been pressing for. Finally, there was some effort to distinguish between pornography and erotica. Women's groups welcomed these changes, but they were still strongly opposed to the bill. It did not recognize power and coercion as defining aspects of pornography, and it provided a defence of artistic merit that could be used to emasculate the rest of the bill.[46] Librarians and civil libertarians joined the fight against the bill. They were afraid of censorship in the schools, and of the police powers that would be needed to implement the bill.

Partly as a result of this widespread criticism, the bill did not proceed to a debate at second reading until six months after its introduction. After five days the debate simply ended. There was no vote, no committee scrutiny, and no more public discussion of the bill. In late 1988 the bill died as Parliament was dissolved for a federal election.

The issue of pornography tells us a few things about our political system. It reminds us that it is very difficult to reach consensus on "moral" issues, especially when there are competing definitions of the issue. The feminist understanding of pornography has become increasingly influential in Canada, as witnessed by the Supreme Court of Canada ruling in *R. v. Butler* (see Chapter 5). Whereas it might have been possible to find a balance between the moral and liberal approaches to pornography, the task is now complicated by the redefinition of pornography as a threat to the physical security and social standing of women.

The outcome of Bills C-114 and C-54 also suggests that the marginalization of women's groups in the political system is not as marked on some issues as it is on others. Women's groups, particularly the CACSW and LEAF, were key players in the pornography debate, and the *Butler* ruling suggests that their influence will continue to grow. Women have decisively changed the terms of the debate on this issue, and policymakers are now forced to come to grips with those changes. Yet the victory for the women's movement was only a minor one. Many feminists felt that it was more important to have a law that banned child pornography. Such a law was passed in 1993. But one key item remains on the agenda: a law that defines pornography as hate literature against women, and that protects women against the harmful effects of pornography. This will remain an item on the feminist agenda for the foreseeable future.[47]

Pornography provides a good example of the factors that can help or hurt women's efforts to influence the policy process. The most important *access points* were public inquiries, the media, and the Charter. Women's groups used those inquiries to promote a feminist redefinition of pornography and a feminist analysis of the threat it poses to women and children. The media helped to popularize the feminist analysis. The Charter was important because it brought the issue of pornography before the Supreme Court, and the court was sympathetic to the feminist analysis.

The *environmental* factors were somewhat important, but not critical. The *social climate* was one of growing concern about pornography, from both a feminist viewpoint and a moral viewpoint. The *economic climate* was not particularly important, but the *political climate* did play a part. In particular, the feminist analysis of pornography was gaining increasing legitimacy, as the *Butler* decision demonstrates.

The *systemic variables* were not very important, except for the Charter. Neither federalism nor parliamentary government played much of a role. Among the *political variables,* the key factors were the moralistic pro-censorship wing of the PC caucus and the hostility to feminism of many PC supporters. The *women's movement* was less effective on this issue than it might have been, because it was deeply split. Some feminists believe that the harms done by pornography are so profound that they justify censorship or even an outright ban. Others oppose censorship, despite their dislike of pornography, while still others argue that a ban on pornography would simply drive it underground. Despite these divisions, those feminists who advocate a ban on pornography were able to stop two unsatisfactory laws and secure a breakthrough Supreme Court ruling.

The *policy* of censoring pornography is fairly controversial, because there remains a constituency that believes free speech is at stake in any attempt to curtail pornography. A *regulatory* policy on pornography would lead to greater *role equity* for women, according to feminists. But not everyone is convinced that such an infringement of the right to free speech is justified. In the end, the Supreme Court had to step in and resolve one issue: the question of whether the obscenity law violated the Charter.

The only area of the pornography issue on which a political consensus exists is child pornography. This is why the Conservatives were able to pass a child pornography law (Bill C-128) through the House of Commons before the 1993 election. The law amended the Criminal Code and the Customs Tariff to forbid the possession, sale, or distribution of any material portraying explicit sexual activity by anyone who is, or is portrayed as being, under the age of eighteen. The maximum sentence for selling or distributing child pornography is ten years; the maximum for possession is five years. There were concerns about the effect of Bill C-128 on artists. These concerns may have been accurate: the first charges laid were against a Toronto artist whose paintings of children were considered by the police to be pornographic, even though the artist denied any such intent. In April 1995 a judge finally ruled that the paintings were not pornographic in intent, although he upheld the law itself. The case illustrates the difficulties in regulating pornography, difficulties that will likely prevent any new legislation for several more years.

Sexual Harassment

As we saw in Chapter 5, the Canadian law on sexual assault has changed significantly in recent years. But the law on sexual harassment has remained largely unchanged for over a decade, despite the huge increase in the attention paid to this issue during that time. After centuries of silence, women finally began to speak out about their experiences of sexual exploitation at the hands of powerful men. The testimony of Anita Hill at the Senate confirmation hearings of U.S. Supreme Court nominee Clarence Thomas was certainly the most widely publicized case, though by no means the only one. At the same time, lurid stories of abuse in residential and religious schools were demonstrating that sexual harassment was not just something that happened to women. Perhaps partly as a result of that realization, the media and the public began to demand harsher penalties for men (and women) who abuse their social, economic, or institutional power over others for their own sexual pleasure.

It is often claimed that sexual harassment is difficult to define. We have all heard men make uneasy jokes about how a friendly hug could land them in court. But the truth is that there is a clear and obvious distinction between sexual harassment and mutually agreeable flirting. That distinction is based on *power*. Sexual harassment is "unsolicited and unreciprocated sexual male behaviour towards women and girls, which may be obscured by what is considered 'normal' behaviour."[48] It is "a social construction founded on inherited male power and gender conditioning"[49] that undermines the autonomy of women and girls. "It may include an explicit or implicit threat for non-compliance."[50]

Catharine MacKinnon offers a similar definition: "Sexual harassment ... refers to the unwanted imposition of sexual requirements in the context of a relationship of unequal power."[51] This definition applies both to the workplace, where a male can have power over a female by virtue of his ability to fire her, and to the university, where a male professor can fail a female student who does not "play along."

We have referred to men sexually harassing women, as if no other type of harassment were possible. In theory, a woman with power over a man can exploit him sexually. But in practice, men sexually harass women and not the other way around. For example, the Canadian Human Rights Commission received 121 complaints of sexual harassment between 1978 and 1986, 97 per cent of which were lodged by women against men. Less than 2 per cent were from men complaining about other men, and the same proportion were from men complaining about women.[52]

As we saw in the *Janzen-Govereau* case (Chapter 5), courts are not always clear about what sexual harassment is. Some people mistake sexual harassment for "flirting," a natural expression of attraction between two adults. But there is nothing natural about sexual harassment. It is the product of a socially constructed power inequality between men and women. In the workplace, men are more likely than women to be the boss. In the university, over half of undergraduate students are female while 80 per cent of professors are male.[53] For men who wish to abuse their power by forcing unwanted sexual attention on women, there are a host of opportunities.

In its preliminary ruling on the case of Bonnie Robichaud (see below), the Canadian Human Rights Commission identified three characteristics of sexual harassment.

1.   The encounters must be unsolicited by the complainant, unwelcome to the complainant and expressly or implicitly known by the respondent to be unwelcome.

2.   The conduct must either continue despite the complainant's protests or, if the conduct stops, the complainant's protests must have led to negative employment consequences.

3.   The complainant's cooperation must be due to employment-related threats or promises.[54]

What specific activities constitute "sexual harassment"? The most common types of activity include "sexually tinged staring, repeated sexual innuendo, frequent reference to their body parts, discussion of their presumed sexual activity, and unnecessary and uninvited body contact of all kinds."[55] It is clear that such behaviours are much more difficult to legislate against than overt acts like rape. But this does not mean that we should resign ourselves to the epidemic of sexual exploitation in workplaces and universities. Studies indicate that 20 to 30 per cent of all female university students in the United States have experienced some form of sexual harassment from their professors.[56] It is estimated that in the United States, between 40 and 60 per cent of women in the workplace have been harassed at some point in their careers.[57] There is no reason to hope that the Canadian statistics are any less shocking.

In July 1983 the Canadian Human Rights Act was amended to make workplace discrimination illegal. Ten specific grounds of discrimination were outlawed, including sex. Sexual harassment is considered to be a form of sexual discrimination under the act. In other words, an employee who wishes to complain about sexual harassment must file a sexual discrimination complaint with the Canadian Human Rights Commission. The commission will set up an independent tribunal to hear the case and to make recommendations to the commission. If the tribunal finds in favour of the plaintiff, it will usually award damages against the harasser or, where appropriate, against the employer. The damages are intended to cover lost wages, in cases where an employee has been forced to leave work because of the harassment, as well as her or his legal costs.

This system does not require a person found guilty of sexual harassment to face criminal sanctions. It is slow, under-funded, and often ineffective.[58] The Canadian Human Rights Commission does not have the capacity to deal with the extent of sexual harassment that goes on in our workplaces and schools. Between 1978 and 1986, 121 complaints were filed with the commission; as of 1987, only 27 (22 per cent) had been settled. These cases represent a drop in the ocean, according to an Angus Reid survey cited by Susan Webb. Of the women surveyed, 37 per cent reported sexual harassment on the job. This is almost four times the reported rate for men (10 per cent). Most of the respondents who reported harassment said that they had done nothing about it, "because they have little faith that their complaints will be taken seriously."[59]

Part of the problem is the cumbersome tribunal system. Another flaw in the system is the definition of sexual harassment as a form of sexual discrimination, which is the only way that it can be litigated under the Canadian Human Rights Act. Why not make sexual harassment a criminal offence? Why not set up a system that provides justice quickly? In the 1995 federal budget the commission suffered a crippling blow; its regional offices were shut down and its staff was slashed. Its capacity to act on behalf of complainants is now even less.

It is clear that this system does not work well enough, and that a new policy is required. But policy-makers are very reluctant to create new laws to define and punish sexual harassment more effectively. This reluctance is partly the result of a more general ambivalence towards the issue. Many people simply refuse to see the sexual coercion of women, in however mild or severe a form, as a crime.[60] Others argue that it is too difficult to distinguish between sexual harassment and mutually agreeable flirting, so that a criminal law would risk convicting innocent men. This is a needless worry, if the humilation of Anita Hill is anything to go by. Any woman who has been subjected to sexual harassment knows that she has been coerced, not flattered. The real problem is that the justice system and the political system are not yet prepared to believe a woman's telling of her own experience when they must weigh her word against that of a man. It does not appear that there will be any legislative action on sexual harassment in the foreseeable future.

As with the issues of abortion and pornography, Canadian superior courts have shown themselves to be ahead of legislatures in this area. The Supreme Court of Canada has issued two rulings on sexual harassment that have reflected feminist analysis and validated women's experience. We have discussed the *Janzen-Govereau* case in Chapter 5. The other case involved Bonnie Robichaud, a cleaner on a Canadian Armed

Forces base who was repeatedly harassed by her male foreman. After years of struggle in the courts, she finally won a Supreme Court ruling that established the responsibility of an employer to protect employees against sexual harassment.[61] After further litigation through the commission, she was awarded the maximum award for damages under the Human Rights Act: $5,000. Her harasser, who had repeatedly threatened and attempted to sexually assault her, was never charged with an offence; instead, he had to pay half of the damages.[62] For this result, Robichaud had to endure years of costly litigation. These costs are prohibitive for most women, and lower courts have not demonstrated great sensitivity to women's perceptions and experiences of sexual harassment.

Despite these two landmark rulings, Canadian women are little better protected from this dehumanizing experience than they were twenty years ago. There must be a change in social attitudes before any action will be taken, either by the political system or by employers and universities, to make women's place in the "public sphere" more secure. Sexual harassment should be regarded as a crime, and those who commit it should be punished.

A step in the right direction was taken in 1993, with the passage of an anti-stalking law (Bill C-126) by the House of Commons. The bill defined a new offence of "criminal harassment." Anyone who persistently follows, communicates with, watches, or threatens someone else, against their explicit wishes, may be liable for a maximum five-year prison sentence. The bill was not specifically aimed at sexual harassment, but some forms of the behaviour may fall under the scope of Bill C-126. Still, this is long way from a recognition of women's right to earn a living, or pursue an education, without suffering mistreatment based on sex.

How well does sexual harassment fit the model of women's influence in policy-making? The only *access point* that may play a role in the near future is the media; consider its coverage of the Anita Hill case in the United States. The *environmental variables* were not particularly influential, except for the growing awareness of the problem of sexual harassment in the *social climate*. The only *systemic variable* that played a role is federalism, and that was only indirect: the case of Janzen and Govereau was heard first at the provincial level and was then appealed to the Supreme Court of Canada. No *political variables* have been significant, because no political party or leader has been willing to speak out on sexual harassment. The *women's movement* has tried to make the public aware of the seriousness of the issue, and has had some success, but the political system has not been moved to respond.

Finally, any new *policy* to crack down on sexual harassment would likely be somewhat *controversial,* because some men feel very threatened by the idea. This may be one reason why policy-makers have shied away from the issue, content to leave it as a human rights issue instead of legislating it into the criminal law. Any law that defines, restricts, and punishes sexual harassment is a *regulatory* statute that promotes *role equity* and indirectly, by empowering women, some *role change* as well.

New Reproductive Technologies

Feminists have debated the value of artificial reproduction since Shulamith Firestone's *The Dialectic of Sex* appeared in 1970. In that book, which we discussed briefly in Chapter 2, Firestone argued that the biological family was the root of women's oppression. Women were weakened by pregnancy and childbirth and enslaved by the demands of nurturing children. Women consequently became dependent on men for physical protection. It followed logically, in Firestone's view, that the only way to end "sex class" oppression was to liberate women from the demands of reproducing the species. She described a utopian society in which babies were conceived and gestated in glass wombs, and where no one could be certain of the parentage of any child. The advancement of reproductive technology would free women from their biological and cultural chains.

The age of the "glass womb" is not yet upon us, but there is no question that reproductive technology has made huge advances in the past decade. These advances have deeply divided the women's movement. There is only room in this section for a brief discussion of a few types of reproductive technology; interested readers are encouraged to consult the works listed in the references to this chapter.[63]

Reproductive technologies fall into three main categories.[64] The first group consists of technologies that prevent the development of new life, including birth control, sterilization, and abortion. The second type of technology is used to "monitor the development of new life": ultrasound, amniocentesis, fetal monitoring and surgery. These first two groups of technologies can pose serious problems for women. The best known problem is "sex selection," in which ultrasound is used to detect the sex of a fetus, and it is aborted if it is the wrong sex (i.e., female). The practice is believed to be fairly common in India and in the Indian communities of North American cities, because of the intense social pressure on women to produce sons.

Most of the new reproductive technologies that concern feminists belong to the third category: "those that involve the creation of new life." The key life-creating technologies are artificial insemination (AI) and *in vitro* fertilization (IVF). Artificial insemination is the process by which sperm, supplied either by an anonymous donor (AID) or by the partner of the woman (AIH), is injected into a woman's vagina through a syringe. Most AI procedures are AID, because the partner is infertile or the woman does not have a partner. IVF is considerably more complicated. The woman is given a fertility drug to stimulate the production of several ova at a time. The ova are removed and mixed with active sperm in a laboratory dish (*in vitro* means "in glass"). Some ova will be fertilized, and these can be either implanted in the woman's womb immediately or frozen for future use. Several fertilized ova (called embryos) are usually implanted at once, because the woman's body will normally reject some of them.

To many observers, AI and IVF are not inherently problematic. The concern arises from the uses to which they have been, and may be, applied. Two examples are the use of AI for impregnating surrogate mothers and the manipulation of IVF to ensure that only embryos with certain qualities – such as maleness – will be implanted. There are also more general concerns arising from these procedures, which we will discuss later. For the moment we will concentrate on surrogate motherhood and sex selection.

Surrogate motherhood is a legally binding agreement between the biological mother of a child and its legal parents (usually a married couple). The parents pay the woman a fee for carrying and giving birth to the child, on top of her medical expenses and sometimes a living allowance during the pregnancy. The woman may be impregnated with the sperm of the legal father, so that the child is, in biological terms, half hers and half his. Or IVF may be used, and the surrogate may be implanted with the mother's eggs fertilized by the father's sperm. In that case the surrogate mother is not biologically related to the child; she is essentially a "womb for rent." When the child is born the woman signs away her rights to it, and it is legally adopted by the couple. Sometimes such arrangements are made informally, between friends or relatives, without money changing hands. A woman offers to have a baby for her sister, or her daughter, out of love. The growing concern about surrogate motherhood does not relate to these informal arrangements, but to the legally binding contracts brokered by doctors and lawyers who charge fees for their services.

There are a host of legal and ethical concerns raised by surrogate motherhood. First, it is against the law in most Western jurisdictions to sell one's child. Does surrogacy amount to selling one's baby, at least in cases where the surrogate contributes the egg? Some courts have suggested that baby-selling laws forbid surrogacy; others have disagreed, ruling that what is being sold is not a *baby,* but rather a reproductive *service.* Second, should the surrogacy contract be enforceable? What about a surrogate who changes her mind about giving up the child before or after the birth? Should the rights of the contracting parents take precedence over the feelings of the surrogate for a child born of her womb? What about cases in which the child is born with a defect of some sort? Third, should the surrogate have any relationship with the family after giving up the child? Would this create enough confusion in the child, and heartbreak for the surrogate, to outweigh any benefits from continued contact?

Fourth, should women be allowed to make money from their ability to reproduce? Some socialist feminists have argued that surrogacy turns women's reproductive capacities into a commodity to be bought and sold, thus reducing women's sole source of power to a commercial transaction controlled by, and for the profit of, men. Others counter that it is only fair for women to earn money by their reproductive labour, instead of being exploited by the capitalist system to reproduce the labour force for free. Meanwhile, some liberal feminists believe that if a surrogate freely chooses to enter into a contract with the parents, her choice should be respected and the contract upheld by the legal system. This debate may never be resolved. It illustrates the dilemmas that confront feminists when they try to deal with the choices and the possible exploitation inherent in the new reproductive technologies.

The process of sex selection has also attracted significant attention. The technology of IVF allows doctors to determine the genetic characteristics of embryos, and to implant only those with the right genes. The other embryos may be discarded. In some cases this practice may be defensible. A couple with a high genetic risk for a terminally ill child may wish to avoid the danger by undergoing IVF and implanting only healthy embryos. In other cases the power to select which embryos will live has very disturbing overtones. We have already seen that some women are pressured to undergo ultrasound to determine the sex of their fetuses, and to abort females. With IVF the same goal can be achieved much more efficiently: only male embryos are implanted in the womb, and the female embryos are discarded. But the potential for genetic manipulation goes much further. Sperm can be separated into those that will produce male and female embryos, and only the "male" sperm mixed with the eggs. Or the embryos can be genetically tested for all sorts of characteristics, including height and eye colour, and only the aesthetically desirable embryos selected for breeding.

Critics of the new reproductive technologies are appalled by these eugenic possibilities. Their fears that we may abuse our power to create a "master race" do not really concern us here. What does concern us is the question of sex selection. In India, men substantially outnumber women — a surprising fact given women's slight majority in other countries. Well over 20 million Indian women are "missing," owing primarily to the combination of ultrasound and abortion, the murder of female infants, and other practices encouraged by the strong cultural preference for male children.[65] India is far from the only culture where sons are preferred to daughters; indeed, son preference is universal, varying only in degree from culture to culture.[66] If parents are given the option of implanting male or female embryos, how many will choose to have only sons? Could the numbers of women be systematically reduced over the next few centuries? What impact will that have on women, and on society as a whole?

A study for the Royal Commission on New Reproductive Technologies (RCNRT) found that while most respondents would prefer one child of each sex, there was no overwhelming desire for boys among Canadian parents. Both men and women displayed a slight preference for male children, but this preference appears to have declined over time.[67] Few parents were willing to consider using technology to determine the sex of a future child, though this may be more likely among parents who already have a child of one sex and want one more child of the other sex.

The more general concerns arising from AI and IVF are legal and ethical in nature. Should AI donors receive custody of their biological children in a divorce? Should AI clinics keep complete records of sperm donors, so that their children can get in touch with them, or be notified of any genetic disorders that crop up in later life? Should children be told about the unusual nature of their conception? Should AI services be controlled by medical professionals, who may be biased in their assessment of applicants? For example, some AI clinics have refused to perform insemination on single women, or on lesbians in committed relationships, because of their fears about the upbringing the resulting child would receive.[68] Should they have the right to impose their morality or their ideas about family life on others?

The current law in Canada is virtually silent on the issues raised by new reproductive technologies. Our capacity to control the reproductive process has progressed faster than our ability to reach a consensus on whether that process should even be regulated, let alone on the content of any possible law. In 1989 the federal government appointed the RCNRT to study the medical, legal, ethical, and political implications of these technologies. The commission was riven with conflict, and required two extensions to its reporting deadline; its report finally appeared in late 1993.[69] The RCNRT called for the creation of a National Reproductive Technologies Commission, which would have the power to license clinics. It would also regulate the use of new reproductive techniques, including sperm collecting, storage, and insemination; egg retrieval and use; prenatal diagnosis; embryo research; and research on human fetal tissue. The commission argued that such a body is necessary because the technology is developing too rapidly for one law to encompass. The creation of a permanent regulatory body, composed of experts in all of the related disciplines (including medicine, ethics, law, and sociology), would ensure the orderly development of NRTs in a way that would benefit all Canadians who sought assistance in reproduction. The commission also recommended that the use of NRTs be publicly funded, but only those that have been proven to be safe and effective; that the prevention of infertility be made a high priority; that NRTs not be used to make money for doctors or brokers; that commercial surrogate motherhood (which the commission called "preconception arrangements") be forbidden and the contracts be unenforceable against the birth mother; that sex selection not be permitted for non-medical reasons; and that AI and IVF be closely monitored for safety, record-keeping, and effectiveness.

Critics attacked the commission for its slowness, its secretiveness, and its alleged failure to take a feminist stand on the issues. The federal government has not moved to set up a national regulatory commission; instead, Health Minister Diane Marleau announced in July 1995 that the government would ask doctors who employ NRTs to regulate themselves.

Whatever its shortcomings, the RCNRT did commission a large quantity of research material that is an invaluable aid to researchers. The issues discussed in the studies include the cost of IVF (about $9,000); the risks of NRTs to the parents and their prospective children; the failure of NRT clinics to inform parents realistically about the small chances of success; and the emotional costs of surrogacy contracts to the women who bear children for infertile couples.

Because health care is a matter of provincial jurisdiction, most of the scanty legislation in this field has been passed by provincial governments. Both Yukon and Quebec have adopted laws that deem the legal father of an AID child to be the husband of the woman who gave birth to it.[70] Feminists find it significant that the first laws to be passed regarding these issues have been designed to protect the institution of fatherhood rather than the interests of women.[71]

Indeed, many feminists believe that the issue of new reproductive technologies can tell us a great deal about a number of crucial issues: the control of women's bodies by medical technology; the attitudes of society and of policy-makers towards women's control of their own reproduction; the tendency for law-makers to avoid dealing with "moral" issues that most directly affect the interests of women. Other issues raised by feminists include the allocation of scarce health-care resources. Should provincial governments pay for couples to undergo IVF, which has a very low success rate and costs tens of thousands of dollars for every successful pregnancy? Or should the money be directed towards preventing infertility? Many of the major causes of infertility can be prevented, including sexually transmitted diseases, IUDs, workplace hazards, anorexia, and amateur abortions.[72] In 1988 the Canadian government spent $3.5 million on NRT research, and $400,000 on preventing reproductive disorders.[73] Why not prevent infertility instead of pouring money into trying to overcome it after the damage has been done? Finally, we must examine the "natural" desire for children that leads thousands of women to undergo painful, risky surgical procedures with little or no guarantee of success. Is it really natural? Or is it a social artifact created by a patriarchal society and reinforced by the paternal aspirations of men?

The report of the royal commission, and the action taken on it by the federal government, will be the strongest indications of the ways in which the political system can deal with this issue. But we can draw some conclusions from the length of time the issue has spent on the back burner, and from the fact that only the women's movement has paid sustained attention to the implications of these developments for women. The state of medical technology is not a "women's issue," although it may affect women's lives most directly. It affects everyone who wants a child, and everyone who pays taxes to support a state health system that prefers expensive heroic intervention to the simple preventive care of women's bodies.

The issue of regulating new reproductive technologies illustrates the complexity of the Canadian policy-making process. The chief *access points* for those involved with the issue include the *bureaucracy,* specifically the Justice departments of several governments and the Ontario Law Reform Commission; the media, which has given NRTs a lot of attention in recent years; and public inquiries, especially the royal commission. One of the key *environmental variables* in the mix is a growing awareness of the new technology in the *social climate,* coupled with apparent support for its use. A Gallup poll taken in 1983 found that 60 per cent of respondents approve the use of IVF, though only 44 per cent were in favour of surrogacy (and 47 per cent felt that the birth mother should be able to keep the baby).[74] Another key environmental factor is the reduction of provincial health care budgets because of the unfavourable *economic climate.*

Among the *systemic variables,* the most important is *federalism.* The provinces are responsible for health care, contract law, family law, and other areas of policy that impinge on issues like surrogacy; but the federal government contributes to provincial health care budgets through the Established Programs Financing Act, so it may have a say in the issue as well.

The *political variables* have been relatively unimportant to this issue; none of the parties has taken a firm stand on NRTs, and it has not become a major issue for the electorate. The *women's movement* has been deeply split on the issue. NAC opposes the use of NRTs, claiming that the medical and scientific communities were turning women into guinea pigs, and condemning the practice of turning poor women into breeders for wealthy couples. This stance has angered many infertile women, who believe that NRTs are their last hope to have children, and who want the research to continue. The split became public and quite bitter, culminating in the resignation of four members of the royal commission.

A *policy* of *regulating* NRTs would be fairly *controversial,* as we have seen. It is not clear whether such a policy would promote role equity or role change. Indeed, one of the reasons why some feminists oppose NRTs is that they increase the social pressure for women to have children. This is seen by some as a backward step, a belief which other feminists reject. All in all, NRTs are a particularly difficult issue for feminists to deal with, because they cut to the heart of the differences between liberal, radical, and socialist feminism. As long as the issue remains unresolved, the women's movement will likely remain divided over the question of whether NRTs are a blessing or a trap for women.

Conclusion

In this chapter we have discussed the following key points:

1. The Mulroney government was forced to confront the issue of abortion when the Supreme Court of Canada struck down the abortion law in 1988. The government held a free vote in the Commons in 1988, which proved inconclusive. A new law, Bill C-43, was introduced in 1989 and was defeated in the Senate in 1991. There is presently no federal law concerning abortion. Provincial governments have tried to restrict access. The principal factors affecting policy-making on abortion are its controversial nature, the influence of the Charter on Canadian politics, the presence of women in the House of Commons, and the success of the women's movement in redefining the abortion issue as one of women's reproductive freedom.

2. Despite an urgent social need, the federal government scrapped its promised national child-care program in 1992. The current federal policies are mostly tax breaks targeted to parents, instead of capital grants to build more spaces. The key factors in the outcome were the government's fiscal restraint programs, the hostility of some PC backbenchers towards the idea of child care, the need to work out an agreement among eleven governments, and the effectiveness of the women's movement in building coalitions and getting the issue on the policy agenda in the first place.

3. Pornography has become big business in Canada. Most feminists agree that it threatens the physical and psychological security of women and children. The existing law is outdated, but repeated attempts to reform it have been defeated by a lack of political consensus on the benefits of censoring pornography. The Supreme Court ruled in 1992, on the basis of an explicitly feminist analysis, that the current obscenity law violates the Charter guarantee of free speech but that it is justified in doing so. The feminist arguments against pornography have become the most legitimate analysis in recent years, although we are still a long way from a consensus. The key factors in policy-making on this issue are the controversial nature of a ban on pornography and the lack of agreement within the women's movement.

4. The present law on sexual harassment is not sufficiently effective, despite the landmark Supreme Court ruling in the *Janzen-Govereau* case. The Canadian Human Rights Commission, which administers the law, has no authority to impose criminal sanctions, and it is overburdened with other types of cases. No action has been taken, largely because of the controversial nature of the issue and because it has not become a high-profile political issue.

5. New reproductive technologies have developed faster than our ability to monitor them or to develop codes of ethics for their use. Feminists are deeply split on the issue of what to do about them. Some are afraid that women's bodies will be even more controlled by male doctors and scientists, and that women will be turned into "wombs for rent." Others see NRTs as a breakthrough for infertile women. There have been a few provincial laws, but as yet no federal policy on NRTs.

6. "Women's issues" usually affect men as well as women. It is time that we started treating them as important social and economic issues, which they are, instead of trivializing them as matters of concern "only" to women.

The issues discussed in this chapter have at least one feature in common: they are among the subjects most commonly referred to as "women's issues." But they are very different in other respects. Canadian governments have assiduously avoided making policy on some issues, including abortion and child care. They have taken little or no action on others, including sexual harassment and new reproductive technologies. And they have made serious but flawed efforts to respond to still other issues, including pornography.

The differences in government response can be partly explained by the differences among the issues themselves. Women's demands for access to abortion and child care have been perceived by many policy-makers and interest groups as a threat to the traditional family. They have used this apparent threat as a rallying point for conservative groups and individuals, and set up very effective resistance to change. The issues of sexual harassment and new reproductive technologies have emerged quite recently, and it is possible that governments may develop more effective responses in the next few years. But the fact that both issues turn squarely on the controversial question of women's control of their own bodies, as well as men's control of property and resources, means that they may be as difficult to resolve as abortion or child care.

Money is also a crucial factor in policy-making, particularly in the past decade, as is electoral appeal. Governments like symbolic policies that pass easily and cost little to implement, such as the "rape shield" law (see Chapter 5) or the sexual harassment section of the Canadian Human Rights Act. Policies for which there is no consensus are avoided (abortion, NRTs, an effective sexual harassment law), as are policies that would cost millions of dollars (child care).

Pornography is a special case, because it appeared to the Mulroney government to be an easy issue to resolve, but proved more difficult in practice. It has been very difficult to build a consensus on the questions raised by this issue. The question of regulating pornography and NRTs has divided the women's movement more deeply than the other issues discussed in this chapter, which helps to explain why a policy consensus has not emerged on these issues: the policy community itself has been divided, which has made it impossible to craft a policy that would appeal to the electorate.

As we have seen repeatedly in this book, policy-makers often categorize issues as "women's issues" in order to downplay their importance. This designation is sometimes supported by feminists, in their efforts to shape the public discourse on these issues. For example, redefining abortion as an issue of women's rights made sense in light of the previous monopoly of the issue by doctors and church leaders. But other feminists are realizing that the tactic can be counterproductive. In the first place, describing a matter of public policy as a women's issue prevents the women's movement from building coalitions with men and with many non-feminist women. Second, as I have already pointed out, a women's issue is likely to receive less serious attention than a serious issue. Third, it strains credibility to argue that issues that affect nearly everyone in society, whether directly or indirectly, are "women's issues." Abortion affects male doctors and the male partners of pregnant women who choose to undergo the procedure. Child care, or the lack thereof, affects fathers, male employers, and children of both sexes. Pornography affects men as well as women. Sexual harassment involves both men and women, and is becoming an issue that employers and managers – the majority of whom are men – must deal with. The questions surrounding new reproductive technologies cut to the heart of our understanding of families, reproduction, motherhood, and fatherhood. To claim that NRTs are a women's issue is clearly inaccurate, and unfair to the men involved (such as sperm donors and fathers of surrogate babies).

It is time to recognize that these issues are important to all of us and cannot be trivialized or ignored as "women's issues." All Canadians, male or female, must have a role in determining the policies with which governments will respond to these issues in the 1990s. Women should not lose any of their present influence in the policy process, which was hard-won in decades of struggle against traditional attitudes and patriarchy. It would be especially disheartening if women's reproductive choices and physical integrity were to be threatened by policies that do not take women's needs and experiences into account. But despite the crucial need for women to participate in designing policies on these issues, we should not pretend that any of these matters are of exclusive relevance to women. For example, child care and sexual harassment, which have been on the back burner for years, would surely receive more serious attention if they were redefined as serious *social* and *economic* issues affecting all Canadians. The struggle for redefinition will remain the focus of women's involvement in the Canadian policy process to the end of the century and beyond.

Appendix: Federal Government Spending on Child Care, 1993–94

	Federal Government Spending ($ millions)	% of Total
CAP	310	43
CEIC training subsidies	90	13
Care on reserves	9	1
Child care expense deduction	310	43
Total	719	100

Source: Canada, Library of Parliament Research Branch, *Child Care in Canada* (Ottawa: Minister of Supply & Services, 1994).

Notes

1 See Lovenduski and Outshoorn, *The New Politics of Abortion.*

2 Collins, *The Big Evasion,* 12.

3 Canada, Library of Parliament, *Abortion,* 16.

4 Ibid., 18.

5 Brodie, "Choice and No Choice in the House," in Brodie, Gavigan, and Jenson, *The Politics of Abortion,* 87.

6 Ibid., 88.

7 Campbell and Pal, "Courts, Politics and Morality," 43.

8 Ibid.

9 Joni Lovenduski and Joyce Outshoorn, "Introduction: The New Politics of Abortion," in Lovenduski and Outshoorn, 4.

10 Ibid.

11 Brodie, "Choice and No Choice," 61.

12 Robin V. Snyder, "The Two Worlds of Public Opinion: Media Opinion and Polled Opinion on the Abortion Issue," doctoral thesis, Rutgers University, 1985.

13 Brodie, "Choice and No Choice," 77–86.

14 Collins, chap. 1.

15 *Gallup Report,* June 3, 1991, 2.

16 Royal Commission on the Status of Women, *Report,* recommendations 115–20.

17 Royal Commission on Equality in Employment, *Report,* 177.

18 National Council on Welfare, *Child Care: A Better Alternative,* 12.

19 Health and Welfare Canada and Statistics Canada, *The National Child Care Study,,* 14.

20 *Child Care: A Better Alternative,* 12.

21 Canada, Library of Parliament, *Child Care in Canada,* 8.

22 Ibid., 14.

23 National Council on Welfare, *The 1992 Budget and Child Benefits.*

24 Ibid., 19.

25 National Council on Welfare, *Child Care: A Better Alternative,* 10–11.

26 Anderson, *The Unfinished Revolution.*

27 Randall, *Women and Politics,* 171.

28 Royal Commission on Equality in Employment, 181–82.

29 *Child Care in Canada,* 3.

30 *Child Care: A Better Alternative,* 8.

31 See Banting, *The Welfare State and Canadian Federalism.*

32 *Child Care in Canada,* 7.

33 *Gallup Report,* January 26, 1989, 2.

34 *Gallup Report,* March 3, 1988, 2.

35 York, "Tory politicians form family compact."

36 Mitchell, "June Cleaver–style moms back in fashion."

37 Canadian Advisory Council on the Status of Women (CACSW), *On Pornography and Prostitution,* 3.

38 Quoted in Robert M. Campbell and Leslie A. Pal, "Sexual Politics: Pornography Policy in Canada," in Campbell and Pal, *The Real Worlds of Canadian Politics,* 116.

39 Ibid., 136.

40 Ibid., 134.

41 Ibid., 117.

42 Ibid., 131.

43 Ibid.

44 Ibid., 140–41.

45 CACSW, *A Critique of Bill C-114.*

46 CACSW, *Pornography: An Analysis of Proposed Legislation (Bill C-54),* brief presented to Hon. Ray Hnatyshyn, Minister of Justice (Ottawa: CACSW, 1988).

47 The 1992 Department of Justice report *Gender Equality in the Canadian Justice System* recommended that the importation of pornography be more strictly controlled, that the law recognize pornography as a source of violence against women, and that pornography be defined as hate literature. See Sallot, "Report links ads to violence against women."

48 Herbert, *Talking of Silence,* 14.

49 Ibid.

50 Ibid.

51 MacKinnon, *Sexual Harassment of Working Women,* 1.

52 Canadian Human Rights Commission, *Casebook on Sexual Harassment, 1978–86.*

53 Statistics Canada, *Universities: Enrolment and Degrees, 1990* and Teachers in Universities, 1989–90.

54 Canadian Human Rights Commission, *Harassment Casebook: Summaries,* 4.

55 Schur, *The Americanization of Sex,* 157–58.

56 See Billie Wright Dziech and Linda Weiner, *The Lecherous Professor: Sexual Harassment on Campus,* 2nd ed. (Chicago: University of Illinois Press, 1990).

57 Webb, *Shockwaves: The Global Impact of Sexual Harassment,* 8.

58 Anderson, *The Unfinished Revolution,* 219–20.

59 Webb, 100.

60 Schur, chap. 4.

61 Anderson, 219.
62 Canadian Human Rights Commission, *Harassment Casebook: Summaries,* 4–5.
63 The collected studies for the Royal Commission on New Reproductive Technology are an excellent resource in this area.
64 Achilles, "Artificial Reproduction," 291.
65 Madhu Kishwar, "The Continuing Deficit of Women in India and the Impact of Amniocentesis," in Corea et al., *Man-Made Women,* 32.
66 See Bennett, *Sex Selection of Children.*
67 Thomas, "Preference for the Sex of One's Children and the Prospective Use of Sex Selection."
68 Fiona A.L. Nelson, "Lesbian Women and Donor Insemination: An Alberta Case Study," in Royal Commission on New Reproductive Technologies (RCNRT), *Treatment of Infertility.*
69 RCNRT, *Proceed with Care.*
70 Brodribb, *Women and Reproductive Technologies,* 56.
71 Ibid.
72 Bryant, *The Infertility Dilemma,* 3, 17.
73 Ibid., 17.
74 *Gallup Report,* March 7, 1983, 1.

References and Further Reading

General

Boneparth, Ellen, ed. *Women, Power and Policy.* Oxford: Pergamon, 1982.

Gelb, Joyce. *Feminism and Politics: A Comparative Perspective.* Berkeley: University of California Press, 1989.

Lovenduski, Joni. *Women and European Politics: Contemporary Feminism and Public Policy* (Brighton: Wheatsheaf, 1986).

Randall, Vicky. *Women and Politics: An International Perspective.* 2nd ed. Chicago: University of Chicago Press, 1987.

Abortion

Brodie, Janine, Shelley A.M. Gavigan, and Jane Jenson. *The Politics of Abortion.* Toronto: Oxford University Press, 1992.

Campbell, Robert M., and Leslie A. Pal. "Courts, Politics and Morality: Canada's Abortion Saga." In Robert M. Campbell and Leslie A. Pal, *The Real Worlds of Canadian Politics.* 2nd ed. Peterborough: Broadview, 1991.

Canada, Library of Parliament. *Abortion: Constitutional and Legal Developments.*
Ottawa, Minister of Supply & Services, 1994.

Collins, Anne. *The Big Evasion: Abortion, the Issue that Won't Go Away.*
Toronto: Lester & Orpen Dennys, 1985.

Lovenduski, Joni, and Joyce Outshoorn, eds. *The New Politics of Abortion.*
Beverly Hills: Sage, 1986.

McDonnell, Kathleen. *Not an Easy Choice: A Feminist Re-examines Abortion.*
Toronto: Women's Press, 1984.

Morton, F.L. *Morgentaler v. Borowski: Abortion, the Charter, and the Courts.*
Toronto: McClelland & Stewart, 1992.

Child Care

Anderson, Doris. *The Unfinished Revolution: The Status of Women in Twelve
Countries.* Toronto: Doubleday Canada, 1991.

Banting, Keith G. *The Welfare State and Canadian Federalism.*
Kingston/Montreal: McGill–Queen's University Press, 1982.

Canada, Library of Parliament Research Branch. *Child Care in Canada.*
Ottawa: Minister of Supply & Services, 1994.

Health and Welfare Canada and Statistics Canada. *The National Child Care
Study: Parental Work Patterns and Child Care Needs.* Ottawa: Statistics
Canada, 1992.

Mitchell, Alanna. "June Cleaver–style moms back in fashion." *Globe and Mail,*
April 20, 1992.

National Council on Welfare. *The 1992 Budget and Child Benefits.* Ottawa:
Minister of Supply & Services, 1992.

———. *The Canada Assistance Plan: No Time for Cuts.* Ottawa: Minister of
Supply & Services, 1991.

———. *Child Care: A Better Alternative.* Ottawa: Minister of Supply & Services,
1988.

Royal Commission on the Status of Women. *Report.* Ottawa: Queen's
Printer, 1970.

Task Force on Child Care. *Report.* Ottawa: Minister of Supply & Services,
1986.

York, Geoffrey. "Tory politicians form family compact." *Globe and Mail,* June
3, 1992.

Pornography

Campbell, Robert M., and Leslie A. Pal. "Sexual Politics: Pornography Policy in Canada." In Robert M. Campbell and Leslie A. Pal, *The Real Worlds of Canadian Politics*. Peterborough: Broadview, 1989.

Canadian Advisory Council on the Status of Women. *A Critique of Bill C-114 as Proposed Legislation on Pornography: Principles and Clause-by-Clause Analysis*. Ottawa: CACSW, 1986.

————. *On Pornography and Prostitution*. Brief presented to the Special Committee on Pornography and Prostitution. Ottawa: CACSW, 1984.

Committee on Sexual Offences against Children and Youths. *Sexual Offences against Children: Report*. Ottawa: Minister of Supply & Services, 1984.

Sallot, Jeff. "Report links ads to violence against women." *Globe and Mail*, July 6, 1993.

Special Committee on Pornography and Prostitution. *Report*. Ottawa: Minister of Supply & Services, 1985.

Sexual Harassment

Canadian Human Rights Commission. *Casebook on Sexual Harassment, 1978–86*. Ottawa: Minister of Supply & Services, 1987.

————. *Harassment Casebook: Summaries of Selected Harassment Cases*. Ottawa: Minister of Supply & Services, 1991.

Herbert, Carrie M.H. *Talking of Silence: The Sexual Harassment of Schoolgirls*. London: Falmer Press, 1989.

MacKinnon, Catharine. *Sexual Harassment of Working Women*. New Haven: Yale University Press, 1979.

Razack, Sherene. *Canadian Feminism and the Law*. Toronto: Second Story Press, 1991.

Schur, Edwin M. *The Americanization of Sex*. Philadelphia: Temple University Press, 1988.

Statistics Canada. *Universities: Enrolment and Degrees, 1990*. Ottawa: Minister of Industry, Science & Technology, 1992.

————. *Teachers in Universities, 1989–90*. Ottawa: Minister of Industry, Science & Technology, 1992.

Webb, Susan L. *Shockwaves: The Global Impact of Sexual Harassment*. New York: MasterMedia, 1994.

Wright Dziech, Billie, and Linda Weiner. *The Lecherous Professor: Sexual Harassment on Campus*. 2nd ed. Chicago: University of Illinois Press, 1990.

New Reproductive Technologies

Achilles, Rona. "Artificial Reproduction: Hope Chest or Pandora's Box?" In Sandra Burt, Lorraine Code, and Lindsay Dorney, eds., *Changing Patterns: Women in Canada*. Toronto: McClelland & Stewart, 1988.

Bennett, Neil G., ed. *Sex Selection of Children*. New York: Academic Press, 1983.

Brodribb, Somer. *Women and Reproductive Technologies*. Ottawa: Status of Women Canada, 1988.

Bryant, Heather. *The Infertility Dilemma: Reproductive Technologies and Prevention*. Ottawa: CACSW, 1990.

Canada. *Treatment of Infertility: Assisted Reproductive Technologies*. Vol. 9 of the collected research studies for the Royal Commission on New Reproductive Technologies. Ottawa: Minister of Supply & Services, 1993.

———. *Treatment of Infertility: Current Practices and Psychosocial Implications*. Vol. 10 of the collected research studies for the Royal Commission on New Reproductive Technologies. Ottawa: Minister of Supply & Services, 1993.

Corea, Gena, et al. *Man-Made Women: How New Reproductive Technologies Affect Women*. Bloomington: Indiana University Press, 1987.

Field, Martha A. *Surrogate Motherhood: The Legal and Human Issues*. 2nd ed. Cambridge, MA: Harvard University Press, 1990.

Guichon, Juliet R. "'Surrogate Motherhood': Legal and Ethical Analysis." In Canada, *Legal and Ethical Issues in New Reproductive Technologies: Pregnancy and Parenthood*. Vol. 4 of the collected research studies for the Royal Commission on New Reproductive Technologies. Ottawa: Minister of Supply & Services Canada, 1993.

Hull, Richard T. *Ethical Issues in the New Reproductive Technologies*. Belmont, CA: Wadsworth, 1990.

Overall, Christine, ed. *The Future of Human Reproduction*. Toronto: Women's Press, 1989.

Royal Commission on New Reproductive Technologies. *Proceed with Care*. 2 vols. Ottawa: Minister of Supply & Services, 1993.

Thomas, Martin. "Preference for the Sex of One's Children and the Prospective Use of Sex Selection." In Canada, *Technologies of Sex Selection and Prenatal Diagnosis*. Vol. 14 of the collected research studies for the Royal Commission on New Reproductive Technologies. Ottawa: Minister of Supply & Services Canada, 1993.

Index

Enlightenment, 24, 25; attitudes to women, 23
Epstein, Cynthia Fuchs, 237, 239, 241
Equal Rights Amendment, 176; vs. Charter, 348–51
Erotica. *See under* Pornography
Estrich, Susan, 205–6
Eugenics. *See* Reproduction: technology, sex selection
Eve, 22
Exploitation of domestic and home workers, 116–18

Fairbairn, Joyce, 284, 284
Fairclough, Ellen, 283
False consciousness, 57, 63; benefits to capitalism and patriarchy, 63
Faludi, Susan, 137, 138
Familism, 28
Family, 314–15; "family values," 143–45; and economy, 93; and legal system, 94; changes in structure ("erosion of"), 130–32; conceptions of, 128–29; conflict with paid work, 108–10; conflict with political career, 243–44; diversity of, 129, 148; explanation of changes, 132–36; ideology of, 129; importance of, 128, 148; resistance to changes in, 136–45, 146, 397
"Family caucus," 138, 143–44, 376
Family wage system, 97–98, 101, 102, 103, 315–16
Federal Task Force on Child Care (Cooke) Report, 374
Fédération des femmes du Québec (FFQ), 80, 326, 330, 337, 345
Female biology. *See* Reproduction
Femininity. *See* Gender roles
Feminism: American vs. Canadian, 340; backlash against, 81–84; black, 69–70; "closet," 292–93; critique of traditional politics, 242–43; currents approach, 39–64; defined, 38–39; different practical strategies, 325–26; disabled women, 73–74; diversity

of, 39; first wave, 43, 48, 75–79, 325; grassroots activism, 325–26, 332–34; identity, 68–75, 68–75; immigrant women, 71; institutionalized, 327–32, 334–35, 340; jurisprudence, 180, 182–83, 184; lesbian, 51, 72–73; liberal, 40–45; Marxist, 56–61; middle-class bias of, 43–44; native women, 71–72; radical, 45–56, 61–63; resistance to, 14, 38, 63, 136–47, 212, 293; revisionist theory, 82–84; second wave, 14, 15, 38, 48–49, 68, 79–81, 325; separatism, 46, 51, 53; socialist, 61–64; strategic practice approach, 64–66; women of colour, 70
Feminist Party, 269
Feminist theory: currents approach, 39–64; identity feminism, 68–75; integrative feminist, 66–68; strategic practice, 64–66
Ferraro, Geraldine, 209
Finestone, Sheila, 284
Firestone, Shulamith, 49–50, 54, 388
Free speech, 378, 379, 380, 382, 396
French, Mabel Penery, 78
Friedan, Betty, 43–44
Funding: Women's Program, 334–35

Gays and lesbians, 27, 350
Gelb, Joyce, 66
Gender gap, 236, 344; in attitudes, 317
Gender roles, 13–14, 35–37, 46, 348; and law (*see under* Justice system); and public policy, 311–12; and radical feminism, 46; and socialization, 36–37; damage done by, 37; division of labour (*see under* Gendered division of labour); in public life, 209–11; resistance to change, 13–14
Gender vs. sex, 35
Gendered division of labour, 16, 24, 26, 96–97, 98–99, 100, 107, 202, 213, 236–40; constraint on female politicians, 243–44; in political parties, 255–57; in politics, 280–81,

284–85, 286. *See also* Occupational segregation